&

Burning and Building
Schooling and State Formation
in Japan, 1750–1890

Harvard East Asian Monographs, 237

&

Burning and Building

Schooling and State Formation
in Japan, 1750–1890

Brian Platt

Published by the Harvard University Asia Center
Distributed by Harvard University Press
Cambridge (Massachusetts) and London, 2004

Printed in the United States of America

The Harvard University Asia Center publishes a monograph series and, in coordination with the Fairbank Center for East Asian Research, the Korea Institute, the Rei-
schauer Institute of Japanese Studies, and other faculties and institutes, administers
research projects designed to further scholarly understanding of China, Japan, Viet-
nam, Korea, and other Asian countries. The Center also sponsors projects addressing
multidisciplinary and regional issues in Asia.

Library of Congress Cataloging-in-Publication Data

Platt, Brian, 1970-
  Burning and building : schooling and state formation in Japan, 1750-1890 / Brian
Platt.
      p. cm. -- (Harvard East Asian monographs ; 237)
  Includes bibliographical references and index.
  ISBN 0-674-01396-4 (cloth : alk. paper)
  1. Education and state--Japan--History. 2. Education--Social aspects--Japan--
History. 3. Educational change--Japan--History. I. Title: Schooling and state
formation in Japan, 1750-1890. II. Title. III. Series.
  LC94.J3P53 2004
  379.52'09'034--dc22

                                                                              2004003854

Index by the author

⊗   Printed on acid-free paper

Last figure below indicates year of this printing

14 13 12 11 10 09 08 07 06 05 04

In Memory of My Mother

Joanne Margaret Shively Platt

1938–1994

&

Acknowledgments

A number of people lent support and guidance to me at various stages of this project. As an undergraduate at Guilford College, Dottie Borei introduced me to Japanese history and inspired me to pursue it as a profession. At the University of Illinois, Ron Toby oversaw every aspect of my graduate studies and provided invaluable advice and encouragement throughout my coursework, my fieldwork, and my dissertation writing—and, in fact, ever since. I owe him an enormous debt of gratitude. Jeff Hanes was also influential early in my graduate work as an outstanding teacher and insightful reader. Bill Kelleher and Nancy Abelmann played important roles in the early stages of this project by guiding me through an interdisciplinary field on the ethnography of modern state formation. I am also thankful to Kevin Doak and Kären Wigen, who read my work carefully at the dissertation stage and provided detailed comments. After the dissertation was completed, Stephen Vlastos and Anne Walthall read the manuscript and provided thoughtful, useful advice about how to revise it into a book. I am also grateful to Abby Schweber for providing me with an advance look at her dissertation during the final stages of revision. Finally, I thank the two anonymous readers for the Harvard University Asia Center, who provided detailed and constructive advice.

In Japan, my research at the Historiographical Institute of the University of Tokyo was made possible by Miyachi Masato. Professor Miyachi's innovative research has continued to be a source of stimulation throughout the preparation of this manuscript. A second research trip to the institute was made possible by Ishigami Eiichi, the current director, and Sugimoto Fumiko, whose practical support and intellectual guidance were indispensable. Yoneyama Mitsunori and Nagura Eizaburō of Keio University also provided guidance at various points during my time in Tokyo. I am also grateful to the staff at the Nagano Prefectural History Museum, who welcomed me warmly and provided me with a wonderful setting in which to conduct my research on Nagano. In particular, Ihara Kesao helped me in innumerable ways at the museum, and Aoki Toshiyuki and many others there provided assistance in reading the handwritten materials held there.

My colleagues in the history department at George Mason University have provided me with an ideal atmosphere in which to rethink and rewrite the manuscript. Their collective influence on this project is too far-reaching to trace fully in this space. In particular, I thank Jack Censer for his constant support and Ben Carton for his encouragement and advice. I also thank Toby Meyer-Fong for her input on various parts of the manuscript.

This book would not have been possible without the generous financial support of a number of institutions. The Fulbright Foundation and the Japan-U.S. Educational Commission funded my fieldwork in Japan, and the Spencer Foundation provided financial assistance during the dissertation-writing stage. Combined assistance from a Spencer Foundation/National Academy of Education Postdoctoral Fellowship, a Mathy Foundation Grant from George Mason University, and a summer stipend from the National Endowment for the Humanities enabled me to enjoy a full year of uninterrupted research and writing as I revised the manuscript. The Dean of the College of Arts and Sciences here at George Mason, Daniele Struppa, provided funds to support a second research trip during the final stages of revision; I am grateful for his assistance.

I am also grateful to my parents, Leland Wesley Platt and Joanne Margaret Shively Platt, for supporting my undergraduate education and encouraging me unconditionally.

I owe my deepest gratitude to my wife, Mary Ann Monk. She has assisted me immeasurably in this endeavor—reading and editing chapters, making maps, and acting as a sounding board for my ideas. Beyond that, she has been a constant source of love, perspective, and fun; it's impossible to imagine accomplishing this without her. As our little one will soon find out, we're lucky she's on our team.

B.P.

Contents

&

Maps, Figures, and Table

Maps

Figures

Table

&

Burning and Building

Schooling and State Formation

in Japan, 1750–1890

Introduction

Each fall the children must endure together
What every child also endures alone:
Learning the alphabet, the integers,
Three dozen bits and pieces of a stuff
So arbitrary, so peremptory,
That worlds visible and invisible
Bow down before it

—From Howard Nemerov,
"September, First Day of School"

Soon after overthrowing the Tokugawa government in 1868, the new Meiji leaders set out to build a modern nation-state. Among the earliest and most radical of the Meiji reforms was a plan for a centralized, compulsory educational system, modeled after those in Europe and America. Envisioning a future in which "there shall be no community with an unschooled family, and no family with an unschooled person," Meiji leaders hoped that schools would curb mounting social disorder and mobilize the Japanese against the threat of Western imperialism.

The sweeping, revolutionary tone of this plan obscured the fact that the Japanese people were already quite literate and had their own ideas about what a school should look like. During the century preceding the Meiji Restoration, commoners in towns and villages had established some 50,000 schools, with virtually no guidance or support from political authorities. Consequently, when the Ministry of Education promulgated its 214-article Fundamental Code of Education (Gakusei) in 1872 and proclaimed its intent to bring modern education to the remotest corners of the nation, the Japanese people were already armed with a set of assumptions concerning the nature and purpose of the local school. What ensued was a process in which local society played an active role in shaping the new educational system from below, variously resisting the government's policies, negotiating compromises, and resolutely pursuing alternative educational visions within the outlines of state policy. In doing so, officials, teachers, and ordinary people within local society ultimately paved the way for the growth and consolidation of the new educational system—a system that bore the imprint of local demands and expectations. This book traces the unfolding of this process in Nagano prefecture and explores how local people, brimming with their own ideas about education and their own memories of crisis and restoration, negotiated the formation of the new order in their communities.

Educated Masses and the Educative State

The Meiji government's decision to create a centralized school system can be viewed in the context of two broad transformations in the concept and practice of education that have occurred worldwide in the past four hundred years. The first is the widespread proliferation of educational institutions for commoners. This transformation began in Western Europe and North America during the seventeenth and eighteenth centuries, when clergy and local elites, convinced that a limited education for local masses would have a positive effect on the moral climate and the level of religious devotion in their communities, established schools for local children. Meanwhile, the expansion of the written word into the social and economic lives of ordinary people enabled them to conceive of the potential value of such schools. This convergence established the context for an unprecedented expansion in both school attendance and popular literacy. In England, France, New England, and parts of Germany and Italy, more than half of the male population and over a quarter of the female population had received some schooling and achieved at least a modest level of literacy by the end of the eighteenth century.[1] At that time, Japan was just beginning to undergo a similar transformation. However, as we will see in the first two chapters of this book, a rapid increase in the number of schools enabled Japan to achieve comparable rates of school attendance and literacy by the time of the Meiji Restoration in 1868.[2]

While these changes were taking place in Japan during the early nineteenth century, a second transformation in education was under way in Europe and America. What defined this transformation was a fundamental change not in the number of schools or the patterns of attendance and literacy but in the organization and control of educational institutions. For the first time in history, the state intervened systematically in the education of ordinary children. Two factors set the stage for this phenomenon. The first was the rise of industrial capitalism. Industrialization may or may not have stimulated a demand for education among the general population;[3] however, it is clear that the demographic shifts and social dislocations associated with industrialization engendered new anxieties among elites about popular unrest. Old fears about the danger of overeducated commoners gave way to the even more threatening specter of uneducated urban masses outside the influence and regulation of social elites.[4] These concerns generated new ideas on preventing unrest through techniques of social management. Schooling came to be conceived as one of these techniques. Social elites, intellectuals, reformers, and government officials realized that the school could be used as a vehicle for socializing the lower classes properly—namely, by teaching them discipline, frugality, and other values conducive to their new role in an industrializing society.[5]

Another major development behind the intervention of governments in education was the emergence of the nation-state. This new political formation was premised on the active involvement of the entire population in the life of the nation. Governments sought to integrate people into the institutions of the state, mobilize them for various kinds of service to the nation, and inculcate in them an identification with the nation. It was soon recognized that schools could facilitate these efforts. Just as schools could prepare people for their new economic roles in an industrialized society, they could prepare people for their new political roles as participants in the nation-state.[6] Schooling therefore became a task too important to be addressed in a hit-or-miss fashion. Nor could the responsibility for schooling continue to be relegated to local elites or the church, who were themselves often rivals of the centralizing state. Thus the rationale of the nation-state required that governments assume an educative role, instructing people in the values and habits that would strengthen the new national community.[7]

By the mid-eighteenth century, then, schooling in Western societies was closely bound up with industrial development and the emergence of a new type of polity that relied on the integration and mobilization of the masses. This was not lost on those Japanese who had opportunity to investigate conditions in the West. They had already discerned that the power of Western nations derived from their industrial might and their ability to tap the collective energies of their populations.[8] In the years following the Restoration, Meiji leaders also concluded that widespread, centralized schooling was essential to Japan's harnessing of these new forms of power. Very early in Japan's state-building project, Japan's leaders linked educational reform to the goals of strengthening the nation and protecting its independence; that much they agreed upon, even though they differed widely over many key aspects of educational policy. Much was riding on the creation of a new educational system, and it became the nation's "urgent business" (*kyūmu*)—one of a number of terms repeated endlessly by local officials during the early years of educational reform. Whereas the public educational systems in mid-nineteenth century Europe and America were the cumulative product of several phases of state intervention, in Japan the urgency of this task would not allow for such a fitful process. Rather, the creation of a new educational system was attempted in one sudden, systematic, sweeping intervention.

But the Meiji government did not start from scratch when it promulgated its plan for a centralized educational system in 1872. Rather, it stepped into a highly variegated field of educational institutions and experiences. The preceding two centuries had seen the establishment of tens of thousands of commoner schools, 276 domain schools, and around 1,500 private academies.[9] The ideological foundations for the expansion in schooling during the Tokugawa period were diverse: Confucianism, Buddhism, nativism, and Shingaku motivated educators at various levels and produced distinctive visions of education and schooling.[10] This diverse field of educational thought and practice was also a shifting one: in the years immediately following the Restoration, intellectuals, village elites, and officials at various levels of government began to rethink the purpose and organization of schooling. Many of these reformists made some provision for the education of the masses, although their goals and the intellectual frameworks for their reforms varied widely. Although the state played a more dominant role in the early stages of educational reform in Japan than it did in many Western nations, as we shall see, the Meiji government's intervention in 1872 occurred during a period of innovation, when voices outside the central government were also calling for reform.

Although Western scholarship tends to frame pre-Meiji educational developments as "preconditions" that help explain the success of the Meiji educational system, such a view can easily obscure the nature and intent of the Meiji government's project in education. As Mark Lincicome has pointed out, the Meiji leaders responsible for the 1872 plan did not view their task as one of "building upon" these pre-existing educational institutions, personnel, and ideas.[11] Rather, they sought to create a new, authoritative educational vision and to effect its supremacy over other visions that were present before and during the Restoration period. The principles that defined the new system—state authority, administrative centralization, standardization, compulsory attendance without regard to status, and the concept of the "school" as a distinct institution in local society—were created in deliberate contrast with the principles that had shaped most pre-existing schools. The challenge facing the government was to make this radical vision of education appear not only reasonable but also commonsensical.

This undertaking, which began in 1872, involved both the propagation of this new vision and the marginalization of alternative visions, an effort treated in detail in Chapter 3. This effort was articulated clearly in government pronouncements: while positioning its own educational policies within a discourse of progress and enlightenment, the Ministry of Education labeled pre-Meiji commoner schools and their teachers "backwards," "narrow-minded," and "corruptive." More effective than rhetoric, however, were a variety of laws, administrative routines (such as surveying and licensing), and rituals that were intended to transform how people thought about "school" and to reserve for the government the authority to define "school," while excluding most pre-existing educational arrangements from that definition. The Meiji government's effort was therefore simultaneously constructive and destructive: even as it involved the building of new schools, the creation of new laws, and the articu-

lation of new ideas, it was also aimed explicitly at sweeping away—
or at least stigmatizing—existing educational arrangements and the
assumptions that underlay them.[12] Even when old elements were incorporated into the new system, they had to be symbolically transformed: teachers were retrained, schools were licensed, curricula
were inspected.

The Meiji government's initial intervention in education can
therefore be characterized as hegemonic—it involved an attempt to
secure the dominance of one particular vision of education over
other visions. Furthermore, this effort was carried out principally not
by means of physical coercion but by a cultural strategy of representation in which the vision promoted by the state was made to appear
commonsensical while competing ideas were branded as marginal or
beyond the pale.[13] Recognizing the hegemonic aspects of early Meiji
educational reform is important, for at least two reasons. First, it
highlights the fact that the formation of the Meiji educational system—and more generally, the Meiji state—was not simply a matter
of building structures and making laws and training personnel.
Rather, it was a cultural undertaking, an effort to transform assumptions and remake meanings. Takashi Fujitani demonstrates this effectively when he traces how Meiji officials transformed the cultural
meaning of the emperor and mobilized his new image for the purpose of consolidating the state's authority.[14] Indeed, the "physical"
and "cultural" elements of state-building were not separate: the educational vision articulated by the 1872 plan was embodied in the
laws, institutions, and administrative routines it created, and it was
in these concrete forms that new ideas about education were most effectively transmitted.

The concept of hegemony also brings the issue of agency to the
forefront of the discussion of educational reform and state formation.
Because of the influence of modernization theory, early postwar
Western scholarship on Meiji state formation generally muted the issues of agency and power, either by de-emphasizing the intentional
or creative acts of individuals or by explaining them within the context of universal processes of development.[15] This has not been a
problem with Japanese scholarship; the Japanese term for "state
formation" (*kokka keisei*) usually implies (and implicates) an actor—
generally the Meiji state—and a project of domination.[16] Recent
Western scholarship has complicated the issue of agency by demon-

strating the ways in which private groups—particularly those associated with the rise of the middle class in the late Meiji and Taisho
periods—cooperated with the Japanese state in setting the agenda
for social reforms.[17] Indeed, it is deeply problematic to treat the Meiji
state as the sole agent in the process of state formation. As I discuss
at length below, to do so is to attribute to the Meiji state a degree of
coherence and uniformity that never existed and to exclude the possibility that those outside the state structure played a role in shaping
the state. Nevertheless, when we examine the Meiji government's
initial foray into the arena of popular education, we should identify
the presence of a project, one designed to integrate a diverse set of
educational experiences and institutions into a centralized system.
We should also recognize the ways in which this project served the
interests of a deeply divided, vulnerable group of elites seeking to
consolidate the authority of the new government. We must ask, as
Philip Corrigan and Derek Sayer have asked in their study of state
formation in Britain, "who is seeking to integrate whom, to what
ends, by what means, and in what forms; and who suffers, which
ends are denied, which means declared illegitimate, whose forms
suppressed, whose histories rewritten."[18]

Negotiating Integration:
Local Responses to Meiji Reforms

In the five years that followed the 1872 promulgation, villagers destroyed over 200 new school buildings. In one incident, farmers in
Gifu prefecture shouted "Down with the new schools!" as they
burned dozens of recently built elementary schools, but steered clear
of the pre-Meiji schools in the area. In Tottori prefecture, villagers
greeted two newly appointed teachers with bamboo clubs, chased
them into the mountains, and beat one of them to death. These protesters perceived new schools and teachers as symbols of the unwanted changes since the Restoration, and they resented the central
government's intrusion into an area of local life previously free from
any extra-village regulation.

Across the mountains from the smoldering schools in Gifu, upon
receiving news of the Meiji government's educational policies, a village headman in Nagano prefecture immediately promoted the construction of a new school in his village. Like many other village elites

of his time, he viewed the educational reforms as a public sanction of his own personal mission to regenerate the moral and economic life of his community. He studied architectural plans of school buildings in Europe, raised funds, and oversaw the school's construction, making every effort to meet—in fact, to exceed—the government's recommendations. For months he prepared the speech he was to deliver at the school's unveiling ceremony and even sent rough drafts to friends in Tokyo. On the day of the ceremony, having fulfilled his personal mission, he announced that "there is no joy that can compare to this."[19]

Acknowledging the hegemonic aspects of the Meiji state's intervention in education should not imply that the formation of the Meiji educational system can be read simply as the unfolding of a government blueprint for educational reform. As we can see from the two examples above, the Meiji government's intervention in education elicited a variety of local responses, ranging from open hostility to enthusiastic cooperation. Much of this book (Chapters 4 through 6) is devoted to exploring these responses. The goal of this endeavor is, in part, to reconstruct the popular experience of Meiji education. But this study seeks not merely to examine the experience of educational reform but to rethink its dynamics. I will argue that local responses to educational reform—in the form of resistance to integration into the new system as well as initiatives toward integration—shaped the formation of the educational system during the first two decades of Meiji rule.

The question of the Japanese people's response to the formation of the Meiji state has been central to the historiography of modern Japan. For the most part, scholars have tended to view the issue of popular response in terms of a dichotomy of "cooperation" and "resistance," a dichotomy that has served as the structuring principle of two dominant narratives of modern Japan. The first was informed by Cold War–era modernization theory, and its goal when applied to Japan was to explain, according to universal patterns of development, Japan's "success" as the only modern non-Western nation. This narrative of Japan's modern history tended to emphasize continuity and consensus rather than conflict, which was presumed to be dysfunctional and counterproductive to the goal of modernization. This view also assumed a fundamentally cooperative relationship between the Japanese people and the Meiji state and often explained such cooperation by pointing to Tokugawa developments that prepared the Japanese people for modernization.[20]

The field of educational history provides an instructive example of the link between modernization theory and the narrative of modern Japanese history as a story of cooperation between the Japanese people and the Meiji state. The pathbreaking work of Ronald Dore, for example, which first revealed to an English-language audience the impressive growth of educational institutions during the Tokugawa period, was framed as an effort to find the preconditions for the successful effort to build a modern educational system in the Meiji period.[21] Tokugawa education was, by all accounts (including Dore's), decentralized, unstandardized, and distinctly local in its organization and orientation—factors that, presumably, could have led people to resist aspects of the Meiji educational reform. However, since Dore and others studied Tokugawa education with the explicit goal of evaluating its contribution to educational modernization during the Meiji period—in Dore's words, its "legacy"—they either deemphasized these seemingly premodern aspects of Tokugawa schooling or treated them as remnants that would be overcome during the process of modernization.[22] When narrating the shift from Tokugawa to Meiji, scholars taking this perspective usually privileged continuity over disruption, characterizing the process as a relatively smooth, consensual transition.[23]

In contrast to this narrative of consensual modernization, most postwar Japanese scholarship (and revisionist Western scholarship) has portrayed Meiji state formation as conflict-ridden. Both Marxist history and People's History (*minshūshi*)—the two dominant historiographical movements in postwar Japan—characterize the Meiji period as an era of clashes between the people and the state. In this story, the people, who symbolize the potential for healthy, democratic modernization, are positioned in opposition to a conservative, absolutist emperor-state that represents the class interests of elites. In the case of People's History, this conflict has an added dimension: in the people resides the true source of Japanese culture and identity—a source that, in the late Tokugawa and early Meiji periods, was poised to produce an indigenous, authentic modernization—whereas the state embodies the homogenizing forces of Western modernity.[24] Scholars writing within this vein invariably sympathize with the cause of the people; indeed, popular struggles against the Meiji state are often used by scholars as precedents for struggles against the conservative postwar government.[25] Ironically, however, this view of Meiji history is heavily invested in the assumption that popular resistance against the state *failed*. By noting (and mourning) the failure of popular resistance against the Meiji state, this tragic narrative of Japanese state formation shields the Japanese people from complicity in the less desirable parts of Japan's modern history.[26]

This narrative of loss, betrayal, and thwarted potential has deeply influenced Japanese scholarship on Meiji educational history. Educational historians often point to the potential in the early Meiji period for a truly democratic, liberal educational system, one that sought as its primary goal the enlightenment and emancipation of the individual. However, they argue that in the 1880s, the Meiji state effectively snuffed out such ideas and instead created a highly centralized, bureaucratic system of education, designed not to empower citizens with the capacity for independent thought but to inculcate in subjects the values of filial piety, obedience, and loyalty to the emperor. The silencing of alternative educational visions, accomplished decisively through the suppression of the Popular Rights Movement, then allowed for the extension of the "emperor system" (*tennōsei*) into the realm of education, resulting in "emperor system education" (*tennōsei kyōiku*).[27] According to this narrative, this system crystallized in the promulgation of the Imperial Rescript on Education in 1890. The narrative continues into the postwar period; an initial period of educational freedom is followed by the imposition of an educational system dominated by a centralized bureaucracy. And, just as the history of popular resistance to the Meiji state has served as a historical precedent for leftist opposition to the postwar government, educational historians have pointed to the suppression of dissenting voices during the formation of the Meiji educational system in order to explain and critique certain aspects of the current educational system, including everything from its bureaucratic character to the examination system to problems with endemic bullying.[28]

The formation of the Meiji educational system was indeed a highly contested process. As I discuss at length in Chapters 5 and 6, popular resistance came in a variety of forms. Protesters destroyed nearly 200 new school buildings in nearly a dozen separate incidents during the five years following the promulgation of the new school laws in 1872. Teachers of pre-Meiji village schools spread rumors about the new schools, sabotaged efforts to collect funds for them, and reopened old schools illegally. Villagers at all income and status levels refused to pay for the new schools, sometimes even in the face of fines and imprisonment. Village elites throughout the country articulated a thoroughgoing critique of Meiji educational policy during the late 1870s, a critique that became a central component of the political vision of the Popular Rights Movement. Ironically, these activists established schools to propagate their dissenting ideologies and presented these private schools as examples of their alternative educational vision. Finally, villagers employed passive techniques of resistance by refusing to send their children to the new schools or sending them only sporadically, thereby revealing their assessment of the importance of schooling in their children's lives.

The element of popular resistance is, therefore, an essential part of the story of the Meiji educational system. We should, however, recognize the problems that result from positioning this resistance in a tragic narrative of failed opposition. First, that narrative tends to make an artificially clear distinction between the state and the people, as if they were discrete entities with uniform interests and perspectives. Irokawa Daikichi's *Culture of the Meiji Period* illustrates some of the problems that result from drawing a sharp distinction between the state and the people and treating these categories as coherent groups. Irokawa deals at length with examples of elite villagers who do not seem to fit neatly within either of these categories. However, his description of a progressive political consciousness among the Japanese people in the early Meiji period is based largely on the writings and activities of these village elites. His argument, therefore, hinges on the assumption that these elites belonged to the category of "the people" and that their activities reveal an indigenous democratic spirit in early Meiji society.[29] However, when explaining popular acquiescence to the emperor system, he vilifies village elites for suppressing the democratic spirit that had welled up among the people during the early Meiji period. It was these local intellectuals, Irokawa contends, who "provided genuine social support for the emperor system."[30] In contrast, Irokawa contends that the people never fully "relinquished their souls to the emperor system."[31] Having grouped village elites with the people in order to demonstrate the possibilities brewing in the early Meiji, Irokawa then recruits these elites to the side of the state in order to explain what appears to have been popular support for ultra-

nationalism and militarism—in effect, framing these elites as col-
laborators and thereby removing from the people the taint of the emperor system. Of course, one can make the argument that these local
elites did, in fact, change sides. However, the fact that one thinks in
terms of "sides" demonstrates the extent to which these categories of
"state" and "people" have been reified as coherent historical actors
and suggests the inadequacy of such an approach when studying the
dynamics of state formation.

A close look at the formation of the Meiji educational system reveals that "the people" did not speak with a uniform voice and were
not aware of a common set of interests. At one extreme were the
many poor villagers who rarely attended school, even at the end of
the nineteenth century; at the other were the village elites who had
always achieved a level of schooling far beyond that of the general
village population and who often acted in an official or semi-official
capacity in the new educational system. In this book, I attempt to
foreground conflicts and divisions within the people and to show
how the different perspectives and interests of each stratum of society led to different conceptions of education and schooling. Similarly,
when I talk about "local society," I am not implying that the interests
and opinions of local people were uniform or that the popular voice
was singular.[32]

Treating "the state" as a concrete historical actor with self-evident
and uniform interests is similarly problematic. First, the structure
and institutions of government were in such a state of flux after the
Restoration that we probably should not talk about the existence of
the "Meiji state," even in a narrow sense, for at least the first decade
of the Meiji period. Furthermore, the "state" is not merely a conglomeration of personnel and institutions; it is also an ideological
project, an effort to represent this conglomeration as a coherent, unified structure, one that (at least in the case of the modern state) embodies the nation. The very idea of the state is an "exercise in legitimation," an attempt to obscure the arbitrary, historically contingent
origins of the power wielded by specific people.[33] This project took
longer than the mere building of institutions and was always, to a
degree, unfinished. Of course, it is impossible to avoid reference to
"the Meiji state" when discussing the historiography of modern Japan. However, in discussing the formation of the Meiji educational
system, I will, whenever possible, identify the actor or speaker pre-

cisely: the Ministry of Education, a central government official, a prefectural governor, and so on. And although it is valid, I think, to speak of the Meiji government's "educational vision" in terms of a common denominator of features or principles, Meiji leaders were often bitterly divided over issues relating to educational policy.[34] Furthermore, central, prefectural, district, and village governmental structures often bargained with one another in pursuit of separate and sometimes contradictory goals or interests. In general, then, rather than making a sharp distinction between the state and the people and positioning them in an adversarial relationship, I seek to disaggregate these categories of actors in order to reveal the complex dynamics of negotiation that took place during the formation of the Meiji educational system.

A second problem that results from interpreting the local response to the Meiji government's educational project as a tragic narrative of failed resistance is that it tends to channel local reactions into a false dichotomy of "resistance" and "cooperation." Many local actions do not fit neatly into either of these categories—or sometimes seem to fit into both. For example, the widespread movement during the 1870s to secede from large, multi-village primary schools and establish single-village schools (see Chapter 5) certainly constituted a form of opposition to the educational vision embodied in early Meiji policy. On the other hand, this "opposition" movement supported the general idea of public schooling, and villages succeeded in earning permission to establish single-village schools only by following proper administrative procedures and by employing rhetoric sanctioned by the government. Similarly, the schoolteachers and educational activists in the Popular Rights Movement opposed key elements of government educational policy but nevertheless affirmed the idea of a national educational system.

Even what appear to be clear-cut examples of resistance or cooperation defy such easy categorization. Incidents of school burnings often expressed not a rejection of the Meiji government or its policies but complaints about specific elements of the new school system— long commutes, inequitable arrangements for school funding, irrelevant content, and so on. Furthermore, the "cooperation" of village elites who worked tirelessly during the early 1870s to build schools and encourage attendance within their communities (see Chapter 4) was usually based on motives and assumptions that were quite different from those of central policymakers. And this cooperation was usually conditional: many individuals who initially responded with enthusiasm to the Meiji government's educational project later flocked to the Popular Rights Movement when their interests diverged from those of the central government. What these examples remind us is that resistance and cooperation were not mutually exclusive acts motivated by unrelated, diametrically opposed sentiments. Charles Tilly has long argued that resistance and cooperation are simply two different strategies by which people attempt to make their voices heard by those in power, and this argument certainly applies to education in the Meiji period.[35] As we will see, resistance and cooperation were simply two sides of the same coin, two related strategies in a single process in which local people negotiated the terms by which they would be integrated into the new state.

Perhaps the most problematic assumption of a tragic narrative of Meiji history is that popular resistance failed to influence the formation of the Meiji state. As noted above, Japanese research on popular resistance to the Meiji state functions mainly to demonstrate that the people tried, nobly but futilely, to change the course of Japanese history. Stephen Vlastos's important article on Meiji opposition movements divests this story of the tragic tone often found in the genre of People's History, but nevertheless it begins with the assumption that these movements failed and then proceeds to explore *why* they failed.[36] In the case of People's History, there is much at stake in this assumption. Carol Gluck has pointed out that these historians' "deep aversion to the nature and direction of Japan's modernity" requires that they attribute only a minimal role to the people in the creation of that modernity. As a result, "those who did not participate in its creation . . . are in some sense pure."[37]

But the dynamics of Meiji state formation did, in fact, allow people at all levels of local society to participate in the creation of the educational system. First, local resistance to Meiji education often persuaded central officials to compromise on certain aspects of educational policy. Local "cooperation"—in the form of educational initiatives generated during the process of implementing reforms—also influenced central policies. The new government made local officials and village elites, informed by their own pre-Meiji educational experiences as teachers, students, benefactors, and reformists, responsible for implementing new policies within their communities. Many of their solutions to the problems that arose while carrying out this task became part of central policy. Consequently, the interplay between intellectuals and the central government that Mark Lincicome and Motoyama Yukihiko describe can be extended to include local society.[38] This dynamic enabled local people to influence the development of the educational system.

If we recognize such a dynamic, must we then dispense with the notion of a "hegemonic project" in education? In other words, if state formation involves negotiation between the state and local society, does that mean that it is not hegemonic? If we view hegemony as a successful, finished project of domination imposed unilaterally by dominant groups, then the concept clearly does not apply here. Indeed, if we define hegemony in this way, we may question whether the concept *ever* really applies. James Scott has shown persuasively how ordinary people's ability to penetrate and demystify ostensibly hegemonic ideologies enables them to manipulate the terms of those ideologies to promote their own interests—or, when open resistance is impractical, to formulate hidden, subversive renderings of power relations even while outwardly consenting to them.[39] However, scholars have recently argued that Gramsci's view of power relations is characterized precisely by the involvement of subordinate groups in what is actually an ongoing, contested process of hegemony. In this view, hegemony is a kind of contract among conflicting interests, one that earns the consent of subordinate groups only when it makes concessions to their demands and perspectives and one that must continually be renegotiated as circumstances change.[40]

Gluck has described such a hegemony in late Meiji Japan, one consisting not of a coherent ideological orthodoxy created by the state but of shared assumptions that existed "in the spaces between the ideological visions, where they seemed so commonsensical as not to merit any comment at all."[41] In the area of education, a similar kind of hegemony had emerged by the 1890s, a new common sense about the purpose and organization of schooling. This did not amount to widespread agreement on all issues relating to education; scholars have demonstrated that ideological conflicts over education continued during the 1890s and the first decades of the twentieth century.[42] Rather, this hegemony took the form of an institutional and discursive framework within which ideas about education could be expressed. This included a common language for talking about education, specific boundaries for acceptable debate, certain patterns of interaction between the government and local society, and procedures for expressing legitimate opposition to educational policy. This framework, which took shape during the first two decades after the state's initial intervention in education in 1872, provided the context for subsequent interaction between state and society on educational matters during the twentieth century. The story of its creation is that of an extended negotiation between the government and local society, a process that transformed all parties involved and produced the basic assumptions that underlay modern Japanese education and society.

Chronological Parameters: Conceptualizing the Tokugawa-Meiji Transition

This study begins in the eighteenth century, when commoner schools began to appear in substantial numbers in Nagano prefecture, and continues through the 1890s, when enrollment patterns changed dramatically and when the broad outlines of the institutional structure and ideological underpinnings of the modern educational system became more settled. This time can be seen as an extended period of innovation in the practice of commoner schooling. The first commoner schools targeted local elites and embodied a concept of schooling rooted in the transmission of high culture and status-specific knowledge. In the early nineteenth century, the decision of many local elites to become teachers resulted in a considerable increase in the number of schools. Then, in the last three decades of the Meiji period, new visions of schooling emerged in response to a perceived crisis in local society. Teachers, inspired by a desire to preserve their status in a time of uncertainty as well as by a desire to regenerate the social and moral life of their communities, began to open their doors to the children of ordinary families—who themselves were seeking ways to ensure their economic well-being in a time of both mobility and insecurity. The years immediately following the Restoration saw an eruption of educational visions at all levels of society, many of which involved some systematic program for the instruction of the masses.

The Meiji government's promulgation of the Fundamental Code in 1872 marks a decisive moment in this long process of innovation and experimentation. The government's intervention was innovative in its own right and was informed by decidedly new assumptions concerning the nature and purpose of the school. What further distinguished this intervention was that it intended not simply to add to an already complex field of possibilities but to displace these possibilities in such a way that the government's new vision would seem authoritative and *a priori* and natural. This effort was, at its core, hegemonic; in Raymond Williams's terms, it was a "cultural activity . . . in which from a whole possible area of past and present, certain meanings and practices are chosen for emphasis, [and] certain other meanings and practices are neglected and excluded."[43]

This task was not limited to the realm of education. Indeed, all revolutionary governments, when attempting to build a stable social and political order after a period of upheaval, face the task of co-opting, marginalizing, or silencing the diverse voices and energies that contributed to the revolutionary moment. Harry Harootunian and George Wilson have spoken suggestively about this aspect of state formation in Japan, pointing out that the Meiji project of state-building was premised on "contain[ing] the vast energies that had been released in the bakumatsu period"[44] and "eliminating precisely the fragmentation, difference, and overdetermination that had defeated the Tokugawa system of control."[45] Scott characterizes this kind of project as a "reconquest" after an interregnum, an attempt to tame the various local visions released during a revolution, to replace them with an official interpretation of recent events, and to attach that interpretation to a project of state-building.[46] Chapter 3 of this book describes such a reconquest in the arena of education — although since political authorities had never before played a significant role in commoner education, the term "conquest" is perhaps more appropriate.

But whatever dreams of conquest may have existed within the unstable, divided early Meiji government, they were doomed from the beginning. Eliminating those educational visions and energies released during the late Tokugawa and Restoration periods was impossible, for they were embedded in precisely those individuals who were mobilized by the Meiji government to build the new system at the local level. This included people like Nagayama Moriteru, the first governor of Chikuma prefecture (later amalgamated into Nagano prefecture), whose educational experiences as a high-ranking samurai in Satsuma domain shaped his program to establish elemen-

tary schools in Chikuma—an effort that actually began several
months before the Meiji government promulgated its Fundamental
Code in 1872. It also included dozens of lower-ranking samurai and
commoner elites who staffed the prefectural and district offices and
hundreds of village leaders whose voluntary participation was essential if the new system were to function. These individuals—and,
of course, the ordinary families whose children were to attend the
new schools—brought their own ideas about education to the project
of state-building. If the creation of the Meiji educational system had
been a unilateral project, one that unfolded strictly according to the
dictates of government policy, these pre-1872 ideas and experiences
would not be crucial to this study; they could be framed merely as
"background." However, the formation of the Meiji educational system involved an active dialogue with local voices. Thus, a chronological focus that spans the Restoration period is essential if we are
to trace how the process of reconquest was shaped by interregnal
energies and ideas.

In choosing such chronological parameters, I am not assuming
that the Tokugawa-Meiji transition was characterized principally by
continuity. Tokugawa education deeply influenced the formation of
the Meiji system, but we should not treat this legacy strictly in terms
of fundamental continuities that bridged the Tokugawa and Meiji
periods and presumably facilitated educational modernization during the Meiji period.[47] The widespread experience of schooling
among pre-Meiji commoners also created firsthand knowledge of
educational arrangements quite different from those designed by the
Meiji government. The Tokugawa legacy included, for example, assumptions about curriculum and pedagogy that were rooted in the
transmission of high culture through master-pupil relationships.
Parents were accustomed to sending their children to the home of a
member of the village elite or to a local temple to receive schooling—
and, even then, only when it did not interfere with the household's
labor demands. Village elites viewed teaching as an activity that
could be linked seamlessly with other forms of political and cultural
leadership in the effort to amass symbolic capital within the community. These and other elements of the pre-Meiji schooling experience were at odds with the educational vision articulated in early
Meiji policy and created memories of educational arrangements that
could be held up as alternatives to those endorsed by the new gov-

ernment. Consequently, although the Tokugawa legacy did indeed facilitate local cooperation with the Meiji reforms, it also informed opposition to those reforms. Rather than ensuring the success of the Meiji government's educational project, this legacy altered the terms of the dialogue through which the new system took shape.

Geographical Parameters: Nagano Prefecture and the Uses of Local History

One of the central tasks of historians studying the Tokugawa-Meiji transition, then, is to identify the energies and ideas released during the late Tokugawa and Restoration periods and to trace their trajectory during the formation of the Meiji state. One way to do this is to explore how those ideas and energies were embodied in individuals whose lives spanned the Restoration, as Walthall has done brilliantly in her recent biography of Matsuo Taseko.[48] This study adopts a similar approach but traces multiple biographies as they intersect with a specific area of life—education—and play out on a specific local terrain—what is now Nagano prefecture. This kind of local history enables us to follow the personal trajectories of individuals who carried out the work of state formation more easily. For example, we can trace the movements of village elites who opened schools during the last decades of the Tokugawa period, then worked tirelessly to implement the early Meiji educational reforms, only to grow disillusioned with the government's policies and join the Popular Rights Movement in the late 1870s. We can follow the experiences of communities as they were amalgamated with neighboring villages during the various administrative reforms of the 1870s and 1880s and explore how these changes informed the efforts of local people to support or obstruct school-building projects. We can also study the trajectory of pre-Meiji village schools that were closed during the early Meiji reforms, then reopened under guidelines set by the new government, and then finally consolidated into larger schools—often despite fierce local opposition. These micro-trajectories illustrate how the national project in education was altered as it played out on a local terrain of people, ideas, and memories.

The bulk of the scholarship on modern Japan that can be categorized as local history has, ironically, functioned to reaffirm the nation as the proper subject of history. In the English-language historiography, postwar modernization theory produced a number of seminal works based on local case studies—most notably, John Hall's study of Bizen and Marius Jansen's book on Tosa.[49] However, in holding up the nation as both the inevitable product of modernization and the unit for comparative analysis, modernization theory relegated local history to a limited role. Hall's book, for example, used the locality as merely a more manageable space within which to trace the process of modernization—to illustrate how modernization "works" at the local level.[50] Although Jansen's study explored in fascinating detail the unique setting of Restoration-era Tosa, it did so within a larger narrative in which the local was ultimately transcended by farsighted individuals (like Sakamoto Ryōma) who built the modern nation-state. In Japan, meanwhile, the postwar decades saw an explosion in the production of research on local history, among both professional and amateur historians.[51] In its account of the Tokugawa-Meiji transition and state formation, most of this scholarship fits neatly within the tragic narrative that is characteristic of the genre of People's History. In fact, "the local" often seems to function as a metonym for "the people" and serves as a site of alterity vis-à-vis the modern Japanese state. In lamenting the failure of localities to resist the centralized, absolutist Meiji state, this scholarship assumes a fundamentally antagonistic relationship between the center and the locality, while paradoxically reaffirming the primacy of national history.

Some scholars have recently disputed this view of the relationship between localities and the Meiji state and have begun to rethink the concept of local history.[52] In particular, several works describe a local response to Meiji state formation characterized neither by passivity nor by antagonism. Kären Wigen argues against the common tendency to position local identities in opposition to forces of nationalization and demonstrates how local identity in Nagano actually facilitated national integration.[53] James Baxter and Neil Waters emphasize the cooperative response to Meiji reforms in Kawasaki and Ishikawa, respectively—areas where, in Waters's terms, "nothing happened."[54] Michael Lewis not only highlights examples of local opposition in Toyama to the effects of economic and political integration into the nation-state but also demonstrates how Toyama residents actively sought to appropriate the benefits of that integration.[55] Gary Allinson has made a similar observation, describing the relationship between the locality and the Meiji government as one of "responsive dependence."[56] Many of these works embody a kind of local history that seeks neither to affirm nor to lament the rise of the centralized state but instead to explore the particularity of a local setting in order to make novel arguments about key issues in modern Japanese history.

I will attempt a similar approach, using Nagano prefecture—and its premodern equivalent, Shinano province—as the setting in which to explore late Tokugawa provincial society and culture, the Meiji Restoration, state formation, and educational change. My choice of Nagano was not guided by the desire to locate a "representative" locality that could then be used to generalize about the rest of the nation. Indeed, if representativeness were a concern, Nagano would appear to be a poor choice. During the century before the Meiji government promulgated its educational reforms in 1872, over 6,000 schools were established in Nagano, more than in any other prefecture. During the first decade of the new system, Nagano's school enrollment rates were consistently higher than anywhere else in the nation, and it was touted by the Ministry of Education as a model prefecture in the area of education. In fact, Nagano's widely recognized interest and precociousness in education has led to its (sometimes disputed) designation as Japan's "education prefecture," a title that continues to shape most Naganoites' sense of local identity.[57]

Indeed, I have chosen Nagano prefecture as the focus of my study in part because its exceptionality throws into sharper relief the dynamics of state formation at the local level. The extraordinary proliferation of pre-Meiji commoner schools in Nagano enables us to explore in concrete ways the kinds of experiences and assumptions that communities brought to the table when they were entrusted with carrying out the Meiji educational reforms. The remarkable vigor with which the project of educational reform was carried out in Nagano not only allows us to identify the ways in which local society was mobilized for this project but also enables us to see the problems and conflicts that this project engendered. The consistent involvement of Nagano's village elites in schooling throughout the Tokugawa-Meiji transition reveals the personal and local trajectories that tell the story of revolution and state formation in Japan. The heightened interest in education, both in the Tokugawa and the Meiji period, also produced in Nagano an explicit dialogue about educational issues that facilitates documentation of the various concep-

tions of "education" and "school" in local society and their development during the formation of the new system.

The diversity of educational conditions and experiences in Japan
during the Tokugawa and Meiji periods cautions against using
Nagano (or any other prefecture, for that matter) to generalize about
the details of educational reform in other areas of the country—for
example, about attendance patterns, the status backgrounds of
teachers, intellectual influences, and so on. In fact, there was a great
deal of diversity *within* the boundaries of Nagano; as a result, a study
of Nagano provides a comparative dimension that is not necessarily
any less revealing than a comparison between different prefectures.
But the aim of this study is not to provide a nationwide, comprehensive account of the details of Tokugawa and Meiji schooling but to
examine the project of educational reform at the local level in order
to explore the dynamics of state formation in Japan. These dynamics,
I suggest, can be seen elsewhere in Japan, even if many of the details
differ. Communities all over Japan confronted the Meiji government's educational project with a diverse set of assumptions forged
through decades of social and moral crisis, ideological ferment, and,
in many areas, educational innovation. As they were mobilized for
the Meiji project, they adopted various strategies to pursue their own
interests and demands—which were by no means uniform within a
given community, much less within the country as a whole. Collec-
tively, these efforts constituted the process by which the Meiji educational system took shape.

O N E

Commoner Schooling
in Tokugawa-Era Shinano

Since the publication in 1965 of Ronald Dore's and Herbert Passin's research, the spread of commoner schooling in eighteenth- and nineteenth-century Japan has served as a major element in the portrayal of the Tokugawa period as "early modern."[1] According to this picture, the explosive growth of schools throughout the country and the high level of literacy, which by 1868 rivaled the levels attained by many contemporary European nation-states, are evidence that social and economic development in Japan had reached an advanced stage before the Meiji Restoration.[2] Commoner schooling is particularly useful for such an argument because of the seemingly spontaneous character of its growth: the lack of any systematic efforts on the part of the Tokugawa bakufu or domain governments to initiate or support popular schooling gives the appearance that it arose spontaneously as part of early modern social and economic development. A similar emphasis can be found in the Japanese scholarship as well. Although most Japanese historians do not share Dore's and Passin's ideological framework, they, too, have been eager to locate a spontaneous, genuinely popular educational tradition in Tokugawa Japan, one that contrasts with the modern Japanese educational system, in which the state's interests are seen to overwhelm those of the Japanese people.[3] In fact, the term that many Japanese scholars use to describe the proliferation of schools in Tokugawa Japan is *shizen hassei*, which doubles as the scientific term for "spontaneous generation."[4]

This chapter attempts to complicate this picture of Tokugawa-era commoner schooling by examining the context for the spread of commoner schools in Shinano province. What scholars might characterize as "early modern" social and economic developments—the orientation of the village toward the market economy, the integration of localities into broader networks of commerce and information, and the formation of large urban areas and an increasingly literate consumer culture—indeed were important parts of this context. However, such conditions alone do not adequately explain the timing and patterns of the growth in commoner schooling, nor do they fully capture what the schools meant to teachers and students. I therefore explore other, less familiar elements of the context for the growth of commoner schooling: patterns of learning rooted in the transmission of elitist cultural knowledge, concepts of commoner schooling informed by Confucian notions of moral suasion (*kyōka*), and the ideological and social movements that emerged in response to the sense of crisis that gripped local society during the last decades of the Tokugawa period. I also address a crucial factor in the spread of commoner schooling that relates not only to the demand for schooling—which has been the main focus of historians—but also to its supply: the increasing orientation of village elites toward aesthetic and literary activities during the eighteenth and nineteenth centuries.

Patterns of Growth

In order to explore the growth of commoner schools in Tokugawa-period Shinano, I have grouped a wide range of educational institutions into one category, "commoner schools."[5] This category encompasses two types of schools, *terakoya* and *shijuku*, that scholars often classify separately. *Terakoya*, which literally means "a hut for temple children," was sometimes used during the Tokugawa period to refer to private schools attended by children belonging to the three non-samurai status groups: farmers, artisans, and merchants. The term stems from the medieval practice of sending young children to temples to study under the tutelage of Buddhist priests—although by the late Tokugawa period, most schools were neither held in temples nor taught by priests.[6] *Shijuku*, while also referring to private schools attended predominantly by commoners (though samurai children often attended *shijuku* as well), generally connotes a school with a curriculum that was more advanced and rigorous than that found in most *terakoya*. Richard Rubinger's rendering of *shijuku* as "private academies" helps distinguish them from *terakoya*.[7] Depending on one's focus, the distinction between these two types of schools can be useful, so long as we remember that the distinction is not always clear and, in fact, was not recognized in Tokugawa society. The words *terakoya* and *juku* did exist in the Tokugawa period, but as abstract categories of schools, they are a product of the Meiji era—more specifically, a product of the Meiji government's effort to investigate and compile statistics on Tokugawa-era schools. Despite the broad variety of institutions, these Tokugawa-era schooling arrangements share a common denominator of characteristics that mark them as "schools," distinct from educational practices that previously had not been separated from household or communal rhythms of work and play.

For a long time, statistical information on these schools came mainly from investigations conducted by local officials in the 1880s at the behest of the Ministry of Education. According to these statistics, the total number of commoner schools nationwide during the Tokugawa period was 11,278; another 1,217 were opened in the five years following the Meiji Restoration but preceding the promulgation of the Fundamental Code of Education.[8] This investigation found 1,341 schools in Shinano, more than in any other prefecture. However, subsequent research by local historians in Nagano prefecture has proved this number to be grossly understated. Supplementing the early Meiji surveys with his own investigation of *fudezuka*, or the small stone monuments built in the Tokugawa and Meiji periods by students to commemorate their teachers, Takamisawa Ryōichirō has uncovered a total of 6,163 schools in Tokugawa-period Shinano,[9] more than four times the Ministry of Education's figure. Recent research in other prefectures has revealed a similar level of undercounting, suggesting that the total number of commoner schools established in Japan during the Tokugawa period may have reached 40,000 or 50,000. Many of these schools were short-lived, but probably 15,000 to 20,000 were in operation at any given moment during the last two decades before the Restoration.[10]

The proliferation of commoner schools in Shinano—in fact, in most areas outside the major urban centers—occurred almost exclusively during the last century of the Tokugawa period. The Meiji

government's investigation identified only 66 commoner schools established before 1750 anywhere in Japan.[11] Ishikawa Ken has located
141 such schools and suggests that their numbers were in fact much
greater—a suggestion borne out by the fact that early eighteenth-
century sources list several hundred teachers in Edo, and local historians have turned up over a hundred pre-1750 schools in Shinano
alone.[12] As a proportion of the total number of schools during the
Tokugawa period, however, the number of schools from the first half
of this period was insignificant. As we can see in Fig. 1, the number
of commoner schools began to increase substantially only in the late
eighteenth century. Starting in the 1780s, the number of schools doubled during each subsequent twenty-year period; this pattern continues until around 1870 (almost all the 1,068 schools opened during
the final twenty-year period were established between 1865 and
1870). But although the rate of growth remained constant over these
eighty-odd years, in terms of absolute numbers, the proliferation of
commoner schools occurred mainly during the last four decades of
the Tokugawa period, and particularly following the Tempō famine
of the mid-1830s. During the 1840s and 1850s, over 100 new schools
opened each year in Shinano; by the 1860s, this had increased to over
200 schools per year. And whereas in the earlier periods the growth
in commoner schooling occurred predominantly in castle-towns and
in villages close to major roads, in these final decades of the Tokugawa period many schools were opened in villages far from regional
urban centers and transportation routes. The nationwide statistics on
pre-Meiji commoner schooling compiled in the Meiji period demonstrate a similar pattern of explosive increase beginning in the 1830s,
when the number of schools opened per year rises dramatically.[13] In
some prefectures, the most significant increase occurs during the
last twenty years before the Restoration.[14] What these statistics suggest is that by 1868, teachers and schools had become a familiar part
of the landscape in most areas of the country; in Shinano alone, there
were 2,675 schools in operation at the time of the Restoration.[15] Only
a few decades earlier, however, commoner schools had not been
so "common," particularly outside the major urban centers and the
castle-towns.

This explosive increase in the number of schools during the late
Tokugawa period meant an equivalent increase in the number of

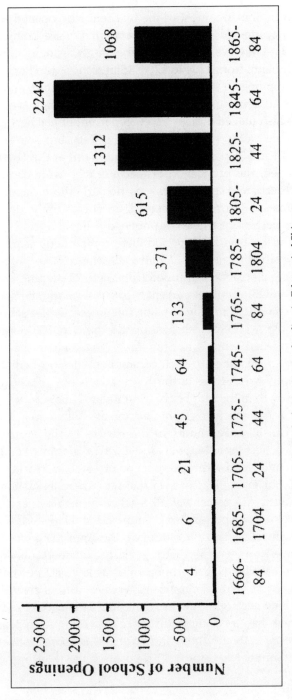

Fig. 1 Spread of commoner schooling in Edo-period Shinano
(adapted from Nagano-ken kyōiku-shi hensan iinkai, *Nagano-ken kyōiku-shi shiryō*, 1: 56)

teachers. And in Shinano, most of the teachers who opened schools in the final decades of the Tokugawa period were commoners. Commoners had always constituted the largest single group of teachers in Shinano; from 1704 to 1764, 45 percent of teachers in Shinano were commoners ("farmers" constituted 35 percent, and "doctors," 10 percent). During this early phase of growth, however, other social groups also played a major role: 35 percent of teachers during this period were clergy (mainly Buddhist priests, but some Shinto priests as well), and 25 percent were samurai.[16] But as the Tokugawa period continued, the proportion of teachers who were clergy and samurai decreased, and commoners—particularly those classified by local historians as "farmers"[17]—played an increasingly dominant role. Sixty-six percent of those who opened schools during the last twenty years of the Tokugawa period were commoners, nearly all of whom are classified as farmers. Meanwhile, the relative proportion of clergy among all teachers dropped from 35 to 23 percent, and that of samurai from 25 to only 8 percent.[18] In absolute numbers, clergy and samurai continued to play a major role in commoner schooling: during these last two decades before the Restoration, 536 clergy and 185 samurai opened schools in Shinano.[19] Nonetheless, the overall trend in Shinano was one in which commoner elites opened schools in droves in the final decades of the Tokugawa period, resulting in a spectacular growth in the number of commoner schools.

When we narrow our focus from Shinano as a whole to individual districts, we can identify important differences in the status backgrounds of teachers (see Maps 1 and 2).[20] In districts composed largely of domain lands, the percentage of samurai teachers was much higher. For example, in Suwa district (where Takashima domain was located), 27 percent of all teachers in commoner schools during the Tokugawa period were samurai; in Hanishina district (where Matsushiro domain was located), the figure is over 30 percent.[21] However, in several districts that contained only small amounts of domain lands, the proportion is as low as 3 percent. The percentage of teachers from religious orders also differs greatly from district to district: because of the large number of temples run by the Jōdō sect (which had a strong tradition of providing formal schooling for its priests) in the northern and northeastern parts of the province, clergy accounted for up to 40 percent of the total number of

Map 1 District boundaries in Tokugawa-era Shinano

teachers in such districts as Minochi, Takai, and Sarashina.[22] However, in the central and western districts (Suwa, Chikuma, Azumi), the proportion of clergy was as low as 13 percent.[23]

The statistical patterns of commoner schooling in Shinano diverge in some ways from the national averages. Although 62 percent of all teachers in Shinano during the Tokugawa period were commoners (excluding clergy), in Japan as a whole commoners accounted for 46 percent of all teachers. Furthermore, whereas there were relatively few teachers of samurai background in Shinano, nationwide almost a third of all teachers were samurai.[24] Thus at first glance, it appears that the figures on the status background of teachers in Shinano are statistical outliers in comparison to the national averages. However, most provinces diverged from the national statistics in some important way; in fact, the national statistics are meaningful only in a limited context, because they are formed by averaging what are in fact a great number of statistical outliers. In contrast to Shinano, most teachers in commoner schools in Edo were samurai. In Kanagawa, where there was a long-standing pattern of wealthy commoners' entrusting the education and discipline of their children to nearby temples, 54 percent of all commoner schools in the Tokugawa period were opened by Buddhist monks.[25] The rural-urban distinction is also significant: for example, teachers from among the clergy were rare in urban areas, and relatively few samurai opened schools outside castle-towns and their nearby suburbs.[26]

Despite this diversity, a few trends identifiable in Shinano are common to much of the country. In particular, we can divide the expansion of commoner schooling in the Tokugawa period into two phases. The first phase, which began roughly in the mid-eighteenth century, witnessed a gradual increase in the number of schools, largely in castle-towns and in settlements along major roads. During this phase, the percentages of samurai, clergy, and commoner teachers were relatively equal. A second phase of growth in the last few decades before the Meiji Restoration produced both a dramatic increase in the number of schools and the expansion of this growth from regional urban centers into the countryside. During this second phase of growth, commoners—and especially village elites—played an increasingly important role as teachers,[27] even in those areas where the overall percentage of commoner teachers was much lower than in Shinano.[28]

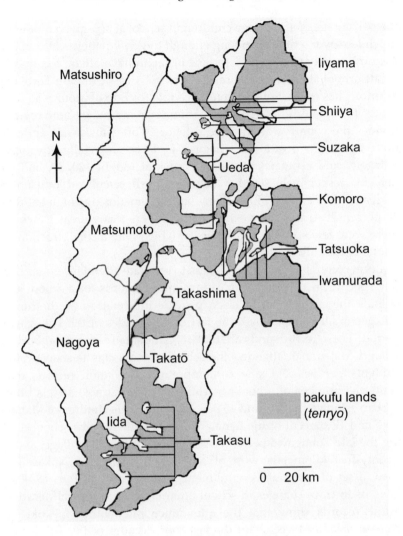

Map 2 Domains in Tokugawa-era Shinano

The exponential increase in the number of schools during the late Tokugawa period might be taken to indicate similarly impressive increases in the number of children attending school, as well as in the overall levels of literacy and educational achievement among the general population. This impression is not necessarily untrue, but it is difficult to quantify: few villages offer both reliable population records and detailed school enrollment records to allow us to calculate the percentage of school-age children in school at any given moment, much less over a time span long enough to verify patterns of change. A number of educational historians in Japan have attempted to calculate school attendance figures for specific areas. Umihara Tōro, for example, has estimated an attendance rate for Edo of around 56 percent.[29] Tone Keizaburō, in his research on schools in the Kantō region, divides the countryside into the categories of "subsistence agricultural villages," "post-town villages," and "commercially advanced villages," and estimates attendance rates at roughly 20, 30, and 50 percent, respectively.[30] Other scholars have calculated unusually high attendance rates for specific villages, sometimes as high as 70 to 80 percent.[31] At the other extreme, there were many areas in which there were few schools, and others in which only a small fraction of school-age children attended.

Local records in Shinano allow us to estimate attendance rates in a few specific areas. For example, enrollment records for a school just outside the castle-town of Ueda provide information on the home villages of all students over the last three decades of the Tokugawa period. These records indicate that 143 students from a neighboring village, Matsunojō, attended the school; the average is sixteen-plus students per year.[32] Using contemporary population records that show the number of school-age children in Matsunojō at this time, we can estimate that around 45 percent of the male children of Matsunojō and 17 percent of the female children attended this school during the late Tokugawa period.[33] At a school in Inekoki village, about twenty-five kilometers west of Matsumoto along the Nakasendō road, a set of continuous enrollment records from 1830 to 1874 allows us to trace changes in school attendance over several decades. These records show that the attendance rate within Inekoki increased steadily throughout the last four decades of the Tokugawa period, from around 23 percent in the 1830s to over 46 percent in the 1860s. Since all these students were boys, it appears that almost all the male children in Inekoki were attending school at the time of the Restoration.

Such statistics suggest that the proliferation of schools in Shinano did indeed result in a sizable and increasing proportion of children who attended school. However, we should avoid making broad generalizations based on these figures. First, there are many potential problems with the statistics themselves, problems common to most statistics on school attendance rates in Tokugawa Japan. For example, in the case of the school in Inekoki village, the increase in attendance assumes that the population figures derived from an 1859 register basically hold for both the beginning of the period (1830) and the end (1874). Furthermore, the Inekoki attendance rates assume that the students at the school came exclusively from Inekoki—an even more dubious assumption. We must also keep in mind that although these schools were located in "villages," both villages were alongside major highways, and one was in the immediate vicinity of a castle-town. Since schools in Tokugawa-period Shinano were highly concentrated in castle-towns and along transportation routes, we should not assume that attendance rates in more remote areas were comparable.

We should also avoid assuming that the growth in the number of schools and the rate of school attendance during the last few decades of the Tokugawa period resulted in a vast increase in the number of fully literate people. A survey conducted in the mid-Meiji period by local officials in the Azumi district confirms the general trend of increasing school attendance but calls into question the common association of attendance with literacy. The investigation took place in Tokoban village, a large village near the provincial town of Ōmachi, located alongside a major road linking Shinano to the Japan Sea. Officials divided the 882 adult members of the village into age groups and then surveyed the level of literacy attained by each individual.[34] What makes this study particularly useful is that literacy was conceptualized in stages rather than as an absolute quality: for example, level 1 signified total illiteracy; level 2 the ability to read (but not write) one's name, village name, and numbers; level 3 the ability to write these basic characters; level 5 added the skill of bookkeeping, and so on, with level 8 signifying the ability to read and understand official documents and newspapers. The survey found that none of the individuals educated before the Meiji Restoration was totally illiterate; however, virtually everyone (82 percent) fell within levels 2 and 3—in other words, most of the village had attained only a very basic level of literacy. In contrast, only 10 percent of the village was able to read and write basic documents, and only a few of these could read official pronouncements or newspapers. This study yields two conclusions. On one hand, it appears that almost everyone in the village had received some formal schooling, very likely at one of the two schools operating in Tokoban village during the late Tokugawa period. On the other hand, the ability to read and write documents and other materials (except those written exclusively in the phonetic *kana* script) was limited to a select few in village society.

In sum, an investigation of conditions in Shinano confirms the general impression of an expansion of commoner schooling in Tokugawa Japan, but it also reveals the patterns and limits of that expansion. After an initial period of gradual expansion in commoner schooling, Shinano experienced a more dramatic increase in the number of schools in the last few decades before the Restoration. This latter phase of growth was marked by an increasingly prominent role for village elites as teachers. Attendance rates also seem to have risen during this phase. Overall, however, the increases in the number of schools and in school attendance produced only a rudimentary level of literacy among the general population, even at the end of the Tokugawa period.

The Initial Spread of Commoner Schooling

The first commoner schools in Shinano opened in the mid-eighteenth century, beginning a modest but steady increase in the number of schools over the next several decades. A number of factors converged to create the context for this early spread of commoner schooling. This section focuses on the role of village elites in this development, particularly on the formation of intra- and inter-regional networks among village elites and the increasing orientation of these elites toward aesthetic and literary pursuits. Another part of the context for the growth of commoner schooling, however, relates to a similar change in the orientation and role of provincial samurai. This development can be traced in part to the movement of Confucian scholars from major urban centers into the provinces during the seventeenth century. Domainal leaders often hired such scholars—many of them students of Hayashi Razan, a Neo-Confucian scholar employed by the Tokugawa family during the first half of the seventeenth century—to act as advisers or as tutors to the daimyo's heirs. Many of them, however, also opened schools. Sometimes these were private schools, operated by the scholars and financed by the tuition of students. Daimyo sponsored other schools to educate their retainers; such schools are referred to by scholars as domain schools (*hankō*).[35]

The fifteen domains in Shinano were relatively slow to open domain schools: the first, in Matsushiro, was not opened until 1758, and most of the other domains did not establish them until the first half of the nineteenth century.[36] In the seventeenth century, however, a number of daimyo in Shinano began to invite Confucian scholars to their domains. The daimyo of Iida domain in southern Shinano was apparently a close friend of Hayashi Razan himself and often invited Confucian scholars from Kyoto and even from Ming China to lecture at the castle in Iida.[37] The Suwa family, the hereditary daimyo family of Takashima domain, frequently brought scholars and poets to Takashima for lectures and poetry meetings.[38] These occasional lectures and study sessions were soon systematized in the form of *shijuku*, or private academies. Although most of these early private academies in Shinano were intended only for elite samurai, other schools quickly sprang up in and around Shinano's castle-towns, thereby making the experience of "school" available to nearly all of the samurai in the province by the mid-eighteenth century. As is true of the private academies studied by Rubinger, most of the private schools opened in Shinano in the seventeenth and early eighteenth century also admitted commoners.[39] These commoners, however, usually traced their lineage to pre-Tokugawa samurai families and were probably not clearly distinguishable from samurai. The presence of commoners in these schools should be seen, in Dore's words, "as a reflection of the still indistinct division between the samurai and the prosperous commoner class."[40]

Although the students at these early private academies in Shinano came from only a small, privileged cross-section of the population, the notion that ordinary commoners might receive an education was not unthinkable. There had long existed within Confucianism a universalistic conception of knowledge and virtue, one that recognized the importance of moral and intellectual cultivation among all people, regardless of status. Itō Jinsai, Kaibara Ekken, and other early Tokugawa intellectuals tapped into this (largely Mencian) strain of Confucian thought and argued that people from all four of Japan's status orders (samurai, farmer, artisan, merchant) could possess moral knowledge and apply it within their own social contexts.[41] And even among those who believed, along with Ogyū Sorai, that formal schooling was strictly for the purpose of training samurai in the art of governance, few denied that a limited sort of education for commoners was useful. In this formulation, education consisted of the inculcation of moral principles necessary to equip people to better perform their social functions, thereby restoring order and stability to the realm. This was the notion of education as "moral suasion" (*kyōka*). At this time, the first element of this compound was usually written with the character meaning "strength" rather than "teaching," and its meaning was closer to "moral strengthening" than to "suasion," giving the term more of a coercive nuance.[42] In either case, the concept of "suasion" or "strengthening" was rooted firmly within the conventional repertoire of proper Confucian government.

We can see this concept of education at work in periodic campaigns by bakufu and domainal authorities to instill in the general population such values as filial piety, frugality, diligence, and respect for law and authority. These efforts usually followed periods of crisis or unrest, when such values were perceived to be in decline. In most cases, these efforts did not involve formal schooling: bakufu and domainal authorities simply dispatched traveling lecturers to sermonize the commoners or compiled books of laws and moral exhortations to distribute to local officials for public readings. During the eighteenth century, ruling elites came to realize that commoner schools could also be an effective means of restoring social order through moral inculcation. In one celebrated example from the 1720s, the shogun Tokugawa Yoshimune arranged for the publication of the *Rikuyu engi taii*, a collection of edicts on popular morality issued by the first Qing emperor in mid-seventeenth-century China, and encouraged teachers in Edo to use the volume as a textbook.[43]

These actions by the bakufu and domainal governments were significant for articulating an authoritative statement on the purpose of commoner education; as we will see, the concept of education embodied in these efforts remained influential throughout the remainder of the Tokugawa period. The efforts themselves, however, were not instrumental in driving the early spread of commoner schooling in the provinces. More significant was the fact that the measures taken by bakufu and domainal authorities to educate their retainers for the purpose of political administration were transforming the provincial castle-town into an increasingly literate, schooled society. In seventeenth- and eighteenth-century castle-towns, there were growing numbers of formally educated samurai, some of whom were unemployed or underemployed, and others who simply had a keen interest in learning and scholarship. This created a pool of potential teachers, and their clientele soon came to include commoners.

In Shinano, too, domainal efforts to educate samurai retainers led to schooling opportunities for commoners. In Matsushiro domain, authorities invited a Confucian scholar from Edo to open up a domain school for elite samurai in 1758.[44] Within a few years, however, other private schools sprang up in the castle-town, either to supplement the domain school's content or to teach lower-level samurai who were not eligible to enter the domain school. And although the domain school forbade commoners from attending, these other private schools in Matsushiro did not; soon, commoners were studying at these schools alongside samurai.[45] In other cases, unemployed samurai wandered from the castle-towns into nearby towns and villages to teach commoners. For example, in the 1750s we find a *rōnin* from Matsumoto domain teaching in a village twenty kilometers south of the castle-town, along the Ina Road.[46] In the 1770s and 1780s, another *rōnin* from Mito domain opened a school in Sasahara-shinden village, located southwest of the castle-town of Takashima along the Nakasendō road.[47] And in 1804, a samurai named Kawanishi Kōshirō, a retainer from Takashima domain who had been expelled for breaking domain laws, settled in a nearby village and taught there for ten years until his death.[48] Formally educated samurai thus helped to transmit the concept of "school" to commoners and from provincial castle-towns into outlying areas.

The reach of these itinerant samurai was limited, however. Their movement into the countryside was irregular and usually precipitated by exceptional circumstances. Village elites, in contrast, were in a better position to convey the concept of school to the commoner population of Shinano. As we have already seen, they ventured into provincial castle-towns to attend private schools and served as patrons for itinerant samurai (or, in some cases, learned individuals of clerical background), thus enabling those individuals to set up shop in rural areas as teachers. In some cases, unusually learned village elites served as teachers themselves, often after the departure of an itinerant samurai or priest left the village without a teacher. The involvement of village elites in education and schooling, therefore, played a critical role in the early spread of commoner schools in Shinano.

Until the mid-eighteenth century, village elites were not equipped, or even interested, in performing such a role. At the beginning of the Tokugawa period, a small number of large landholding families stood atop the hierarchy in rural society, possessing a near monopoly of wealth, status, and political power within their communities.[49] In many cases, these early Tokugawa elites were former samurai who had chosen to relinquish their status and entrench themselves in rural society. In Shinano, as in other areas of the Kantō region, many of these rural elites were former retainers of the Takeda family who had used military stipends to buy large blocks of land in rural areas during the 1590s.[50] Such elites had expansive landholdings, supported large numbers of dependents, and usually held a political office—either village headman (*nanushi*) or village group headman (*ōjōya*). This local sociopolitical structure was in part a medieval inheritance; the "characteristic" features of the early modern village— the *murauke* system (village-wide, collective responsibility for tax payment), the large numbers of independent small landholders, and so on—had not yet materialized.[51]

By the eighteenth century, however, many of these features were beginning to take shape and produce changes in the role and position of village elites. First, a growing parity in landholding within rural society had eroded the economic basis of the authority of these local elites. Acutely aware of this fact, an emerging stratum of small landholders began to challenge the authority of local elites and demanded that their voices be heard in local decision-making.[52] The scale of the authority of early Tokugawa village elites also began to be curtailed, as elites who had once exercised control over large, multi-village units (*gō*) found their sphere of leadership reduced to a single village.[53]

But even as the position of village elites within their own communities was being contested from below and curtailed from above, their horizontal ties with elites in other communities were being strengthened. This phenomenon was in part the result of the conduct of local administration, which over time involved increasing cooperation and interaction among village elites. First, headmen were required, beginning in the late seventeenth century, to attend meetings with all the headmen in their *kumiai*, or village league.[54] In addition, village officials were expected to communicate with one another on a regular basis for the purpose of circulating their overlord's decrees and instructions from village to village. Finally, as Anne Walthall explains, the tasks of shipping tax rice to Edo, maintaining hawking grounds for the shogun, and organizing irrigation systems required extensive regional cooperation among village officials.[55] These kinds of practices began to create regional networks of communication and social interaction among village elites.

The expansion of regional commercial activity also strengthened ties among village elites.[56] In the case of Shinano, castle-towns functioned as the regional hubs of such commercial activity, serving as centers of consumption, production, and mercantile networks.[57] Merchants bought materials in the hinterlands and brought them into the castle-towns, where finished goods were manufactured and, in many cases, shipped to other areas for final sale. The destinations for such products ranged from nearby castle-towns in Shinano and neighboring provinces to distant urban centers, including Edo and Kyoto. For example, tobacco produced in and around the castle-town of Matsumoto was shipped and sold for cash in provincial urban centers such as Iida, Takato, Suwa, Ueda, and Zenkōji, as well as in the larger, more distant markets of Nagoya, Okazaki, and Yoshida in the Nōbi plain and down the Nakasendō road into Takasaki and Edo.[58] Paper bought by merchants in Zenkōji in northeastern Shinano was sold throughout northern Shinano, as well as in Echigo province and other neighboring provinces to the northeast. By the late eighteenth century, dozens of products from various parts of Shinano were shipped to Edo, from foodstuffs (*soba* noodles, for instance) to lacquerware to commercialized agricultural products; hair cords from Iida were sold as far as Kyūshū in southwest Japan and Matsumae domain in the northeast.[59] "Made in Shinano" (*shinshūmono*) became a well-known label throughout most of Japan and could be found on a number of different goods.

For the purposes of this study, what is important about this commercial integration is that it also involved the integration of people, particularly local elites (or would-be local elites) who took advantage of the new opportunities created by the expanding commercial market. At first, intra- and interregional commercial exchange did not usually involve personal interaction among village elites, since the exchange of goods was monopolized by castle-town merchants. During the eighteenth century, however, monopolistic trade associations in the castle-towns were progressively undermined by unlicensed merchants in villages or post-towns who established their own connections with outside markets.[60] In Shinano, this kind of interaction was enhanced by the fact that several major transportation arteries passed through the province, making it accessible to both the Kantō and the Kansai areas, as well as northward toward the Tōhoku region and southward toward Nagoya and the Nōbi plain.

Established village elites were not the only ones to take advantage of the opportunities created by the expanding commercial market. In some cases, these opportunities disrupted local hierarchies, as older elite families were forced to share the stage of local leadership with upwardly mobile families who had achieved wealth and status through commercial activity. And of course, not all village elites became interregional merchants or entrepreneurs. Nonetheless, the expansion of commercial activity and proto-industrial production forged new kinds of ties within and among regions and thus diversified the networks of interaction among village elites. This was especially true in Shinano, because the highly fragmented nature of political authority in the province made it inevitable that commercial ties would transcend the existing boundaries of political administration.[61] The resulting networks of information and interaction tied village elites together at several levels: first, within each region, centered around a particular castle-town; second, in larger circles of trade and commerce that encompassed other castle-towns, both in Shinano and neighboring provinces; and finally, in a remarkably broad circle encompassing Edo, Kyoto, and much of central Honshū, linked together through common webs of personal and material contact. In only one manifestation of these expanding networks, commoner elite families in Shinano began to send their teenage children to a samurai or rich merchant family far away—ideally to Kyoto or Edo, depending on where in Shinano the family lived—in order to teach them discipline and manners and to allow them to "see the world."[62]

As village elites began to strengthen horizontal ties with other elites through administrative and commercial activities, their orientation also shifted toward aesthetic and literary pursuits, a trend that continued throughout the late eighteenth and early nineteenth centuries. This shift can be explained in part by recalling some of the changes addressed above. Namely, as domainal leaders began to emphasize scholarly training among their retainers, castle-towns soon emerged as regional centers of learning and literate culture. In turn, as village elites were increasingly connected to these same regional centers through administrative and commercial networks, they were inevitably exposed to this culture and its accoutrements—most notably, books and schools.

This explanation addresses the issue of opportunity but not that of motive. We must ask, in other words, why village elites began at this time to invest so much time and money in aesthetic and literary pursuits. The answer to this question lies, in part, in the changes in the role and position of village elites during the late-seventeenth and eighteenth centuries. During this time, the dominant position of early Tokugawa village elites grew more precarious, in part because of the erosion of the economic basis of their authority. The families of many headmen and elders (*toshiyori*) faced difficult financial circumstances: in addition to the financial attrition caused by the custom of dividing family landholdings fairly equally among at least two male offspring, the burdens of public office were a significant drain on the time and resources of elite families.[63] As a result, some hereditary headmen in Shinano renounced their families' position and the privileges and responsibilities it entailed. The house rules of one elite family in Ueda domain forbade family members from seeking public office on the grounds that it took time away from the family businesses, often resulted in troublesome lawsuits, and incurred the jealousy of other villagers.[64]

Meanwhile, many landholders—especially those whose holdings had increased significantly over the seventeenth and eighteenth centuries or who had profited from commercial opportunities—began to challenge the monopoly of political office held by the hereditary elite families. One strategy of up-and-coming families was to petition for the creation of additional elder positions, thereby opening up political office to previously ineligible families, some of whom were of small landholder (*kobyakushō*) status.[65] A directive issued by Matsumoto domain in 1800 noted this development: "In recent years," the author lamented, "we see [officials] from among men of small landholder status. In fact, there are some villages where all the officials are small landholders."[66] The decree stipulated that henceforth only one official in each village could be of small landholder status; the other two had to be from traditional elite families. Although this decree was intended to constrain the political power of families of small landholder status, it also sanctioned their inclusion in the political leadership of the village. Up-and-coming families also challenged the status trappings of older elite families. Many families of small landholder status—and even some non-titled peasants (*kakae,* *kadoya, mizunomi*)—became quite wealthy and sometimes used their newfound wealth to purchase the status of titled peasant (*onbyaku-shō*).[67] Others violated village laws by wearing types of clothing and materials customarily restricted to titled families; more than a few village disputes (*murakata sōdō*) in Shinano started over such seemingly trivial matters.

For those established elite families who sought to preserve their local position—as well as for those up-and-coming families who aspired to elite status—such matters were far from trivial. As Pierre Bourdieu has argued, it is precisely when the economic or political foundations of status are being shaken that such symbolic sources of status become more valuable.[68] This claim is based on the notion that symbolic capital is fully convertible with economic or political capital and can therefore function to bolster status even when its material foundation has eroded. Herman Ooms has used this concept in his study of intravillage conflict, viewing titles (like *onbyakushō*), clothing materials, and types of housing as forms of symbolic capital that functioned to maintain or create status differences.[69] This concept is also useful in understanding the involvement of village elites in aesthetic and literary pursuits. Facing various challenges to their economic and political dominance in village society, village elites invested in such pursuits as a means of creating a new foundation for status. They recognized that cultural expertise was, in Bourdieu's words, "rare and worthy of being sought after" and thus could function as a valuable source of symbolic capital.[70]

Village elites began to engage in such aesthetic and literary pursuits around the mid-eighteenth century. One such pursuit was that of *haikai* poetry, which became phenomenally popular among village elites during the second half of the Tokugawa period. There is little evidence of commoners practicing it before this time, and even the passage of nationally renowned poet Matsuo Bashō through Shinano in 1688 received little attention from the people of Shinano.[71] By the mid-eighteenth century, however, a few Shinano natives had begun making a name for themselves in Edo or Kyoto poetry circles. One such individual was Ōjima Ryōta (1718–87), who was born into a wealthy commoner family in the Ina district but left the family business as a young man to live in Edo and study with some of Matsuo Bashō's pupils. Ryōta eventually achieved fame and status as one of Edo's top poets. Upon reaching this pinnacle, however, he returned to Shinano and opened up a *haikai* school in the castle-town of Matsu-shiro, organizing the publication of over 200 poetry volumes and teaching over 3,000 pupils, who ranged from merchants and members of the rural elite from nearby villages to the daimyo of Matsu-shiro domain, Sanada Yukihiro.[72] Similarly, Kaya Shirao (1737–91) was the second son of a samurai in Ueda domain who achieved nationwide fame as a *haikai* master in Edo. Shirao operated a school in Edo during the spring and autumn, but in summer and winter he returned to Shinano and taught thousands of aspiring poets (mostly commoners) from throughout the province—many of whom would eventually become *haikai* teachers themselves and who raised money to publish ten volumes of Shirao's poems after his death.[73] Through the movements of provincial elites like Ryōta and Shirao, cultural forms were transmitted from national to regional urban centers.[74]

These regional urban centers, however, did not serve merely as provincial outposts of Edo and Kyoto culture. For after nationally known masters like Ryōta and Shirao returned from Edo to the provinces, they—and the castle-towns in which they usually set up shop—became hubs in the generation of regional cultures. And if Ryōta and Shirao were the hubs of such regional cultures, then the spokes (to continue the metaphor) were individuals like Kobayashi Issa (1763–1827), a native Shinano poet from a later generation of local *haikai* masters. Issa came from a humbler background than most other Edo-trained Shinano poets. His family lived in Kashiwabara, a small post-town in northern Shinano, near the primary roadway connecting Shinano to northeastern Japan. His father held about six *koku* of land, which would classify him as a small landholder—enough for agricultural self-sufficiency (the conventional dividing line is five *koku*) but definitely not enough to be considered among the economic elite of the village.[75] The family had once had significant holdings, but generations of partitioning among multiple offspring had dissipated their holdings considerably. At age fifteen, Issa went to Edo for a term of domestic service (*hōkō*); this was not, it seems, the "grand tour" type of domestic service mentioned above but a one-year term involving unskilled manual labor. His encounter with poetry, however, kept him in Edo for the next fourteen years.

During his time as a domestic servant, he found time to study poetry briefly with some friends he met in Edo. Later, he formally entered the tutelage of a poetry master in the Katsushika school of *haikai*. He gradually climbed his way up in Edo poetry circles and traveled extensively throughout western Japan teaching and writing poetry. He eventually returned to Shinano, but, unlike earlier *haikai* masters like Ryōta and Shirao, Issa did not establish a permanent school in a regional urban center. Rather, he became an itinerant poetry teacher with a clientele scattered in villages throughout northern Shinano. According to Issa's diary, during the last fifteen years of his life, he spent nearly two-thirds of his time away from his home in Kashiwabara, staying in the homes of village elites who had entered his tutelage. The individuals to whom he taught poetry (at least, those whose names can be located on local tax and population registers) were the upper crust of village society: headmen, sake brewers, large landlords.[76] These individuals were not merely students but patrons, with whose support *haikai* culture reached further into village society through regionally prominent poets like Issa.

We can witness a similar dynamic in the spread of other aesthetic pursuits as well. Terajima Sōhan (1794–1884), for example, was a regional *ikebana* (flower arranging) master from a wealthy farming family in northeast Shinano who had studied in Edo with the nationally renowned *ikebana* master Shōfū Enshū. Like the poet Issa, upon returning to his hometown, Sōhan spent decades journeying around the province, teaching both *ikebana* and Noh to village elites in exchange for temporary room and board; according to Sōhan's records, he taught over a thousand students in Shinano during this period.[77] The popularization of the *waka* form of poetry in Shinano can also be traced to the movements and teaching activities of commoner elites. Momozawa Mutaku (1737–1810), for example, was the son of a village headman in the Ina district who, according to one of his pupils, "developed a passion for *waka* as a youth and traveled to Kyoto at the age of thirty to study with master Chōgetsu."[78] Upon returning to his home in 1801, Momozawa founded a *waka* society; hundreds of samurai, castle-town merchants, and village elites from throughout southern and western Shinano flocked to his home to study with this prestigious figure in regional poetry circles.

The transmission of new ideologies in eighteenth-century Shinano followed a similar pattern and played a key role in the early spread of commoner schooling. Particularly important was Shingaku, a religious movement that flourished in the merchant communities of Kyoto and Edo and was carried into the provinces by disciples during the last few decades of the eighteenth century. Although Shingaku originated in the major urban centers and diffused outward into the provinces, the agency behind this diffusion lies not only in the center but also in the periphery—namely, in the activities of commoner elites in villages and provincial towns. The spread of Shingaku in Shinano is usually attributed to the efforts of two natives, Nakamura Shūsuke (1732–1816) and Uematsu Jiken (1749–1810). Both were born in villages alongside major highways in Shinano and spent much of their time in Japan's major urban centers: Shūsuke spent part of each year in Kyoto as a silk thread merchant; Jiken went to Edo as an apprentice and eventually opened a bookstore there.[79] Both became disciples of Shingaku in their forties after studying at Shingaku meetinghouses (*kōsha*) in Kyoto and Edo, and both returned to Shinano to establish meetinghouses in their home villages.[80] More important to the spread of Shingaku than these meetinghouses, however, were Shūsuke's and Jiken's traveling lectures. Shūsuke traveled throughout most of Shinano, teaching nearly 5,000 students from 350 different villages.[81] The geographic scope of Jiken's preaching was even larger, extending to the provinces of Kai, Kōzuke, Bishū, and much of central Japan.

But the spread of Shingaku in Shinano was not due only to the efforts of two exceptional individuals who traveled to the center and returned to transmit new forms of knowledge throughout the periphery. For once they returned to Shinano, it was only through the patronage and connections of village elites that Shingaku became a prefecture-wide phenomenon. Shūsuke's case is illustrative here. After returning to Shinano, he initially concentrated his teaching activity in castle-towns (particularly Matsushiro, Suzaka, and Ueda) and in nearby post-towns on major highways.[82] During this time, many of his pupils were from villages near these towns; these pupils were probably similar in background to those village elites who traveled to castle-towns to study at private schools or with regionally renowned poetry masters. After studying Shingaku with Shūsuke and returning to their home villages, these elites served as a kind of human infrastructure for Shūsuke's evangelistic activities, housing and feeding him as he traveled throughout the province. In the process, they enabled not only the propagation of Shingaku but also the spread of a concept of "school" forged in the patterns of group learning under the leadership of a teacher in a Shingaku meetinghouse. This concept was in some ways different from that embedded in the master-pupil relationship common in the transmission of high culture: Shingaku meetinghouses were less hierarchical, and teachers saw themselves more as discussion leaders than as professional dispensers of knowledge.[83] Furthermore, as Janine Sawada shows, the Shingaku movement developed texts and teaching methodologies specifically for children, thus fostering the idea that childhood schooling was both distinct from adult learning and important in its own right.[84] In Shinano, we find at least one instance in which a Shingaku meetinghouse was used during the day as a school to teach children reading and writing and during the evening as a site for lectures and meetings among adults.[85]

What was occurring at this time was not merely what Nishiyama Matsunosuke has dubbed the "diffusion" of Edo and Kyoto culture to the peripheries but the formation of new, regional communities of cultural production. Castle-towns served as the nodal points for these communities. This was where the poetry of regionally renowned masters was compiled and published, usually through the initiative and funding of their students. This was also where village elites from throughout the region gathered to study and socialize with other aspiring literati. Upon returning to their respective villages, they sometimes took on their own pupils; in other cases, they formed local poetry associations with likeminded elites from nearby villages. These regional communities had their own "who's who" catalogues of local literary figures, as well as their own hierarchies of masters; famous poets like Ryōta and Shirao occupied the top of such hierarchies, and part-time connoisseurs in the countryside the bottom. These communities sometimes had their own local histories, written by regional poets or artists who sought to legitimize their local field of cultural action and make a name for themselves within it.[86]

These active regional cultures, sustained in large part by the activities of village elites, formed the context for the initial spread of commoner schooling in Shinano. Participation in aesthetic and literary pursuits did not necessarily require that children attend a school; one could, as village elites had long done, acquire the foundations of literacy at home. Nevertheless, the enthusiasm of so many village elites for their new role as literati undoubtedly helped to drive the demand for more systematic arrangements for the schooling of children. Furthermore, the experience of cultural training familiarized village elites with a particular concept of "school," a model easily transferred to the context of childhood education. The personal contacts they forged through their administrative, economic, and cultural activities also provided village elites with access to a network of potential teachers and made it possible to secure the services of a teacher. Finally, the extensive training of many village elites in aesthetic and literary pursuits created a growing pool of literate, formally schooled village elites who could open up their own school. During this first phase of commoner schooling, relatively few village elites took such a step. In the last few decades before the Meiji Restoration, however, they would do so in droves and, in the process, dramatically transform the patterns and purposes of commoner schooling.

The Late Tokugawa Crisis and the Transformation of Commoner Schooling

The conception of school described above, one in which local elites achieve familiarity with rarified forms of knowledge with other village notables under the tutelage of a locally or regionally recognized expert, persisted in Shinano throughout the second half of the Tokugawa period. However, during the last few decades of this period, beginning roughly with the Tempō era in the 1830s and continuing until the Meiji Restoration, a different conception of school emerged alongside it. This new conception was generated in response to the sense of crisis that pervaded late Tokugawa society; it was the extraordinary vigor of this response that fueled the opening of nearly 5,000 schools in Shinano alone during the last three decades of the Tokugawa period. In this new conception of school, the attendance of ordinary villagers was actively encouraged. In fact, many of those who articulated this new conception envisioned mass schooling as a public responsibility—although they defined "public" in diverse ways. The exponential growth in the number of schools, and the new conception of school that informed this development, together constitute a new phase in the history of commoner education in Tokugawa Japan.

Explaining this new phase has not been a priority among historians of Tokugawa education, principally because most historians have viewed the proliferation of schools in the last decades of the Tokugawa period simply as an acceleration of existing trends in the economy and society of the Tokugawa village. Specifically, scholars usually argue that the orientation of farm households toward production for the commercial market stimulated popular demand for literacy, and this, in turn, led to the proliferation of schools. The commercialization of the village economy indeed constitutes a critical part of the context for the long-term growth of commoner schooling in Shinano. However, causal connections between production for the commercial market and the demand for literacy are difficult to establish.[87] At the very least, even if we assume that such a connection exists, the development of commercial integration and the growth in the number of commoner schools are only roughly congruous. This suggests that many other factors were involved.

In Shinano, and elsewhere in Tokugawa Japan, the household economy of village families became increasingly oriented toward the commercial market. This was not a sudden development, however. By the mid-eighteenth century, many ordinary families in Shinano were already investing a significant amount of their time and resources in the production of tobacco, paper goods, oil, cotton, lacquer, and a number of other products to be sold for cash.[88] These trends intensified in the late eighteenth and early nineteenth century, particularly because of the surge in silk-related production in parts of Shinano. The silk industry was not entirely new to Shinano: as early as 1706, in Ueda domain (in northeast Shinano) over 80 percent of all villages were involved in raising silkworms, and 90 percent devoted some land to the growing of mulberry trees to feed the worms.[89] But by the early nineteenth century, Shinano had overcome competition from the silkworm-producing areas of Gumma and Fukushima to become the dominant supplier of silkworm cocoons, mulberry leaves, and silk thread to the Kantō, Kansai, and Chūbu areas. To meet the growing demand, families in villages throughout many areas of Shinano began spending much of their time in silkworm cultivation or silk reeling, and other villages converted much of their dry land, and even some paddy land, to mulberry tree plantations.[90] As a result, by the early nineteenth century in Shinano, the level of rural integration into the commercial market had intensified to the point that it was unusual for a farm family not to devote significant portions of its land and labor resources to the production of cash crops, often destined for distant markets. And of course, along with this intensified production for the market came an increase in the reliance on that market for consumer goods, and farm families perforce began to experience the risks of commercial production along with the opportunities.

These developments are also reflected in the change in landholding patterns in Shinano. Although the late seventeenth and early eighteenth centuries saw the breakup of expansive landholdings by rural magnates, the late eighteenth and early nineteenth centuries saw the re-emergence of large landlords—although this time, often on the basis of fortunes earned through commercial activity. Simultaneously, the average landholding of ordinary peasants shrank considerably. In most villages, the number of families with five to ten *koku* of land (the range usually considered enough to sustain small but self-sufficient owner-cultivators) decreased throughout the eighteenth and nineteenth centuries, and the number with under five *koku* increased steadily. The group that swelled most noticeably—especially during the first three decades of the nineteenth century—consisted of farm families with less than one *koku*, who were compelled to make ends meet through tenant farming, commercial side-employment, and day labor.[91] And during the last few decades before the Restoration, the children of households unable to subsist solely on agriculture began attending local schools in large numbers.[92]

Faced with similar evidence in the Kantō region, Tone Keizaburō argues that school attendance by these children was made possible because many of their families had earned, through the opportunities created by the commercial market, the surplus time and money necessary to pursue a formal education.[93] Despite the small size of their holdings, Tone argues, commercialization had provided them with enough cash and surplus labor that they could now afford to send their children to school. Thomas C. Smith, too, maintains that school attendance was fueled by an overall surplus in the material conditions of farmers: "It is impossible to believe that this voluntary expenditure on education was at the expense of other forms of consumption."[94]

This argument should be revisited in light of the fact that the exponential increase in the number of commoner schools began in the midst of an extended period of famine and material insecurity among ordinary families, both in Shinano and in most other areas of the country. The Tempō famines of the mid-1830s were the worst of a series of famines that began in the 1820s and produced a level of anxiety and desperation in rural Japan not seen since the Temmei famines of the 1780s. In Shinano, the famine began in 1833, as over-abundant rains and cold summer temperatures resulted in abnormally low crop yields, particularly in the southern part of the province.[95] This was followed by similar conditions in 1835 in northern and central Shinano, and then again in 1837–38, this time on a more widespread and disastrous scale. In Kajiashi, a small village with only 40 households, more than 50 people died from starvation. In a 150-household village along the Suga River, over 300 people died in 1838—an astonishing rate of two people per household. In the 28 villages that supplied packhorse labor to the post-town of Karuizawa—an area with a total population of 10,998—the death toll reached nearly 1,300.[96]

It is possible to view the Tempō famines as a brief downturn in what was otherwise an extended period of economic growth encompassing much of the Tokugawa era, a period characterized by declining mortality rates and improving standards of living in the Japanese countryside.[97] The spread of commoner education would indeed be a logical outgrowth of such an environment. That is, declining death rates enable parents to expect with greater certainty offspring to survive, thus making it reasonable to invest a greater amount of household resources in the upbringing of each child. Formal schooling constitutes one such form of investment. In this model of educational modernization, economic development provides families with the resources to make such an investment, while creating a more complex social and economic environment in which parents are less capable of providing their children with the knowledge and skills necessary to provide for themselves—thus requiring parents to entrust the education of their children to specialized institutions like schools.[98]

But even if we recognize the long-term trend of declining birth and mortality rates, the growth of commoner schooling during and immediately following a period of famine suggests that the popular demand for schooling was driven more by scarcity and anxiety than by surplus and security. The desperate circumstances that befell rural society during the 1830s probably intensified popular awareness of the shortage of household resources, thus raising the stakes of any decision about how to allocate those resources. In this context, the decision to send one's children to school involved calculations of both the costs and the potential benefits of such a decision. Tuition was not exorbitant, but neither was it inconsequential. Teachers in Shinano generally collected a few hundred *mon* from each student at the beginning of the year (or in installments at various points of the year), which amounted to roughly 5 percent of the income an adult earned for a season of wage labor (usually two to three *ryō*) in late Tokugawa Shinano.[99] Families also gave teachers seasonal gifts— usually something like rice cakes, sake, handkerchiefs, or fans—at various points in the year. And because most school-age children could contribute to the family income in a variety of ways (weaving straw sandals, picking mulberry leaves, babysitting younger children, and so on), families also had to consider the opportunity cost of the time children spent in school—although, as I discuss below, most parents sent children to school only when it did not interfere unduly with the household's work schedule. Taken together, the costs were significant enough that the economic implications of a decision to send one's children to school were serious—particularly since formal schooling for the children of ordinary farm families was a new concept, a marked deviation from existing patterns.

At some point during the first decades of the nineteenth century, many ordinary farm families determined that the potential benefits of schooling were enough to outweigh the costs. Economic factors undoubtedly entered into this decision. In particular, the increasing involvement of farm families in commercial exchanges may have convinced them of the value of being able to make sense of business-related documents or to perform simple bookkeeping tasks. Especially in the midst of the famine of the 1830s, anxiety-ridden families may have believed that such skills offered security or protection from the circumstances that plagued their communities. Production for the commercial market did not require literacy: middlemen or rural entrepreneurs often organized production and arranged for the exchange of goods for cash. Furthermore, the level of literacy achieved by the children of ordinary families who began attending school at the end of the Tokugawa period was quite limited. Although the children of village elites usually received several years of formal schooling, the majority of children attended school for only two or three years. During those "years"—which, for families who relied on their children's labor contribution, usually began in November/December and ended in March/April—students learned the Japanese phonetic symbols (*kana*) and, at most, 200 basic characters.[100] Nevertheless, the rudimentary knowledge acquired in this brief period of schooling may have indeed been useful in some circumstances, for after learning the *kana*, most students learned the characters for numbers, local and regional place-names, and common family names. And even if retention was minimal, at a time when distant market forces impinged on many families' economic circumstances, the mere familiarity with such knowledge may have lessened one's sense of vulnerability.

Any calculation of the benefits of formal childhood schooling, however, must extend beyond the realm of purely economic factors. For example, the major events in the social life of a farm family were also shaped by the written word. Marriage, divorce, lawsuits, travel, and other central events of rural life were marked by the production of documents. Most villagers entrusted the writing and reading of such documents to village elites, but total illiteracy could be disastrous. According to Takahashi Satoshi, such factors created a popular association of literacy with security—and conversely, instilled a fear of the written word in those to whom it was inaccessible.[101] Furthermore, the world of culture and entertainment in rural society had become increasingly saturated with the written word during the eighteenth and nineteenth centuries. Although villagers could still enjoy theater, painting, and other entertainments without being literate, the written word was still visibly present in almost all such activities: on theater props, on the margins of illustrated books rented to villagers by itinerant peddlers, on the awnings of shops depicted in prints of Edo street scenes, and so on. As a result, villagers who partook of such entertainments were dipping their toes into a world of literate culture, which may have stimulated a demand for literacy and schooling among those villagers who wanted to deepen their level of participation in that culture.

Finally, farm families may have also perceived the symbolic benefits of receiving a formal childhood education. Just as elite families had used schooling to distinguish themselves from other villagers, ordinary farm families might have perceived the potential symbolic value of rubbing shoulders with children of village elites and gaining access to knowledge and practices associated with people of high status in their communities. From a child's perspective, this may have amounted simply to a desire to be included. Children likely knew who was going to school and who was not, and as more and more children in a particular neighborhood began to attend, those who did not would inevitably feel left out. Many teachers led their students on field trips or other activities that would have undoubtedly caught the attention of non-attending children: public handwriting contests, pilgrimages to the local shrine to Tenjinsama (the spirit of the tenth-century poet and scholar Sugawara no Michizane), and other seasonal parties. In one instance, a teacher led his students on a parade through the village during the annual New Year's festival, organizing the students to chant "Join us!" to neighborhood children. One student recalled, "This method must have worked quite well, because there were almost no children in the village who did not go to school."[102]

Considering all these possible reasons why ordinary villagers began to send their children to school at this time, it is reasonable to assume a correlation between early modern socioeconomic developments and a rising demand for literacy among ordinary commoners—especially if we view socioeconomic developments broadly, so as to include status conflicts in village society and the growth of a literate culture. However, in order to explain the extraordinary proliferation of schools in the last few decades of the Tokugawa period, it is useful to shift the emphasis from issues of demand to those of supply. Specifically, we should look again at the sense of crisis that gripped the social consciousness of late Tokugawa Japan, focusing not simply on how it stimulated a popular demand for literacy but on how it informed unprecedented efforts by political and social elites to educate the masses. Bad weather, crop failures, and starvation were certainly of dire concern for ordinary villagers, but they also weighed heavily upon the minds of elites, for whom these ominous portents signified a threat to the existing sociopolitical order. This crisis prompted a response by elites at all levels of the Tokugawa order, a response that took the form of various programs to curb social and moral disorder. Some of these programs entailed the provision of schooling for ordinary people, thus marking the emergence of a new concept of school.

Attempts at educational reform occurred first at the domainal level, within the context of a broader effort by domain officials to strengthen

the financial condition of the domain and the moral condition of its retainers. As Mark Ravina and Luke Roberts have shown, this effort can
be traced to the eighteenth century,[103] but particularly in smaller domains like those in Shinano, educational reforms associated with this
movement did not intensify until the first half of the nineteenth century. The domainal project of educational reform was directed principally at the education of samurai: the daimyo, in the interests of
strengthening the domain by cultivating talent and rejuvenating
moral and martial discipline among their retainers, began reorganiz-
ing haphazard conglomerations of private schools into unified domain academies. In some cases, domainal authorities encouraged elite
commoners to attend these academies in the hope of broadening the
pool of talent available to the domain.[104] But in many domains, educational initiatives went beyond the systematization of samurai schooling. The most notable early nineteenth-century efforts in Shinano involved the official sponsorship of Shingaku education for commoners.
In Suzaka and Matsushiro domains, for example, daimyo not only established Shingaku meetinghouses to provide a supplemental education for samurai but also dispatched instructors on lecture tours to
provide instruction for commoners.[105] In the 1820s, the bakufu intendant in Nakanojō took the additional step of compiling Shingaku
tracts and distributing them to the villages under his jurisdiction.[106]

Other domains sought to intervene in commoner education in the
last decades of the Tokugawa period by using the existing infrastructure of private commoner schools. In most domains, this amounted
to nothing more than issuing official directives encouraging villagers
to attend schools.[107] Matsumoto domain went further by collecting
handwriting samples from commoner schools once a month for inspection by domain authorities.[108] Owari domain officials even organized the opening of 32 commoner schools in Shinano's Kiso valley, and republished the *Rikuyu engi taii* (the Chinese book of moral
exhortations for commoners that Yoshimune had published in the
1720s) so that teachers would use this text in the schools.[109] Finally,
the noted teacher and scholar Sakuma Shōzan (1811–1864) took concrete measures to encourage commoner schooling while serving as a
minor official in Matsushiro domain. In the 1840s, Shōzan worked on
a project to develop timber and mining resources for the domain.
While scouting one area of the domain as a possible site for development, Shōzan observed that the people in the area were "back-

wards" and "unfamiliar with reading and writing," and he called upon a literate older man in the area to teach the local children to read and write.[110] This was important, Shōzan argued, because "if people cannot read, they will not understand anything, and they will neglect to serve their parents or respect their elders." Shōzan even wrote a textbook for the teacher to use, one that taught moral principles while familiarizing students with common characters and expressions used in writing letters.[111]

The concept of commoner education that informed these efforts in Shinano did not mark much of a departure from long-standing Confucian notions about strengthening the masses through moral exhortation (*kyōka*). However, these domainal efforts are significant for two reasons. First, the authorities initiated these measures explicitly as a response to a perceived crisis in the sociopolitical order. An intendant in the Saku district of Shinano who opened up a Shingaku meetinghouse to provide moral instruction for commoners gave this explanation for his initiative: "The Way of human morality has been lost: farmers have neglected their occupation, and merchants struggle for profit, abandoning themselves to extravagance. The Way of the Sages has been obstructed."[112] In the intendant's Confucian worldview, the contemporary crisis was a manifestation of the failure of individuals to perform their ascribed function within the sociopolitical order. This failure was ultimately a moral failure; therefore, the solution to the various social problems within his jurisdiction lay in moral instruction. Again, such ideas were not new. But what is significant is that such sentiments were so prevalent during the last decades of the Tokugawa period and that they produced increasingly active intervention by political authorities in the education of commoners.

What is also significant is that these educational initiatives were devised not simply by bakufu officials or scholars in major urban centers but also by minor daimyo and bakufu intendants stationed in the provinces. Certainly, minor daimyo and bakufu intendants took their cue from bakufu officials in Edo or from large, powerful domains. But although the various reform programs adopted by daimyo and bakufu intendants shared certain generic principles with reforms initiated by the central government (for example, financial retrenchment and moral discipline), the application of those principles to local circumstances produced a variety of specific measures.[113] In many cases, these measures included the provision of moral instruction, and in some cases, rudimentary training in reading and writing, for commoners. Such measures did not challenge bakufu authority or ideological orthodoxy. As Harry Harootunian has argued, however, they signified a dynamic of secession from the Tokugawa order: perceiving that the bakufu was no longer able to respond properly to the current crisis, domainal authorities took it upon themselves to create a new, autonomous space—the morally reconstituted domain—within which virtuous leaders could restore order and provide security and relief for the people.[114] And many daimyo and bakufu intendants, interpreting local conditions as signs of social and moral disorder, adopted educational reforms as one means of establishing such a reconstituted space.

Although these initiatives by daimyo and bakufu intendants were in some ways novel, they played a relatively small role in the dramatic increase in the number of schools in late Tokugawa Shinano. Only a handful of the nearly 5,000 schools opened in Shinano during the last few decades of the Tokugawa period were the direct result of bakufu or daimyo efforts. Far more consequential were the educational initiatives of village elites. Village elites had always been literate, and during the eighteenth century, many of them attended school at some point in their lives. But in the early nineteenth century—particularly in the aftermath of the Tempō famines—village elites throughout Shinano decided to open their own schools, largely in their spare time. And most of these village elites actively encouraged the attendance of ordinary commoners in their communities.

Like bakufu and domainal authorities, village elites felt threatened by the signs of crisis in late Tokugawa rural society. The Tempō famines not only brought starvation and death but also triggered an exodus of adult men from many villages. As noted above, the area around Karuizawa suffered nearly 1,300 deaths as a result of the 1837–38 famine, but in addition, nearly 2,500 residents fled their villages in search of wage labor.[115] In Koida village, only sixteen out of a pre-famine population of over 200 able-bodied male residents remained in the village in 1838; starvation and illness had claimed many, but dozens of others were either working outside the village for wages (*dekasegi*) or had simply fled in desperation.[116]

For elite families hit hard by crop failures or unable to adapt to the changes in the rural economy, this crisis brought personal hardship: a number of headmen in Shinano were forced to flee their village and seek employment as day laborers.[117] More commonly, however, the wealth and position of village elites were threatened by the insolvency of other families in their community. Village depopulation was extremely troubling to elite villagers: not only did it destabilize the village tax base, but it reduced the local labor supply for elite households that depended on hired help. In many cases, the peasants who had died or decamped owed them money.[118] The increase in the number of migrants flowing through rural society also disturbed local order and safety. Furthermore, village elites increasingly faced direct, usually hostile challenges to their position and authority from within their own villages. In these internal village disputes, ordinary peasants contested local elites' monopoly of social and political privileges—mainly political office, but often extending to their titles, their clothing, and other forms of status differentiation.[119]

Village elites perceived these changes as signs of a profoundly disordered world. These elites, highly literate and connected through networks of commercial exchange and cultural transmission, proved ready converts to ideological movements aimed at fixing this disorder. This was particularly the case in Shinano and other neighboring provinces in central Japan; as Walthall points out, Shinano's proximity to major transportation routes provided access to new ideas, and its political fragmentation created open spaces in which unorthodox ideologies could flourish.[120] The restorative ideological movements that erupted in the last decades of the Tokugawa period were remarkably diverse in their intellectual provenance: particularly prominent in Shinano was Hirata Atsutane's brand of nativism, but other rural ideologues positioned themselves within various schools of Confucianism, and still others identified themselves with Shingaku. What they shared was a desire to restore social and moral order within the context of a regenerated community.

Nativism provides an instructive example of these restorative ideologies. Hirata traced the origin of all human and natural life to the ongoing work of the Shinto creation deities, a view that emphasized the connectedness of all things and sacralized the world of ordinary life and work.[121] In the hands of Hirata's followers, this connectedness and sacrality was applied specifically to the space of the village community; this was seen as offering a solution to the problems of exodus and conflict that plagued rural society. Like the advocates of domainal restoration, Hirata and his followers had lost confidence in the ability of existing political arrangements to preserve order and provide relief and were determined to create a space for themselves—the village community—within which the current crisis could be resolved.[122] Village elites in Shinano provided an unusually receptive audience for this message: following Hirata's death in 1843, 639 people from Shinano became his posthumous disciples—more than twice as many as in any other province.[123]

Many of the restorative ideological movements that spread through Shinano and surrounding provinces during the late Tokugawa period explicitly advocated education as one strategy for restoring social and moral order within the village community. One such advocate was Ōhara Yūgaku (1797–1858), a former retainer of Owari domain who, after being disowned by his family and losing his samurai status, traveled through Shinano and neighboring provinces observing at first hand the hardship suffered by many farm families during the Tempō famines. Ōhara was particularly distressed by the self-interest that he believed was tearing the village community apart. Drawing from an unusual mix of Confucianist, Buddhist, and nativist concepts, he sought to rebuild a self-sufficient farming community through a strategy of moral cultivation and practical training, preaching the virtue of social harmony while organizing credit associations and disseminating new farming techniques.[124] Ōhara argued that schooling could play an integral part in this effort by providing village elites with an opportunity to teach practical skills and to inculcate moral virtue within their communities. Education was also adopted as a strategy for rural renewal by followers of Ninomiya Sontoku's (1787–1856) Hōtoku movement. Sontoku, like Ōhara, sought to improve the desperate condition of villages during the Tempō famines by teaching values of self-discipline, diligence, and thrift and by providing practical assistance. The Hōtoku movement found many adherents among village elites in central Japan, some of whom applied his ideas in their communities by opening schools for local children.[125]

Many of Hirata's disciples, too, viewed schoolteaching as a practical application of restorative ideology, as evidenced by the fact that so many of them became teachers themselves. The most explicit theorization of the link between Hirata's vision of rural restoration and schoolteaching can be found in the writings of Miyaoi Yasuo

(1797–1858), a village headman in Shimōsa province. Deeply concerned with conditions in rural society, Miyaoi perceived moral decay to be at the root of desperate material circumstances: "The hearts of the people are not right; they do immoral things, defiling their hearts, their bodies, their houses, and their country."[126] Miyaoi was particularly disturbed by the practice of infanticide, which he saw as proof of the current state of moral decay in rural society and a threat to the viability of the village community. Like Ōhara and Sontoku, his prescription for rebuilding the village community involved both moral cultivation and practical assistance. Accordingly, when discussing the role of schoolteachers in this effort, he spoke of a "Way of teaching" in which teachers not only taught reading and writing but also provided moral instruction.[127]

Matsuo Kōan (1795–1844), a teacher who lived near the castle-town of Iida, viewed his calling in a similar fashion. Matsuo, however, was not one of Hirata's disciples; on the contrary, he was a Chinese Learning scholar who was trained in Tang poetry and wrote commentaries on classical Confucian texts. After studying at an academy in Nagoya and spending time in both Edo and Kyoto, Matsuo returned to Shinano and settled in a village near Iida and opened a school there.[128] His school is perhaps better characterized as a "private academy," since the instruction was advanced and his clientele tended to be the sons of other doctors and village headmen. Yet he used his school to propagate among village elites a kind of reformist Confucianism that encouraged them to apply Confucian virtues in concrete ways to improve conditions in their communities.[129] Matsuo himself set an example of such local activism: in 1833 he donated 30 *ryō* to his village—3 *ryō* to be distributed immediately for famine relief, and another 27 to serve as a fund to provide no-interest loans for poor farmers during future famines. Deeply moved by the suffering in his community, he even adopted an abandoned infant and raised him as his only child.[130]

Many of the village elites who opened schools in Shinano during the last decades of the Tokugawa period neither officially joined one of these restorative ideological movements nor articulated the connection between rural regeneration and schoolteaching. Given the extent to which village elites in Shinano were integrated into networks of information and commercial exchange that extended throughout the region, as well as to Edo, Kyoto, Nagoya, and other urban centers, it is reasonable to assume that most of them were at least aware of such movements. In any case, the sheer variety of these movements indicates both a pervasive sense of crisis among village elites and a common impulse to open schools as one possible means of resolving this crisis. By opening a school, village elites could teach villagers skills and virtues that could assist local households in times of economic distress—which, in turn, might prevent the flight and unrest that were so troubling to village leaders. By providing an opportunity for elites to interact socially with non-elite families, teaching also enabled them to rebuild personal ties that could hold the community together in a time of fragmentation and conflict. In this sense, elites viewed schoolteaching as a public act, undertaken in part for the benefit of the collective—in this case, the village community.

Village elites who were unable to open schools themselves sometimes went to great lengths to find someone outside the village to teach the children in their communities on a full-time basis. In one case, the headman and elder of Sasahara-shinden village in the Suwa district wrote to the officials of a village in neighboring Kai province (southeast of Shinano) in 1823 to ask if a man named Ontake would come to their village to teach. They explained that there had been no teacher in their village in the fourteen years since the death of a previous teacher—a masterless samurai from Mito domain who had taught in the village for 40 years. As a result, parents had to send their children to teachers in distant villages, and the commute "causes them great hardship."[131] The officials of the village in Kai agreed to the request. Verifying that Ontake was indeed "a man of considerable learning" and acting as his guarantors—in a document resembling the letters of guarantee sent by village officials when a *hōkōnin* from their village was sent into the service of a family in another village or town—they sent him to Sasahara-shinden to teach on a three-year contract. Paying him from the interest earned on a fund collected from the "prominent people" (*omodatta hito*) in the village, the officials of Sasahara-shinden wrote back to Ontake's home village on three separate occasions, each time extending his contract five more years. He eventually died in Sasahara-shinden in 1838, leaving the village without a teacher once again. But in 1847, the village officials wrote to request the services of another teacher, this time from the northern Ina district of Shinano. This man taught in

Sasahara-shinden for 26 years, until the Meiji government's promulgation of the Fundamental Code in 1872 and the official closing of all pre-existing schools. During the last decades of the Tokugawa period, this practice of bringing someone from outside the village to teach on a contract basis became relatively common. Sometimes, village elites took turns housing the teacher;[132] in other cases, they pooled their resources to build the teacher a house and provide him with food and other necessities.[133] In all these instances, village elites used their wealth, political capital (to arrange for the transference of village registration for the incoming teacher and encourage the officials in his village to serve as a guarantor), and social connections to provide a formal education for their children.

Considering the value of educational credentials in determining status distinctions within village society, it may seem odd—or counterproductive—for village elites to provide schooling for the children of ordinary families in their communities, particularly at a time when intravillage status distinctions were being contested so fiercely. Put another way, after having enjoyed the real and symbolic benefits of a near-monopoly of literacy and cultural knowledge for over two centuries, why would village elites take the initiative in tearing down that monopoly? We might expect to find opposition to the schooling of poor farmers, like that articulated by Iijima Isen, a village official in the Ina district of Shinano. In 1825, Iijima wrote a "Famine Record" chronicling local conditions during each of the previous five famines, beginning with the Temmei famine of the 1780s; Iijima seems to have written this record as a didactic text for future generations of his household, exhorting them to avoid extravagance and teaching them how to deal with local crises.[134] Iijima, like the various village intellectuals discussed above, was extremely concerned about problems of poverty, flight, and unrest. He urged his descendants to reduce rents during famines and to "save the poor from hardship." But although Iijima emphasized to his descendants the importance of education—which was necessary, he argued, in order to govern the village benevolently, without self-interest—he also warned against the overeducation of ordinary villagers: "It's better if the poor (*chū yori ika no mono*) know nothing. People are becoming increasingly clever, and if even the tenants know how to calculate taxes, there will be disputes. If the masses (*komae*) want to become group leaders (*kumigashira*), the village cannot be governed."[135]

But such sentiments are not necessarily contradictory to the vision of commoner education articulated by Ōhara, Miyaoi, or other village intellectuals. Indeed, these sentiments shed light on a key assumption that informed the efforts of village elites who opened schools in the last decades of the Tokugawa period. That is, by opening schools and encouraging ordinary children to attend, village elites were not seeking to facilitate social or economic mobility in rural society or to erase the status distance between themselves and ordinary villagers. On the contrary, the "schoolteaching movement" of the late Tokugawa period, like many of the restorative ideological movements that informed it, was fueled in part by the desire to reaffirm the status hierarchy within village society. The self-sufficient, harmonious, autonomous village community envisioned by rural intellectuals was not an egalitarian one; it assumed distinct roles for ordinary farmers and the village elites. Miyaoi, for example, stressed that the role of the farmer was to produce food and to pay taxes and rents.[136] However, he articulated a separate role for village elites, a position of leadership granted to them as a divine trust. By stressing the sacred responsibility of village elites to promote the well-being of the community, he also provided a divine sanction for their claim to local leadership.[137] As a former samurai, Ōhara was concerned more with the distinction between samurai and commoner than with the distinctions among commoners. His portrait of a harmonious village community, however, assumed that village elites would play a special role in that community as leaders and teachers. This assumption was shared by most of the restorative ideological movements popular among village elites during the last decades of the Tokugawa period. Even as village elites became increasingly aware of themselves as a distinct social and political group with common concerns and perspectives that transcended the village, they devised measures to strengthen the village community and root themselves firmly within it. In Harootunian's words, they sought to "enforce a community of interests among the upper and lower peasantry" and thereby "overcome the apparent ambiguity stalking the relationship between the village leaders and followers."[138]

There are a number of reasons why schoolteaching was an attractive proposition to a stratum of village elites seeking to strengthen the village community while clarifying their leadership position within it. Assuming the role of "teacher" in the community could bolster their image as both benevolent leaders and local men of culture and constitute a considerable symbolic investment in their own local authority. In addition, having experienced the power of the master-student bond in their own education and cultural training, they may have also seen teaching as an opportunity to re-establish personal bonds of obligation with the lower strata in the village and thus to restore hierarchical order to their community. Schoolteaching enabled village elites to bring local children into their homes, to teach them on a daily basis, to exchange gifts with their parents. Such activities forced the various actors to engage in a personal but hierarchical relationship: they reminded students and their families of their position of dependence and of their roles as followers and pupils, while reaffirming the teacher's role as leader and educator.

Furthermore, there seems to have been little fear among village elites that opening schools to the children of ordinary families would erode their monopoly of literacy or the prestige that accrued from it. As noted above, the education received by most ordinary villagers at the end of the Tokugawa period was rudimentary, and their daily agricultural tasks did not systematically reinforce the knowledge they might have gained while in school. Village elites' literary mastery, by contrast, was not built on a few years of intermittent schooling as a young child. Rather, it was created through several years of study, sometimes at private academies or under the tutelage of regional experts in high culture, and was reaffirmed through travel, work, and hobbies. Two or three winters of exposure to reading and writing was probably just enough for ordinary villagers to peer into the mysterious world of poetry, documents, and ancient texts and to understand the gulf that stood between themselves and those who had seemingly mastered this world. The fact that ordinary villagers likely perceived such a world as irrelevant to their daily lives would only have increased the symbolic value of elites' unfettered access to it.

My intent is not to view the efforts of late-Tokugawa elites to open schools in their communities as a cynical strategy of domination. It is, rather, to take into consideration the intravillage power relationships and status conflicts that informed these efforts. There is, in fact, a debate among Japanese historians whether Tokugawa commoner schools functioned as a liberating, modernizing, revolutionary force in Tokugawa society or as a tool for ruling authorities to preserve the feudal class structure.[139] But this debate is somewhat misguided, since it hinges on a separation of Tokugawa society into "ruler" and "ruled" that effaces the ambiguity inherent in the role of village elites. It also tends to overlook the dual nature of the restorative ideological movements that fueled the growth of commoner schooling in the last decades before the Restoration—movements that sought to rebuild community while reaffirming hierarchy and that echoed the basic assumptions undergirding the Tokugawa order while seceding from that order.

Conclusion

The early growth of commoner schooling in Shinano had its roots in two separate developments. The first was the establishment of castle-towns and their emergence as regional centers of learning and scholarship. The second was the orientation of village elites toward aesthetic and literary activities during the eighteenth century. Fueling this second development was economic competition within the early Tokugawa village, which led village elites to broaden the foundation of their status to include social networks and cultural training. As more and more of these local elites engaged in aesthetic and literary pursuits, the practice of master-centered cultural training became widespread and led to a recognition among elite families of the usefulness of formal childhood schooling outside the home. During this early stage in the spread of commoner schooling in Shinano, school attendance was confined largely to the children of village elites, who spent several years studying under the guidance of a full-time teacher.

Shinano experienced a new phase in the growth of commoner schooling during the first half of the nineteenth century, particularly in the aftermath of the Tempō famines of the 1830s. It was at this time that the number of schools began to increase exponentially, and the children of ordinary farm families began to attend in significant proportions. For these families, the desperate circumstances of the 1830s triggered an awareness of the connectedness of the household economy and the commercial market, as well as a recognition that rudimentary literacy might alleviate their vulnerability during crises. More important, the rural crisis—particularly the incidents of starvation, flight, and unrest among the village poor—prompted thousands of village elites in Shinano to open schools and to encourage the attendance of non-elite children in their communities. This development was informed by the various ideological movements that spread among village elites during the last decades of the Tokugawa period. These movements attempted to resolve the contemporary crisis by rejuvenating the village community through moral cultivation and practical assistance and articulated an implicitly educative role for village elites, who were responsible for leading this rejuvenation. Schoolteaching was adopted by many elites as one strategy of rural restoration. Opening a school provided elites with an opportunity to teach skills and moral values that would improve the lives of local families and strengthen the village community while clarifying the local hierarchy and shoring up their own position of leadership within it. These two patterns of schooling—one rooted in the transmission of high culture among village elites, and another that emerged in the context of the late Tokugawa rural crisis—coexisted during the last decades before the Restoration, bequeathing to the Meiji period a complex and shifting set of assumptions concerning commoner schooling.

T W O

Village Elites and
the Changing Meaning of "School"
in the Late Tokugawa Period

The lead roles in the story of modern state formation have generally been given to "the state" and "the people." The role of village elites, who occupied an ambiguous space between these two categories of actors throughout the Tokugawa and Meiji periods, tends to be subordinated to either of these two categories or ill-defined. In this study, village elites are given center stage; as I hope to show, they played critical roles in the history of schooling and modern state formation. During the initial spread of commoner schooling in the eighteenth century, their thirst for literary and aesthetic training helped to fuel the growth of private schools in and around provincial castle-towns, thus serving as a medium by which the concept of school was transmitted from center to periphery and from samurai to rural commoners. In the last decades of the Tokugawa period, they opened schools in their communities as a response to the ongoing crisis and encouraged non-elite villagers to send their children. In the early Meiji period, the new government mobilized them to carry out educational reform at the local level.

As with the categories "state" and "people," we should not assume that "village elites" were a uniform group whose members were clearly identified by rigid, objective criteria. There were, of course, visible signs that helped to distinguish village elites from others in their communities: wealth, political office, titles. But in order to understand how these signs functioned in village society, we need to examine how people read them. Indeed, what was important to village elites was this subjective dimension of status—that is, how others viewed them and how they viewed themselves. In this chapter, I explore this issue by examining the lives of one family of village elites and schoolteachers in Shinano as seen through the eyes of an elderly member of this family during the final years of the Tokugawa period. These writings detail the family's teaching activities and present a portrait of the late Tokugawa village school and the role of "teacher" in the lives of village elites. In addition, these writings demonstrate how many of the developments addressed in the preceding chapter—the orientation of village elites toward literary and aesthetic pursuits, the spread of schooling in the late Tokugawa countryside, the response by village elites to the perceived crisis in the years leading up to the Restoration—affected the lives and schooling experiences of specific people in the context of a single community.

A caveat is in order. The source materials for this chapter are the very personal writings of an old man, and we need not assume that the author's representations of his own family are factual. Not only were his writings subject to the same practices of selection and omission inherent in any relating of personal or historical memory, he probably exaggerated certain details either to enhance his family's claims to local position and status or to create more interesting stories for posterity.[1] The likelihood of embellishment (conscious or unconscious) does not diminish the value of his account; on the contrary, it brings into clearer relief those virtues and practices that generated status distinctions within the Tokugawa village.[2] The events in his account may not have occurred just as he depicts them, but his stories of his father and grandfather describe activities and character traits that would have been recognized as appropriate for individuals of high status in rural society. The question we should ask is not whether he remembered correctly, but why these particular "memories" would have been useful or meaningful to an elderly member of the village elite in a time of social and political upheaval.

From Samurai to Headman to Literatus

Writing down the unremarkable events of today
becomes tomorrow's enjoyment[3]

This poem was written in the spring of 1868 by Ozawa Watoku (1796–1869), then a seventy-two-year-old teacher and former headman in the village of Ono in Shinano province. For Watoku, this poem served as a guiding principle of life during his twilight years. After his retirement as family head in 1861, he kept a journal until 1869, recording the details of his daily life, his travels, and his teaching, as well as some of the startling and epochal events of the final decade of the Tokugawa period. Motivated in part by the sense of crisis that gripped rural society at the time, Watoku also decided in 1867 to write a detailed family history recounting the major events in the lives of his paternal grandfather, Shisan (1736–91), and his father, Kameharu (1762–1834).[4] In these writings, Watoku dealt extensively with his own teaching activities, as well as those of his father and grandfather (and his uncle and great-uncle). For over a century, teaching and literary expertise had served as a pillar of the Ozawa family's position within the community.

During the early Tokugawa period, the family's position rested not on literary credentials, but on its landholdings and the residual prestige accruing to it as a former samurai lineage. According to a sketchy family tree and a few brief notes at the beginning of Watoku's family history, his pre-Tokugawa ancestors were titled retainers of the Takeda family in Kai province who fought against Nobunaga during the wars of unification in the latter half of the sixteenth century. After the defeat of the Takeda in 1582, the Ozawas moved northward into Shinano province, eventually settling in Ina district. With the implementation of the various policies that served to demarcate samurai from villagers, most samurai were faced with the choice of either moving out of the countryside into castle-towns or relinquishing their swords and becoming peasants. The Ozawa family chose the latter course, abandoning their samurai status and settling in Ono as farmers.[5]

In terms of long-term household stability and income, this was probably a wise decision. It is unclear where the Ozawa family

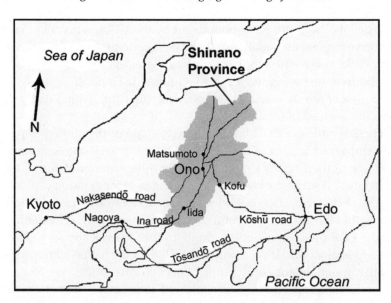

Map 3 Important places in the life of the Ozawa family

would have been positioned along the spectrum of samurai status and income gradations had it retained its samurai status and moved into a castle-town (probably Matsumoto, Suwa, or Iida). As farmers, the Ozawas were well situated to carve out a place for themselves in Ono as rural magnates. During the 1590s, they probably used their military stipends to buy up large blocks of land and thus built an economic foundation for the family based on landowning.[6] Although there are no specific landholding data from this period, it is clear from inheritance records that the family had expansive holdings and large numbers of dependents. And, like many other such families, the Ozawas were able to translate their status as former samurai into political power and social prestige within the village by securing a hereditary hold over the position of headman (*nanushi*) of Ono throughout the seventeenth century.[7]

As noted in the preceding chapter, the growing parity in land-holdings during the seventeenth and early eighteenth centuries—and, in turn, demands by ascendant landholders for increased participation in village politics—began to constrain the local dominance of rural magnates like the Ozawas. Watoku's writings do not provide details about this early period, but by the 1730s, when Watoku's narrative begins, the family faced one economic problem common to early Tokugawa elite families: Watoku's great-grandparents raised six children, including five sons, to adulthood. To partition a largely fixed pool of family assets among so many offspring would dissipate even the greatest of family fortunes.[8]

The fate of these six children suggests some of the strategies parents employed to ensure their collective wealth and status. Because only one of the five male offspring could inherit the headship of the main house (*honke*), the Ozawas faced an important decision concerning their other sons. One option was to retain them and their dependents within the main family compound, thus creating a large extended family. Like many in a similar situation, the Ozawas appear to have decided against this; in so doing they followed the historical trend for smaller, independent family units.[9] One son (the fourth son, Shisan, the grandfather of Watoku) was allowed to separate from the main house soon after marriage and establish a branch house (*bekke*), taking with him a significant portion of land and other resources. Establishing such branch houses placed an obvious strain on the family's considerable, yet still finite, resources. Undoubtedly aware of this fact, the family arranged for their two eldest sons to be adopted into the homes of wealthy merchant families in Ono.[10] In comparison to the alternatives, adoption was not a financially onerous burden on the main lineage.[11] And although maintaining a large extended family or multiple branches may have had some symbolic value, those sons who "left" the Ozawa house could still benefit the family in the long term, for such adoptions broadened and diversified its connections.[12]

Broadening of this sort is also evident in the marriages arranged for the Ozawa sons. According to Watoku's diary, three of the five sons (including the third son, Kozaemon, who was selected as the main heir)[13] married daughters of headmen from other villages in the Ina district. Such marriages had several advantages. Horizontal ties among status equals could help to cement the status difference between those families and other villagers. This kind of marriage publicly displayed a family's extra-village connections, which ordinary villagers were less likely to possess.[14] On a more practical level, developing close ties with the leaders of other villagers could, as we will see with subsequent Ozawa generations, provide a family with resources, opportunities, and contacts that otherwise might be difficult to obtain.[15]

The importance of social connections was undoubtedly a factor in the decision to invest in another strategy for maintaining status: education. Ozawa children (especially male children) had customarily received some sort of education, since literacy was necessary to perform the routine administrative tasks required of village leaders. Until the mid-eighteenth century, this most likely meant home schooling by a family member or a tutor. Beginning with the generation of Shisan and his five siblings, however, the Ozawa family made a concerted effort to invest in formal schooling outside the home. Watoku's family history records that one of Shisan's younger brothers traveled to Kyoto to learn poetry and that an elder brother was sent to Nagoya to study medicine.[16] Shisan began his formal education at a school taught by a *rōnin* named Okamoto in Matsumoto, about fifteen kilometers north of Ono. More detailed records are available for Shisan's son, Kameharu, who pursued his advanced education in a highly specialized fashion, learning noh, Shinto, flower arranging, and poetry from different teachers in southern and central Shinano province. It is noteworthy that the Ozawas were investing in what we would not normally consider to be a "practical" education: for children who would likely become village officials or rural merchants, noh, poetry, and flower arranging do not appear to be critical, or even relevant, skills.[17] Generations of Ozawas had served as headmen in Ono without receiving formal, specialized training in these pursuits. With the relative economic decline of many early Tokugawa village elites, however, aesthetic expertise became both a symbolic and a practical means of preserving—or achieving—status within the village. At a symbolic level, aesthetic pursuits represented a form of knowledge historically associated with the court and samurai aristocracy and inaccessible to most villagers.[18] At a practical level, many political and business contacts among elites were forged while participating in cultural activities. And increasingly, the way to gain access to such knowledge and social circles was through formal education.

Teaching Status: The Ozawas and Their Schools

Schoolteaching occupies a central place in Watoku's diary and family history. His diary contains a great deal of information about his school, and his family history relates a number of unusual stories about his father's and grandfather's experiences as teachers. In this section I use these materials to investigate some of the central features of Tokugawa village schools. In addition, I explore what teaching meant to the Ozawas and how it overlapped with the family's other roles and functioned to bolster the family's status during the second half of the Tokugawa period.

Sometime in the 1750s, the Ozawa family's investment in their children's education began to reap dividends beyond those of prestige or social connections. It was at this time that Ozawa Shisan became a schoolteacher and made education his profession. As noted above, Shisan had been studying in Matsumoto with a *rōnin* named Okamoto. According to the family history, the Ozawas invited Okamoto to teach in Ono. When he returned to Matsumoto a few years later, the parents of the children who had been studying with him asked Shisan, the most advanced pupil in the village, to take over his teaching responsibilities.[19] Shisan, still a teenager, accepted the challenge, and became one of the first commoner (non-samurai, non-clergy) teachers in Shinano.

The story of Shisan's first teaching job allows us to observe the dynamics of the early spread of formal schooling from the castle-town into the countryside and from samurai to commoner elites. In this case, the carrier of the concept of "school" was an unemployed samurai who ventured from the castle-town into the hinterlands at the invitation of a wealthy and well-connected rural family. By the time this initial carrier left, the family was equipped to continue this practice on its own. In the spread of commoner schooling to Ono, they acted as facilitators, as consumers, and eventually as providers. This early school was indeed a product of demand, in the sense that certain families, perceiving some value in formal schooling, were willing to pay the teacher's salary. But in this case, the demand came from a limited segment of the local population. Furthermore, the demand was for schooling, not literacy, for it came from those commoners who had long been literate anyway.

Shisan did not intend for this initial stint as a teacher to be permanent. After teaching for a few years, he married, established his own branch house in Ono with property received from the main house, had two children, and seemed to settle down to the life of a wealthy farmer. His initiation into a life of high culture, however, left him ill prepared for the daily routine of running a farm household. Watoku writes of his grandfather:

Because Shisan had been raised in such splendor at the main house, he was unaccustomed to the affairs of the real world. He was praised for his learning and culture, especially for his noh singing and his playing of the drums and the *shamisen*. However, even though he was born into a farm family, he never picked up a hoe, sickle, or abacus once in his entire life, [but thought] only of things practiced by people above his station.[20]

Within only three years, Shisan had racked up debts totaling the considerable sum of 83 *ryō*, and to pay off his creditors he had to pawn his land, his house, and most of his furniture. His father told him, "You have to find some sort of a job!" and managed to convince friends in Matsushima village (about fifteen kilometers south of Ono) to hire Shisan as a schoolteacher. In exchange for his teaching services, the leading families of Matsushima and two neighboring villages agreed to take care of all of Shisan's living expenses. From this point on, teaching became Shisan's primary occupation. Watoku remarked that his grandfather "had neither an official name nor a seal, relying on the main house for everything, and despising all public matters, official business, lawsuits, and the like." Instead, Shisan spent all his time "teaching, writing poetry, practicing traditional-style flower arranging, playing *kemari* [a game resembling Hacky Sack, most commonly played in court circles], and socializing with notable families in and around Matsushima."[21] He "never saved a penny in his entire life, although he lived quite well."[22] For Shisan and his parents, the returns on their investment in his education were now concrete: it (coupled with rich, well-connected, forgiving parents) enabled a son lacking the disposition to make a living as a farmer or merchant—and who otherwise would have been a financial drain on his parents—to hang onto the elevated status of his family while living a fairly comfortable life as a teacher.

The role of teacher and literatus was also central to the life and livelihood of Shisan's son Kameharu, despite his markedly different personality and career path. Unlike his father, Kameharu seems to have been a responsible, business-oriented individual. Perhaps this was due to his father's surprising decision to send him at age twelve to Edo as an apprentice. This apprenticeship was not undertaken at the exclusion of more lofty educational pursuits—as noted above, Kameharu later studied noh, poetry, and flower arranging. Shisan, possibly regretting the lack of direction in his own life, secured this apprenticeship "to make [Kameharu] start thinking about a future profession."[23] Upon returning home at age sixteen, Kameharu opened up a store and became a prosperous businessman, apparently earning a great deal of money during his time in Matsushima.

Before long, however, Kameharu faced a financial crisis. First, he had to make several trips to Edo to testify on behalf of his younger brother, Ryōnosuke, who had been fired from his job as a clerk at the bakufu intendant's office in Iida and fled to Edo to petition against the dismissal.[24] The trips were expensive and took time away from his business. Kameharu also felt obliged to find a new husband for Ryōnosuke's ex-wife, incurring debts and favors along the way. Then came expenses related to his father's funeral, which was, according to Watoku, "the largest funeral ever in Matsushima."[25] Finally, Kameharu's house in Matsushima was destroyed by fire—only one of several such disasters suffered by the Ozawa family. Consequently, Kameharu sold his land to repay his debts and decided to return to Ono with his wife, mother, and two young children, penniless—35 years after his father had left Ono under strikingly similar circumstances. In Kameharu's own words, repeated frequently by Watoku in the family history, "In this world, at one moment there is prosperity, and in the next, decline. That is the way of this world for everyone."[26]

For Kameharu, however, the periods of decline were short-lived.[27] And, as with his father, teaching served as a safety net, softening the impact of economic hardship. Upon Kameharu's return to Ono, his uncle (head of the main house of the Ozawa family) declared that due to his age and increasing senility, he would turn his school over to Kameharu. After only a short time of living at the main house, Kameharu was able to earn enough money through his teaching and newfound business prospects to re-establish his own household on a firm footing. And within ten years, he achieved political standing within the community, for in 1812 he was selected headman of Ono. Undoubtedly, this would not have been possible without the support of the main house of the Ozawa family, which had remained in Ono throughout Shisan's and Kameharu's wanderings and misfortunes. But Kameharu's educational credentials and his influence within Ono as a schoolteacher must have enhanced his qualifications, particularly among the other village leaders whose children he taught. Once again, the decision to invest in education and in the lifestyle of a literatus had proved an effective strategy for maintaining wealth and status.

After retiring from his position of village headman in 1815 and turning over the family headship to his son Watoku, Kameharu retreated to a life much like that of his father, spending most of his time teaching school, writing poetry, and drinking sake with his friends.[28] Two years after he retired as headman, Kameharu was invited to teach in Minamidono village, about twenty kilometers south of Ono. Watoku recounted that one day in 1817, two representatives from Minamidono came to Kameharu's house to ask if he would come to their village to teach. Two days later, they returned, entreating Kameharu to grant their request:

"Please, we beg of you. At first there will be only a few students, but a group of four or five of us from Minamidono and the surrounding area will provide for you, so you will want for nothing. If you will only teach our children, we will take care of you. You won't have anything to worry about."[29]

After consulting with his family and the parents of the children attending his school in Ono, Kameharu consented to the request and arranged for his son Watoku to take over his students in Ono. On the day he set out for his new position, the people from Minamidono dispatched a group to meet him halfway between the two villages; there they presented him and his traveling companions with box lunches and sake. Then, according to Watoku, "they waved off our porters, telling them, 'Go back to Ono with your horses. The people from Minamidono will take it from here.' They provided a special horse and saddle on which father could ride for the remainder of the journey."[30] Finally, when Kameharu arrived in Minamidono on horseback, he and his companions were treated to a tremendous two-day feast. Watoku recorded the event in detail, commenting that they were treated "as if they were the guests at a wedding ceremony."[31]

This was only the first of three occasions in which Kameharu was hired to teach in other villages. All occurred in the Bunka and Bunsei eras (1804–29), the period when the number of commoner schools in Japan began to increase more rapidly. During this period, in Shinano alone 30 new schools were opened each year—more than ten times the rate when Shisan began teaching in the 1750s. Whereas most earlier schoolteachers had been learned men passing through Shinano, by the early nineteenth century there was a pool of formally educated commoners capable of providing this service. This was a significant development, since it enabled children to receive formal schooling within their own village rather than at the nearest castle-town or in distant urban centers. In turn, schools could target not only young adults but younger children, too—and, at least in theory, children from families who, unlike the Ozawas, could not afford to send their children great distances to receive a formal education.

The story of Kameharu's experience as a teacher-for-hire in Minamidono village suggests, however, that schooling was as yet not widely available. The individuals who asked him to come to Minamidono said that although there would be only a few students, four or five families from the village would supplement tuition revenues with their own funds so that Kameharu could live comfortably. From this we can infer that what motivated the leaders of Minamidono to hire a teacher was not a pressing demand for education from the people of their village; rather, these elite families took the initiative to hire a teacher and start a school knowing that the lack of students would require them to shoulder the burden of paying Kameharu. This suggests that the number of teachers had increased because of the efforts of village elites *before* the general population began demanding formal schooling. Later, Watoku notes, as Kameharu's reputation spread through the area, the number of students at his school increased to as many as 40. Watoku also notes that these students came from at least six different villages, with only a handful from each village. It thus seems safe to assume that Kameharu's school was quite exclusive, a school taught by a gentrified village notable and attended by the children of wealthy parents who wanted their offspring to achieve a certain level of literary and aesthetic expertise.

This pattern of rural schooling had changed considerably by the time Watoku, following in his father's and grandfather's footsteps, began teaching full-time after his retirement from the family headship. The time was the mid-1850s, when much of the Japanese countryside was experiencing a new phase in the expansion of commoner schooling: the number of new schools was increasing exponentially, and the middle and lower classes of rural society had begun attending in large numbers. Watoku's journals confirm some of these trends, in particular the attendance of non-elite villagers during the last decades of the Tokugawa period. During peak seasons (from late fall to early spring), the number of students attending his school was often above 70, the majority of whom were from Ono. Furthermore, there were four other schools in Ono at the time; the five counted among them a combined peak attendance of well over 200 students.[32] Ono was a large village, with a population at the end of the Tokugawa period of about a thousand. Even if we assume that many of the students at the other schools came from outside the village, we can surmise that most of the children in Ono were attending school at the end of the Tokugawa period, and that many of them were not from wealthy families.[33]

Watoku's journals also suggest that we cannot necessarily equate wider access to schooling during the late Tokugawa period with the breakdown of status distinctions within the village. Even though the school was now accessible to a much larger segment of the village population than before, there were significant differences in the level and extent of the education received by Watoku's students. An examination of the names in Watoku's periodic enrollment records shows that most students attended Watoku's school only briefly — often for only one year. In contrast, a few of Watoku's students remained in his school for as long as seven years. Furthermore, whereas many of these advanced students attended Watoku's school year-round, the vast majority of the beginning students attended for only a few months.

The difference between one or two years of intermittent schooling and seven years of regular, concentrated schooling cannot be overestimated. In a student's first year of schooling, he would have learned *kana* and a few basic characters — mainly those used in numbers, personal names, and village names.[34] In his second year, he would have continued studying characters using workbooks Watoku made from two Buddhist morality texts, *Teachings for the Young* (*Dōjikyō*) and *Teaching the Words of Truth* (*Jitsugokyō*).[35] If a child quit school at that point, his retention would likely have been minimal, and his schooling would most likely have had little impact on his life. In contrast, children who studied in Watoku's school for many years gained access to an entirely different social and intellectual world. Not only did they learn high culture (noh, flower arranging, poetry), but they also studied the classic Confucian texts—*Doctrine of the Mean* (*Chūyō*), *Great Learning* (*Daigaku*), *Analects* (*Rongo*), and *Mencius* (*Mōshi*). Rarified knowledge of this sort imparted prestige to those individuals who acquired it. Cultural accomplishments, furthermore, facilitated interaction with others who shared them, whether in a social, political, or business context. Even after the children of ordinary villagers began attending school in large numbers during the last decades of the Tokugawa period, education continued to be a source of distinction among villagers; existing status divisions within the village were confirmed in the schools by differences in the duration, content, goals, and effects of education.

Just as these schooling practices reflected the existing status hierarchy within the village, they also conformed to existing rhythms that structured the economic and social life of rural society. As did all Tokugawa-era village teachers, Watoku adapted his schedule of instruction to the agrarian and ritual calendar of his community. Watoku's schoolyear began on the twenty-first day of the first month, following a month-long break coinciding with New Year festivities. Unlike most other breaks during the year, this one was "official": Watoku recorded an annual year-ending school party on the twentieth of the twelfth month and a back-to-school celebration on the twenty-first of the next month, and each year the dates of the break remained fixed. During this peak time of year for school attendance (which usually began in the eleventh month and continued until late in the third month, an off-season for agriculture), as many as 70 students would show up at Watoku's house for instruction.[36] However, this coincides with the period of severe weather in Shinano; consequently, it was quite common for Watoku to write that students who lived far away did not attend because of snow, cold, or heavy rain. Beginning in April, attendance tapered off to 20 to 30 students as farm families prepared paddies and dry fields for cultivation. Then came the major events of the agrarian calendar: the planting and harvesting of paddy fields. In most of Shinano, these tasks took place in June and October, respectively; during these busy times of year Watoku's journal entries mention other happenings but not students or school. However, unlike many late Tokugawa rural teachers, Watoku continued to meet with his students during the months between planting and harvesting (July through September), when dry-field crops like sesame, millet, and wheat were sown. Attendance dropped off precipitously at these times—Watoku often recorded as few as three or four students—but Watoku's school remained open. Watoku sometimes noted the specific tasks that prevented students from attending, citing everything from grass pulling to chestnut gathering to fertilizer application. Indeed, his own agricultural tasks often required him either to cancel instruction or adapt it to his own schedule. At various times he suspended class, usually for a half-day, so that he could weed, wash radishes, pick plums, or, most commonly, perform some task related to his family's involvement in the cultivation of mulberry trees. One day he even had his students help him weed the mulberry field during the lunch break.[37]

The village's ritual calendar placed similar constraints on Watoku's schedule of instruction. In addition to the month-long New Year's break, we find in his diary many other ritual events that caused him to change his normal teaching activities. For example, on 1866/3/9, Watoku noted, "We're having a Kompira festival in the evening; so I dismissed the students before noon so they could go play."[38] Eight days later, his students left at noon to attend a Kannon festival. The following month, he again dismissed them early because it was a local deity's festival (*chinju matsuri*). Other more widely celebrated occasions such as the seasonal festivals (*gosekku*) in March, May, and October and the Tanabata festival in July resulted in a full day's suspension of class.

Watoku sometimes organized activities to coincide with such events. For example, before the Tanabata festival in July, Watoku prepared special workbooks to teach the children about the festival during the week preceding the event. Then, on the day of the festival, he held special Tanabata writing contests attended by the children, their parents, and neighbors. Watoku ranked the students' papers and displayed them as part of the festival. Similarly, to commemorate the coming New Year, Watoku wrote workbooks to help children practice for the writing contest to be held during a village-wide celebration on the last day of school before the New Year's break. On 1863/12/8, Watoku wrote about the progress of the students' practice for this occasion: "New students finished practicing for the writing contest. Even though I break my back every day trying to help them, there are so many new students that we don't accomplish much. In any case, students who have no desire and who can't remember anything tend to do poorly anyway. I'm very disappointed."[39] On the day of the contest, however, Watoku commented happily, "The students all did much better than I expected."[40]

Like most teachers, Watoku scheduled the collection of tuition and other forms of remuneration to coincide with the ritual calendar. According to his diary, he collected 100 *mon* from each student on two occasions during the year: before the New Year's break, and around the time of the midyear festival (Obon). In addition, there were several other times of year when students were expected to bring a gift to Watoku: the beginning of the schoolyear after the New Year's holiday, the seasonal festivals in the third and fifth months, and the Tanabata festival in the seventh month. The gifts varied, but usually consisted of such mainstays as rice cakes, sake, and handkerchiefs. In terms of total income, Watoku received about two *ryō* each year—roughly the amount an adult could earn as a seasonal laborer—plus all the sake and rice cakes he could consume. His net pay, however, was considerably less, for Watoku used some of this money to cover the operating expenses of his school. Watoku bought brushes, ink, and paper to make the workbooks used by the students. A few times a year Watoku made bulk paper purchases costing several hundred *mon*. Because Watoku held class in his home, there were no major overhead expenses beyond the extra fuel needed for heat and light; however, we do find in Watoku's journal that he replaced the paper on his sliding doors an inordinate number of times each year, suggesting that the daily traffic of dozens of students took its toll on his house.

Regardless of its immediate financial value, teaching was very meaningful to Watoku and central to his sense of identity and purpose. Particularly important to Watoku were the personal, lifelong ties he and his family were able to create with their students. Watoku's family history is replete with evidence of such ties. Over 300 people attended Shisan's funeral in 1791, for example, mainly because so many of his former students came—not only from Matsushima (where he died) but also from fifteen kilometers away in Ono. Watoku stated proudly in his family history that people "from both high and low" attended, and that "it was the first great funeral in Matsushima, I hear."[41] When Kameharu died in 1834, students from each of the four villages in which he had taught made the journey to Ono for the funeral. Watoku remarked, "Because he was a teacher for so many years, we were able to give father a lively send-off at the funeral."[42] Earlier, when Kameharu's house was destroyed by fire, Watoku notes, his former students helped rebuild it.[43] Perhaps the most unusual example of this teacher-student bond occurred when a group of Shisan's former students carried their palsy-stricken teacher fifteen miles to see a play:

While [Shisan] was stricken with palsy, a group of young men from Kino-shita said to each other, "The famous actor Hatsuzō is putting on a play along the riverbed of the Obinashi river. We ought to take him to see it—it might cheer him up." So they put him on a palanquin, carried him [to the play], opened the gate, spread out a futon in a private gallery they had made ahead of time, and laid him down on top of it. There, the pupils from Kino-shita and Matsushima surrounded him and brought him lots of sake and fish. Then, distinguished people from nearby villages came to pay him a visit and brought him food and drink all day. The actor Hatsuzō was surprised, and went to the gallery and said to [Kameharu], "We've been to many different provinces doing kyōgen, but seeing all these distinguished people visiting [Shisan] and giving him this feast, I am truly impressed."[44]

This kind of close teacher-student relationship often extended to parents as well. Watoku's diary reveals that parents frequently invited him to their homes to exchange gifts and drink sake. Whenever he organized school festivals or held special writing contests for his students, he invited the parents to view their children's work and join the festivities. On the last day of school before the New Year's break in 1863, for example, he noted, "The children gathered early this morning for the contest. Their parents came later, bringing red-bean cakes with sesame seeds, and each brought some kind of gift. We invited a good-natured group of people from around the village, with people of both high and low status, and we ate, drank, and celebrated until evening."[45]

These ties between teacher, student, and parent highlight a defining characteristic of most pre-Meiji village schools: they had no permanent institutional existence apart from the individual instructor and his relationship with the students and parents. This was due in part to the absence of regulation by the bakufu and han governments as well as to the schools' origins in a type of master-pupil relationship experienced by most teachers themselves in learning poetry and other forms of high culture. When a teacher was sick or busy with other work, the school disappeared for as long as he was away (unless there was a relative available to teach in his stead, as Watoku did for his father); if a teacher fell ill or died, the school disappeared altogether. Conversely, if parents chose not to send their children to a school and pay for their tuition, there was nothing to prevent it from ceasing to exist. Of course, all schools are shaped by the personal relationships between the teachers, students, and the community at any given time; most pre-Meiji village schools, however, were wholly defined by that nexus. This is why the various Japanese terms used to refer to pre-Meiji educational arrangements (*terakoya*, *tenaraijo*, and so on) are somewhat misleading. As Rubinger points out, there was no generic term for "school" in common use in Tokugawa Japan: there were commonly used terms for entering a teacher's tutelage for the first time (*terahairi, tōsan, tenaraihajime*) and leaving a teacher's tutelage (*terakudari*), but people rarely referred to the institution itself.[46] Most often, people simply used the name of the instructor. When the Meiji government began compiling statistics on the Tokugawa-period schools, it had to adopt some sort of institutional nomenclature; it was from this point that terms like *terakoya*, *shijuku*, and *kajuku* became widely used. But the children who attended the schools had no reason to conceive of them in this abstract manner; for them, "school" was the teacher-student relationship.

It was perhaps this close, personal nature of the teacher-student-community relationship in pre-Meiji village schools that made teaching so attractive to village elites. During Shisan's and Kameharu's time, the relationships forged in the context of the school solidified the Ozawa family's position in a regional network of leading families and created among them a body of shared knowledge that reaffirmed their own status while excluding others. For Watoku, who taught in the last two decades of the Edo period, the more diverse social composition of his school enabled him not only to strengthen horizontal ties of this sort but also to form direct and personal strands of obligation and loyalty with students from the wider group of small landholders and tenants within his village. At a time when village elites were increasingly becoming the targets—rather than the leaders—of peasant protests, the value of these relationships could not have been lost on families like the Ozawas.

The Ozawa Family's Non-Teaching Roles

Village elites enthusiastically accepted the role of teacher because it complemented and overlapped with their other roles and functions in local society. This overlap was due in part to the nature of the pre-Meiji village schools; the absence of the distinct and permanent institutional presence commanded by most modern schools blurred some of the lines separating schooling practices from other aspects of social and cultural life. Performing the role of teacher could, therefore, strengthen and broaden a reservoir of authority founded on other functions. One of these was the role of headman, a post occupied by Kameharu in the 1810s and later by Watoku.

In his family history, Watoku recorded several incidents from his father's term in office, focusing on those situations in which Kameharu was compelled to act as mediator—within Ono, between Ono and neighboring villages, and, in one case, between Ono and the overlord authorities. This last incident occurred in 1814, when the bakufu directed Ono and other villages to contribute portage corvée to assist the passage of authorities through the post-town of Shiojiri (just north of Ono) for the bicentennial celebration at Nikkō Shrine.[47] After Kameharu had promised that his village would fulfill the request, the poor farmers (*komae*) of Ono plotted to interrupt the procession to complain about the unreasonable corvée obligations. According to Watoku's account, two representatives from the bakufu intendant's office in Iida sent word to Kameharu that they were arriving to investigate the matter personally. He was to gather all the men of the village together at his house by the time they arrived. The sun set as Kameharu frantically made the necessary preparations. Then the authorities appeared, clothed in formal robes and flanked by spear-toting bodyguards who lit candles and took out handcuffs and ropes to intimidate the villagers. The two officials proceeded to scold Kameharu in front of his fellow villagers for the trouble they had caused:

Reneging on one's labor obligations is the height of insolence. . . . For if we are questioned by the authorities (*gokōgisama*) when they pass through . . . it will reflect badly even upon our own office. If someone does not show up [for *sukegō* service], it will mean trouble, not only for that person, but for the village officials as well. In fact, the blame will fall even on us. Fearlessly committing such selfish acts demonstrates contempt for our office![48]

According to Watoku, the perpetrators "trembled with fear, and said not a word," and the authorities made the entire village sign a pledge promising to comply with the corvée request.[49]

As Ooms points out, overlords usually left villages alone to con-duct their own affairs as long as they maintained public order and did not openly challenge overlord authority; for their part, villages sought to preserve a semblance of internal harmony so that over-lords would leave them alone.[50] In this case, an open challenge to overlord authority pierced what Ooms terms a system of "mutual avoidance." The overlords had to enter the community and interfere in its affairs, and the village officials, who were entrusted by over-lords with the responsibility of ensuring that such disruptions did not occur, were held accountable along with the perpetrators. Kame-haru experienced firsthand the pressures of serving in the Janus-faced role of headman, acting as both "representative of the village community" and "terminus of the state's institutional apparatus."[51] Yet Kameharu also experienced the benefits of serving in this capac-ity. To be sure, he temporarily lost face with his superiors due to the momentary disruption of village harmony and solidarity. His posi-tion as point man in this kind of direct interaction with overlords, however, unquestionably lent him a great deal of authority in the eyes of the people of Ono. Hosting the officials from Iida in his home and even being scolded by them reaffirmed Kameharu's position at the pinnacle of Ono society.[52]

Kameharu's activities during his term as headman likewise helped solidify and expand his extra-village contacts. As one might expect, his responsibilities required him to communicate (and social-ize) regularly with officials from other villages in the area.[53] And since Ono was bakufu land (*tenryō*) ruled from the intendant's office in Iida, he was frequently required to make the two-day trip to Iida, usually to testify in some sort of village dispute. Whenever disputes arose between Ono and a village under a different political jurisdic-tion, he was summoned to Edo. Because Ono was bordered by villages ruled by the domains of Takatō and Matsumoto, such incidents were common. When he traveled to Edo as the representative of Ono, Kameharu stayed in the homes of acquaintances established through his economic or cultural activities; conversely, Watoku noted that while on a post-retirement trip to Edo, Kameharu visited the homes of individuals he had met while serving in the capacity of head-man.[54] Thus not only did his position as headman affirm his author-ity as a local leader, it also strengthened his extra-village contacts and further integrated him into a regional society of village elites. The Ozawa family's political activities, like their cultural and eco-nomic pursuits, took them into a different world from the one in which most of the people of Ono lived. This was a world in which Edo and Kyoto were not distant abstractions but real places directly relevant to their own lives—and a world in which a much broader range of knowledge, information, and social contacts was both avail-able and necessary.

Among the roles most important to the self-image of the Ozawas was that of connoisseur of high culture. Watoku clearly enjoyed writing poetry; in fact, poems were fundamental to the narrative format of his journal, inserted to convey emotions and observations at strategic moments. His diary reveals that he taught noh singing to both children and adults and also sang occasionally at wedding ceremonies and other special occasions in Ono and the surrounding area. His father, too, was an enthusiastic practitioner of noh: Watoku commented that "during Kameharu's youth and continuing through his prime, kyōgen [a form of noh] was very popular in the town of Ina as well as in Matsushima. Every year kyōgen performances were staged, and Father participated. He was an expert in *onnagata* [the female impersonation roles], and he worked with only the most skilled actors from the area and put on kyōgen plays."[55] Among Wa-toku's relatives, however, it was his grandfather, Shisan, whose aes-thetic prowess was nonpareil. Watoku commented repeatedly in his family history about his grandfather's expertise in poetry, flower ar-ranging, flute (*shakuhachi*), and *kemari*.[56] He seems to have admired Shisan's orientation toward such refined pursuits more than his fa-ther's keen eye for business and local politics.

For Watoku, this artistic, literary, and musical expertise appar-ently translated into a position of de facto leader of village cultural activities. I noted above that he frequently organized special celebrations for his students at New Year's and other seasonal holidays and that these student-centered celebrations often incorporated parents, neighbors, and other segments of the village population.[57] His diary suggests that he also helped organize cultural or ritual activities within the village at large, outside the context of his role as teacher. In the summer of 1863, for example, he collected contributions for the construction of a local shrine and then sent hand towels or sake to all those who contributed or otherwise assisted with the preparations.[58] On other occasions, we find him securing stonecutters and listing the people who contributed their labor to the construction of a memorial,[59] or choosing among different lumber contractors to supply the wood for a Tengu deity festival.[60] His journal contains dozens of lists recording the kind and amount of food and other party favors individual villagers brought to community festivals, an indication that he must have been involved in organizing these events. Why or how Watoku was selected to perform such a function is not certain; however, his role as organizer of school-centered festivals and his expertise in matters of culture undoubtedly made him a strong candidate for village leader in such matters.

Outside the village, the Ozawa family's education and their aesthetic pursuits initiated them into loftier social circles based in nearby towns and regional urban centers. Watoku was conscious of this connection, for his discussions of his father's and grandfather's talents are always followed by details about their social networking. After proudly recounting his father's noh skills, Watoku wrote that "he often made friends [at these performances], and so he was close to many of the notable families in Ina. After he moved back to Ono, they frequently visited him during their trips from Ina up to Matsumoto."[61] Similarly, after writing about his grandfather's *kemari* prowess, Watoku commented, "He often fraternized with the great families (*taika*) and dignitaries (*rekirekishū*) around Matsushima, for at this time, *kemari* was in fashion with the wealthy crowd in the Ina district."[62] Watoku tells an odd story about how Shisan and two friends would go to Matsumoto disguised as mendicant monks and walk around the castle playing the flute. Afterwards, according to Watoku, "He would socialize with samurai and attend elegant feasts."[63] In Watoku's eyes, the family's aesthetic expertise gave it access to social circles that would otherwise have been out of reach; such social interaction, in turn, lent status and prestige to the family.[64]

In addition to providing access to the social circles of superiors, the family's training in aesthetic pursuits provided a forum for building valuable friendships with other village elites from throughout the region. Kameharu, for example, while studying noh, poetry, and other subjects with noted masters in the area, developed a circle of what Watoku calls *gakumon no hōyū*, or fellow disciples of the same teacher. While in his twenties, Kameharu and about a dozen of these fellow disciples traveled to Ise, Osaka, and Kyoto on a pilgrimage and sightseeing trip; while in Kyoto, they visited their poetry teacher's former master, a noted poet named Chōgetsu. Kameharu and his friends stayed with Chōgetsu for several days, writing poetry under his tutelage and listening intently to his words of wisdom. They brought back to Shinano shared experiences and knowledge, as well as a common connection to a well-known poetry master.[65] Kameharu maintained contact with his fellow students for the rest of his life, mainly through poetry gatherings held periodically in Matsumoto, Suwa, and various villages in the Ina district. Connections of this sort played an important role in Tokugawa history. As Miyachi Masato has pointed out, relationships forged among village elites in the context of cultural activities often served as private channels for the spread of political information, especially during the final decades of the Tokugawa period.[66] These connections were critical to the process of cultural integration in Tokugawa Japan, linking Edo and Kyoto to the provinces in a reciprocal exchange of cultural knowledge.[67] But for the Ozawa family, these extra-village connections held an additional significance, since they symbolically reinforced the family's status *within* Ono.

Aesthetic expertise and social connections also served a very practical function. Networks of local elites, established in the context of cultural pursuits, facilitated the transmission of economic capital. Kameharu, in particular, capitalized on his cultural contacts in his business career. Watoku wrote that, after returning from his apprenticeship in Edo, Kameharu opened up a wholesaling business handling "large and small goods, brushes, ink, and the like" not only in south-central Shinano but also in several surrounding provinces.[68] "Well thought of by everyone," he "received the favor of various people from many different areas." For this reason, Watoku claimed, "he was able to raise investment capital quickly and easily," to the point that he "was able to buy and sell freely even while having twenty-five to thirty *ryō* in outstanding loans, and thus could pay the loans back on time." After recording the names of some of the well-known *gōnō* with whom Kameharu had done business, Watoku mentioned that they would often stay over for extended periods at an inn in Matsushima while engaged in transactions with his father. During those stays, Kameharu "would become very friendly with them. After a while, he was able to interact with these men from distant provinces as if they were his real brothers." Because of such contacts, Watoku asserted, his father was able to expand his business, and during the Temmei famine and other periods of crisis, he "bought up soybeans in Iida and sold them in Kai province at a huge profit. He also made a killing in the grain market. Consequently, they lived comfortably, and he was praised for ensuring the security of his parents and being filial toward them."[69]

From Watoku's perspective, the contacts and reputation his father had established through his education and cultural pursuits were essential to the success of his business. Particularly suggestive is the statement that Watoku could interact easily with merchants from different parts of the region. Undoubtedly, Watoku's ability to participate in—and excel at—various aesthetic pursuits was instrumental in establishing this kind of common ground. Indeed, Watoku's account of Kameharu's talents appears within a larger discussion of Kameharu's business interactions, a placement that suggests that the extended commercial transactions also included writing poetry, playing *kemari*, discussing literary texts, and talking about the latest trends in Edo and Kyoto—all of which Kameharu could perform confidently among people from regional centers of culture and information (Kōfu, Iida, Matsumoto).[70] Because the price of entry into these indispensable networks of capital, information, and culture included such expertise, Kurushima Hiroshi has argued that cultural training was in fact a necessary, rather than optional, investment for village elites. Aesthetic talent, he states, "was as indispensable to leadership in local society as administrative competence."[71]

The role of the Ozawas as book collectors and lenders was both a symbol and a product of this access to extra-village connections and information. In his family history, Watoku made a point of recording many of the books collected by his father and grandfather. Ranging from Confucian classics and Tang poetry to the *Kokinshū* and the *Tale of Genji*, they are too numerous to list here. Shisan and Kameharu apparently borrowed these texts, copied them, and returned the originals while adding the copy to their collection.[72] Watoku not only borrowed and copied books but also lent them out to various individuals in the village. On dozens of occasions he recorded in his journal the name of a particular book and the person to whom he had lent it or from whom he had borrowed it. Occasionally, we can trace the movement of a specific book; for instance, in the summer of 1868 Watoku borrowed *Record of Faithful Subjects* (*Gishiden*) from an individual in Ono, spent several weeks copying it, bound it himself, and then lent it to someone else in Ono.[73] Watoku provides evidence of great diversity in the types of books circulating in Ono: there are Confucian classics and Chinese poetry, but we also find *A Record of the Sanada Family* (*Sanada sandaiki*), volumes of Matsuo Bashō's poetry, and *A Record of the Sakura Uprising* (*Sakura sōdōki*).[74] In addition, he often borrowed printed matter other than books. In a journal entry for 1868/7/14, he noted that he "borrowed three Edo newspapers and one shogunal document from the Kichijima store."[75] On other occasions, he recorded borrowing and copying official notices (*ofuregaki*) from Edo, documents written by the Office of Deities (Jingikan) in Kyoto, and the pro-bakufu newspaper *Chūgai shinbun* from Edo.

Watoku's book borrowing and lending activities underscore the crucial role networks of village elites played in the circulation of books from major cities and regional urban centers into the hinterlands.[76] Just as Kameharu and Watoku in their role as village headmen acted as the channels through which overlord political authority was transmitted into Ono, they also functioned as conduits for information—whether it be scholarly knowledge of the Confucian classics and high culture or information on current events. Furthermore, as teachers, they were in a particularly powerful position to convey—and, undoubtedly, to censor—that information. But whereas Watoku seemed to relish his family's function as a mediator between Ono and the larger world, his journal also reveals that it became increasingly difficult in the 1860s, as chaos in the outside world began to cause disorder within his own community.

"A World on Thin Ice"

Despite substantial continuity in the lifestyles and experiences of Shisan, Kameharu, and Watoku, Watoku often emphasized the differences among the three generations, employing distinctive metaphors to characterize each. He described his grandfather's time as one of "elegance" (*fūga*), a quality exemplified in Shisan's aesthetic talent and refined aloofness from mundane matters. It was an age when aesthetic sensibility was valued more than money—when, according to one anecdote, Shisan could pay his bills by leaving a basket of money (consisting of the tuition payments he had just collected from his students) outside his door, trusting his creditors to take what he owed them.[77] In contrast, Watoku remembered his father's time (which he associated with the Bunka and Bunsei periods, from 1804 to 1829) as one of economic prosperity. His practical, responsible father had taken over the reins of the family from his genteel grandfather, ushering in an era of stability. In this period, "the realm was at peace," evidenced by the low price of rice and "people of high and low status living in harmony."[78] Watoku's account of his father's term as headman makes it clear that these years were not without conflict; nevertheless, he portrayed these disputes as intermittent disruptions of an otherwise peaceful age. And this peace was brokered at the local level by his father, who repeatedly succeeded in restoring order to the village following episodes of unrest.

As is always the case with nostalgia, these characterizations of previous generations tell us less about Watoku's family's past than about his own present. In Watoku's writings, the present is an age of decline and disorder in contrast to past times of elegance and prosperity. This contrast can be perceived most sharply after the mid-1860s, when the tone and content of his journal changed noticeably. Whereas entries for the first several years primarily record his financial transactions and daily activities at school and in the community, after 1865, interspersed with such information are news, commentaries, and poems relating to the upheavals of the Restoration period. By this time Watoku was in his early seventies, and his journals reveal that he had begun to experience frequent bouts of illness and fatigue; perhaps his views of the decline in the society around him were colored by a consciousness of his own physical deterioration. It was at this time that, in Watoku's view, disorder became chronic and pervasive—rather than anomalous and manageable, as in his father's generation. Such disorder was not the reason he became a teacher. Teaching had become something of a hereditary avocation in the Ozawa family and had been central to their identity well before the perception of crisis led thousands of other village leaders to begin teaching in the last decades of the Tokugawa period. But it is clear from Watoku's journal that his teaching acquired newfound meaning at the end of the Tokugawa period. After recording incidents of unrest or signs of moral decay in the world around him, he described his teaching activities with newfound urgency; mundane entries that once read "Taught reading and writing today, and prepared workbooks in the evening" were replaced by entries like "I teach my pupils earnestly each day, encouraging them constantly, and working unfailingly to instruct them in the truth."[79] Facing the end of his own life, and responding to what he perceived to be a cataclysm in the social and moral structure of his world, he seems to have found refuge and purpose in teaching.

In describing this disorder, Watoku focused on certain signs, visible manifestations of chaos undermining the world around him. The first such sign was that of inflated rice prices. We see this in Watoku's journal entry for 1866/4/25; after recording current rice prices, he added: "Such prices are unheard of. The lower classes are in dire straits, and the nation is on the brink of chaos. It is as if the world is on thin ice."[80] Just as low rice prices symbolized the stability and prosperity of his father's generation, the inflated rice prices at the end of the Tokugawa period were a sign of the disordered state of his own society. He believed, in particular, that they were impoverishing the lower classes. Poverty and suffering among the "lower classes" (*naka yori ika no banmin*) may have been, in and of itself, a genuine concern for Watoku, but he probably also feared the protests such conditions might encourage. The "thin ice" metaphor, adopted from the classic *Book of Odes*, was perhaps meaningful to him because it captured his own tenuous position as a village leader in a time of social upheaval.

For Watoku, rural unrest was an indication of a larger collapse in the social and moral structure of the country. In one passage, reflecting the influence of his education in the Confucian classics, he spoke of a breakdown in the five relationships fundamental to human society. Disloyalty between lords and retainers, coldheartedness between friends, betrayal between brothers, and unfiliality between fathers and sons had grown rampant; as a result, "the spirit of benevolence, righteousness, propriety, humility, and honesty are forgotten more and more each day."[81] Particularly disturbing was a rumor that the lord of Matsumoto domain was selling the titles of village officials (*nanushi, kumigashira,* and *hyakushōdai*) in order to pay for military expenses and had raised over 10,000 *ryō* in this manner. Watoku commented: "Truly, this shows that the signs of a world in chaos are converging. What is the world coming to? (*kono yo no naka ikaga aran ya*)."[82] For him, the position of the Ozawas at the pinnacle of village society was the result of generations of cultural, social, political, and educational leadership. That someone could simply purchase such a position was a sign of profound social, even cosmological, disorder.

A major cause of this disorder, according to Watoku, was the encroachment of westerners on Japanese soil. He expressed this sentiment several times, usually in the form of satiric poems about the impact of the foreigners' arrival. Representative of this genre are the following poems written on 1867/5/11:

> The English creep toward us like a squash vine
> It ends with opening the port of Hyōgo
>
> We have licked too much American candy
> Because of this so-called revolution, we are indeed
>   becoming an "open" country[83]

Although these verses are not explicitly critical of the opening of the country, the images of both the West (the English "creeping" throughout the country) and those Japanese who have embraced the West too readily (licking too much American candy) are clearly not positive. On 1868/4/22, Watoku again linked the country's disordered condition with the arrival of the foreigners:

> The world has been thrown into chaos
> I wonder what the future holds
>
> Since the arrival of foreign countries
> Japan has become an impossible place to live[84]

Watoku's attitude toward the West would appear to make him sympathetic to the "expel the foreigners" (*jōi*) ideology that had spread throughout Shinano—and especially the district of Ina, in which Watoku lived—through the efforts of local nativists during the last decades of the Tokugawa period. Not only did more of Hirata Atsutane's disciples come from Shinano than from any other province, but among these, five times as many (387) came from the Ina district as from any other.[85] A list of disciples by village reveals that 25 of these 387 were from Ono, the second highest number of any village.[86] Ono was in the eye of a storm of nativist activity, and Watoku would have had many acquaintances among the networks of rural elites promoting Hirata's brand of nativism.

Given such circumstances, it is tempting to draw an analogy between Watoku and Hanzō in Shimazaki Tōson's novel *Before the Dawn*. The nativist Hanzō (modeled on the author's father) was also a local leader in an Ina post-town during the bakumatsu period, and, like Watoku, he was deeply concerned with preserving order in his community and resentful of the foreigners who had thrown Japan into confusion and made it more difficult for him to accomplish this task.[87]

In many regards, however, Watoku and Hanzō took quite different perspectives on the events occurring around them. One was the anti-Buddhist movement that swept through Shinano during the Restoration period. Unlike Hanzō, whose initial reluctance to reject Buddhism and its traditions subsided over time (evidenced in part by his attempt to burn down the local temple), Watoku remained steadfast in his support of Buddhist traditions and institutions, and he condemned the nativist destruction of temples and Buddhist icons (*haibutsu kishaku*). On the night of 1867/3/18, temples in three villages adjacent to Ono were ransacked. Watoku reported in his journal: "The Kannon, Jizō and Batō Kannon statues were all overturned, and the heads were cut off and thrown into the river; the children came to school today and told me about it."[88] The next night, temples in Ono—including Sairinji, the temple where his father's funeral had been held—were vandalized in a similar way. Watoku responded: "Such unprecedented lawlessness. It is beyond words."[89] When the temples were vandalized again a few days later, he castigated the perpetrators: "What kind of person would do such a thing? Such evil is beyond words. I fear what the future holds for us."[90] Despite his apparent sympathy for *jōi* ideology, he could not countenance the desecration of local institutions important to his family and community.

Similarly, although both Watoku and Hanzō embraced a restorative vision for their own communities, they differed on whether the Meiji Restoration offered a real solution to the local disorder they faced. Whereas Hanzō initially supported the Restoration and genuinely believed that it would bring about a spiritual rebirth of the Japanese nation,[91] Watoku seemed at best ambivalent. Much of the time he recorded the information he received about Restoration developments carefully but matter-of-factly, without adding his own commentary. On 1868/3/1, for example, he wrote that the imperial commander Iwakura Tomomi and his troops had passed through the nearby post-town of Shiojiri on their way to Edo. *Before the Dawn's* Hanzō, too, witnessed the event and hailed Iwakura's passage as a sign of the triumph of Restoration forces.[92] Watoku's journal entry confirms the sense of excitement surrounding the event, and he noted that boys and girls from Ono made the journey to Shiojiri to cheer Iwakura as he passed through. But he did not express strong feelings one way or the other—except for mild disapproval over the fact that none of his students showed up for school on that day. "Probably they went to see Iwakura," he remarked.[93] In the summer of 1868, Watoku received information regarding the Boshin war and the fall of Nagaoka castle to Restoration armies. Once again, these developments came close to home, as troops from Iida passed through Ono on their way north to confront the pro-bakufu armies at Nagaoka. He simply noted, however, the crowded roads and the number of "high-speed palanquins" carrying important people through his neighborhood.

Meanwhile, at the local level, popular excitement over the Restoration took the form of *ee ja nai ka* celebrations. The diary of a relative, Ozawa Tōzaemon, noted that in the eleventh month of 1867, such events were precipitated in Ono by an *ofudafuri* incident—the mysterious falling of paper talismans bearing the names of Shinto deities.[94] Tōzaemon reported that the talismans fell on the homes of a number of village notables in the area—one being none other than Ozawa Watoku. The people of Ono, taking the talismans as a fortuitous omen from the gods, turned the occasion into a week-long party. Tōzaemon wrote that the people on whose homes the talismans fell provided *mochi* and red bean cakes for all the villagers. Everyone got drunk, and "young people, old people, and even women and children danced until sunrise."[95] Since Watoku did not keep a journal during the last several months of 1867, we do not know his reaction to these local events. Several months later, however, he wrote the following poem, entitled "The Spirit of the Times" ("Tōji no jinki"):

Everything is running high: popular sentiment, the
    price of rice
The only thing "low" is our hearts[96]

Watoku, clearly, did not share fully in the excitement generated by events of the Restoration. Seeing the feverish anticipation of the time as masking an erosion of basic norms and values, he was skeptical and ambivalent about the momentous events taking place around him.

At times Watoku expressed direct criticism of the Restorationist movement, as in these two poems from the summer of 1868:

In this strange time of so-called change, nothing
    good has happened
Due to this "great revolution," our country is
    actually in great chaos

Since spring, the nation has been in disorder, with
    East fighting against West
This world—I'm sick of it![97]

His disgust with the chaos of the time was elsewhere tinged with sadness. On the fifteenth of the eighth month of 1868, Watoku and his friends continued an annual tradition of writing poetry to celebrate the full moon, although the occasion was dampened— literally—by the heavy rains that prevented them from seeing the object of their attention. In previous years this event had resulted in what might be termed "stereotypical" moon-viewing poems; however, in 1868, Watoku's anxiety about the state of the world seeped into the creative act:

The world is in confusion, and the Way of humankind
    has been destroyed
Even our footpaths have crumbled and washed away

In the strife, wars and disputes of the samurai
We witness the evanescence of the flowers of young
    trees being scattered[98]

Where some villagers (including *Before the Dawn*'s Hanzō) at first saw grounds for hope in the upheavals of the Restoration, Watoku sensed a wave of disorder and destruction that pervaded both the human and the natural realm.

On occasion Watoku seems to have grudgingly supported the Restoration precisely *because of* his overriding concern for the problem of disorder. Such sentiments can be detected in his comments on a pro-bakufu essay that he copied into his diary on 1868/4/12.[99] How he obtained this essay is unclear; considering the frequency with which Watoku borrowed documents, newspapers, and other materials from Edo and Kyoto, it could have come from any number of sources. It evidently impressed him, for this entry is one of the few instances in which he copied verbatim something acquired from elsewhere. The main thrust of this essay is a refutation of the claims of the former allies of the bakufu, who, by 1868, were seeking to overthrow it. It blames the current state of rebellion on such self-seeking men and maintains that the chaos of the times is not a sign of the shogunate's loss of a mandate to rule the country. If such evil men are not punished, it concludes, they will "corrupt the reputation of our imperial nation (*kōkoku*) among the countries of the world."[100]

After copying out the essay, Watoku added: "I wonder who wrote this. There are certainly some valid points here. But as the saying goes, if [the country] is in chaos at the core, it will not be pacified." In other words, Watoku agreed in part with the sentiments expressed in the essay; indeed, he himself had often written with contempt about the activities of traitorous retainers and the distressing breakdown in the traditional moral order. The chronic disorder of the bakumatsu years nevertheless suggested to him that the Tokugawa political order was beyond repair. To restore order, he implied, "revolution" was necessary. Then, in the very next sentence, he noted how difficult it was for him to advocate such a course: "Yet is it not extremely regrettable that we have come to the point where we could be overturning the laws of our sacred ancestors for nothing?"[101] It remained uncertain whether the Restoration was the will of heaven or the handiwork of pernicious, selfish men seeking power.

Eventually Watoku seems to have resigned himself to the former proposition. On 1868/10/1, in the last "political" commentary in his journal, after once again recording the inflated price of rice (which had stirred his first commentary on the Restoration), he wrote: "This change (*henka*) is the fate of heaven. If there is no change, then it will be difficult for the world to get back on its feet."[102] He proceeded to compare the present situation to his own experience in cultivating his vegetable garden. He could not control how his vegetables grew, he remarked, all he could do was prepare the ground, add fertilizer, and plant the seeds. "Once that is done," he concluded, "all I can do is leave it up to nature."[103] In commenting on the struggles and tragedies faced by his own family over three generations, Watoku often compared human society with nature, at one point declaring, "Truly, the vicissitudes of human life are no different from the changes in the seasons."[104] He evidently applied a similar reasoning to the political realm: the Tokugawa "season" had passed. All that was left for him to do was to wait anxiously as the new order unfolded.

Conclusion

While Watoku was coming to grips with the momentous changes taking place in Japan during the Restoration, a rural doctor named Hayama, living over three hundred miles away in Kii province, was facing similar issues. Better informed about current affairs in Kyoto and Edo than Watoku, Hayama had begun in the late 1850s to write regularly about the movements of foreigners and the changing fortunes of the bakufu.[105] Like Watoku, he lamented the impact of the foreigners' intrusion into Japan in recent years and desperately sought a solution to the chaos that had ensued. He used many of the same words to describe the situation. He, too, for example, characterized the current situation as "absolutely unprecedented" (*zendai mimon*) and borrowed the "stepping on thin ice" metaphor (*hakuhyō o fumu ga gotoshi*) from the *Book of Odes* to capture the sense of anxiety pervading society at the end of the Tokugawa period.[106]

Watoku and Hayama were simply two of the thousands of village elites who participated in what Harootunian has called a "public realm" in late Tokugawa society, one based on widespread efforts "to resolve problems of common concern."[107] Some rural activists, like Matsuo Taseko, flocked to Kyoto in hopes of participating in the Restoration and resolving these problems on a national scale.[108] Watoku and Hayama, like the nativist Miyaoi Yasuo and the Confucianist Matsuo Kōan discussed in the preceding chapter, perceived a disorder of cosmological proportions, but their sphere of action—their restoration—was local. Their shared perspective illustrates their common struggle to restore local order while protecting their own economic and political interests in the midst of upheaval. Their shared language reflects the fact that they had received a comparable education, read similar texts, and visited the same places in their travels; had they lived closer, they might have shared common business interests and even participated in the same poetry associations. Taken together, these various elements constituted a distinctive lifestyle, one that was remote from the lives of most villagers in Ono.

For the Ozawas, schoolteaching was an essential part of this lifestyle. It was central to their status and identity and overlapped with their other pursuits. Teaching enhanced their credentials and honed their skills as literati, helping them to cultivate extra-village contacts through the practice of poetry, noh, and other literary and aesthetic practices. Such activities aided the Ozawas in their business careers by providing them valuable contacts in the business world and facilitating their interaction through shared knowledge and hobbies. Business activities and aesthetic pursuits, in turn, gave the Ozawas greater access to books and information, which not only was advantageous to them as book lenders but also lent legitimacy to their selection as local political and ritual leaders. Finally, in the last decades of the Tokugawa period, Watoku's role as teacher provided him with a concrete way to restore moral and social order within his community, which was crucial to his family's wealth and local political position.

Watoku's views about teaching, status, and restoration invite us to cast our eyes forward to the formation of the Meiji educational system. Watoku died in the fall of 1869, when the collapse of the bakufu was complete, but the exact nature of the new order was still unclear. Other teachers with similar backgrounds and ideas about education, however, went on to play key roles in building the new school system at the local level, as teachers, administrators, local political leaders, and unpaid volunteers. The post-Restoration trajectories of these individuals and their ideas, as well as their efforts to promote, obstruct, and alter the new system, will be the focus of subsequent chapters. One such individual who deserves mention here is Watoku's son, Masaaki. In the early 1860s, Masaaki followed in his family's footsteps by opening a school in Ono. In 1871, however, he closed his school and joined with several other teachers from the upper Ina district to establish a new kind of educational institution: a "local school" (*gōkō*), which was designed to provide public education for commoners. The Meiji government ordered this and all other pre-existing schools to close when it promulgated the Fundamental Code of Education in 1872, but when a new elementary school was established, Masaaki was able to secure a position as an instructor. In

1879 he was promoted to an administrative post in the school district, and four years later, he was appointed district head (*kuchō*), thus making a common jump from a position of educational leadership to one of political leadership within the new Meiji state. After retiring from this position, he returned to the field of education as a member of the local educational committee (*gakumu iinkai*), a post he would retain until his death in 1910. There are no documents that reveal how he felt about the new government or what motivated his service in the new educational system. What is clear, however, is that, as with earlier generations, his investment in education and literary skills paid off by providing continuity in status and identity during a period of radical change.

THREE

Post-Restoration
Innovation and the Fundamental
Code, 1868–1872

As Ozawa Watoku and other rural activists were responding to the perceived crisis in late Tokugawa society by opening schools and devising other strategies for local renovation, momentous events were occurring elsewhere in Japan. On January 3, 1868, the domainal armies of Chōshū, Satsuma, and Tosa carried out a coup d'état and declared the formal restoration of imperial rule. This event marked the end of Tokugawa rule but did little to clarify what would replace it; even the most general outlines of the new order were yet to be drawn. A civil war between the insurgent domains and forces loyal to the Tokugawa had yet to be fought, and several basic questions about the new political structure were unanswered. More broadly, the ideas and energies that had contributed to the bakufu's demise had been remarkably varied, and the overthrow of the Tokugawa government only multiplied and intensified them by injecting a new sense of possibility into the atmosphere as they jostled for a place in the new order. The next several years constituted a kind of interregnum, one characterized by fluidity and openness, permitting, in Tetsuo Najita's words, "a flowering of large and small visions based on an anticipation that unusual things were about to happen."[1]

This spirit of innovation and urgent indeterminacy also marked the realm of education. The century preceding the Restoration had already seen basic transformations in the concept and practice of commoner education. Shoguns, domainal officials, intellectuals, local clergy, and village elites had engaged in a discussion about the nature and purpose of schooling. In this chapter, I trace this discussion into the early post-Restoration period and explore how it took shape within a rapidly changing domestic and international political context. Key figures in the new government interjected revolutionary ideas about the role of education in the new nation into this discussion but were unable to implement them. Meanwhile, village elites and domainal and municipal leaders continued to carry out their own visions for educational reform within their spheres of influence. The post-Restoration atmosphere of fluidity and possibility permitted diverse reformist visions at all levels of leadership to coexist and flourish. In 1872, however, the Meiji government stepped decisively into this variegated field of educational thought and practice by promulgating the Fundamental Code of Education (the Gakusei). In doing so, it announced its own vision for education and began its attempt to displace other visions generated before and during the interregnum.

New Visions of Education and Schooling: The Central Government

Immediately after the Restoration, as the new government struggled to keep the Western powers at bay while it carried out military campaigns against pro-bakufu forces, a number of government leaders began to turn their attention to matters relating to education and schooling.[2] The political context for these discussions was volatile: the samurai who engineered the Restoration and led the imperial forces coexisted with court nobles, domainal leaders, and the emperor himself in a constantly shifting political field. Each of these groups was involved in a struggle to secure a place in the new order. This struggle was not simply about political power; rather, it concerned the very meaning of the Restoration. The Restoration movement was broad enough to encompass a variety of agendas and aspirations; what followed was an effort by various groups to ascribe a specific meaning to the event—one that would legitimize that group's claim to leadership in the new political order—and to secure the dominance of that meaning over others. The various educational visions articulated at this time reflected both the contest for political power and this larger struggle among competing interpretations of the Restoration.

One such interpretation was that the restoration of imperial rule (*ōsei*) entailed the return to the ancient Japanese system of government (*fukko*). The new government's first official statements regarding education reflected such an interpretation. Only two months after the Restoration, the Sōsaikyoku—one of eight departments in the new government, supposedly modeled after the structure of government in the Nara period (710–94)—appointed three nativist scholars to the position of school superintendent (*gakkō gakari*). One of them was Hirata Kanetane, the son of Hirata Atsutane, whose strain of nativism had inspired the activism of so many village elites in the years leading up to the Restoration. Their first goal was to resurrect the Gakushūin, which during the Tokugawa period had provided court nobles with a Confucian education, and to transform it into a Shinto-centered institution of higher learning that would train nobles for service in the new government. In doing so, the Gakushūin would help accomplish the ideal of the "unity of rites and rule" (*saisei itchi*)—a return to an ancient form of government supposedly based on proper Shinto ritual and doctrine. Training court nobles for government service was also important to entrench the aristocracy within the leadership of the new government. Indeed, during the first several months after the Restoration, court nobles filled the majority of high-ranking posts in the government, and the Department of Rites—a body designed to align government with Shinto ritual and doctrine—occupied the highest position within the institutional structure of the government. The structure and personnel of the new government reflected, to some extent, the nativist interpretation of the ideal of *ōsei fukko* and *saisei itchi*; the Gakushūin was to maintain this ideal by securing a place for the nobility in the new political order and by establishing Shinto as the ideological basis for that order.

These goals were challenged from the start. The Shintoism espoused by nativists fought for space in a crowded ideological field with Confucianism and Western Learning, and court nobles were vulnerable when competing with domainal leaders and samurai for leadership positions in the new government. The nativists' plan for a system of higher education dominated by Shinto was never realized: they eventually established their own school (the Kōgakusho, or Imperial Studies Institute), but it shared the stage in Kyoto with a separate school for Chinese Learning (the Kangakusho, or Chinese Studies Institute). This marked an early stage in a three-year battle with Confucianist and Western Learning scholars over the ideological orientation of Japan's institutions of higher learning. The nativists' cause was further damaged by the shift in the political center in 1868–69 from Kyoto—the ancient capital and the locus of the nativists' primary sphere of influence—to Tokyo. This shift was accompanied by the decline of the two Kyoto schools and the increasing importance of a new university in Tokyo, the Daigakkō.[3] The move to Tokyo signified the influence of different voices within the new government, many of them belonging to the younger, lower-ranking samurai who had been a driving force in the Restoration movement.[4] These individuals did not reject the notion of returning to the ancient pattern of imperial rule, but they also stressed the need to take innovative measures to secure Japan's place among the powerful nations of the world and asserted the value of Western Learning in accomplishing this goal. They had already made their presence felt in the creation of the Charter Oath, a public statement of purpose proclaimed by the new government in April 1868. Although the progressive nature of this document is often overstated, its call to "throw off old customs from the past" and to "seek knowledge from throughout the world" offered an interpretation of the Restoration and a vision of the post-Restoration order that stood in contrast to those of many nativists.[5]

This segment of the Meiji leadership also articulated a rather different vision of the role of education in the new political order. They, too, were concerned about cultivating talent for service in the new government but advocated a university that included samurai of all ranks and that offered an intellectual foundation of Western Learning as well as Shinto and Confucianism. More significant, a few prominent leaders in the new government also began to consider the possibility of providing schooling for the entire population. Among them was Iwakura Tomomi (1825–83), a court noble who had played a major role in negotiating the fate of the imperial court in the years immediately surrounding the Restoration. Iwakura was deeply concerned with Japan's instability at a time when Western nations were maneuvering to take advantage of the chaos and gain a foothold in the country. His solution to Japan's vulnerable diplomatic position was national unity, which he perceived as the key to strength and prosperity—and, by extension, independence. A unified system of education, he believed, was essential to this goal. As early as March 1867, he advocated the creation of a centralized school system. He seems to have been concerned primarily with university education and the cultivation of talent for government service, for he focused mainly on the construction of five universities that would teach Western Learning as well as Chinese Learning and Shinto. But he also urged the construction of several hundred elementary schools in each district, which would be charged with teaching children "the five principles of morality." Such a system, he argued, would allow the government and the people "to cooperate as if of one mind" and thereby "promote imperial prestige throughout the world."[6] In a subsequent proposal made in June 1869, he reiterated that the goal of primary education was to enable Japan "to present a unified front to the foreigners, both in times of peace and in times of war."[7]

In these proposals, Iwakura essentially advocated two separate school systems, both of which embodied concepts of education articulated in the Tokugawa period. First, we see the principle of schooling as a means of training men of talent for government service—a concept that many domains had been applying in earnest, particularly in the last decades of the Tokugawa period. In addition, Iwakura articulated the goal of achieving harmony and unity through moral instruction for the masses; as he expressed in an 1869 statement concerning elementary education, "Clarifying the eternal Way of morality is the key to governing the country."[8] This notion was rooted in the long-standing Confucian concept of education as moral suasion (*kyōka*), a concept that had informed many Tokugawa-era educational initiatives. What was new, however, was Iwakura's effort to coordinate these educational initiatives through a unified system of educational administration.

Two other central figures in the early Meiji government stressed the importance of government-directed schooling for ordinary people but espoused somewhat different ideas on the nature and function of that schooling. In February 1869, Itō Hirobumi (1841–1909), then governor of Hyōgo prefecture, expressed a vision of mass schooling in which ordinary people were more than passive recipients of moral inculcation:

Today the world situation has changed dramatically. Engaged in intercourse with all the world, men vie with each other to keep their ears and eyes open, gaining information that spreads from one person to another and eventually reaches ten thousand. Accordingly, we have initiated a policy of civilization and enlightenment. Now is our millennial opportunity to reform the bad old habits that have been followed in our Imperial Land for centuries, and to open up the eyes and ears of the people of our realm. If, at this juncture, we fail to act quickly and make our people broadly pursue useful knowledge from throughout the world, we will in the end reduce them to a backward folk without eyes and ears.[9]

Itō urged the government not merely to establish universities but to open elementary schools "in every locality, from metropolitan districts, domains, and prefectures on down to every district and village."[10] Like Iwakura, Itō hoped that mass education would encourage unity, but he emphasized the role of education in achieving a form of national strength built on the collective strength of the Japanese people. This collective strength, in turn, could be tapped only if the abilities of the individual were developed through education. Although he did not mention it here, moral instruction was certainly part of Itō's educational vision; equally important, however, was the pursuit of "useful knowledge."

Kido Takayoshi (1833–77) used a similar argument in stressing the importance of mass education. He, too, drew a connection between national strength and the collective strength of the individuals who constituted the nation. In a proposal from January 1869 entitled "Recommendation on the Urgency of Promoting Mass Education," he stated, "If ordinary people are poor and illiterate, the wealth and power of the entire country cannot be summoned." An additional consequence, he argued, would be that "imperial rule will degenerate into despotism."[11] His ultimate concern was not the political participation of the individual but national strength; he conceived of political participation quite narrowly and mainly as a precondition for the latter. Neither can be fully realized without a state-run system of education. "For this reason, it is urgent to adopt regulations from each civilized nation and to gradually establish schools throughout the country in order to develop the knowledge of ordinary people."[12] In 1871, the Iwakura Mission provided Kido the opportunity to observe the schools of Europe and America firsthand. When he visited three elementary schools in San Francisco in January 1872, he was struck by the sight of over a thousand students learning in unison and following common rules and regulations. The experience seems to have impressed him deeply and prompted him to write in his diary that the goals of "civilization" and "national independence" were attainable only through the involvement of the entire population. This involvement, in turn, was possible only by "cultivating knowledge among the masses."[13]

Itō's and Kido's statements articulate not merely a concept of education and schooling but a vision of the post-Restoration political order, one in which the Japanese people were integrated into the institutions of the state and actively involved in the political and economic life of the nation. Their statements reflect a specific interpretation of the Restoration. Kido, repeating a sentiment expressed above, remarked that if ordinary people were left poor and uneducated, "the goal of standing alongside the powerful nations of the world will inevitably be unrealized." In the process, he argued, "the glorious phrase 'Imperial Restoration' (ōsei ishin) will be rendered absolutely meaningless."[14] His Restoration—here coupled with the term ishin (renovation) rather than fukko (revival)—was not principally one of returning to an ancient system of government; rather, his goal was to achieve national strength and independence through innovation and reform.[15] And that Restoration required a system of education that went beyond the scope of moral suasion, a system designed to mobilize the collective strength of the entire population by imparting skills and knowledge to ordinary people.

We should avoid seeing Itō's or Kido's statements as evidence of what Passin calls a "liberal dominance" stretching back to the late Tokugawa period.[16] Not only were there key differences between Itō's and Kido's views on education and those of contemporary liberal educators in Europe and America,[17] but their views were only one of many diverse visions in early Meiji educational thought. Nevertheless, it was such views that informed the Meiji government's first directive concerning primary schooling, a document from February 1869 entitled "Procedures for Local Government." The document urged metropolitan and prefectural governments to establish primary schools to teach reading, writing, and arithmetic to local children, so that they would become competent in "writing petitions and letters, bookkeeping, and using the abacus."[18] In addition to teaching such skill-based knowledge, the schools were also entrusted with the tasks of "making students understand the national polity and current conditions, instructing them in loyalty and filial piety, and inculcating morality."[19] The proposal envisioned primary schools not unlike those of the Tokugawa era: schools that transmitted practical skills and instructed children in morality. Even so, the limited education received by the masses was intended to prepare them for a certain level of active participation in the life of the nation.

Meanwhile, the Shinto priests and officials within another segment of the new government, the Department of Rites, were formulating a very different plan for educating the Japanese people. In July 1869, the Department of Rites created an Office of Proselytizers (*senkyōshi*) within its ranks and charged it with propagating Shinto—the "Great Teaching of the Gods" (*Kannagara no daikyō*)—to the entire population.[20] The method of propagation—proselytizers were to "read the scriptures aloud, lecture on them, and instruct people gently"[21] while traveling throughout the country—was basically similar to that employed by bakufu and domainal officials of the Tokugawa era when they dispatched Confucian or Shingaku teachers to deliver lectures to the people in their jurisdiction. The concept of education behind the campaign was also familiar: it embodied the notion that the purpose of mass education was to make the population governable through moral suasion, or *kyōka*. Tanaka Chihō, a Shinto priest involved in the campaign, referred to the Great Teaching as "the root of governance" and "the foundation from which to pacify the people." "No matter how stubborn the people are, when we teach them the message of reverence for the gods and loyalty to the emperor . . . they will naturally understand and follow the five principles of morality."[22] Although Tanaka's notion of education as moral suasion had extensive precedents in pre-Meiji Japan, the doctrine being propagated—Shinto—was unfamiliar to its audience.[23] Moral principles of obedience, reverence, loyalty, and filial piety were now to be separated from their familiar Buddhist or Confucian context and directed toward the nation and the emperor. And while not yet in place in 1870, the administrative structure eventually created for this effort was unprecedented: soon there was a Great Teaching Institute to coordinate the campaign nationwide, as well as Middle Teaching institutes to train future proselytizers and Small Teaching institutes to carry out the work of bringing the message to the Japanese people.[24] The campaign represented another early Meiji experiment in education: one grounded in old assumptions concerning the method and purpose of education but propagating a new creed through new administrative machinery.

But throughout the first three and a half years of the Meiji period, any ideas concerning education and schooling faced a basic problem of implementation. Because of the continued existence of administratively independent domains, any policies devised by the central government could be implemented only in the 20 percent or so of Japan directly administered by the Meiji government—and even in these areas, the unstable new government was unable to enforce its educational policies systematically. The limitations of the new government were highlighted in February 1870, when the Council of State created a proposal for a truly national educational system, outlined in a document entitled "Regulations for the University and for Middle and Primary Schools."[25] The plan called for middle schools and elementary schools to be established in each metropolitan district and prefecture, as well as in the domains. These schools would be administered by the University in Tokyo, which would create policy and regulations for the entire system. The ultimate purpose of the system was to "nourish talent, diffuse knowledge, and serve the needs of the state." As Motoyama Yukihiko points out, the plan itself did not envision universal education; the primary schools were intended to feed into the middle schools and the University as a means of cultivating talent among elites.[26] In this sense, the proposal reflected a conception of schooling different from that of Kido and Itō, who sought to develop talent among the entire population for purposes beyond that of mere government service. Nevertheless, it was envisioned as a national educational system, administered by a single, central body. Naturally, the University sought to publish the proposal and distribute it throughout the country. The Council of State, however, fearing that the domains would not implement the proposal, chose not to publish the plan. The new educational visions generated in the aftermath of the Restoration existed in an ideological field bounded by the administrative constraints of the new government; as we will see below, the removal of those constraints—namely, the abolition of the domains in August 1871—fueled more ambitious attempts to make mass schooling an integral part of the new political order.

New Visions of
Education and Schooling: Shinano

The limited administrative reach of the new government left room for local activists, working independently or in concert with local government bodies, to experiment with new ideas and institutions. Many of the conditions that had fueled educational reform during the late Tokugawa period were still in place. In particular, popular uprisings—which in the last decades before the Restoration had inspired domainal authorities and village leaders alike to devise arrangements for the schooling of the general population—intensified in the years after the Restoration. There were fifteen large-scale uprisings in Shinano during the first three years of Meiji rule; some targeted wealthy villagers or merchants, others the political authorities at the domain or prefectural level.[27] Herbert Bix sees this spate of protests in Shinano as a reaction to increased impoverishment and suffering; Selçuk Esenbel interprets it as a proactive effort by commoners to negotiate more advantageous tax conditions in the midst of political change.[28] In either case, the reformers considered conflict evidence of disorder, and their goal of eliminating conflict continued to inform efforts for educational reform at all levels of leadership in Shinano. But the Restoration itself created a substantially new environment for experimentation in the realm of schooling and education. The sense of expectation and possibility in the aftermath of the Restoration stimulated new thinking, and the fluidity of the post-Restoration political order created relatively open spaces in which new ideas might be implemented. Leaders at the village, domainal, and prefectural level took the initiative in creating educational arrangements for a political order that was still undetermined.

Domainal leaders focused their reform efforts primarily on institutions of higher education. The urgency of training men of talent for government service intensified after the Restoration and stimulated widespread reforms in domain schools. Forty-eight new domain schools were established nationwide between 1868 and 1871,[29] and many existing schools underwent significant changes following the Restoration. In Shinano province, seven such schools were established during this period. In all these domains, some form of officially sponsored school for retainers had already been in operation, but the Restoration prompted a reorganization or reorientation of these schools, as well as the formal adoption of the name "domain school."[30] In Matsushiro, the domain school hired Takeda Ayazaburō, a former instructor at the bakufu's Institute for Western Learning (the Kaiseijo), and made Western military techniques a major component of the new curriculum.[31] In 1868, authorities in Takashima domain, one of the hotbeds of nativism in the years leading up to the Restoration, hired a prominent disciple of Hirata Atsutane to open a "National Learning School" (Kokugakkō) for both retainers and elite commoners; this represented a clear shift from the Confucian focus of the previously existing domain school.[32] The Matsumoto domain school issued a new statement of purpose following the Restoration; however, unlike those in Matsushiro and Takashima, the school reaffirmed its focus on Chinese Learning as the core of the curriculum: "We want to include the study of England, France, Germany, and other countries, but if we do not have students read [the Confucian Classics] . . . we will incur the scorn of other countries, both East and West."[33] In all these cases, the shift in the ideological basis of domain school curricula was accompanied by efforts to open domain schools to lower-ranking samurai and elite commoners and thereby widen the pool of talent available for service in domainal governments—a trend seen in many domains in the early Meiji period.[34]

The impulse behind such reforms was similar to that which motivated late Tokugawa reforms in domain schools: in the face of popular unrest and fiscal crisis, domainal leaders sought to invigorate schooling as part of a larger effort to build an economically viable and morally reconstituted domain. The secessionary thrust of this movement softened after the Restoration, however, as school authorities began to draw explicit connections between the function of their own school and the fate of the nation. After the Restoration, the domain school in Matsumoto declared its mission to be one of "expanding knowledge and fostering talent so that we may be of use to the state."[35] Many Tokugawa-era domain schools expressed similar sentiments but used "state" (*kokka*) to refer to the domainal government.[36] However, the immediate context for this mission statement is a discussion of the importance of loyalty and service to the "imperial nation" (*kōkoku*); furthermore, the insertion of the term "realm" (*tenka*) before *kokka* suggests that the referent was indeed the central rather than the domainal government. The leaders of the Matsushiro domain school made this distinction explicit in a revised mission statement in 1870 by affirming their loyalty to both the domain and the nation: "We struggle day and night," the statement begins, to "examine our national polity" and "to expand the authority and force of our imperial nation," thereby "fulfilling our mission as military retainers for the sake of our house (*ie*) and our country (*kuni*)."[37]

The language of reform shared by so many domain schools at this time suggests that the secessionary impulse of the late Tokugawa now coexisted with a recognition of the need for reintegration—or perhaps, by 1870, domains simply acknowledged the inevitability of such a reintegration. But this shared language also reflects the fact that domains were in close touch with political and educational developments in the center (first Kyoto, then Tokyo). In general, the domestic and international crises of the late Tokugawa and Restoration periods heightened domainal interest in and access to news from Kyoto (as well as from Nagasaki, Tokyo, and other key locations).[38] The domain schools seem to have played a key role in transmitting such information: at the domain school in Matsushiro, recent government directives were posted on the school's bulletin board, along with urgings from school authorities for students to "read [the directives] carefully and follow them diligently, day and night."[39] In addition, many domains throughout the country began sending students from the domain schools to study Western subjects at the University in Tokyo, and their letters and communications provided another means of acquiring information on recent educational developments.[40] Although the ideological foundations of higher education remained highly contested, the Restoration and its aftermath gave domains the impetus to rethink the organization, content, and purpose of schools for samurai.

Although most domains were concerned primarily with institutions of higher learning, the first few years following the Restoration were also a period of experimentation in popular schooling. Prominent among these experiments is what is thought to be Japan's first modern elementary school, established in Numazu, Shizuoka prefecture, in 1869.[41] The school was attached to the Heigakkō, the bakufu military school that moved to Numazu after the fall of the Tokugawa government. A driving force behind the elementary school was Nishi Amane, a scholar of Western Learning who argued that government should "exercise jurisdiction over children" by taking an active role in popular schooling.[42] Many of Nishi's ideas were novel: for example, his proposal that moral education be taught only once a week, in the mold of Sunday schools in the West, defined public elementary schools as sites for secular, practical instruction.[43] The elementary school in Numazu did not, however, apply such ideas; as the preparatory school for entry into the military academy, its purpose was not to provide education for the general population but to train samurai and commoner elites for government service.

This was not the case in Kyoto, where municipal authorities designed a citywide school system in 1868 to provide formal education for ordinary children. This was an articulated system, with 64 elementary school districts feeding into two middle-school districts. The system was also centralized: the city government administered exams, appointed teachers, and designed the curriculum.[44] The system was publicly subsidized, with half the expenses coming from the city government and the other half from the contributions of wealthy families in each district.[45] The system was in operation by the summer of 1869; Fukuzawa Yukichi toured the schools at that time and was deeply impressed. He particularly admired the division of the city into relatively uniform school districts: "Anyone who sees these schools and is not inspired is lacking in patriotism."[46] The schools performed community functions outside the realm of education, serving as clinics for vaccination, stations for civil guards, and meetingplaces where governmental orders could be explained to the populace.[47] Schools were thus mobilized for the task of governance in a new way. In the Tokugawa period, the authorities hoped to use schools to render the population governable through moral instruction; the Kyoto system did not reject this concept, but it also treated the school as a local arm of the machinery of government, one that integrated the general population into the state and complemented its functions.

It is perhaps somewhat misleading to describe these early experiments in popular schooling as "local" initiatives. True, they were implemented on a local rather than a national scale, but the initiative came from individuals close to the center of national political life. The elementary school in Numazu was attached to the military academy of the recently overthrown national government and was influenced by nationally prominent Western Learning scholars. The Kyoto system was spearheaded by Makimura Masanao, a colleague of Kido Takayoshi; as Richard Rubinger points out, Kido had apparently charged Makimura with the task of applying locally the ideas that Kido hoped to implement nationally.[48] But novel experiments in primary schooling can be found much farther from the center. Local activists and educators, who had been the driving force behind the expansion in popular schooling during the last decades of the Tokugawa period, began to devise new kinds of educational institutions and new ideas about popular schooling.

In Nagano these efforts were inspired in part by the same restorative ideological movements that had stimulated the late Tokugawa expansion in popular schooling. One teacher who explicitly incorporated such ideologies into his ideas about schooling was Kitahara Inao (1824–81). Kitahara's father and grandfather had been headmen and teachers in their home village of Zakōji, near the castle-town of Iida. In 1859 Kitahara became a disciple of Hirata Atsutane, and like many other Hirata disciples in Shinano, he opened a school of his own. This school provided basic instruction for local children, but it also served as a meetingplace for Hirata disciples during the late Tokugawa period—one of whom was his cousin Matsuo Taseko, a prominent female disciple of Hirata who traveled to Kyoto in the final years of the Tokugawa period and witnessed firsthand the events of the Restoration.[49] Kitahara remained in Zakōji during this period, but the events of the Restoration prompted him to devise a plan for a new kind of school, one that embodied a number of novel ideas concerning content and pedagogy.

It is not surprising that Kitahara, as an ardent disciple of Hirata, would make Shinto (what he calls *hongaku*, or "fundamental learning") the foundation of the curriculum for his model school. But unlike most prominent nativists in Kyoto—who, at that very moment, were advocating an exclusively Shinto curriculum for higher education—Kitahara stressed the value of a broad education, one that included both Chinese and Western Learning. He recognized the unprecedented nature of "the Revolution" (*goisshin*) and argued that a new approach to learning was necessary: "At this time, when circumstances have changed so dramatically, to adhere to our own traditional way of learning is of no value to the state."[50] He criticized scholars for studying a single path of learning to the exclusion of all others and urged Japan to "sweep away this evil of stubbornness." Citing the example of Western countries, where people first learn "the history and writings of their own country" and then study the rest of the world, he argued, "If we do not learn in a fashion appropriate to the times, we will be unable to expand our knowledge or cultivate talent." Such ideas were common among contemporary scholars of Western Learning, but it is notable that such statements came from a rural nativist only a few months after the Restoration, when nativists could still harbor realistic hopes for the kind of thoroughgoing *ōsei fukko* they envisioned. To be sure, Kitahara had not abandoned such hopes, and he was quick to distinguish his own approach from that of most advocates of Western Learning. He argued that Chinese and Western Learning should be undertaken only after building a firm foundation in the nativist canon and excoriated those who "are roused by the study of other nations without comprehending the ways of our imperial nation." Furthermore, after justifying the inclusion of Chinese and Western Learning in his model curriculum, he warned that such knowledge must not compromise Japan's claim to divinely ordained uniqueness. "Students should know," he continued, "that this imperial land, which lies at the foundation of the globe and has an eternally unbroken line of emperors, should not be placed in the same category as other nations."

Kitahara's pronouncements on the content of education are grounded in a detailed statement about the curriculum and pedagogic techniques to be employed in his school. He designed an articulated curriculum composed of three stages of learning ("beginning," "intermediate," and "advanced"). Each stage was organized not only around texts but also around different pedagogic techniques designed to impart different skills. The goal of the beginning stage was to teach basic literacy skills by reading through texts word for word and emphasizing character recognition and pronunciation. This resembles the practice of *sodoku*, or recitation, which was the customary method of instruction for beginning students in Tokugawa-era schools; however, Kitahara emphasized that students should not simply memorize the readings of the characters but understand the meaning. "It is of great benefit," he stated, "that students remember what they learn as they get older." Once students can read the beginning texts without a mistake, they progress to the intermediate-level curriculum. This level incorporates both a new set of texts and a new learning technique: the "reading group" (*risshokai*), in which students gather in a circle and read the texts under the guidance of an instructor or a more advanced student. Students who proceed to the advanced level also encounter both new texts and a new method of learning. It is at this point that students begin reading such nativist standards as the *Kojiki, Nihon shoki,* and the *Manyōshū,* as well as medieval chronicles such as the *Taiheiki* and *Heike monogatari.* Students at this level participate in a kind of seminar, in which they not only read texts aloud (as do the intermediate-level students) but also discuss their meaning.

This curriculum represents an attempt to rethink the pedagogy of Tokugawa-era schools. Kitahara repeatedly criticized the practice of memorization without comprehension—the method of teaching that later critics would derisively call "pouring in."[51] He also argued against the practice of imposing a rigid curriculum on all students; instead, teachers "should set the curriculum in consideration of the academic abilities of the student." In his own school, each successive stage of learning was targeted to a specific audience and built on knowledge and skills acquired in previous stages. In these respects, Kitahara's concerns are remarkably similar to those of the advocates of developmental education (*kaihatsushugi*) in the 1870s. These educators, influenced by Enlightenment ideology in the West, espoused a pedagogy that, in Mark Lincicome's words, aimed to "cultivate the unique, innate abilities of every child . . . according to the child's individual learning level and capacity."[52] Kitahara also made several statements on the practical value of education that would be echoed several years later in the Fundamental Code of Education. For example, "Learning is the foundation of a person's character and enhances one's abilities in whatever task he chooses." He urged students to read materials outside the regular curriculum that would assist them in their chosen occupation, so that their schooling would become a "foundation for success."

I do not cite these statements in an attempt to locate in Japanese local society an indigenous enlightenment that preceded the influx of Western ideas. Kitahara's critique of conventional pedagogy and his emphasis on practical learning were not unprecedented; such issues were already part of the intellectual field in late Tokugawa Japan, and Kitahara's ideas are best seen within that context. But his writings call attention to the impulse for educational reform among village elites, an inclination generated by the extraordinary circumstances surrounding the Restoration. This desire prompted village elites to rethink basic issues regarding the content, method, and purpose of schooling and to consider new possibilities in education.

One manifestation of this spirit of innovation was the spread of *gōkō*, or "local schools," during the first five years after the Restoration. A handful of *gōkō* existed in the Tokugawa period as well, but those that were established after the Restoration were markedly different from most Tokugawa-era *gōkō*, and their proliferation constitutes an entirely separate movement; it is these early-Meiji *gōkō* that I will examine here.[53] These schools were intended for commoner children and were the product of cooperative efforts by local elites and government authorities at the prefectural or domainal level. At least several hundred *gōkō* were established in Japan between the Restoration and the promulgation of the Fundamental Code of Education in 1872; the precise number depends on which institutions are included in the category. Their appearance was a nationwide phenomenon, but their numbers were concentrated in several specific areas. In Yonezawa domain, for example, where the *gōkō* were intended for the cultivation of talent among commoner elites, 28 schools were established.[54] Authorities in Aichi prefecture, hoping to reach a much larger proportion of the local population, established over 400.[55] The primary school in Numazu discussed above is classified as a *gōkō*, as are the 64 schools established in Kyoto in 1868–69. The variety of names used to refer to these schools—*gōgakkō, shōgakujo, gikō, keimōka*, among others—reflects the fact that they were founded locally, even though they belonged to a nationwide movement.

There is a contentious debate among Japanese scholars concerning these *gōkō*. Some scholars emphasize their "top-down" character and cite them as an early intervention of the state into the arena of popular education, an arena previously free from government intrusion. Others, however, see them as a product of popular energies, an alternative to the state-controlled system imposed on the people (*minshū*) in 1872—an event that, according to this view, marked the demise of genuinely popular education in Japan.[56] The debate is somewhat misguided, however, because it assumes a clear, categorical distinction between the state and the people. Such a distinction is particularly dubious in the case of the early Meiji period, when the institutional framework of the state was highly fluid. Amid this fluidity, local elites from both inside and outside local government mobilized themselves to create new kinds of public institutions and programs. The *gōkō* were a product of this mobilization and represented the ambitions and educational concerns of local elites as they strove to influence the post-Restoration order.

The origins of *gōkō* in modern-day Nagano prefecture reflect these patterns of mobilization. When in the 1880s the Ministry of Education asked village officials and educational administrators to write local educational histories, they almost invariably attributed the beginnings of the *gōkō* to the "cooperation of volunteers" (*yūshi no kyōgi*). An investigation of these volunteers turns up the names of village officials, literati, and schoolteachers from the late Tokugawa era. Nagano's first *gōkō*, for example, the Nisshinkan in Imasato village, was established when a small group of men—three of whom were former village headmen, and three others who were schoolteachers—from Imasato and surrounding villages gathered in April 1869 to establish a new kind of school.[57] They envisioned a large, multi-village school, one that would replace several pre-existing commoner schools in the area. Rather than nominating one of their own to serve as instructor in the new school, they arranged to hire Kobayashi Tsuneo, a regionally renowned scholar of Chinese Learning from nearby Matsushiro domain.

Although the founding of the Nisshinkan was undoubtedly the work of these local notables, the idea probably came from the "Procedures for Local Government" issued by the Council of State in February 1869, two months before planning for the Nisshinkan began. Imasato village was former bakufu land that had been reorganized as Ina prefecture and transferred to the jurisdiction of the Meiji government; as village officials in Ina prefecture, they likely would have received, or at least heard about, the directive from the new central government. The directive seems to have produced an immediate response in other areas of Ina prefecture, both inside and outside the local government. At some point between February and March, three doctors from the town of Iijima, the site of the Ina prefectural office, petitioned the prefectural authorities concerning "middle and primary schools" (a phrase used in the government's directive).[58] The authorities responded by summoning seven local elites and schoolteachers from the immediate area to the prefectural office and urging them to speak their minds: "Because this is a time of revolution (*goisshin*)," they remarked, "please say whatever you think."[59]

Several months after these discussions, the seven local notables asked permission from the prefectural office to establish a school in an inn in Iijima. The authorities, citing their "desire that people learn to discern the way of morality," approved the proposal, and in August 1870, they circulated a directive throughout the prefecture announcing the establishment of the school.[60] The school, the authorities explained, would offer instruction to children "without regard to the status divisions between warrior, farmer, artisan, and merchant" and would provide tuition exemptions for "poor children who, unable to pay tuition fees, cannot read or write." For children who faced long commutes, the school provided dormitories. The directive characterizes the founding of the school as a private undertaking: "A group of volunteers have collected funds out of a spirit of benevolence and established an elementary school." However, the authorities also pointed out that they had appointed an administrator from the prefectural office to oversee the school. The directive thus sent the clear message that the prefectural government endorsed public activism among the local population to further education and that the government would supervise the schools.

News of such experiments soon reached beyond the areas directly administered by the Meiji government, inspiring local elites in Shinano's domains to clamor for educational reform. In September 1870, one month after Ina prefecture announced the founding of its first *gōkō*, Fujimori Jūbei, a literatus and schoolteacher from a wealthy family in Toyoshina village, petitioned the authorities in Matsumoto domain on the establishment of primary schools. As was true of so many other local activists in the region, the Restoration stirred in Fujimori a recognition of the need for educational reform:

In this age of the Restoration of Imperial Rule and the Return to Antiquity (*ōsei fukko*), establishing primary schools is our first priority in the effort to restore the ancient spirit of reverence and gratitude. . . . If we lecture to the ignorant masses on the Way of the Five Relationships and patiently help them understand the meaning of imperial proclamations, then imperial rule will prosper, social mores will return to the timeless ways of the ancients, and we will cleanse ourselves of two hundred years of evil customs.[61]

Fujimori's concept of education is similar to that of the Tokugawa-era authorities who hoped to make the masses governable through moral suasion, although the Way of morality he advocated includes both that of Confucius and that of Shinto gods. He saw the entire Tokugawa period as a time of disorder and moral decline; following the overthrow of the bakufu, he sought to restore order—both within his local community and, more broadly, throughout the "imperial nation." But Fujimori's petition went beyond these familiar calls for moral rectification; he proposed a concrete plan for a domain-wide education system. The existing institutions of commoner education, he argued, are insufficient for this new age; in particular, he derided the schools held in Buddhist temples as "a waste of time," and the priests who taught in them as "worse than scoundrels." The anti-Buddhist movement had been especially vigorous in this area, and Fujimori's essay represents the application of this movement to the issue of commoner education. In fact, the eradication of Buddhist influence from local society was central to his plan: he urged the authorities to establish new elementary schools in every district, funded not only by village levies and voluntary contributions, but by funds confiscated from local temples. His desire to "cleanse ourselves of evil customs"—a sentiment echoed by the rhetoric of "civilization and enlightenment" that soon swept through local society—here carried a specifically anti-Buddhist meaning.

Fujimori's plan illustrates the changing scope of public activism among village elites. The sense of crisis during the final decades of the Tokugawa period had strengthened regional and national ties among village elites, but the reformist efforts of these elites were mainly confined to the village—excepting, of course, that small minority who left their communities and went to Kyoto in the final years before the Restoration. However, in the wake of the Restoration, Fujimori applied his reformist vision to a larger space by devising a plan for a domain-wide system of primary education and urging the domainal government to coordinate the system. He did not mention his own village, focusing instead on the domain as a whole; he even identified unique character traits among the people in the domain—namely, a simplicity and stubbornness born of geographic isolation—that made primary education all the more necessary. But although the scope of his proposed reforms was domainal, his reformist vision was motivated by events at the national level. His efforts for domainal educational reform were inspired by, and perceived as contributing to, a larger revolution within the imperial nation. Furthermore, his proposal for educational reform was informed by similar efforts in other areas of the country—he concluded by urging domainal authorities to investigate other domains that had already established elementary schools.

Soon after Fujimori sent his petition to the authorities in Matsumoto, domain authorities began plans to coordinate commoner education. Over the next few months, contrasting proposals were formulated: one by the domain school, and one by the domain government. In October 1870, the domain school expressed the need to establish elementary schools throughout Matsumoto.[62] The school's intent was to widen the pool of talent for government service; elementary schools could serve this purpose by channeling outstanding students from among the commoner elite into the domain school.[63] One month later, the domainal government issued a very different statement on elementary education. Like Fujimori, the domainal authorities sought to use elementary schools to "instruct [people] in the way of human morality," thereby "expanding the domain's efforts at moral suasion (*kyōka*)."[64] We do not know if Fujimori's petition played a role in prompting these two plans. But as in Ina prefecture, it is clear that government efforts in Matsumoto domain to coordinate elementary schooling articulated sentiments already expressed by local educators and village elites.

For the first few years following the Restoration, domainal and prefectural authorities in Shinano moved sporadically into the arena of elementary education, spurred from below by educators and village elites; indeed, governmental initiatives consisted mainly of supervising or sanctioning the efforts of local activists who had already mobilized for the cause of educational reform. In late 1871, however, the newly formed prefectural governments began to take a more active and systematic role in coordinating elementary schooling. This effort followed soon after the Meiji government took the momentous step of abolishing the domains and establishing a nationwide, centralized structure for local administration. In Shinano, this reorganization resulted in the amalgamation of thirteen domains and dozens of former bakufu territories into two new prefectures: Nagano in the north and Chikuma in the south. On the heels of this sudden enlargement in the scale of local administration, the new prefectural authorities began to implement more systematic measures to further the schooling of the local population.

Administrators in Nagano prefecture were the first to act. In September 1871 the prefectural office issued a directive calling for the establishment of *gōgakkō*, or local schools.⁶⁵ The directive dealt mainly with the issue of funding and created a hybrid system in which tuition fees and voluntary contributions from local benefactors were to be supplemented with moneys from the prefectural government. The financial commitment of the prefectural government was minimal—only 0.01 percent of the prefecture's total tax revenues—but it nonetheless signified a governmental stake in the provision of elementary schooling. The schools were to target children between the ages of seven and fifteen, but according to the directive, "anyone who is interested may enroll, regardless of age." The stated purpose of the schools to "cultivate human talent among the general population" embraced a familiar refrain but expanded its scope beyond the limited circle of samurai or elite commoners. The directive was distributed along with a notice instructing village officials how to nominate children from the local schools for admission to the newly founded prefectural school; together the two notices created a structure by which ordinary children could, at least theoretically, use schooling as a means of social advancement.⁶⁶

Prefectural administrators in Chikuma were slower to encourage and coordinate the establishment of *gōkō*, but they pursued this goal with unusual vigor. The initiative within the government came from Nagayama Moriteru, a former retainer of Satsuma domain who had held positions in the Ministry of Civil Affairs and the Ministry of Finance before being transferred to Ina prefecture in 1870. He became a senior councilor in the Chikuma prefectural government after its formation in November 1871 and then was named governor in 1873. Nagayama is known as a pioneer in modern Japanese education, an activist who left the inner circles of the Meiji government to bring enlightenment to Japanese local society through schooling; his many stirring proclamations on the urgency of education reveal that he saw his own role in such terms. In February 1872 he issued his first directive concerning the importance of establishing schools:

The strength of the state lies in the development of the intellectual powers of the people. However, until now the establishment of schools in remote areas has not been carried out sufficiently. As a result, those with ambition and talent are stuck in the mud; I am constantly grieved by such conditions. Starting now, we will build schools throughout our jurisdiction. In doing so we will unite our subjects, exhaust the powers of their diligence, and take the initiative in bringing to fruition their loyalty to the country. I implore you, volunteers, to contribute your energies and your money so that our schools will prosper rapidly.[67]

Several key strains of early Meiji educational thought are revealed in Nagayama's statements. Like all late Tokugawa and early Meiji leaders, Nagayama gave priority to the task of cultivating talent among samurai and commoner elites. His experience as a high-ranking retainer in Satsuma probably ingrained such concerns into his views on education and schooling. A second component of Nagayama's educational vision, however, was the schooling of ordinary people. In his view, national strength is linked not merely to the training of competent officials but to the development of the character and abilities of the general population—which, he argued, can only be accomplished through schooling. This concept of popular schooling reflects some of the ideas articulated by educational reformers in the early Meiji government. Like Itō and Kido, Nagayama based the strength of the state on the intellectual powers of the people. However, his main concern in the area of primary education seemed to reside less with the abilities of the individual than with the collective virtues of the people as a whole—namely, the virtues of unity and loyalty. In this respect, his views most closely resemble Iwakura's early statements regarding the purpose of popular schooling. As an official in the central government during the first two and a half years after the Restoration, Nagayama would likely have been familiar with these arguments, and he carried them with him to Chikuma.

The most critical part of Nagayama's proclamation is his entreaty to "volunteers" to "contribute [their] energies and money" to the project of building schools. In the first sentence of a document distributed along with this appeal, he explained: "The establishment of schools . . . is today's urgent task. But you must establish them by collecting private moneys, not by relying on official funds. Volunteers must therefore contribute according to their means, regardless of how much or how little."[68] The document set out guidelines for the management of such school funds, directing local officials to place the contributions in an endowment, the interest from which would be used to pay for the operation of the school. Records of all contributions were to be kept at the prefectural office, and each do-nor received a certificate of commendation from Nagayama. However, the prefectural government provided no funding for the schools, nor did it administer the funds collected in each locality. The only prefectural support came in the form of voluntary contributions from Nagayama and his staff. In an internal memo to prefectural government employees, he pledged 100 *ryō* to the effort—an enormous sum—and urged other officials to "help clear the path to progress and enlightenment." Most responded generously, giving at least 10 *ryō*.[69]

But the local contributions constituted the core of each school's endowment. The prefectural office in Matsumoto was soon flooded with reports from volunteers reporting the results of fundraising campaigns in each locality. In the small village of Muraimachi, 21 donors contributed a total of 56 *ryō*.[70] In Katagiri, a much larger village on the Nakasendō road, village officials collected 150 *ryō* from 102 donors.[71] In the town of Matsumoto, fundraising efforts raised 2,639 *ryō* from 298 donors.[72] The diary of Kitahara Inao, the Hirata disciple who had been calling for educational reform since early 1868, paints a simple picture of how these fundraising campaigns were conducted. In April 1872, Kitahara wrote, "The village officials have been walking around the village encouraging people to contribute to the school fund; in 34 days, they have raised 147 *ryō*." Several months later, when funds began to run low, Kitahara recorded that volunteers met again to organize another fundraising campaign.[73] In Suzaka, the former castle-town of Suzaka domain, organizers hoped to supplement voluntary contributions by earmarking the licensing fees of local brothels for the school endowment campaign; if school funds came up short, they remarked, "civilization and progress will be far off."[74] By April 1872, only two months after Nagayama issued his call to local volunteers, these local fundraising efforts in Chikuma prefecture had produced over 13,000 *ryō*—an endowment large enough to fund a dozen or more elementary schools.

Local volunteers not only supplied the funds for the school-building effort but coordinated virtually every other aspect of this endeavor. These volunteers consisted of local elites already involved in education; most commonly, they were village officials, literati, and former teachers. Many of them had already called for some sort of educational reform before the prefectural governments of Nagano and Chikuma became involved, and some had already taken the step of establishing *gōkō* as an alternative to existing primary schools. Soon after Nagayama issued his call, he created the official, but unpaid, position of *sewayaku* to give formal recognition to those volunteers who had already mobilized for the project of establishing schools. The term *sewayaku* can carry various meanings depending on the context and is often translated as "sponsor," "manager," or "mediator." The dozens of largely self-selected *sewayaku* in Chikuma prefecture performed all these roles as they organized local school-building projects: they not only donated their own money to the school endowment funds, but also collected funds, selected the location for the schools, and arranged to find school buildings, hired teachers, encouraged attendance, kept records, and handled all correspondence with the prefectural office.[75] Nagayama sometimes called them together to issue instructions and encouragement, but in reality, they directed policy as a kind of consultative group to Nagayama, offering guidance concerning various aspects of the school-building effort.[76]

The *gōkō* built by these local volunteers represented a new type of school, one that embodied many elements of various reformist educational visions generated during the first four years following the Restoration. The schools admitted children of all status and income backgrounds, but their goal was to reach the general population. Nagayama was explicit on this point. He acknowledged that such a goal would be difficult "due to old habits," but he nevertheless declared in a statement to the *sewayaku*, "I expect all subjects to attend."[77] However, the *sewayaku* were even more insistent on the need for universal education: whereas Nagayama proposed that all students pay tuition—an annual enrollment fee of two *shu*, plus a monthly fee of one *shu*, which was not exorbitant but nevertheless exceeded charges at most pre-Meiji commoner schools—the *sewayaku* opposed the collection of any fees.[78] They also intended the schools to serve a specific geographic area. In the earliest *gōkō*, the geographic scope varied, but after promulgation of the Registration Law in April 1871, most local organizers adopted the newly created "small districts" (*shōku*) as the area to be served by the schools. Since most small districts in Nagano and Chikuma prefecture encompassed several pre-Meiji villages, the establishment of the *gōkō* involved local coordination on a new, and broader, scale. The curriculum at the *gōkō* resembled that at most pre-Meiji commoner schools, but with a few important distinctions. In addition to reading and writing, the *gōkō* also offered instruction in arithmetic, which had been quite rare in Tokugawa-era schools in Shinano. Most of the textbooks were the same as those used in Tokugawa-era commoner schools, but many *gōkō* also used newspapers, history texts, and books on the West (such as Fukuzawa's *Conditions in the West*).[79]

The *gōkō* represented an intentional departure from many aspects of pre-Meiji commoner schools. Some pre-Meiji teachers had allowed children from poorer families to attend for free—particularly those village officials who opened schools for the children of ordinary villagers in the final decades before the Restoration; however, all schools relied almost exclusively on the tuition payments of the children who attended. In contrast, the *gōkō* were funded mainly through voluntary contributions to a school endowment. The mere fact that the *gōkō* served several villages did not distinguish them from pre-Meiji commoner schools, most of which also drew children from more than one village; some private academies, in fact, attracted a regional, or even a national, clientele. However, the element of multi-village cooperation in the administration of the school was new, as was the concept of a single school serving a specific jurisdiction. This, along with the principle of communal funding, calls attention to the public character of the *gōkō*. The notion of schooling as a public service for local children can be traced to the efforts of late Tokugawa village schoolteachers, but the *gōkō* manifested this idea more fully. In keeping with this concept, most *gōkō* met not in private homes but in newly built structures, temples, or some other rented space.[80]

Finally, the teachers of *gōkō* were different from those in late Tokugawa village schools. Many late Tokugawa schoolteachers, particularly those who were village officials or were otherwise rooted firmly in a specific community, were actively involved in the establishment of *gōkō*. However, rather than assuming the role of teacher, they worked together to select new teachers, most of whom were samurai or commoner literati with more extensive training and more renown in regional literary circles than the average village schoolteacher. In doing so, these former teachers created a distinction between "teacher" and "administrator"—a distinction that was not recognized in Tokugawa-era commoner schools—and delegated to themselves the role of administrator. When the Chikuma prefectural

office created the position of *sewayaku* in March 1872, it formalized
the role of *gōkō* administrator; however, this separation of instruction
from administration was evident in the *gōkō* established in Nagano
and Chikuma before any sort of prefectural intervention: village officials and educators had already conceptualized a new kind of school
that was distinct from their pre-Meiji experience. The Chikuma prefectural government expressed this distinction in a more categorical
fashion when, in May 1872, it formally terminated the activities of
tenaraishishō, or "writing teachers," the term by which Tokugawa-era
teachers were most commonly known:

Until now there have been so-called writing teachers throughout the countryside, who teach only basic characters. We hear that there are many people
with innate ability and ambition who live their whole lives thinking that
[such an education] is sufficient, and therefore remain undiscovered. . . . Today, in view of the imperial effort to cultivate talent, this is unacceptable.
Consequently, we must abolish all so-called writing teachers at once.[81]

The fact that the prefectural office could count on the support of
local volunteers—a great many of whom fell into this maligned category of writing teachers—reveals both the tenor of the period that
followed the Restoration and the nature of the *gōkō* movement. Many
village officials, educators, and literati felt strongly that the unprecedented changes of the recent past necessitated the adoption of a new
model of commoner schooling. This sentiment was articulated in a
petition sent to the Chikuma prefectural office by two local advocates of educational reform. One was Fujimori Jūbei, the village official who had written an earlier petition urging Matsumoto domain
officials to dissolve the Buddhist temples and apply their assets to
the establishment of new schools. After writing that petition, Fujimori had established a *gōkō* and hired Takahashi Keijūrō, a samurai
scholar from Takato domain in the Upper Ina district of Shinano, to
serve as instructor. Their relationship had been forged in late Tokugawa literati circles that often transcended status divisions, linking
elite commoners and samurai together through aesthetic pursuits
and ideological movements. Takahashi actually wrote the petition,
based on his discussions with Fujimori and on their common effort
to reform schooling practices; the document is undated, but textual
clues place it between late 1871 and mid-1872.[82]

Takahashi believed that Japan was in a time of "cosmic upheaval,"
a time that compelled those with "spirit" or "will" (*kokorozashi*) to take

action for the benefit of the imperial nation. Action, Takahashi argued, should not take the form of the "extremist violence" or "divisive obstinacy" that had recently manifested itself in those patriots who "clenched their fists and gnashed their teeth in vexation while shouting 'Revere the emperor; expel the barbarians!'" Rather, he called for constructive action consistent with both the "spirit of fervent patriotism" and the "law of civilization and enlightenment." For Takahashi, the most crucial arena for such action was that of schooling and education. Schooling, he maintained, was necessary to train talented individuals for service to the country and would foster unity and loyalty among the general population; consequently, Japan's future depended upon it. But in his view, the old pattern of schooling in which scholars simply opened up private schools in their own homes was no longer sufficient. Rather, he envisioned a distinctly public form of schooling, an integrated school system comprising primary schools, middle schools, and universities. Contributing to the construction of such a system constituted, in Takahashi's words, a form of "service to the public of our imperial nation."

The sense of crisis and possibility inherent in the late Tokugawa and early Meiji periods triggered in Takahashi an impulse toward public activism. This was not the activism of extremist samurai who responded to the crisis by offering militant protection from foreign corruption. Nor was it the secessionist activism of the late Tokugawa period, in which leaders withdrew from the dominant order to create a reconstituted order within their own sphere of influence—which for samurai like Takahashi was the domain, and for Fujimori, the village. His criticism of those who "focus only on their own locality" and "know nothing about the public of the entire country" could be directed at either form of late Tokugawa secessionism. In his view, the very purpose of the Restoration was to create an "imperial public" that transcended these divisions; in turn, his own service to this imperial public—in the form of building schools—was a way to "begin the Restoration anew."

The attempts by prefectural governments in Nagano and Chikuma to coordinate the school-building effort merged unproblematically with such sentiments. Prefectural authorities explicitly relied on the initiatives (and money) of "volunteers" like Takahashi; this public sanctioning of local initiatives could only have encouraged individuals seeking to link their own personal contributions to a larger collective effort. The prefectural government did make a clear distinction between "official moneys" and "private moneys" and repeatedly reminded local volunteers that the *gōkō* would be funded solely by the latter. However, prefectural authorities did not exclude the contributions or efforts of these local activists from the realm of public service. Indeed, the fact that prefectural financial support came strictly in the form of voluntary contributions from individual officials undoubtedly convinced local volunteers that they were engaged in a common effort, an effort that involved men of spirit from both inside and outside local government. One local activist, Nishihara Jūbei, clearly understood his involvement in these terms. In a petition to the Nagano prefectural office in March 1872, Nishihara lamented that the recent progress in the realm of schooling had not reached the isolated parts of the prefecture, which remained mired in "extreme stupidity and utter darkness."[83] What upset him most was that people in those benighted areas would feel isolated from the affairs of the country: "How will [such people] recognize that they have a stake in our great system of government?" His solution to this problem was to build a new school, an endeavor he referred to repeatedly as his "public mission." The name he gave his proposed school, a *kyōritsu gakkō*, or a "jointly established school," signified that the school would be funded privately but serve a public function.

There is no sense in Nishihara's petition, or in any other materials relating to the *gōkō* movement, that the private sources of funding and initiative behind the *gōkō* were inconsistent either with the schools' public mission or with the notion of government coordination. This is due in part to the fact that the *gōkō* embodied many concerns and aspirations shared by both prefectural authorities and local volunteers. One can identify certain differences between the rhetoric in prefectural directives and that in petitions by local activists. For example, most activists stressed the value of the *gōkō* to the "imperial country" (*kōkoku*); the prefectural government, in contrast, never used the term and instead focused on the role of schools in strengthening the state (*kokka*). Such differences in emphasis, however, would have been overwhelmed by the many points of consensus in their shared vision. But the willingness of local activists to accept the prefectural government's coordination of the *gōkō* can also be attributed to the fact that nothing in the prefectural government's intervention constrained the initiatives of local activists. Indeed, this "intervention" amounted to the official encouragement of initiatives already under way and an attempt to link those initiatives under the nominal guidance of the prefectural government. The naming of the *gōkō* reflected the nature of prefectural involvement. Local organizers usually gave their school a name that reflected their own backgrounds and their goals—for example, the School for Faithful Thought (Shiseikan), or the Society for Proper Practice (Shōsenkan). The prefectural government assigned numbers to them according to the order in which they were established (for example, Primary School No. 24).[84] The prefectural government did not, however, require the local organizers or students to adopt that number, and most did not do so, even in official correspondence. Although the prefectural government had come to view each individual school according to an overarching administrative rationale, there was nothing to prevent local organizers from continuing to perceive the schools as a product of their own initiative and educational vision.

The rapid proliferation of *gōkō* so quickly after prefectural governments in Nagano and Chikuma identified the goal of building new schools reflected the presence of local activists already mobilized for the cause of educational reform. In Nagano prefecture, more than a hundred *gōkō* were established between October 1871, when the prefectural office issued its first public statement on schools, and August 1872, when the Ministry of Education promulgated the Fundamental Code.[85] In Chikuma, the effort to establish *gōkō* continued unabated until mid-1873, by which time there were 143. In the sense that these schools were in large part the product of local activism, it is appropriate to refer to the spread of *gōkō* in Nagano and Chikuma as a "movement." This term might be misleading to an audience of Japanese scholars, who generally use the term "movement" (*undō*) to characterize phenomena that derive exclusively from popular energies—usually in opposition to state oppression or regulation. It is problematic to view the spread of *gōkō* as this type of movement. First, the initiative came from a stratum of highly literate, usually wealthy, commoners, many of whom held some sort of official position (headman, elder, *sewayaku*) during the late Tokugawa or early Meiji period; it would be somewhat inaccurate, therefore, to view these initiatives as "popular." Nor were these initiatives conceived in opposition to the government (the relevant government

body being the prefectural office). Local activists welcomed the involvement of the prefectural government; prefectural coordination
was consistent with their own desire to locate their own initiatives
within a broader effort to serve an expanded, though still undefined,
public. Furthermore, this coordination was not intrusive or oppressive, or even regulatory. Rather, the prefectural office took a collegial
and affirming stance toward local activists. Just as this was not a case
of reformist popular energies being dampened by an autocratic state,
nor was it like the situation William Kelly found in early-Meiji Shō-
nai, in which progressive prefectural leaders were pitted against the
"inertia" of local elites.[86] The crisis of the late Tokugawa period and
the post-Restoration atmosphere of fluidity and possibility generated
reformist visions among village elites and prefectural officials alike;
the many common points among those visions—combined with the
nebulous quality of the administrative framework in the early Meiji
period—allowed the initiatives of local activists to mesh unproblematically with the early state-building efforts of prefectural authorities.

Ending the Interregnum: The Promulgation of the Fundamental Code

In August 1872, just as the *gōkō*-building efforts in Chikuma and
Nagano were gathering momentum, the Meiji government brought
them to a formal end when it promulgated a new vision for educational reform, the Fundamental Code of Education. The Fundamental Code was one of a series of momentous reforms by the Meiji government that together constituted the initial thrust of modern state
formation in Japan. The first of these reforms was the Registration
Law of April 1871, which mandated that all households register with
the government for the purposes of a national census. Yamamuro
Shin'ichi emphasizes the importance of this step; it legally integrated
all Japanese people into the institutions of the Japanese government
on an equal footing—a precondition to national mobilization.[87] Subsequent measures abolishing the status category of "outcaste" and
removing the vestiges of samurai privilege reinforced this effort,
since they made possible a relationship between the Japanese people
and the new government that was unmediated by formal status distinctions. Just as the Registration Law established the legal basis for
national integration, the abolition of the domains and the establish-

ment of the prefectures (*haihan chiken*) in July 1871 established the administrative apparatus by which such an integration might be achieved. The abolition of the domains allowed the Meiji government to assume administrative jurisdiction over the entire country for the first time, and the centralized prefectural system constituted a governmental structure capable of implementing central policies on a national scale. Once the legal and institutional basis for national mobilization was in place, the Meiji government then created national systems to carry out that mobilization for specific purposes. In addition to the Fundamental Code, the Conscription Law of January 1873 created the legal means by which the entire Japanese population—rather than samurai alone—bore the collective burden of military service to the nation. Beginning in July 1873, the Meiji government also created a new taxation system in which the land tax became a fixed-rate tax based on land value rather than yields.[88]

This flurry of reforms served the goals of integration and mobilization and thus furthered the larger cause of national strength and independence. Most Meiji leaders recognized that a centralized educational system was crucial to these goals. Such a system would integrate families and children into the institutions of the new government on a daily basis, train them for responsible and effective participation in the life of the nation, and enhance mobilization efforts by inculcating a personal identification with the nation. Centralized schooling would, in Bruce Curtis's words, allow the government to "anchor the conditions of political governance in the selves of the governed."[89] It is telling that the Meiji government's first official act after assuming administrative control over the entire country in July 1871 was to extend this control to the realm of schooling by creating a Ministry of Education.[90] Just as several key figures in the Meiji government were departing for Europe and America with the Iwakura Mission—one purpose of which was to investigate school systems in the West—the Ministry of Education began in late 1871 to engage in the project of educational reform. Its first step was to experiment with reforms on a limited scale by creating a public elementary school for girls and exercising administrative control over a small network of elementary schools in Tokyo.[91]

At the same time, it began to prepare for the creation of a national educational system. In November, it enlisted the help of prefectural offices in conducting a preliminary investigation of educational conditions throughout the country.[92] In December, Minister of Education Ōki Takatō, a former retainer of Saga domain and cousin of Ōkuma Shigenobu, appointed twelve officials to draw up a plan for an educational system. Almost all these officials, as well as Ōki himself, were scholars of Western Learning; their preparation for this task involved studying educational laws in Europe and America.[93] By January 1872, the committee of scholars had already created an initial draft of the Fundamental Code, one that outlined most of the key principles that would define the new system.[94] The Council of State approved of the basic thrust of the Fundamental Code, but the cost of the plan proved to be a sticking point: some councilors were not willing to commit three million *ryō* to the project from a severely strapped budget.[95] The debate seemed intractable at the time, and in the end the Council of State agreed to approve the plan itself without the budget, and in August 1872 the Fundamental Code was promulgated and distributed to prefectural offices throughout the country.

The promulgation of the Fundamental Code was without question an epochal moment in the history of Japanese education. Whereas most Western countries moved incrementally toward a centralized, compulsory school system over a span of several decades, the Fundamental Code represented an effort to a do so in a single step. In this sense, the promulgation of the Fundamental Code can be seen as the definitive start of the modern school system in Japan. But this moment should be recognized not merely as one of creation but also as one of displacement. The Ministry of Education was stepping into a broad, variegated field of thought and practice relating to popular schooling. This field had been shaped by over a century of development and experimentation and consisted of several distinct strains of thought on the purpose of popular schooling. It also consisted of tens of thousands of teachers who had invested heavily in existing forms of schooling, and millions of adults and children with their own personal memories and experiences of "school." Almost immediately following its creation in 1871, the Ministry of Education proclaimed these pre-existing educational arrangements insufficient and expressed the need for arrangements that were decidedly new and distinct. The Fundamental Code was the product of this revolutionary impulse. It represented an effort not merely to create new laws and institutions and to train new personnel but to redefine "school" and to displace and marginalize existing definitions.

This dual nature of the Meiji project is evident in the text of the Fundamental Code and the two documents appended to it at the time of its distribution. One of these documents was a notice from the Ministry of Education stating that all existing schools were to be abolished at once. "Hereafter," it noted, "schools can reopen if they conform to the Fundamental Code and carefully consider its intent."[96] This document created an unoccupied space into which the Fundamental Code might enter. The second document appended to the Fundamental Code, known as its "Preamble," critiqued existing schooling arrangements and outlined the principles underlying the new system.[97] The Preamble is widely recognized as expressing the intent of the new government to bring modern schooling to the entire nation and for espousing schooling in terms of its economic value to the individual. "It is only by building up his character, developing his mind, and cultivating his talents," the Preamble states, "that a man can make his way in the world and make his business prosper." Schooling, in turn, is justified because of its instrumental role in accomplishing these goals. The Preamble reflects a utilitarian conception of the school informed by an Enlightenment emphasis on the intellectual and moral development of the individual.

These and other statements in the Preamble about the new purpose of schooling are accompanied by criticisms of the assumptions that underlay previous schooling arrangements. For instance, the Preamble comments that in the past, people "did not know that [learning] was the very foundation of success in life," believing instead that the pursuit of learning was "for the sake of the state." This critique is ironic, given that the implicit assumption behind the Fundamental Code—one that was made explicit in many other statements by the Ministry of Education—was that the government was taking control of education for the purpose of enhancing its ability to mobilize the Japanese people for state-defined goals. In any case, it is significant that the Ministry of Education framed its justification for popular schooling in opposition to previous conceptions of education. Elsewhere, the Preamble elaborates on its critique of Tokugawa education:

Learning being viewed as the exclusive privilege of the samurai and his superiors, farmers, artisans, merchants, and women have neglected it altogether and know not even its meaning. . . . This was due to our evil traditions and, in turn, was the very cause which checked the spread of culture, hampered the development of talent and accomplishments, and sowed the seeds of poverty, bankruptcy, and disrupted homes.[98]

This passage, too, explains the new conception of schooling embodied in the Fundamental Code as a deliberate contrast to pre-Meiji assumptions. As evidence for its contention that the purpose of schooling is to provide economic stability to the household, the Preamble cites the "poverty, bankruptcy, and disrupted homes" caused by the absence of popular schooling during the Tokugawa period. The Preamble conspicuously fails to mention the thousands of schools that were in existence at the time the Fundamental Code was written; in other documents, the Ministry of Education recognized these schools, but simply emphasized their shortcomings. In either case, pre-Meiji schooling practices are represented in such a way as to make the new government's intervention appear necessary.[99]

After abolishing, then delegitimizing, all existing schools in the appended documents, the Ministry of Education provided its own authoritative definition of "school" in the Fundamental Code itself. Like the Preamble, the 109-article Fundamental Code (eventually expanded to 214 articles) explained the basic principles underlying the proposed school system but it did so in the form of detailed regulations on institutions, personnel, and procedures. Whereas the Preamble focused on the benefits of schooling for the individual and the household, the Fundamental Code dealt with the administration of schooling, affirming the principle of government control on a national scale. Indeed, the first article of the first section of the Fundamental Code begins with the statement: "The educational affairs of the entire country will be under the control of the Ministry of Education." In subsequent articles, the Fundamental Code explained that this control would be exercised through a nationwide administrative structure linking all schools directly to the central government. The Fundamental Code divided the country into eight university districts (with one university per district), each under the direct supervision of the Ministry of Education in Tokyo. In turn, each university district was divided into 32 middle-school districts, each of which was divided further into 210 primary-school districts, for a grand total of eight universities, 256 middle schools, and 53,760 primary schools.[100] Together these districts formed a rationalized pyramidal structure with the Ministry of Education at the top generating policy for all the institutions below.

The creation of "elementary-school districts" (*shōgakku*) was also intended to facilitate centralization by supplanting the village as the administrative and educational unit of Japanese society. The effort had begun one year earlier with the 1871 Registration Law and the establishment of "large districts" (*daiku*) and "small districts" (*shōku*), to replace the village league (*kumiai*) and the village as the units of general administration for the new state.[101] The *gōkō* established in Nagano and Chikuma prefectures in the months before the promulgation of the Fundamental Code had been based on these *shōku* units and thus involved cooperation among the leaders of several different villages. The new elementary-school districts designated by the Fundamental Code were also intended to encompass several villages in a single unit of educational administration, but these units were to have different boundaries altogether and operate independently of the *shōku* unit of political administration. As Michio Umegaki has argued, this effort to redraw and rename existing boundaries of local political life (and in this case, educational life) was intended "to foster the sense of discontinuity and impress areas with the presence of the new central government."[102] In addition, since the new boundaries for educational administration did not match those of political administration, they highlighted the distinction between the various leadership functions in local society and limited the authority of local elites to a single sphere of activity.[103]

Although the Fundamental Code asserted the principle of centralized administration, it rejected the principle of centralized funding. The Ministry of Education had already stated in the Preamble that one of the "evil traditions" of Tokugawa education was the tendency to "depend upon the government for the expenses of education" (here referring to samurai education rather than commoner education, which was funded through tuition payments). The Ministry of Education reaffirmed this sentiment in the Fundamental Code. Because the Council of State could not agree on a budget, the version promulgated and distributed in August 1872 did not mention financial assistance from the central government. The three million *ryō* budget initially proposed by the Ministry of Education was approved by the Council of State in September 1872, and the funds were distributed to prefectural offices in April 1873. However, most of these funds went toward normal schools and middle schools; only a small percentage went to individual school districts to help fund primary schools.[104] As a result, the costs of popular schooling were borne primarily by the families within each school district. Indeed, this was consistent with the new rationale for popular schooling as outlined in the Preamble: since it is individual households that enjoy the benefits of schooling, it is they who should bear its costs.

One of the most significant steps in marginalizing pre-existing schooling arrangements was the creation, through the various regulations and classificatory schemes articulated in the Fundamental Code, of an abstract concept of "school." The abstract character of the new vision of school is reflected in the use of a distinct term for school: *gakkō*. Rubinger discusses the contemporary connotations of this term and remarks that it "denote[d] a sense of restriction, limitation, or conformity to a uniform standard." Perhaps more significant is his observation that this term was a generic one.[105] A number of different types of schools were addressed in the Fundamental Code, but these types were named by adding prefixes to the generic word *gakkō*—for example, *shihan gakkō* (normal school), *chūgakkō* (middle school), *senmon gakkō* (professional school), and so on. Such prefixes created variations of "school" but reified the abstract concept of *gakkō*, the essential characteristics of which each variant presumably shared. The creation of this abstract concept, in turn, enabled the Ministry of Education to define those "essential characteristics" and to apply the appellation of *gakkō* only to those particular schools that possessed such characteristics.[106] The Fundamental Code did, in fact, withhold this appellation from all pre-existing schools, thus marking their difference from the new schools sanctioned by the Ministry of Education and denying them access to the legitimacy inherent in this abstraction.

In addition, the Fundamental Code created new names for pre-existing commoner schools—which, as noted above, were not generally identified by a generic term during the Tokugawa period. The two names given to these schools can be seen as subtly derogatory. *Shijuku*, the term used in the Fundamental Code to refer to private schools with a licensed teacher, were marked by the character *shi*, or "private," thus symbolically positioning them outside the public system sanctioned by the imperial government. *Kajuku*, which referred to private schools without a licensed teacher, bore the stigma of *ka* (the character *ie*, or "home"), which linked the *kajuku* to premodern schools held in the home of a teacher—schools that were criticized in other Ministry of Education pronouncements as insufficient, even harmful. Even if the Ministry of Education's intent was not to stigmatize, the mere act of withholding the term *gakkō* from these schools clearly identified them as being something less than "school."

The Fundamental Code contained a variety of regulations and bureaucratic procedures that both fleshed out this new, abstract concept of school with detailed content and, in the process, delegitimized various aspects of pre-existing schooling arrangements. For example, the Fundamental Code created licensing procedures for all teachers and schools. In Article 40, the Fundamental Code stated: "If [a teacher] does not obtain a graduation certificate from a normal school or middle school, he/she is not permitted to assume a post." In Article 43, the ministry acknowledged that since no normal schools had been established, it would have to wait a few years before enforcing this rule rigorously. However, in establishing the procedure for teacher licensing, the ministry was claiming the authority to define who could teach and what qualifications that entailed. The assumption behind this rule was, of course, that existing teachers lacked those qualifications and were not yet fit to serve in the new schools. The Ministry of Education had already expressed this sentiment elsewhere. For example, when the ministry submitted a proposal for a normal school in April 1872, it justified the urgency of the proposal by disparaging the abilities of pre-Meiji schoolteachers, "scoundrels" who "have no other way to make a living," and whose instruction is "superficial and shallow."[107] The procedure of licensing simply rooted this delegitimation of old teachers in the bureaucratic procedures of the new system and required them to submit to the Ministry of Education's definition of "teacher" if they wished to participate in the new system.

Schools, too, were subject to this process of licensing. In order to open a new school—or to reopen an old school closed when the Ministry of Education promulgated the Fundamental Code—local authorities needed to submit a "school establishment petition" to the prefectural authorities. Article 177 of the Fundamental Code established guidelines for the format and content of these petitions, providing a sample petition with eleven different categories of information that had to be supplied by the petitioning parties: location, school name, curriculum, instructional rules, school rules, building rules, teacher qualifications, teacher salaries, number of students, tuition revenues, and school finances (with recommended concluding remarks, required signatures, and correct title of addressee included at the end of the form).[108]

Although these forms might appear to belong to the realm of objective fact gathering, they enabled the Ministry of Education to transmit throughout the country its new conception of school. Each category contained in the form reflected a different component of this definition. For example, the first question on the form, the "location" of the school, could be answered in any number of ways, particularly considering the rapid changes in the structure of local administration during the early Meiji period. However, the sample form in the Fundamental Code specified a precise definition of "location": the university district number, followed by the prefectural name, followed by the middle-school district number, followed by the elementary-school district number, followed by the village name. All these administrative units (except the village) were recent creations; the various levels of "school districts," in particular, would have been meaningless outside the context of the Fundamental Code. The petitions, however, required people to conceive of their school, if only for a moment, as one component of a network of hierarchically organized institutions. Other categories in this petition functioned in a similar way: the category of "school name" was to be designated as "elementary school no. X"; the category of "curriculum" was to be answered simply with the phrase "in accordance with the standard elementary-school program found in the Fundamental Code," and so on. All these informational categories made some sort of statement about the conception of "school" articulated by the Meiji government and functioned to transform local knowledge about schools according to that conception.

We can see these dynamics at work in two separate petitions submitted by Kyōwa Elementary School in Chikuma prefecture.[109] The first petition is dated September 1873, less than a year after the Fundamental Code was first sent to the prefectures. One glance at the petition reveals that the writers—the small district head (*kuchō*) and the registration district head (*kochō*)—were either not fully aware of the Ministry of Education's formatting guidelines or did not deem it necessary to follow them closely. For example, they did not, as was suggested in the Fundamental Code, simply open with the title "School-Building Petition" and move directly to the informational questions; rather, following the language and format of Edo-period documents, they opened with a formal, all-purpose petition title (*kakitsuke o motte otodoki mōshiage tatematsurisōrō*) and then requested in petitionary prose that their application be considered by the authorities. Then, in the "location" section, they omitted the prefecture name and middle-school district number and instead gave the old province, district (*gun*), and village league (*kumiai*) names. They made the additional mistake of including here (instead of in the separate "school name" section) not only the name of the school but the information that the school was formerly a pre-Meiji private school with the name "Kyōwa gijuku." In the "curriculum" section, the authors listed the texts and subjects to be taught. To make matters worse, the texts were those typically used in pre-Meiji commoner schools, and the subjects did not fit the classificatory schemes found in the Fundamental Code. Similarly, other categories were either out of order, combined with other categories, or recorded in a way that deviated from the official format. All the desired information was included in the application in one form or another, but not in the form specified in the guidelines provided by the government.

These deviations reflected not only an unfamiliarity with new administrative procedures but also a conception of the school that clearly differed from that embodied in the Fundamental Code. It was for this reason, and not simply on the grounds of administrative conformity, that such petitions were rejected. Such was the fate of the application submitted by Kyōwa Elementary School. The village officials went back to the drawing board in order to make sure that their school, which had been operating before the promulgation of the Fundamental Code, could reopen with the sanction of the Ministry of Education. Their second petition, submitted three months later, conformed precisely to the model provided in the Fundamental Code. Of particular interest is the "teacher qualification" category: the petitioners preceded their account of each teacher's educational training with the statement, "lacks graduation certificate from the teacher-training school," even though such a school had not yet been established in Chikuma prefecture. The rewriting of this petition presumably did not transform the operation of the school itself; most likely, community leaders simply learned what they needed to say in order for the application to be approved. In the process, however, they learned to think according to the concepts and in the language endorsed by the Meiji government.

Another bureaucratic procedure that served to reinforce the definition of "school" found in the Fundamental Code was the inspection. Inspection was performed at various levels during the first several years after the promulgation of the Fundamental Code: even prefectural governors and Ministry of Education officials periodically traveled the country to observe local schooling conditions. The most common, and systematic, inspections, however, were performed by *gakku torishimari*, or "school district administrators," a position I discuss in more detail in the next chapter. Article 181 of the Fundamental Code charged the *gakku torishimari* with the task of inspecting schools within each middle-school district; as in the case of the school establishment petitions, the Fundamental Code provided a sample form indicating the kinds of information to be gathered by the *gakku torishimari* and the format in which that information should be communicated to the prefectural office. The information that *gakku torishimari* were to gather for each school was, in fact, quite similar to that to be included in the school establishment petitions: the school name, location, funding, the number and names of teachers, the number of boys and girls who attended the school, and the number of boys and girls who did not. In addition, the *gakku torishimari* were to instruct the *sewayaku* for each school to investigate and report the names of non-attending children and the reasons for their absence.

Inspection served a number of different purposes for the new government. First, since it was a means by which the central government confirmed whether localities were acting in conformity with central policy, inspection played an instrumental role in the process of centralization. In addition, as Takashi Fujitani has argued in reference to imperial tours and ceremonies, the practice of educational inspection made possible the panoptic modes of power that are essential to the modern state.[110] By collecting information about localities and individual households, the government let people know that education was subject to the vision, and regulation, of the authorities; this, in turn, eventually led to some level of self-regulation. Finally, as in the case of licensing, the classificatory schemes embedded in the practice of inspection helped to disseminate the abstract concept of "school" described in the Fundamental Code and imposed the condition of "lack" or "defect" on schools that did not conform to this concept.

Scholars of colonial administration have long recognized what Frederick Cooper and Ann Stoler have called the "culture-defining" effect of bureaucratic routines, particularly those of a classificatory nature.[111] Such routines are, in fact, employed by all modern bureaucratic states as a means of consolidating authority, whether in a domestic or a colonial setting. In Japan, they were a crucial part of the repertoire of the Meiji government in its effort to create a national, centralized school system. Particularly after a period of unregulated experimentation in educational thought and practice, the Ministry of Education's task was one of redefining "school" and displacing alternative definitions. In the Fundamental Code it defined "teacher" as an individual with a certificate from a state-run normal school; "school" as a "*gakkō*," a public institution subject to government regulation and distinct from the other areas of social and cultural life in local society; and "education" as something that takes place within this "school." By reaffirming these definitions—and by requiring people to *use* them—the routines outlined in the Fundamental Code helped to create a common discursive framework for talking and thinking about schooling. This framework was essential to the consolidation of the new system: because alternative visions of schooling could not be advocated effectively from within that framework, the new conception of "school" articulated by the Ministry of Education in the Fundamental Code could gradually be accepted as common sense.

Conclusion

The Meiji Restoration initiated a new phase in the ongoing effort to rethink existing schooling arrangements, particularly those directed at the general population. Officials within the new imperial government participated in this effort, recognizing that control over educational institutions would play a key role in the struggle among competing interpretations of the Restoration and visions of the post-Restoration order. At a time when both the structure and the ideological orientation of the new government were still unsettled, officials and scholars in Tokyo and Kyoto fought over the direction of Japan's institutions of higher learning, and a few began to devise a new rationale for mass schooling and its role in building a modern nation-state. The impact of such efforts, however, was constrained by the limited administrative reach of the new government.

This indeterminacy at the center was seen by many activists and officials within local society as a moment of opportunity and possibility. The crises of the last half of the Tokugawa period had prompted local elites to devise their own strategies to provide order and relief within local society—strategies that often included measures for popular schooling. The Restoration, however, inspired many of these elites in Shinano to expand the scope of their initiatives. The overthrow of the Tokugawa order had created a broad, undefined public space over which no particular group or vision held a decisive claim. Local elites from both inside and outside the government flocked to this space, injecting into it their own interpretations of the Restoration and their hopes for the new order. The fluidity of the immediate post-Restoration government allowed for few constraints on either the direction or scope of local initiatives. One product of these initiatives was the *gōkō*, which was conceptualized as a public institution but reflected the concerns and ambitions of local activists. Attempts by prefectural governments in Chikuma and Nagano to coordinate these *gōkō* into prefecture-wide school systems consisted mainly of an effort to encourage local initiatives already under way and to build an official structure to encompass the activities of local elites who were already mobilized for public activism.

The Fundamental Code, however, represented a different kind of government intervention. Faced with the task of creating a school system that would help to consolidate the authority of the new government, Meiji leaders could not afford to leave the project of educational reform to the initiatives of local activists and prefectural leaders. Their project was not merely one of creating a network of schools and teachers under the centralized leadership of the Ministry of Education. Rather, their task was to transform local knowledge pertaining to schooling and education, to create a new conception of school while displacing alternative conceptions that had been generated in the late Tokugawa and early Meiji periods. This was one part of a larger effort by the Meiji government to define and constrain the vast space of public activism created in the wake of the Restoration. It had to sort out which ideas and energies could survive in the new order and which needed to be transformed or marginalized. In the realm of education, the regulations and routines established by the Fundamental Code began this sifting process. As we shall see in subsequent chapters, however, this process proved to be a delicate undertaking, for it constrained precisely those local activists whose participation was needed if the new system was to take root.

FOUR

National Policy
and Local Mobilization,
1872–1876

Although it is important to recognize the hegemonic intent of the Fundamental Code—its effort to redefine "school" and to displace pre-existing definitions through rhetoric and bureaucratic routines— we must not assume that the Meiji government successfully and unilaterally carried out this intent. As James Scott points out, even stable regimes with extensive administrative apparatuses are forced to negotiate the terms of rule with subordinate groups;[1] in early Meiji Japan, the central government was much less capable of imposing its will on local society. The new government had only shortly before emerged from a period of revolutionary upheaval and faced several years of serious challenges before its survival was secured. Its monopoly over the means of violence was tenuous. The domains had been abolished only a year earlier, and the nationwide administrative system drawn up to replace them was still very much in flux. The implementation of the Fundamental Code assumed the operation of administrative structures and personnel that did not yet exist, and the financially strapped central government could offer local governments few resources to realize its new policies.

To implement the Fundamental Code, therefore, the central government needed to secure the cooperation of both prefectural officials and a critical mass of subprefectural leaders functioning in official and unofficial capacities. To a certain extent, this is what happened. But the initial dynamics of the implementation of the Fundamental Code were more complex than is usually implied by the term "cooperation." With only a weak and constantly shifting administrative structure to enforce the Fundamental Code, the central government tapped local movements for educational reform under way before the Fundamental Code's promulgation. These movements were driven by a voluntaristic, collegial spirit among local elites and were characterized by an ambiguous—and sometimes nonexistent—distinction between the roles of educational and political leadership. This mobilization was oriented toward national integration, but local elites viewed integration not in terms of administrative centralization but as a means of linking their efforts to a larger campaign of public activism. These patterns had driven the *gōkō* movement of the early post-Restoration period, and they subsequently shaped the formation of the early Meiji educational system. The purpose of this chapter is to trace this process by highlighting the ideas and activities of local participants in educational reform during the years immediately following the promulgation of the Fundamental Code.

The Prefectural Response to the Fundamental Code

Nagano's claim to the title "education prefecture" stems in large part from its seemingly rapid and successful implementation of Meiji educational reforms, particularly in the first few years after the promulgation of the Fundamental Code. At the time, modern-day Nagano prefecture consisted of two prefectures, Nagano and Chikuma (Map 4). Both prefectures—particularly Chikuma, which was amalgamated into Nagano prefecture in 1876—were praised by the Ministry of Education for their "vigorous mindset toward education."[2] Figure 2, derived from statistical surveys conducted by prefectural and local officials, reveals a remarkable increase in enrollment rates for both prefectures between 1873 and 1875. The rates in Chikuma prefecture were by far the highest in the country until the prefecture was joined with Nagano in 1876; even after the amalgamation, the rates were at or near the top for decades.[3] The vigorous

Map 4: Nagano and Chikuma prefectures (former Shinano
province), with prefectural capitals

response in Nagano and Chikuma to the Meiji government's educational reforms can also be seen in the relatively rapid increase in the
number of "new" schools established according to the Ministry of
Education's guidelines for primary education: from some 30 new
schools in Nagano prefecture in mid-1873 to 221 in late 1873 to 327 in
1874 to 343 by 1875 and from 537 new schools in Chikuma at the end
of 1873 to 614 by 1874 to 656 by 1875. The Ministry of Education often cited Nagano and Chikuma as "model" prefectures for other localities.

Given the unusually high number of commoner schools in late
Tokugawa Shinano, as well as the vigorous efforts in both Nagano
and Chikuma to establish *gōkō* during the years immediately follow-

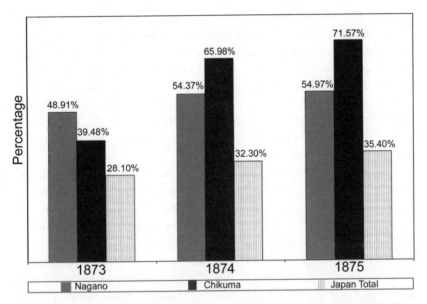

Fig. 2   Percentage of elementary school–age children enrolled in schools, 1873–75

ing the Restoration, this positive response might appear to have been a foregone conclusion. However, the Ministry of Education's attempt in the Fundamental Code to denigrate existing schooling arrangements and espouse a radically new concept of "school" ran the risk of alienating local activists who had invested so much time and money in these earlier forms of schooling. These were the same individuals whose cooperation was necessary for the implementation of the Fundamental Code in local society. Some persons in Nagano and Chikuma did, in fact, feel such a sense of frustration and alienation. In Chikuma, for example, the prefectural government noted "resentment over the betrayal of the *shōkō* [the term for *gōkō* commonly used in Chikuma]" and its negative effect on the implementation of the Fundamental Code.[4] In the records of one school in Nagano, community leaders reported that "the local sentiment was one of dejection" in the wake of the abolition of a nearby *gōkō* that people had worked so hard to establish. They observed that local people were "very discouraged. . . . They feel that building a new elementary school once again would be very difficult, and they will not be able to get people to help."[5]

But whatever resentment may have been felt toward the Fundamental Code seems to have been muted, at least at first, by the enthusiasm of many officials and activists. They lauded it as "a grand undertaking, unprecedented in discernment from eternity past." Within months, both prefectures launched campaigns to establish new schools according to the Fundamental Code's guidelines.[6] Many participants in these campaigns had been active in the *gōkō* movement, and they were now eager to contribute at the local level to this national undertaking.

The prefectural governments in Nagano and Chikuma took the lead in coordinating these campaigns, even though the Ministry of Education had not intended that prefectural governments would assume a comprehensive role in education. According to the Fundamental Code, the chief subnational coordinators of the new system were to be the new administrative offices (*tokugakukyoku*) in each of the country's eight university districts (*daigakku*). The ministry had designed these offices—and the school-district system in general—as an institutional framework for educational administration separate from the framework for political administration. However, partly because the prefectural governments quickly assumed an active role in educational administration, these administrative offices were never established.[7] As a result, the loose alliance of local activists and prefectural officials seen in the *gōkō* movement continued and drove the early campaign to implement the Fundamental Code.

Upon receiving the Fundamental Code from the Council of State, the chief policymaking body in the new government, the prefectural offices in Nagano and Chikuma made copies and distributed it to lower officials. In Nagano, the prefectural government sent one copy to each of the 28 large-district (*daiku*) offices and, citing the difficulty of copying such a large document, instructed all small-district officials (*kuchō* and *fukukuchō*) who wished to read it to go to the large-district office.[8] The Chikuma prefectural government, led by its governor, Nagayama Moriteru—the same governor who had been so active in coordinating the *gōkō* movement in the months before promulgation of the Fundamental Code—went to much greater lengths. The prefectural office made hundreds of copies of the entire Fundamental Code and distributed them to all small-district officials, directing them to deliver additional copies to each *gōkō* so that teachers and *sewayaku* administrators could read and discuss it.[9] Further, it sent a copy of the Fundamental Code's Preamble to all village-level officials and urged them to "warmly explain its meaning to the people in an easily understandable manner."[10]

In both prefectures, the distribution of the Fundamental Code produced a flood of questions from local leaders. Despite its length, the Fundamental Code was often vague and identified goals without explaining how they were to be achieved. Rather than throwing up their hands in frustration, however, local officials quickly identified the problems they had to address in order to implement the Fundamental Code. For example, the large-district heads in Nagano prefecture assembled to discuss the Fundamental Code and produced an extensive set of questions on virtually all aspects of the new system—such as the selection of educational administrators at the district and the village levels, the collection of funds, and the location of schools.[11] Both prefectural governments, in turn, compiled a list of these administrators' questions, added some of their own, and sent it to the Ministry of Education. The prefectural office in Chikuma, for example, asked the ministry:

In the Fundamental Code it says that each university district should be divided further into 32 districts called "middle-school districts." It also says that "local officials" are to draw up these middle-school districts based on local considerations. But are we supposed to draw them up, or will the Ministry of Education or the university district administrative offices? And should they be divided according to the amount of arable land or according to population?[12]

Inundated with questions from prefectural offices throughout the country, the Ministry of Education selected sample questions and distributed its official responses to all prefectures.[13] In effect, these official responses became policy. This process initiated a dynamic in which central policy was driven by queries from local governments generated by local officials as they encountered problems relating to the implementation of the ministry's plans.

The Ministry of Education's responses to prefectural queries resemble those of a teacher responding to a group of overly eager, rule-minded pupils: it restated the general guidelines provided in the Fundamental Code but reassured prefectural governments that they were free to adapt central policies to local circumstances. Such reassurances stimulated a flurry of activity in Nagano and Chikuma. Beginning in spring 1873, both prefectures issued a spate of directives explaining the intent of the Fundamental Code and outlining their strategies for implementation. Because the language of these directives was peppered with key phrases from the Fundamental Code's Preamble, the claim that learning was "the foundation for success in life" and predictions of a future in which there would be "no community with an unlearned family and no family with an unlearned individual" began to work their way into the local discourse on education. These general principles resonated among prefectural officials already convinced of the need for educational reform.

Faced with the task of implementing these general principles, prefectural governments adopted a variety of strategies based both on local exigencies and on previous experience. The question of funding, for example, generated a broad variety of solutions from prefectural governments. Articles 99–101 of the Fundamental Code explained that the Ministry of Education would distribute ¥3 million, in the form of grants called *itakukin*, to school districts through the prefectural governments. During the first few years after the Fundamental Code's promulgation, Nagano and Chikuma each received over ¥4,000 every year, around half of which was distributed to individual schools to bolster their endowments.[14] Distributed among hundreds of elementary schools, however, this amounted to less than ¥10 per school. As a result, prefectures had to devise additional strategies for funding local schools. Both Chikuma and Nagano adopted a funding strategy from the *gōkō* movement: each school used local contributions to set up an endowment; the interest from this fund, along with tuition fees, was used to pay for the operating expenses of the school. Envisioning large schools with new facilities, officials in the Chikuma and Nagano prefectural governments set a goal of at least ¥1,000 for each school's endowment. Authorities in Nagano prefecture chose to build such endowments primarily through a combination of tuition payments and, in an unprecedented move, mandatory school levies. The prefectural government established a uniform scale of payments, with farmers paying 5 *sen* per *koku* of income, and merchants between 25 *sen* and ¥3, according to a four-tiered income scale.[15]

Seeking to avoid relying so heavily on levies and tuition payments, authorities in Chikuma devised other means of building school endowments. First, Governor Nagayama, as he had during the *gōkō* movement, exhorted local elites to contribute to the endowments. In addition, authorities hoped to exploit the anti-Buddhist movement, which had been particularly intense in Chikuma prefecture. In March 1873, Nagayama issued a circular urging people not to destroy temples (as had been common in the early post-Restoration years) but to convert them into new school buildings and to apply the profits from the sale of temple articles to school endowments.[16] The next month, he urged communities to appropriate not only temples but also all common lands for schools: "In the past . . . people have held common lands under the pretense of helping out with village finances, but in reality, [the money from the lands] was thrown away wastefully on sake or food at kabuki or kyōgen productions, or other kinds of gatherings."[17] Such activities, he argued, "incite arguments" and "throw popular morality into confusion." He recommended an end to all such celebrations and the conversion of these common lands into "school lands" (*gakuden*), the income from which was to be applied to the local school endowment. Soon after, he also called for the conversion of local theaters into school buildings; within a year, eighteen former theaters were serving as schools.[18] In his view, schooling was a means of eradicating a retrogressive mindset, of which Buddhism, festivals, and popular entertainments were manifestations. It was therefore highly symbolic—and, indeed, logical—to build the new schools on the ruins of these practices.

The prefectures diverged widely in forming school districts. Articles 5 and 6 of the Fundamental Code specified that each of the 256 middle-school districts was to contain 130,000 people, and each of 53,760 elementary-school districts 600 people. The creation of school districts according to these guidelines would have required basic transformations in previous patterns of mobilization in local society. Indeed, the goals of the school district system were not only to facilitate centralization and standardization but to initiate a departure from the customary ways of local organization.

Almost immediately, however, it became clear that the "school district," as defined by the Fundamental Code, could not function as the organizing principle for local efforts to establish new schools. As noted above, the university districts were almost immediately stripped of any substantive role in the new system, and their functions were either dispersed among prefectural governments or absorbed by the Ministry of Education. Middle-school districts met a similar fate, with their functions redistributed upward to the prefectural government and downward to the large districts. Elementary-school districts, in contrast, played a critical role in the new system. Their boundaries, however, were drawn according to previous administrative borders and patterns of local mobilization.[19] Most elementary-school districts in Nagano and Chikuma were formed through a temporary and strategic alliance among a handful of villages (usually between three and ten) with a history of intervillage cooperation. On such occasions, village leaders—who ostensibly served as registration-district officials (*kochō* and *fukukochō*), but usually functioned as de facto village headmen[20]—negotiated with one another in the interests of their own villages and hashed out the location of the new school and the distribution of the financial burden. Some elementary-school districts corresponded with the "small district" (*shōku*), an administrative unit created by the Meiji government in 1871 as the smallest unit of political administration. Many of these had served as the unit of organization for many of the *gōkō*. Other school districts were based on Tokugawa-era village leagues (*kumi*), which were larger groups of villages (in Shinano, usually around ten to twenty) that cooperated for various administrative purposes, such as the shipping of rice for tax payments.[21]

Because elementary-school districts were based on such a range of geographic and administrative units, the number of people per school district varied widely. The largest elementary-school districts served populations of over 10,000; others only 1,000—although this number, too, was larger than the Ministry of Education's recommendation of 600, which was generally too small to provide an adequate financial basis for a school patterned after the Fundamental Code's specifications.[22] Nationwide, the variation was even greater: in some areas of the country, elementary-school districts consisted of only 300 people; in others—particularly in northeast Japan—local officials created enormous school districts, in terms of both geography and population, in order to reduce per capita school levies.[23] After being flooded with queries from prefectural governments, the Ministry of Education issued a revised version of the Fundamental Code in May 1873; among other changes, it inserted the phrase "depending on local conditions" to the article that addressed the criteria for creating districts, so as to reassure local officials that they had some leeway to create districts that deviated from the recommend guide-lines.[24] In doing so, the Ministry of Education reaffirmed the notion that certain aspects of central government policy were negotiable, while allowing existing patterns of local mobilization to function on behalf of the new system.

Sometimes local variations reflected differences not only in local conditions but also in the interpretation of the basic intent of the Fundamental Code. One such variation concerned the *gōkō*. In Naga-no, as in Gunma, Tochigi, and most other prefectures, authorities in-terpreted the Fundamental Code as mandating the abolition of all ex-isting schools.[25] Early communications from the authorities in Nagano to district officials assumed as much, and in November 1873 the prefectural governor issued a directive explicitly abolishing all schools predating the Fundamental Code and requiring anyone who wished to reopen a school as a private institution to "submit a peti-tion based on Article 179 of the Fundamental Code."[26] In Chikuma, too, the prefectural office noted that previous forms of schooling "do not embody the intent" of the Fundamental Code and ordered that they be "abolished at once."[27] However, whereas the authorities in Nagano included *gōkō* in the category of "pre-existing schools" to be abolished, the Chikuma prefectural office did not.[28] The authorities in Chikuma continued to coordinate the effort to establish *gōkō* through mid-1873—not in defiance of the Fundamental Code or of the Ministry of Education, but because they felt that the *gōkō*-building effort, even though it was initiated locally months before the Fundamental Code, was consistent with the intent of the Funda-mental Code. This difference in interpretation derived partly from the differences between the two prefectures' *gōkō*-building efforts: much of the initiative behind the *gōkō* in both prefectures came from networks of local elites, but in Chikuma the prefectural government had taken a more overt coordinative role in the months before the promulgation of the Fundamental Code and had emphasized the public nature of the schools. It was only in July 1873, almost a year after the promulgation of the Fundamental Code, that the authorities in Chikuma became aware of the Ministry of Education's desire that all *gōkō* be closed.[29]

Although prefectural authorities in Nagano and Chikuma adapted some aspects of the Fundamental Code to fit local condi-tions and pre-existing patterns of mobilization, they were deeply committed to the principle of standardization. This commitment is clearly visible in the two prefectures' efforts to make local curricula and teacher-training practices conform to guidelines set by the Ministry of Education and the Tokyo Normal School. Almost immediately following the promulgation of the Fundamental Code, both prefectures distributed curricular guidelines to local authorities and teachers.[30] Authorities in Chikuma even asked the permission of the Ministry of Education to make a large number of woodblock prints of the Fundamental Code's curricular regulations, explaining: "We want all schools, even those in distant, isolated areas, to be based on the [Fundamental Code's] curricular regulations."[31] In addition, both prefectures petitioned the Ministry of Education to be allowed to publish for local distribution the textbooks recommended in the Fundamental Code. Beginning in late 1873, the prefectural governments published thousands of woodblock-print versions of several texts and other teaching materials, such as the *Primary School Reader* (*Shōgaku yomihon*), *Elementary Geography* (*Chiri shoho*), and *An Outline of History* (*Shiryaku*), as well as various syllabary charts and arithmetic tables recommended by the Ministry of Education.[32] Authorities in Chikuma explained that locally printed versions of these texts were necessary because "purchasing necessary materials from Tokyo is an exorbitant expense and a hardship to communities."[33]

In order to achieve a better understanding of the new curricular guidelines, both prefectural governments endeavored to study these guidelines at their source: Tokyo Normal School. In June 1873, the Nagano prefectural government sent seven local educators to Tokyo Normal School to investigate the curriculum and pedagogical techniques used in its laboratory elementary school in order to "move forward in conformity with its example."[34] Several months later three of these educators requested permission to return to Tokyo for an additional period of study, because "upon returning to our prefecture, we realized that there were several things we don't understand concerning local implementation."[35] In September 1873, Chikuma authorities dispatched a similar mission; among its members was Takahashi Keijūrō, the *gōkō* teacher discussed in the preceding chapter who had petitioned the Chikuma government in early 1872 to carry out educational reform on behalf of the "imperial public." Immediately on their return, the members of these missions worked closely with prefectural officials to establish a normal school (initially called *kōshūjo*, but later renamed *shihan gakkō*) in each prefecture. Both schools opened in the fall of 1873. To help these schools keep up with the latest developments in curriculum and pedagogy, both prefectures independently petitioned the Ministry of Education to send teachers from Tokyo Normal School to the prefectural schools.[36]

The prefectural governments in Nagano and Chikuma did not take such steps as a result of prodding by the Ministry of Education. The Fundamental Code stated that all teachers must have a normal-school or middle-school graduation certificate but acknowledged that, because of the absence of normal schools, this standard could not be applied for several years. By mid-1873, however, Nagano, Chikuma, and several other prefectures convinced of the value of teacher training had initiated plans to establish prefectural normal schools.[37] Authorities in Nagano voiced concern about "the lack of people who are fit to become teachers,"[38] and those in Chikuma expressed the need for new teachers who can "open the minds and train the bodies of local children, so that they can be of use to the state."[39] Within a week after announcing the opening of their normal schools and summoning all existing teachers for "retraining" (*saikō-shū*), these schools began herding candidates through the two- to three-month program and issuing teaching certificates to those who completed it. They proceeded quickly: in late 1874, less than a year after the schools were established, more than half of the over 1,000 primary-school teachers in Nagano and Chikuma had undergone retraining and received certificates.[40]

Perhaps the most striking example of how these prefectural governments exceeded the requirements of the Fundamental Code despite the absence of any real political or legal pressure from the center can be found in the prefectural authorities' efforts to visit each local school. Officials in both prefectures conducted such tours, but those in Chikuma were more extensive and better documented. The Chikuma prefectural office organized fifteen different tours from 1873 to 1876, each of which lasted around two months and included visits to over a hundred schools. The purpose of the tours, as stated in a circular to district- and village-level officials, was to "scrutinize the land and the people . . . and to investigate the extent to which official directives have been implemented, so that there will be no place where the official will is not carried out."[41] The prefectural office instructed local officials to prepare for these visits by reading prefectural directives on education to their communities "in a friendly way" so as not to "obstruct the expression of feelings between those above and those below." The prefecture also informed local officials that, during the tours, materials from the "model" schools in the prefecture would be distributed so that this model could be replicated in other communities.[42]

But the tours were more than a mechanism to distribute documents and verify the conformity of local practice with central expectations. They were, by all accounts, dramatic spectacles that reflected the profound sense of mission behind the movement to implement the Fundamental Code. The central figure in these tours—although he participated in only two of them—was Governor Nagayama. Nagayama cut an imposing figure as he swept into town with his entourage. However, in contrast to the pomp and splendor that characterized the imperial tours of this era, Nagayama's tours were conspicuous for their austerity. He assured local officials that they need not send welcoming parties and urged them instead to appoint a single person to meet him at the boundary of the village and serve as both guide and informant.[43] Nor did local officials need to arrange elaborate accommodations or exquisite meals. Nagayama apparently relished the idea of "sleeping under the stars" and existing on a diet of "mixed grains." The kind of "special treatment" customarily given to government officials, he argued, "only increases suffering among the people."[44]

The official chronicle of the tours, written by prefectural official, noted literatus, and member of the governor's entourage Nagao Muboku, describes Nagayama's activities in vivid detail. Nagao's mission report depicts the struggles and accomplishments of Nagayama and his band of faithful activists as they "traverse mountains and streams to observe remote villages, waving the banner of education wherever they go."[45] The governor delivered pep talks to local officials, entreating them to redouble their efforts to establish new schools and encourage attendance within their communities. He gathered local people around him—"both young and old, male and female, rich and poor"—and made stirring speeches on the value of education. "When he spoke," wrote Nagao, "the people were moved to tears, and roused to action."[46] Along with his colleagues—usually an instructor and several advanced students from the prefectural normal school—Nagayama conducted model classes in each local school, employing the latest pedagogical techniques and curricular regulations. "Imagine," wrote Nagao, "a group of eight- and nine-year-olds surrounding [Nagayama]. When he asks a math question, they call out the answer. When he writes a character, they read it aloud. . . . Ordinary people reading, writing, counting—this is the urgent purpose of our efforts."[47] The tours were also used as fundraising campaigns for local schools. Reminding people that education was the source not only of national strength but of personal prosperity, Nagayama urged local people to contribute to their elementary school's endowment. The Ministry of Education took note of Nagayama's fundraising activities and reported in an 1874 issue of the *Journal of the Ministry of Education* that during his latest tour 82 new people had come forward to offer contributions. According to the report, these contributors were not wealthy families but "the elderly, the poor, women and children" who "scrounged up money by spinning thread or making rope, working hard in the early morning or late at night."[48]

The rhetoric and imagery of the Japanese enlightenment resonated powerfully with those prefectural officials and normal-school instructors who participated in these tours. These earnest reformers, in turn, spoke of their tours as a civilizing mission. The prime targets of their mission were the "remote villages" of the prefecture, which were replete with "backward people" and "old, evil customs." The presence of such areas within their jurisdiction provoked in these leaders a sense of both dismay and profound responsibility: as carriers of enlightenment, they bore the burden of penetrating those areas still shrouded in darkness and exposing them to the light of civilization. For them, the principles of civilization and enlightenment were embodied in the Fundamental Code. The act of making local schools conform to the Fundamental Code, in turn, was essential to the civilizing process. Nagao Muboku wrote with eager anticipation of a future in which "the endowments of all schools will be over a thousand yen; all teachers will be graduates of the prefectural normal school; old methods of instruction will be eliminated; [all schools] will have standardized curricular regulations. . . . Ordinary people, even those in mountain villages, will understand them."[49] Their standardizing mission was motivated not by the dictates of administrative rationality, but by the desire to see the dark corners of local society exposed to the light of civilization.

From the perspective of the prefectural government, enlightenment (*kaika*) was a project to be carried out by elites on the people— who are usually represented in Nagao's account by the Tokugawa-era terms "stubborn people" (*ganmin*) or "stupid people" (*gūmin*). The mechanism by which this enlightenment would occur is captured by the word *setsuyu*, a term prefectural leaders used repeatedly when discussing their role in implementing the Fundamental Code. The term most often meant "exhortation" but also carried the meanings of "instruction" and "admonition." In Nagao's chronicle of the tours—which he entitled "Setsuyu yōryaku," or "An Account of Our Exhortation"—we find examples of all three meanings: officials instructing local people on the meaning of the Fundamental Code, exhorting communities to implement it, and admonishing those who obstructed this effort.

The role played by prefectural officials in reforming local society through exhortation and admonition closely resembles the late Tokugawa concept of moral suasion (*kyōka*). In fact, *kyōka* appears in Nagao's text more frequently than *kaika*. The concept of *kyōka* was at work not only in the method but also in the content of enlightenment: although Nagao sometimes spoke of the importance of cultivating the intellect, he more often described enlightenment as the inculcation of moral principles. "The purpose of the school," he wrote, is to foster "loyalty to authorities, filiality to parents, reverence for those above, and mercy for those below."[50] Enlightenment educators in Europe had also emphasized the importance of moral cultivation, as did the Tokyo-based leaders of the Japanese enlightenment. The view of moral cultivation embraced by Nagayama and his colleagues in the prefectural government, however, emphasized not the cultivation of an independent moral sensibility within each child but the transmission of specific moral principles to the people as a collective, with the ultimate goal of facilitating the task of governance (*minji*).

Although the prefectural office justified the tours in terms of enlightenment and moral suasion, the tours were perhaps more significant for another reason: they gave the prefectural government an opportunity to enter communities physically and impress on them the reach of the new government. It is telling that prefectural officials made a point of scheduling their tours to coincide with two important occasions in the life of each school: examination days and school-opening ceremonies. The inaugural festivities were particularly grand occasions, the likes of which many communities had never seen. Even at small schools, these ceremonies could attract several hundred people, including students, parents, and officials. For example, some 400 people from the three villages that had consolidated to form the Sōtatsu Elementary School district attended the opening ceremony for the school. The ceremony began at 10:00 A.M.; following the official proceedings, school administrators provided sake and bean cakes and led the three communities in a party that lasted until late in the evening.[51] The opening ceremonies at large schools were media events. Over 13,000 people—among them, the school's 28 teachers and 1,000-plus students—attended the ceremony to celebrate the construction of the new school building at Kaichi School in Matsumoto.[52] This event, as well as the openings of several other large schools in Chikuma, were covered in detail by the *New Day Newspaper* (*Shinpi shinbun*), a Matsumoto-based paper run by local intellectuals sympathetic to the cause of educational reform.[53] More significant than the size of these ceremonies, however, was the presence of prefectural and district officials, which demonstrated to teachers, students, and local residents that each new school was, from the moment of its inception, a part of a larger movement coordinated by the new government. As if to make this point clear, the prefecture distributed elaborate regulations regarding the order and position of seating for the various officials in attendance; by specifying the location of local teachers and school administrators, the regulations in effect situated them within the larger hierarchy of prefectural administration.[54]

Examination days were also heady occasions for students and their families. According to Article 48 of the Fundamental Code, elementary schools were to hold examinations every six months to determine which students could proceed to the next grade. The Fundamental Code recommended some sort of official presence at the examinations that came at the end of the fourth and of the eighth grade, which determined graduation from lower- and upper-elementary school, respectively.[55] Once again, prefectural authorities in Nagano and Chikuma went beyond these guidelines and urged the presence of district educational administrators and, whenever possible, at least one prefectural official, at all examinations. As at school-opening ceremonies, the prefectural offices distributed seating charts for the examination ceremonies, with students, teachers, local educational officials, local political officials, and officials from the prefectural office positioned in a manner that reflected their relative roles in the new system.[56] During his tours, Nagayama often attended examinations himself; according to an 1874 article in *New Day Newspaper*, after the tests had been graded, he handed out a variety of awards to successful students, such as physics primers, maps of Japan, poetry books, and fans.[57]

The prefectural government's goal in attending examinations was to verify that local testing procedures, as well as the schools themselves, were operating in conformity with the Fundamental Code. In the process, the examinations also subjected local society to a new form of inspection. Of course, communities had always been subjected to certain forms of government inspection, particularly in the areas of landownership and population. The attendance of prefectural officials at school examinations, however, symbolized the expansion of this power. The prefectural government was now able to step into each local school and examine each child, evaluating whether he or she was "useful material for the state." As in the imperial tours described by Takashi Fujitani, these examinations rendered local people visible before the new government; they mapped out the geographic scope of the new government's authority and generated the panoptic forms of power essential to modern rule.[58] We should, however, recognize the limited nature of these examination ceremonies and prefectural tours in general. The presence of prefectural officials in the life of the local school was sporadic, and their tours were not meant to gather information. More broadly, the rationale behind the tours was to allow officials to be present rather than to institute a bureaucratic regime of inspection, and their goal was to exercise moral suasion over a collective rather than to reconstitute the individual subject. Regardless of their intent, however, the tours had the effect of exposing new areas of local life to the gaze of the government and reminded local society of the government's stake in each local school.

Activist Bureaucrats
and Subprefectural Mobilization

The handful of prefectural authorities who dealt with educational affairs constituted only one segment of a larger circle of activists who worked together in this common cause. This circle was, for the most part, the same as that mobilized for the *gōkō* movement: in addition to a few prefectural officials, it consisted of a few dozen regionally renowned literati and teachers (who often became instructors at the prefectural normal school or at one of the large, urban elementary schools), and several hundred local activists with ambitions for a wider form of public service. Many of this last group found a home in the new system as one of two types of subprefectural administrators, both of which allowed activists to continue to play a leadership role in education. These positions were "school manager" (known in Chikuma as *sewayaku* and in Nagano as *sewakata*)[59] and "district administrator" (*gakku torishimari*). Unlike other local officials, the *sewayaku* and the *torishimari* served school districts (rather than general administrative districts), and their responsibilities were confined to the realm of education—although as we will see, they viewed their own role in much broader terms. The efforts of the individuals who served in these positions shed light on the rationale behind the movement to build the new educational system in Nagano and Chikuma. Furthermore, their initiatives functioned as a driving force in the process of state formation, for they facilitated the bureaucratization of the movement to implement the Fundamental Code.

The Ministry of Education's creation of the position of *sewayaku* marked a departure from pre-Meiji commoner schooling practices, because it separated the roles of teacher and administrator in the local school. Although this innovation had been realized in the early-Meiji *gōkō*, the Fundamental Code's nationwide enforcement of this separation brought a more definitive break from pre-Meiji patterns. The Fundamental Code was not very specific, however, as to the nature or responsibilities of this position. In Nagano prefecture, authorities were at first unsure of how many *sewayaku* each elementary-school district should have and how they should be selected. The prefectural government eventually created guidelines for *sewayaku*—but, as was usually the case, only after it received queries about the matter from local officials. The prefectural office recommended that four or five *sewayaku*, serving part-time on a rotating basis, should be selected by the district official (*kuchō*) to serve at each school.[60] In Chikuma, the prefectural government had created the position of *sewayaku* in early 1872 for volunteers who had spearheaded the *gōkō* movement at the local level. In the first two years after the promulgation of the Fundamental Code, these *sewayaku* continued to function in a volunteer capacity, receiving no salary for their efforts.

Although they were appointed by district officials, the *sewayaku* were, to a large extent, self-selected. In Chikuma, many had served in the same position during the *gōkō*-building effort; in Nagano, some were registration-district officials who decided to take up the additional responsibility of serving as *sewayaku*.[61] Since they received little or no pay, those who nominated themselves to district officials must have possessed some interest in educational matters. And it is clear that not all village officials shared that interest: on two occasions, the Chikuma prefectural office noted that it had received reports that some registration-district officials "look upon the schools with scorn" and "recklessly vilify the *torishimari* and *sewayaku*."[62] But for those village leaders who were not teachers and could not find a position in local political administration, the post offered a substantive position of leadership and an opportunity to contribute to the creation of the new order.

The nonspecific title of the position—"school manager"—was appropriate, because these men were expected to perform a variety of administrative and clerical functions on behalf of the school. Their primary administrative responsibilities were to collect school levies, manage the endowment, secure and maintain school buildings and equipment, supervise personnel, and process all documents relating to the operation of the school. In addition to these administrative functions, however, they were charged with encouraging attendance among local children and acting as a representative of the school in the community. They were expected to be the first to arrive at the school each morning and the last to leave; during the day, they were to keep the school clean, reprimand children when they fought or wandered away from the school, and "watch over students when they have to commute in cold, hot, windy, or rainy weather."[63] As the only nonfaculty employee at the school, they were to act as principal, trustee, secretary, hall monitor, crossing guard, community liaison, and janitor.

Diaries kept by the *sewayaku* of Isetsu Elementary School in Chikuma prefecture and Sōtatsu Elementary School in Nagano prefecture give a picture of their various responsibilities.[64] Both diaries begin in the months before the opening of their schools (January 1875 for Isetsu and July 1873 for Sōtatsu). During this period, the *sewayaku* met with one another almost every day to address a number of pressing issues. One of these issues was funding: the four *sewayaku* at Isetsu held meetings with the general population to discuss the new school levy, and the three *sewayaku* at Sōtatsu traveled door to door to collect funds and obtain signatures from contributors. They also faced the urgent task of locating a building that could serve as the new school. This task was especially onerous for the *sewayaku* at Sōtatsu: since this school was formed through the cooperation of three different villages, each of which proposed a different site for the school, the *sewayaku* had to meet repeatedly with village leaders to reach a compromise. The *sewayaku* at Isetsu reported no such problems, but a controversy in their community over the name of the new school provoked a debate that kept them occupied for an entire day. At both schools, the work involved in preparation for the schools' opening was intense; the *sewayaku* at Isetsu even met until late at night on New Year's Day to plan for the occasion.

After the schools opened, the amount of work trailed off a bit, but the *sewayaku* remained busy. On most days, only one *sewayaku* was on duty, but the entire group continued to meet at least once a week to address special issues, and all the *sewayaku* gathered to prepare for the semiannual examinations. On another occasion, the illness of an instructor at Sōtatsu required the *sewayaku* to assemble repeatedly and make use of their connections to procure a substitute teacher from another district.[65] In a more remarkable case, the *sewayaku* at Isetsu organized a meeting with other teachers and *sewayaku* in the area to devise a plan to improve and standardize the level of education: the group decided to have teachers collect the best essays and handwriting samples; the *sewayaku* would have them printed in book form and distribute them to all students.[66]

Their work was, in many ways, typical of the village leadership exercised by local elites in the late Tokugawa and early Meiji periods.

In particular, it required the *sewayaku* to remain embedded in their communities while demanding close communication and interaction with extra-communal officials. The *sewayaku* at both schools had to worry about hosting visiting prefectural officials and *torishimari*; those at Sōtatsu traveled to the prefectural office to consult with authorities on various matters relating to the schools.[67] More common were meetings with village- or district-level political officials, usually to discuss the operation of the school at which the *sewayaku* worked. These two diaries also reveal frequent interactions with *sewayaku* from other schools; during these meetings, they discussed educational matters, shared relevant documents issued by the prefectural government, and, of course, socialized over food and drink. The job was, therefore, suitable for Tokugawa-era village elites and literati who were comfortable in such situations and were already embedded in these kinds of extra-village networks. By mid-1873, these networks were being mobilized for the purpose of establishing and operating new schools according to the principles identified in the Fundamental Code.

The mobilization of *sewayaku* was harnessed for the project of modern state formation through the movements and activities of the *gakku torishimari*, their immediate superiors in the hierarchy of educational administration. The *torishimari* played a critical role in transforming the movement for educational reform into an educational system and in channeling the voluntaristic efforts of local activists into a bureaucracy. They lived a peripatetic life, traveling from village to village to deliver pep talks to local personnel, instructing the unenlightened, admonishing the recalcitrant, passionately debating educational matters among themselves, and drafting earnest petitions to prefectural authorities. They lacked a permanent institutional presence; their "office" consisted of nothing more than their own persons. Indeed, their position was abolished only seven years after it was created, squeezed out of the bureaucratic system before it coalesced. Yet they were largely responsible for creating the structures and pathways of that system.

Articles 8–11 of the Fundamental Code declared that a dozen or so *torishimari* should be appointed in each middle-school district, chosen from among those in each district deemed to be "of good reputation" (*meibō aru mono*)—a term often used in a generic sense to refer to local notables, particularly those who demonstrate a spirit of public activism on behalf of their communities. The responsibilities of the *torishimari* overlapped with those of the *sewayaku*: as defined in the Fundamental Code, their purpose was to exhort the local population, encourage attendance, and assist communities in the establishment of schools and the administration of school funds. But whereas the *sewayaku* were attached to a specific school, the *torishimari* served the newly created unit of the middle-school district, each of which, according to the Fundamental Code, was to consist of approximately 130,000 people. The *torishimari* were, in fact, the only public officials who served the middle-school district, a unit of educational administration that was intended to remain entirely separate from the units of political administration (*daiku* and *shōku*) into which local society had already been divided. Although in Gifu the prefectural government established a permanent office in each middle-school district to serve as the institutional home of the *torishimari*, in Nagano and Chikuma, as in most prefectures, the middle-school district functioned as nothing more than an arbitrary boundary within which the *torishimari* operated.[68] After being appointed by prefectural governments in early 1873, the *torishimari* in each district met, divided up the district into roughly equal units (with each *torishimari* responsible for an average of seventeen elementary schools),[69] and went to work.

In late 1873, there were 23 *torishimari* in Nagano and 32 in Chikuma; together they served a total of seven middle-school districts. This amounted to eight *torishimari* per district, a considerably lower ratio than that recommended by the Fundamental Code. Several of these early *torishimari* served simultaneously as local political officials (usually at the large-district level); apparently the Ministry of Education's concern with separating educational administration from political administration was not necessarily shared by prefectural and subprefectural officials.[70] Nearly half the *torishimari* were former samurai, and the rest were chosen from among the more wealthy and well-connected commoner elites. All were highly learned, and whatever gap may have existed between samurai and commoner *torishimari* was undoubtedly mitigated by the master-pupil ties that had crisscrossed literate society in late Tokugawa Japan and transcended commoner-samurai status divisions. For the samurai—who, at that time, were in the process of being disestablished as a privileged status group—the position of *torishimari* provided a place in the new government, as well as a stable source of income (unlike the *sewayaku*, the *torishimari* received a salary and were reimbursed for travel expenses). For commoner elites, the position offered the attractive opportunity to serve in a position of leadership alongside former samurai. For both, the position provided a niche from which they could enlighten the local population through public schooling, a cause in which many of them had long labored.

On the very day their appointment was approved, the *torishimari* in one district of Nagano prefecture assembled to discuss the task ahead of them and produced a set of queries for the prefectural office concerning their work.[71] One question addressed the issue of travel expenses—a significant matter, since the diary of one *torishimari* reveals that, from late 1874 through 1876, he spent an average of thirteen days a month away from home, either inspecting local schools or meeting at the prefectural office.[72] The other questions reveal that they had already read the Fundamental Code carefully and had thought seriously about their role in its implementation. They asked, for example, "If [a school] does not yet have a teacher, should we wait until after it has one before we meet to talk about opening it, or should we have it open with the status of 'irregular school' [a category created in the Fundamental Code]?" In another question, they urged the prefectural office to send an official notice to village leaders in advance of a *torishimari*'s visit, so that all local leaders would be prepared to meet with him when he arrived. Still another question attempted to test the boundaries of the *torishimari*'s authority; if confronted by complaints from communities concerning school fees, were they free to devise solutions for each community as they saw fit? On their first day at work, they were already anticipating problems relating to the local implementation of the Fundamental Code and were beginning to devise strategies to solve them. In fact, many of their "questions" are proposals followed by the query "Shall we do it this way?" And in most cases, the Nagano prefectural office responded simply with "Do as you propose" (*ukagai no tōri*).

In their efforts to establish and supervise local schools, the *torishimari* continued to follow similar procedures. As they encountered problems, the *torishimari* formed committees and proposed solutions, usually in the form of queries to the prefectural office. From 1873 to 1876, the prefectural office was flooded with questions generated by the *torishimari* assemblies that had sprung up in every district; increasingly, these questions came in the form of "*torishimari* conference reports," in which the assemblies submitted dozens of queries, usually grouped under several different headings—"School Endowments," "Encouraging Attendance," "School Districts," and so on. In response, the prefectural office usually approved the *torishimari*'s suggestions, sometimes with minor revisions. Furthermore, following the pattern they had observed in their own communications with the Ministry of Education, prefectural authorities usually distributed the questions, along with the prefecture's "answers," to other districts. In other words, the *torishimari* not only set the policymaking agenda but also devised the content of specific reforms. Furthermore, since the prefectural governments in Nagano and Chikuma often forwarded the *torishimari*'s questions to the Ministry of Education, which then published its responses and distributed them throughout the country, these local officials could boast a modest degree of influence over national educational policy as well.

Sometimes, the questions posed by *torishimari* to the prefectural government were aimed at adapting rigid central guidelines to local realities, similar to the pattern that Neil Waters identified among early Meiji local officials in Kawasaki.[73] One such set of questions was generated by a group of *torishimari* in Chikuma in March 1873, only weeks after their appointment. Noting that "in isolated villages there is not enough cash to pay tuition fees," they asked the prefectural government if it would be acceptable for students to pay tuition in kind (specifically, firewood and charcoal).[74] The *torishimari* also requested that parents be allowed to send their children to a school outside the community under the guidance of a specific teacher—a request probably motivated by the desire to accommodate the wishes of wealthy families whose concept of "school" was that of a master-pupil relationship rather than a local institution organized on the basis of geographic proximity. Furthermore, after commenting on how difficult it was for young children to commute long distances, they proposed a compromise. Although they agreed that upper-elementary-school students (ages 10–13) should be required to attend a licensed elementary school, they suggested that children in lower-elementary school (ages 7–10) be allowed to attend school at pre-existing commoner schools in their own villages. Finally, demonstrating their familiarity with Ministry of Education policy, they noted that "in Article 99 of the Fundamental Code, it says that 'hereafter the amount of the endowment in each school district should be fixed.'" They argued, however, that since in their area the people are "isolated" and "stubborn" and "do not understand the meaning of enlightenment and civilization," most districts would not be able to raise such amounts. The *torishimari* asked for permission to open schools that did not meet the Fundamental Code's endowment guidelines, but they also suggested strategies to help these communities make adjustments for their lower endowments—for example, by consolidating school districts and by sharing textbooks and equipment among area schools. These proposals suggest that some *torishimari*, like the local officials studied by Waters, can be characterized as "pragmatists" who attempted to modify central reforms and soften their disruptive effect upon local society.

Far more often, however, the *torishimari* in Nagano and Chikuma expressed the need for greater standardization. A report from one *torishimari* conference in 1874, for example, lamented that most schools did not conform to the curriculum outlined in the Fundamental Code because they had neither the new texts nor instructors qualified to teach them. Instead of calling on the prefectural office to permit local deviation, the *torishimari* emphasized the importance of following the Fundamental Code's regulations and warned that letting each school operate according to the whims of the individual teacher would be to "bring about the evil of utter disorder."[75] Their remedy was for teachers throughout the prefecture to hold regular assemblies to discuss the new curricular regulations, so that all teachers would understand them properly. At a *torishimari* conference in another district, the participants suggested that *sewayaku* and local political officials should also hold quarterly assemblies, "so that there will be no inconsistency among those responsible for education."[76] These *torishimari* viewed assemblies as a means of rectifying the "problem" of local deviation from the Fundamental Code. In fact, in early 1876 the *torishimari* organized a prefecture-wide meeting on education of not only *torishimari* but representatives from each level of the local administrative hierarchy: the prefectural office, large-district officials, and registration-district officials, as well as teachers. When the prefectural office approved the idea, the *torishimari* set an agenda of 57 specific proposals for discussion.[77]

Another strategy adopted by *torishimari* to achieve the goal of standardization was to press the prefectural government to take a more active, interventionist role in local schooling. They urged the prefectural office, for example, to act more decisively against unlicensed private schools.[78] In an effort to eliminate small, substandard schools and curb the school-deconsolidation movement that spread throughout the two prefectures after 1874, they asked the prefectural office to establish a minimum size for school districts based on geographic area rather than population.[79] They asked repeatedly that prefectural officials visit each local school more frequently, so as to impress upon the local population the importance of education.[80] They also envisioned a more active role for *sewayaku* and village-level political officials in the lives of local children and their families. They wanted *sewayaku*, for example, to investigate every family whose children were not enrolled in school. They also urged the prefectural government to require political officials to visit the homes of nonattending children and "amicably admonish" the parents.[81] Although the prefectural office generally agreed in principle with the *torishimari*'s suggestions that it standardize and regulate schooling practices, it sometimes had no choice but to reject specific proposals due to the lack of available funds and personnel.[82]

The various proposals and activities of the *torishimari* played a key role in fueling two processes fundamental to modern state formation. The first was the rationalization of local administration. The Fundamental Code had imposed a structure on the local movement for educational reform by assigning formal positions and responsibilities to what had been a loosely organized group of activists held together only by personal relationships and a commitment to a common cause. This new structure, however, was still malleable, and the functions of those who served in it were not always clearly defined. The *torishimari* were able to perceive the ambiguities in this structure and took the initiative to clarify them. For example, the *torishimari* carefully defined the responsibilities of the various local officials involved in educational administration. They paid particular attention to the *sewayaku*, arguing that the part-time, voluntaristic nature of the position worked against accountability and compromised the goal of standardization.[83] After continued pressure from the *torishimari* to make the *sewayaku* into fulltime, paid officials, the prefecture followed their advice and ordered schools to earmark a portion of their funds to provide salaries for the *sewayaku*.[84]

The *torishimari* sought to clarify another key ambiguity in the new system: the incomplete separation between the administrative realms of politics and education. Such a separation had not previously been recognized as desirable, either in pre-Meiji commoner schools or in the *gōkō* movement. In both cases, schooling was viewed as one of many tools in the repertoire of benevolent governance; as a result, it was natural for local elites to serve simultaneously as teachers and as political officials. By creating a separate educational administration, the Fundamental Code tried to draw a clearer distinction between the two realms. In the process of implementation, however, political authorities at all levels assumed many of the functions of educational administration; this in turn created a large, undefined overlap between the two administrative hierarchies. Indeed, the *torishimari* in Nagano and Chikuma did not always hold to a rigorous distinction between the two realms. They participated actively in local assemblies that dealt with areas of public service other than education (such as public works and economic development), and they did so not in their capacity as *torishimari* but as "men of good reputation" devoted to public service at the local level.[85]

However, when faced with the task of implementing the Fundamental Code, *torishimari* repeatedly attempted to clarify the chain of command in matters relating to education. They asked, for example, whether documents submitted by *sewayaku* and *torishimari* needed to be signed by district heads as well[86] and urged the prefectural office to define more clearly the role of district officials in the administration of elementary schools.[87] In an attempt to clarify the status rankings of local leaders, they inquired about the order of seating when political authorities and teachers met in public.[88] At an assembly devoted specifically to educational matters, they forbade discussion of politics—and this was in early 1876, several years before the Popular Rights Movement prompted central and prefectural governments to take a stance against the participation of teachers in political assemblies.[89] Although the *torishimari* did not seek to exclude political officials from involvement in educational administration, they worked to clarify the various functions and positions within local officialdom and thereby contributed to the bureaucratization of local leadership.

A second enterprise fundamental to the formation of a modern state is the collection of information about the governed. In this enterprise, too, the *torishimari* played an important role. Although some of their time was spent assembling, debating, and exhorting, the rest was spent collecting information and organizing it into readable form for the benefit of the prefectural and central governments. The implementation of the Fundamental Code necessitated such an endeavor. Drawing school districts, calculating school levies, and enforcing attendance required officials to collect information about the land and the people within their jurisdiction. Although the tours conducted by Governor Nagayama and other officials within the prefectural office also served this purpose, it was the *torishimari* who carried out the bulk of the inspections and did so in an increasingly systematic manner. *Torishimari* also took the initiative to expand the investigative project into new categories of knowledge. For example, they seemed particularly concerned with evaluating local sentiment toward schooling and devised various ways of quantifying it. One *torishimari*, eschewing a simple accounting of population, enrollment, and financial conditions, developed an elaborate chart with six categories of evaluation: "diligence/laziness of instructors," "quality of students," "enrollment level," "level of attention [to education] by village officials," "level of attention by *sewayaku*," and "popular sentiment toward the school"—and gave each school a ranking of 1, 2, or 3 in each category. When the *torishimari* delegated certain information-gathering tasks to *sewayaku* (such as inquiries into the health and family circumstances of children not enrolled in school), they created standardized forms to ensure that *sewayaku* would collect the "right" information.[90]

The importance of information on residents of a school district to the new educational system is not surprising, since the system was modeled on the example of Western nations in which modern techniques of rule were already manifest. As states in Europe began to integrate their entire populations into both the life of the nation and the institutions of government, they developed mechanisms for gathering information about the populace. This very project was built into the Meiji educational system, as well as into the new systems of taxation and conscription created in 1873. What occurred in such systems was not merely the collection of new kinds of information about the nation's subjects but also the production of new subjects—and, in the case of the educational system, the production of a new conception of school embedded in the categories of information being collected. Like the school inspectors Bruce Curtis examines in his study of nineteenth-century Canada, the *torishimari* produced hundreds of reports about "improperly furnished" schools, "irregular attendance," and "unlicensed teachers." And, in Curtis's words, these reports "were intelligible only within the terms of an implicit model of desirable educational organization."[91] The inspectional activities of the *torishimari*, then, provided a means by which that implicit model penetrated local society while also producing the kinds of information essential to the functioning of the modern state.

Despite their important role in gathering information and bureaucratizing local administration, an image of the *torishimari* as paperpushers or bean counters could not be further from the truth, or at least from their own self-image. To local notables eager to serve the new, suddenly expanded public, the Fundamental Code represented, in the words of one *torishimari*, "an effort to extend the emperor's influence throughout the world by cultivating talent within the realm, and to bring the masses inside the boundaries of civilization and enlightenment."[92] Filled with such sentiments, *torishimari* grieved over local people who "stubbornly adhere to their old ways" or who "conform only outwardly and temporarily" to the Fundamental Code; such people, they lamented, "cannot truly bask in the beautiful meaning of 'civilization.'"[93] They believed themselves to be in a position to understand the true meaning of the "imperial intent" and "enlightenment"—two phrases frequently coupled and interchanged in the rhetoric of activists in Chikuma and Nagano—and as local notables, they considered it their moral responsibility to convey such meanings to those below them. Aoki Ekino, a *torishimari* and one of the founders of the first *gōkō* in Nagano prefecture, expressed it in this way: "Above us is our great debt to the exceeding kindness of the emperor, which we must do everything we can to repay; below us is the task of enlightening the people. If we do not accomplish these tasks, we bring disgrace to our posts and corrupt our mission."[94] Their emphasis on standardization, their attempt to rationalize the structure of local leadership, their endless inspections—all were an expression of this goal of serving an imperial public by bringing enlightenment to the dark corners of local society. In the process, the *torishimari* generated a powerful local momentum for the Meiji government's goals of centralization and integration.

Early Meiji Teachers and Schools

The opening ceremony of Keichi Elementary School in November 1873 included a ritual that, although unusual, symbolized the transformation effected by the Fundamental Code. On the morning of the ceremony, the teachers of the three existing commoner schools in the area assembled their students and led them in a procession to the site of the new elementary school. When the ceremony began, the teachers deposited their students at the new school, completing a formal, highly symbolic transfer of authority in the education of local children.[95] Such was the intent of the Fundamental Code: to make a decisive break from earlier forms of educational practice and to place the task of schooling Japanese children firmly in the hands of the new educational system.

Of course, the conditions in each local school did not always reflect this sudden, epochal transformation. In fact, the three teachers who participated in this ritual transfer of authority joined the faculty of Keichi Elementary School, providing students and parents with an obvious point of continuity in what was otherwise a moment of rupture and dislocation. This incident highlights the difficulties inherent in any campaign to standardize local schools according to a new model when the teachers themselves are the products of previous schooling arrangements. The purpose of this section is to explore the backgrounds and experiences of those teachers who served in the new system during these early years and to examine the extent to which their schools conformed to the new model of "school" advocated by the Ministry of Education.

The Ministry of Education's decree abolishing all existing schools forced more than 2,000 teachers in Nagano and Chikuma to close their schools. Those who had taught only part-time were undoubtedly dismayed at having to give up an avocation so central to their identity, but they did not suffer significant economic hardship. Teachers who depended on tuition payments and gifts as their main source of income faced the prospect of attending the new prefectural normal school for retraining or finding other employment. Some teachers realized that the new regulations allowed a third option: petitioning the prefectural government for permission to reopen their old schools as "private schools" (*shijuku*). A doctor and former teacher from Hanishina district, for example, informed the prefectural office that his former students were suffering; "How painful it is to see them," he wrote. He entreated the prefectural office to allow him to reopen his school, explaining, "If, in your esteemed and generous will, you would grant the request of an idle old man to teach, I would be grateful and happy." To support his case, he noted that "it is my wish to instruct students in accordance with the intent of the Restoration."[96] Another petitioner, a 63-year-old doctor, explained to the prefecture how he began his teaching career: "In this isolated area there was no teacher; so about 40 years ago, at the request of a family, I began teaching five or six students; however, over time I was urged to teach the entire village, and as a result, without consciously intending to do so, a private school formed." In response to the prefecture's requirement that all prospective private schools submit a list of school regulations, this teacher wrote, "I teach reading and writing to children, ages seven to twelve or thirteen; my purpose is to preserve the way of morality and obey the national polity. I have no other rules."[97] These petitions—and most others like them—were unsuccessful, although the prefectural office did approve some requests from private-school teachers who possessed more impressive educational qualifications and whose schools offered more advanced, rigorous curricula.[98]

Many former teachers made the journey to the normal school to undergo retraining and receive a license to teach at the new elementary schools. The decision to do so would not have been a casual one. Obtaining a license required two to three months of full-time study at the teacher-training school. Tuition and room and board during this period would have cost ¥4–6, plus travel expenses—more than most teachers received for a year's worth of teaching.[99] For many of those who lived outside the cities of Nagano and Matsumoto (where the two training schools were located), the extended period away from home was likely to have been a serious hardship. As a result, some former teachers decided to obtain a teaching license only with great reluctance.

Such an attitude is revealed in a series of letters written by a former teacher at a commoner school, Miyashita Keizō, as he underwent retraining at the normal school in Matsumoto. Before the promulgation of the Fundamental Code, Miyashita had been an instructor at a private school in Iida founded by his grandfather that had been in operation for nearly a century. While in Matsumoto,

Miyashita wrote home several times to update his family on his plans and to ask them to send clothing and money. He also took the opportunity to express his frustration and displeasure over his experience at the normal school. He remarked on several occasions—particularly after learning of a fire in his home village—that he wished he "could sprout wings and fly home," but he concluded that he could not afford to do so, because that would prolong his training and require him to pay another month's tuition.[100] He complained bitterly about the fact that "young men, even those who are totally incompetent, are rising through the ranks, while older, more capable men are falling." Ultimately, he resigned himself to completing his retraining: "I'm regretting that I ever came here, but unavoidably I must trudge on."[101] Considering Miyashita's position as a well-known teacher who was now being forced to jump through hoops simply to continue doing what he and his father and grandfather had been doing for almost a century, his sentiments were understandable.

On the other extreme was Chimura Kyokai, a poet and Hirata disciple who had opened a commoner school in the Kiso valley before the Meiji Restoration. After the promulgation of the Fundamental Code, Chimura had organized a local campaign to build a new elementary school in his village. His efforts came to fruition in 1875 when the new building was completed. As the instructor of the new school, Chimura delivered a speech at the opening ceremony. He began by articulating the importance of the school to the Japanese nation:

The nation prospers or declines according to the strength or weakness of its people. The strength or weakness of the people, in turn, depends on the strength or weakness of education, as the ancient sages often explained. Perhaps we can say that the nation is like the fruit and the people like the petals, and education is like the stalk and the roots. Therefore, if we wish for the petals to be beautiful and the fruit to be good, we must cultivate the trunk, prospering through education.[102]

Chimura then proceeded to recount the specific accomplishments that had already been made in the area of education, noting the establishment of universities and middle schools and the furnishing of schools with the "implements of learning." He likened the healthy structure of the newly completed school building (dry floors, excellent air circulation, proper arrangement of the desks in the classroom) to the health and strength of the community and the nation at large. He also explicitly positioned his own contribution to the new school system within a national hierarchy of leadership, one that began with "activists" (*yūshi no mono*) like himself and stretched upward to district officials, the prefectural government, the central government, and, finally, the Meiji emperor. His students, too, were implicated in a much larger undertaking: "The establishment of our school is not merely for the honor and welfare of the people within this village. It is no exaggeration when I say that these children here play an important role in the fate of the entire realm." Reflecting on his efforts to establish Narakawa Elementary School, he concluded by remarking proudly, "There is no joy that can compare to this."

Chimura clearly identified with the Meiji government's project of education reform and was eager to link his own local efforts as activist and teacher to that project. He even took his school-opening speech seriously: he wrote a draft and sent it to fellow nativist scholar and poet Takei Yōsetsu, who was residing in Tokyo at the time, and included Takei's suggestions in the version that he ultimately delivered at the ceremony.[103] His initial enthusiasm is noteworthy when we consider that Chimura was someone from whom we might expect recalcitrance rather than cooperation. Not only had he invested time and effort into a now-illegitimate form of schooling, but he had been active in the nativist movement during the late Tokugawa and Restoration periods. Considering the rapid decline in the influence of nativist ideologues on educational policy during the 1870s, we might expect him to feel some disillusionment toward the Meiji government.[104] However, either Chimura perceived no divergence between his own vision of educational reform and that embraced by the Ministry of Education, or he believed that his own efforts and interests could be accommodated within the new system.

The experience of Miyashita and Chimura, who decided to undergo retraining after the mandatory closure of their old schools, was relatively common: in Chikuma, 32 percent (173) of the 541 elementary-school teachers in 1873 had served as teachers in the older forms of schools.[105] One reason the percentage was not higher was the fact that, in the first few years after the promulgation of the Fundamental Code, former samurai flocked into the new profession of teaching. These samurai were more likely to follow the proper channels by obtaining a license from the prefectural normal schools: in both Nagano and Chikuma, the first few cohorts of students to enter the normal school were almost exclusively of samurai background.[106] Since hundreds of elementary-school teachers did not attend the normal schools, the percentage of samurai among all teachers was not so overwhelming: in Chikuma, 60 percent of all elementary-school teachers in late 1873 were commoners.[107] Nevertheless, in an area where the vast majority of pre-Fundamental Code schoolteachers had been commoners, the presence of such large numbers of samurai among the ranks of teachers was an important development. Most of these samurai were relatively young; more of them were in their twenties than in their thirties and forties combined. Recognizing that, unlike their fathers, they could no longer count on the prospect of a guaranteed stipend, many young, educated samurai in the early Meiji period viewed teaching as a desirable way to earn an income and make use of their talents. In contrast to their samurai colleagues, teachers of commoner background were usually older; over 60 percent of the total number of commoner teachers were at least 40 years of age. For the most part, these commoners did not come from the ranks of ordinary village officials, who, in the last decades of the Tokugawa period, began to teach local children on a part-time basis in the agricultural off-season. Rather, those of commoner background who found employment at the new elementary schools were among the more literate of the broader stratum of educated commoners in late Tokugawa society. Most had acquired impressive educational credentials and had achieved considerable status as local literati.

In fact, the educational background of these elite commoners who became teachers in the new elementary schools was remarkably similar to that of their samurai colleagues. Although the domain schools had been closed to most commoners, elite commoners had used the same texts as their samurai colleagues and could trace their academic lineage to the same pool of regionally renowned scholarly figures. According to the early Meiji records compiled in Chikuma prefecture, more than nine out of ten elementary-school teachers listed Chinese Learning as the central component of their training. Teachers generally added some other area of study to their résumé (usually mathematics, National Learning, medicine, or Western Learning), but in most cases, they had pursued those subjects after building a foundation of Chinese Learning. Consequently, although the social backgrounds of early Meiji teachers in Chikuma appear quite diverse—there were farmers, priests, doctors, monks, and samurai from fourteen different domains—they shared a significant amount of common ground in terms of their educations. Furthermore, all were deeply experienced in previous forms of educational practice—if not as teachers, then as students—and undoubtedly shared similar assumptions concerning such central issues as pedagogy and curriculum.

For this group of teachers, the training (or retraining) they received at the prefectural normal schools must have been something of a shock. If they were not already familiar with the regulations published by the Ministry of Education, they would have discovered on arriving at the teacher-training school that Chinese Studies was totally absent from the curriculum. According to the journal of Miyashita Keizō, their training consisted mainly of an in-depth study of the texts advocated by the new curricular regulations—many of which were direct translations from Western texts, and almost none of which had been used in pre-Meiji schools.[108] The organization of the curriculum, too, was decidedly different: whereas the curriculum of the older schools had been structured around specific texts, the new regulations divided the curriculum into subjects—handwriting, vocabulary, grammar, geography, physical science, and arithmetic, among others.[109] In an effort to standardize this new curriculum among all elementary schools, both prefectural governments created charts based on the new regulations and distributed them to all elementary schools. For a school to receive an official license from the prefectural government, local organizers had to state in their "school-opening petition" that the school's curriculum would be based on the new regulations.[110]

The prefectural governments and the normal schools also sought to accomplish the more difficult task of reforming and standardizing pedagogical techniques. As noted above, prominent educators in Tokyo had been highly critical of traditional teaching methods and had begun to produce new texts and guidelines that embodied new pedagogical assumptions. Although the prefectural governments in Nagano and Chikuma rarely mentioned the issue of pedagogy, the instructors at the prefectural normal schools—many of whom had received some training at Tokyo Normal School—produced detailed pedagogical guidelines for teachers. Students at the school in Nagano received a handbook that described, in minute fashion, how teachers should act, speak, and move in the classroom. For example: "At 9:00, upon arriving at the school, the teacher should clap the wooden blocks and have the children sit in their seats. The teacher should then approach the students' chairs and correct the form of the students."[111] The handbook then proceeded to give pedagogical guidelines for each subject; the following set of instructions on the proper technique for leading a class in reading is typical:

The teacher should distribute the book called *An Elementary Reader* and have the students open the book. Positioning himself in front of the students' desks, the teacher should read the book aloud. He should read it a second time while passing along the rows of desks, and a third time while standing behind the students in the back of the room . . . then [the teacher] should have the first student sound out a character three times, and then have each student do the same thing, and finally have the entire class sound out the character in unison.[112]

The handbook also paid particular attention to the bodily movements of both teacher and student—explaining, for example, how teachers should point at the blackboard and how students should raise their hands. Such movements were seen as essential to the proper functioning of the new curriculum.

The teacher-training schools also perceived a need for the temporal rhythms and material accoutrements of the school to reflect the new regulations. Both prefectures distributed annotated timetables to all schools and local officials. These timetables served the purpose of linking the new educational content with the new scheme of temporal organization—explaining, for example, that arithmetic would be taught on specific days of the week, for specific periods of the day. In Nagano, the schoolday (which ran from 9:00 A.M. until 3:00 P.M.) was divided into five 50-minute periods, with 10-minute recesses each hour and an hour's break for lunch; Chikuma's schedule was similar, except that students were allowed only three 5-minute recesses.[113] This campaign of standardization was also extended to the material life of the school. Prefectural governments created samples of various school-related materials—seating charts, attendance charts, diplomas, and so on—and distributed them, via the *torishimari*, to all elementary schools.[114] The instruction handbook given to teachers in Nagano prefecture included drawings—complete with detailed measurements—of the various accoutrements of learning, including desks, benches, tables, syllabary charts, blackboards, chalk, erasers, and swing sets (see Fig. 3).[115] The prefectural government in Nagano even issued a directive concerning the height of flagpoles and the size and design of school flags.[116] Such accessories were seen as embodying the enlightened principles behind the new curricula, and their presence in every school functioned both to symbolize and to effect the assimilation of these principles in local society.

As one might expect, these vigorous efforts at standardization were not immediately and completely successful. The records of several elementary schools, for example, demonstrate the continued influence of previous assumptions regarding the content and organization of learning. A late-1873 curricular chart from Nakahara Elementary School illustrates this point. In conformity with the Fundamental Code, the teachers divided the curriculum into eight grades. However, the curriculum of each grade was structured according to texts rather than subjects—that is, students in first grade worked with one set of texts, students in the second grade moved on to a new set of texts, and so on. Furthermore, although some of these texts were those recommended by the Ministry of Education and Tokyo Normal School, many were the same texts that had been used in pre-Meiji commoner schools.[117] The curriculum of another school, Bun'ya Elementary, adhered more closely to the new regulations, in that the curriculum was structured according to subjects rather than texts. However, the subject divisions corresponded neither to the fourteen-subject curriculum found in the Fundamental Code nor to the eight-subject curriculum recommended by Tokyo Normal School. Rather, the curriculum was divided into three subjects—reading, writing, and arithmetic—and the texts used consisted almost exclusively of pre-Meiji materials.[118] Extant records from other elementary schools in Nagano and Chikuma show similar patterns of deviation from the new regulations. It is significant, however, that all these schools made some attempt to rethink their curricula in light of the new regulations—for example, by dividing the school into grade levels, organizing the content into subjects, or simply incorporating new texts. Dozens of directives from the prefectural office and

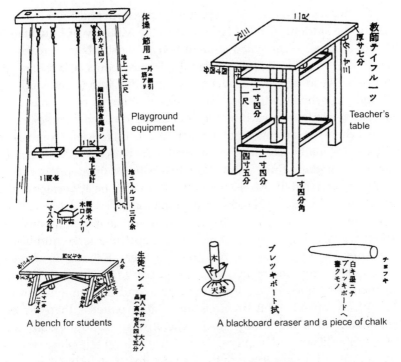

Playground equipment

Teacher's table

A bench for students

A blackboard eraser and a piece of chalk

Fig. 3   Prefectural specifications for school-related equipment, 1873

repeated visits by prefectural authorities and *torishimari* had, it seems, convinced teachers that their schools were now subject to some kind of external regulation.

In other ways, too, most elementary schools deviated from the model described by the Ministry of Education. The most visible deviation lay in the school buildings themselves. Neither the central nor the prefectural government required that schools be housed in newly constructed buildings, but the prefectural authorities and *torishimari* in Nagano and Chikuma often expressed to local officials the importance of building new schools that embodied the Fundamental Code. A few of the large, urban school districts were able to raise the funds necessary to build new schools during these first few years, the most high-profile of which was the new Kaichi School building, which cost over ¥10,000; in 1876, however, almost nine out of ten schools in the two prefectures still met in temples or rented buildings.[119] Similarly, the interior space of the school and the organization of the students rarely conformed to the Ministry of Education's model of an age-segregated student body. The shortage of teachers, the lack of school buildings with multiple classrooms, and the incongruity between age and academic background among the students resulted in schools with large numbers of students of various ages and academic levels, learning together under the leadership of a single teacher—an arrangement similar to most pre-Meiji commoner schools.[120] Finally, despite the impressive increases in school enrollment during these three years, the actual patterns of attendance were still far from what the Ministry of Education and the advocates of the Fundamental Code in Nagano and Chikuma hoped to achieve. I address this issue at length in Chapter 6; here suffice it to point out that when we take into consideration, for example, the large number of students who were enrolled but rarely, if ever, attended or who left school after only one or two years, the early Meiji campaign to implement the Fundamental Code in Nagano and Chikuma had much less of an impact upon previous attendance patterns than the enrollment figures might indicate. In general, despite the standardizing efforts of officials and activists, the realities of local schooling were in many ways quite distant from the abstract image of "school" embodied in the Fundamental Code.

Conclusion

It seems rather unnecessary, even petty, to point out such local deviations from the expectations of the central and prefectural governments. Considering that the Meiji government had issued its radical proposal for a nationwide school system only three years earlier and had offered little financial or institutional support to ensure its implementation in local society, the achievements in Nagano and Chikuma were considerable. Fortunately for the still unstable and financially strapped central government, the promulgation of the Fundamental Code prompted a vigorous campaign in Nagano and Chikuma to carry out the new educational policies at the local level. This movement consisted of a relatively small group of several hundred highly motivated and literate former samurai and elite commoners who were already mobilized for the cause of educational reform. Most of these activists stepped quickly into the new administrative or teaching roles created by the Fundamental Code, which imparted a formal structure to their movement and channeled their energy in support of this nationwide undertaking. It was largely due to their active, constructive response (and that of local activists in other parts of the country) that the Fundamental Code is remembered as the definitive starting point of the modern Japanese educational system, rather than as simply an ambitious, but unrealized, statement of intent by the new government.

Explaining this response is of critical importance to the comparative study of modernization and state formation. Postwar scholars in the West, working within the interpretational framework of modernization theory, observed this response and formulated a question that continues to influence the study of Japanese educational history: Why did the Japanese people consent to the central government's policy of educational modernization? The most common answer is that Tokugawa-era advancements in education prepared the Japanese people for educational modernization and predisposed them to consent to, and participate in, the Meiji government's reforms. This line of reasoning is somewhat off target, in part because the question is derived from the inaccurate assumption that the Japanese people as a whole did, in fact, support the Meiji government's educational policies. The vigorous local response described in this chapter was characteristic of a specific segment of the local leadership, not the entire populations of Nagano and Chikuma, which in the early Meiji period numbered nearly a million.[121] As we will see in the next chapter, many local people, including some village elites, were indifferent or hostile to the Fundamental Code.

One explanation for the active response to the Meiji reforms among many local leaders can be found in the handful of regional studies of modern state formation in Japan.[122] Most of these works argue that local elites' cooperation with the central government was motivated in large part by local interests. In Neil Waters's book, for example, we find local elites cooperating with the Meiji government in a pragmatic attempt to mitigate the disruptive effects of its new policies.[123] In Michael Lewis's recent work, local elites in Toyama strategically pursue various initiatives from the central government as a means of securing benefits from the center, a dynamic that Gary Allinson has described as "responsive dependence."[124] The movement to implement the Fundamental Code in Chikuma and Nagano, however, does not quite correspond to either of these models. First, the local leaders who participated in this movement are much better characterized as "idealists" and "activists" than as "pragmatists." They embraced the standardizing spirit of the Fundamental Code, along with its categorical renunciation of existing schooling arrangements, and their commitment to this mission made them reluctant to deviate from central policies. Second, although the notion of responsive dependence clearly applies to center-periphery relations beginning in the late 1870s—when the new government had finally consolidated its position and secured its monopoly over military force, political power, and economic resources—this model does not apply as well to the early 1870s. At this time, the military and political presence of the new government was still weak, and it had few resources to distribute in return for local compliance with central expectations. Consequently, local elites in Chikuma and Nagano did not cooperate with the center either because they were afraid not to or because they sought to obtain material benefits for the locality.

Rather, the movement to implement the Fundamental Code represented a convergence of interests between a central government seeking to create a centralized administrative system and a group of local activists eager to contribute to a broader campaign of public service. Just as these activists had welcomed the efforts of the prefectural government to coordinate the *gōkō* movement in early 1872, they initially viewed the Fundamental Code and the intervention of the central government not as an intrusion but an opportunity for public service on an even larger scale. This convergence of interests was made possible by the fluidity of the early Meiji government: because its administrative structures and bureaucratic routines had not yet hardened, the new educational system could accommodate the energies of these local activists and their loosely organized, voluntaristic movement. Ironically, as local activists worked through the practical aspects of their movement—establishing schools, encouraging attendance, collecting funds, disseminating curricular regulations—they drove the processes of bureaucratization and administrative centralization from below. In doing so, however, they were able to influence the formation of central policy on education and set in motion a dynamic in which localities could negotiate the terms of their integration into the state.

FIVE

Local Resistance
to the Fundamental Code

The activists in the movement to implement the Fundamental Code in Chikuma and Nagano believed that they were involved in something unprecedented. Although they perceived that the Fundamental Code was in some ways consistent with their own pre-1872 reform initiatives, they also recognized that it was, in other crucial respects, decidedly new. This newness attracted them: "new" connoted enlightenment, renovation, and possibility.

These activists, however, constituted only a narrow segment of the local population. Others were less sanguine about the Fundamental Code and its implications for local society. Many teachers were forced out of work because of the Fundamental Code, and those who found employment in the new elementary schools experienced a considerable loss of autonomy. Local officials who did not see the value of mass schooling resented this new responsibility. Those officials who understood the importance of education now had to deal with the intrusion of the central government into a previously unregulated area of local life. Finally, ordinary people had to send their children to this unfamiliar institution even though many were skeptical of its usefulness; furthermore, they had to pay for this institution, an institution over which they had little control. These people, too, recognized the newness of the Fundamental Code—but to them, "new" often meant unwanted, disruptive, even threatening. In response, people adopted a variety of strategies for resisting these policies. At one extreme, this resistance took the form of violent uprisings that rejected categorically the new educational system. More commonly, people opposed specific elements of the new system or resisted passively by refusing to send their children to the new schools.

In this chapter I explore the range of local dissent. I begin with the most overt manifestations: the early Meiji "uprisings against the new order" (*shinsei hantai sōjō*), in which protesters destroyed schools, attacked teachers, and violently opposed the central tenets of the Meiji government's concept of education. I then narrow my geographical focus to Nagano and Chikuma prefectures in order to explore the less overt techniques employed by teachers, officials, and ordinary people to contest specific points of Meiji educational policy and, further, to transform it from below.

The "Uprisings Against the New Order"

The most obvious outbreaks of resistance to the Meiji educational reforms were the dozen or so incidents (the number depends on whether some uprisings are counted as separate episodes or as one linked event) during the first decade of the Meiji era in which rioting villagers destroyed new elementary schools. These uprisings, in which nearly 200 schools were damaged or destroyed, occurred in two waves: the first, in 1872–73, around the time of the promulgation of the so-called enlightenment reforms, such as the Fundamental Code, the adoption of the Gregorian calendar, the Conscription Law, and the liberation of *burakumin*; and the second, in 1876–77, during the widespread opposition to the implementation of the new tax law adopted in 1873. These moments of intense hostility and violence open a direct window onto the issue of the local reception of the Meiji reforms.

One striking feature of these "anti–new order uprisings" was the circulation of fantastic—or, depending on one's perspective, frightening—rumors concerning the intentions and institutions of the new Meiji government. The most famous of these rumors concerned the Conscription Law. The injudicious use of the phrase "blood tax" in its text spawned rumors that conscripts' blood would be extracted and, in some variations of the story, sold to foreign countries.[1] In an earlier uprising, villagers in Kōchi prefecture had protested the replacement of a long-serving daimyo after the abolition of the *han* in

1871 in the belief that he would be replaced by an evil official who would sell Japanese people (especially women and children) to foreigners as slaves. It was even reported that the foreigners would throw their Japanese slaves into large furnaces and render their body fat to drink.[2] In one case, there were even rumors that the head of the Council of State was a foreigner and a Christian.[3] The frequent appearance of *burakumin* in the rumors also provided another bogeyman to spark the anxieties and anger of rural people. Finally, the new schools were embroiled in this swirl of threatening images. For instance, people often feared that the schools were simply a method of rounding up conscripts to be sent abroad, and teachers and inspectors were sometimes rumored to be foreigners, Christians, or *burakumin*.[4] It did not help that the new school buildings—which in 1873 were actually quite rare—could easily be mistaken for, and indeed often doubled as, local conscription offices.

Fueled at least in part by these rumors, groups of villagers in different regions of Japan expressed their suspicion and anger toward the new government by destroying schools, conscription offices, official bulletin boards, officials' houses, and other structures. For example, in May 1873, over 3,000 people from some ten different villages in Okayama prefecture destroyed eighteen schools, two temples, the residences of 52 officials, and over 300 *burakumin* homes.[5] That same year, over 10,000 protesters in Kagawa prefecture, wielding bamboo sticks and beating drums as they marched, burned 34 schools, 34 local government offices, five temples, three public bulletin boards, and over 300 homes of local officials.[6] Three years later, in 1876, a second spate of uprisings broke out in Ibaraki, Mie, Gifu, and Aichi prefectures. This time, tax offices, police stations, courts, and post offices served as additional targets of animosity.[7] The burning of public buildings (even though the total number of private homes destroyed exceeded that of public buildings) and the theft or destruction of public documents distinguish these early Meiji uprisings from Tokugawa-era protests, in which such acts were, as a rule, considered outside the bounds of accepted means of expressing grievances.[8]

The general hostility toward the changes associated with the new Meiji regime, which can be inferred from the rumors as well as from the specific structures and people targeted for destruction by the uprisings, is confirmed by the specific complaints and demands expressed by protesters. In addition to customary grievances concerning rice prices and general economic distress, these uprisings also conveyed opposition to a number of specific policies initiated by the Meiji state. In particular, nearly all the uprisings targeted the new schools, the new conscription system, and the abolition of *burakumin* status. Other grievances focused on the recent intrusion of cultural influences from the West, which protesters generally blamed on the new Meiji government. For example, protesters in Fukui in 1873 carried banners emblazoned with the picture of Amitahba and voiced opposition to the influence of Christianity in the new schools, in the belief that behind the new trends toward short hair, Western clothes, the eating of meat, the adoption of the Western calendar, and the pursuit of Western learning in general lurked the insidious influence of Christianity. The leader of this protest, a literate villager named Fudemori Magotarō, asserted, "Short hair and Western clothes are a custom of Jesus, the [new] calendar is a calendar of Jesus, and the [new] landholding system is the law of Jesus!"[9]

An uprising in Tottori in 1873 illustrates the various elements that came together in these early Meiji protests. The uprising apparently began when two strangers in Western clothing watched a group of young children playing.[10] One of the strangers reportedly said to the other, "If we could only get children this young into the schools, education would surely improve." The children, hearing only snippets of the conversation, grew afraid and ran away. As the incident was transmitted from child to parent to neighbor, a rumor spread that the two strangers were foreigners who had come to extract the blood of Japanese children and take it back to their home country. A large group of villagers wielding bamboo sticks gathered and chased the two men (who were actually schoolteachers en route to their new jobs in nearby villages) into the mountains and killed one of them. After destroying the homes of five officials, the protesters then submitted a ten-point petition to prefectural officials. Their demands included a lowering of rice prices, the expulsion of all foreigners from the prefecture, the freedom to wear old hairstyles (instead of the new, shorter Western cut), the abolition of the new elementary schools and the voluntary reopening of the old village schools, the abrogation of the Conscription Law, the destruction of government bulletin boards, and the abandonment of the Western calendar. In this case, as in most other early Meiji rebellions, the protesters were dispersed by military force—specifically by bands of samurai employed as peacekeeping forces by the new Meiji government—with no concessions on the part of the prefectural government.[11]

But even though these uprisings were unsuccessful, it is important to look at what villagers *wanted* to accomplish, what they were trying to say, by destroying public buildings and opposing the policies of the Meiji government. Of course, we could conclude that rural people simply reacted negatively to any change, particularly the kind of disruptive changes planned by the Meiji government. In fact, Western historians' neglect of these very visible social movements suggests that many scholars view them as a knee-jerk reaction. One could also argue that the uprisings were motivated by economic concerns, with the various rumors and demands serving merely as red herrings or as more noble-sounding justifications. Indeed, it would be naïve to ignore the financial factors involved: the new land tax, conscription, and schools imposed new financial burdens on villagers, either to pay for the new reforms or institutions or, in the case of conscription and schools, to make up for the opportunity costs of the labor of participating family members. It is also possible to discuss these uprisings in more general terms as constituting an "anti-modernization" movement.[12] Protesters never articulated an explicit Luddite stance against capitalism or technology or modernity *per se*, but all the policies targeted by villagers as objectionable—tax reform, conscription, centralized education, the liberation of *burakumin*, the Gregorian calendar, short hair, and so on—were fundamental to contemporary views on the meaning of becoming modern. And in fact, "new religions" such as Tenri-kyō and Maruyama-kyō—which Hirota Masaki argues emerged from the same social and cultural forces that produced the anti–new order protests—explicitly decried the destructive influence of capitalist industry and modern culture in their critique of "civilization."[13]

The particular combination of rumors, complaints, and demands surrounding these uprisings, however, allows us to speak more precisely about the specific sources and meanings of the fears and hostilities people felt at this moment. Above all, their reaction calls attention to the sudden, revolutionary, and disruptive character of early Meiji reforms. The common view of the Restoration as a smooth and consensual "transition" often obscures the fact that most of the early Meiji "civilization and enlightenment" policies were perceived as radically undermining the foundations of life and thought. Policies that in hindsight appear quite reasonable—and sometimes even morally right, as in the case of the *burakumin* liberation—and crucial to Japan's modernization were often viewed with a combination of fear and disdain.[14]

For example, the new systems of land taxation (based on the value of the land rather than a negotiable percentage of the yield) and of land tenure (which formally granted people the right to buy and sell land freely) were not necessarily seen as opportunities. Rather, villagers often saw these measures as destroying whatever security they had been able to derive from the old system of land tenure, as well as the elements in the old taxation system that allowed them to appeal to the "benevolence" and "protection" of overlords during times of poor harvests.[15] Similarly, unlike the "civilization and enlightenment" ideologues, ordinary people did not necessarily see the dismantling of Edo-period status distinctions as a liberation. As Herman Ooms explains, the notion of a status-based social and cosmological order had become completely internalized during the Edo period;[16] as a result, many perceived the elimination of those distinctions as the breakdown of order itself. At the very least, people could see that their release from the burdens of the Tokugawa status system also meant the shouldering of new burdens—most notably compulsory military service and school attendance.[17] Popular opposition to the end of the status system crystallized around the issue of the *burakumin* liberation. On a concrete level, liberation meant that *burakumin* were freed from their hereditary duties of dealing with prisoners, disposing of dead animals, and so on. But in addition, Tsurumaki Yoshio argues, because *burakumin* had shouldered the responsibility of removing physical and spiritual pollution from the village, their liberation heightened the sense of crisis by rendering communities that already felt besieged by new sources of pollution even more defenseless.[18] Finally, contributing to the sense of disorder and crisis was the ever-growing presence of foreigners. Like the status system, the conception of foreigners—and especially Christians—as dangerous and barbaric Others had become naturalized during the Edo period.[19] The inability of the Tokugawa political authorities to resist the influx of foreigners and foreign influence was distressing enough, but the unabashed embrace of things foreign by the Meiji government aggravated the already resentful attitude of many villagers toward the new policies.

Given these perceptions of early Meiji policies, the opposition of many villagers and their willingness to take such extreme actions as burning public buildings and petitioning for the repeal of these policies are understandable. At one level, the protesters' association of the new government and its policies with traditional bogeymen reveals the unease many felt and their suspicions toward the new government. In addition, the "feeling of powerlessness and vulnerability to the new government's arbitrary decisions," as Stephen Vlastos puts it, undoubtedly contributed to this antagonism.[20] Moreover, the protesters' demands suggest that the uprisings expressed not only a vague sense of unease or a resentment over the lack of popular input into policy changes but also a more specific opposition to the content of those policies. Some Japanese scholars even see the anti–new order uprisings as Japan's first political movement. Makihara Norio, for example, argues that the seemingly "irrational" rumors and demands surrounding the uprisings had distinctly political undertones and reflected opposition to the new imperial government.[21] Hirota Masaki contends that the uprisings demonstrate the rural masses' consciousness of the principles governing their premodern peasant world and their rejection of the early Meiji reforms as an assault on that world.[22] Indeed, it is possible that a statement by Fudemori Magotarō, the leader of the 1873 peasant uprising in Fukui, may contain an alternative political vision: "Recent state policies [conscription, the land tax, *burakumin* liberation, Western hairstyles, and schools] are totally unacceptable. We cannot submit to them, and we earnestly seek to abolish them and return to the way things were before."[23] Of course, categorization of these uprisings as political or apolitical depends on our definition of those terms. The uprisings did, however, express rejections of specific policies of the new government and proposed alternatives to these policies—alternatives that often reflected the (idealized) conditions of the pre-Meiji social, political, economic, and educational order.

But why did protesters include the new schools on their lists of objectionable institutions and policies? The scant attention paid by Western scholars to this point reveals the common assumption that the protests were not about the new schools.[24] However, nearly 200 schools were damaged or destroyed in the uprisings. In three incidents, protesters attacked teachers or teachers' homes. In several other incidents, protesters demanded either the abolition of the schools or the repeal of the policies requiring villages to shoulder the costs of teachers' and administrators' salaries. Even if the demand for the abolition of the new schools was secondary to other issues, and even if protesters destroyed new schools principally as symbols of the new order, opposition to the new schools was clearly one of the *meanings* of the uprisings. Consequently, we must attempt to understand the reasons for this opposition.

This opposition may seem puzzling, since schooling had already been a part of most people's lives before the Meiji Restoration. In contrast to many other parts of the world, where modernizing states have had to force schools on a largely unschooled agrarian populace, the Tokugawa period bequeathed a strong tradition of rural schooling. By the Meiji period, schooling was no longer a strange concept; many rural people had already faced the question of whether the household economy was better served by sending a child to school or by keeping the child at home. Historians have generally seen the impressive legacy of Tokugawa education as the primary reason for the rapid acceptance of centralized compulsory education during the Meiji period; the assumption behind this argument is that the pre-Meiji schooling experience was essentially similar to that of the new Meiji schools. I argue, however, that people perceived the new schools as different and often resented that difference.

For most participants in the 1873 uprisings, this perception of the new schools was not based on extensive firsthand experience. The Ministry of Education had promulgated the Fundamental Code only about six months earlier, and although new schools were being established, the full effect of the new conception of education was yet to be felt: teacher-training schools had not been established, new textbooks and instructional techniques had not been widely disseminated, and the ministry's myriad rules concerning the organization and administration of primary education were yet to be fully understood, much less fully implemented. Furthermore, although some prefectural authorities had begun collecting funds from the local population to finance new schools, in many areas those funds came largely from voluntary contributions, and school levies were neither systematic nor substantial.[25] Consequently, we should not assume that protesters in

1873 were fully aware of the differences between the Fundamental Code and pre-Meiji educational arrangements. More likely, protesters perceived the Fundamental Code and the new school buildings as symbols of the unwanted changes initiated by the Meiji government. The popular association of the schools with objectionable policies (conscription, land reform, and so on) as well as with traditional bogeymen (foreigners, *burakumin*) suggests that the new schools served as a symbol of all things different and foreign and threatening. By destroying this symbol, protesters expressed their opposition to all those things, including the new government itself. By investing so much symbolic weight, so broad an array of meanings, in a single institution, the Meiji government enabled people to reject the entire new order by rejecting that one symbol.

The second wave of education-related uprisings in 1876–77 differed from these earlier protests in a number of ways. First, whereas almost all the participants in the 1873 incidents were lower-level peasants, the 1876–77 uprisings were led by wealthier villagers.[26] Second, although tax reform had not been a major issue in the earlier uprisings (largely because the new land tax had not been fully implemented by the time of the 1873 uprisings), in 1876–77 it was central to the protesters' demands. In particular, villagers identified the new rice-cash calculation rate and the rice-classification system—rather than the land tax itself—as the most objectionable elements of the new system.[27] Third, the nature of popular sentiment against the new schools was different in the 1876–77 uprisings. In contrast to the absolute rejection of the new schools expressed in the earlier incidents, in 1876–77 the protesters' grievances and demands regarding the new schools were quite specific. They particularly objected to paying the school tax, the property-based levy collected in most areas to finance the new schools and pay for teachers' and administrators' salaries.

People had long been accustomed to the idea of paying for schooling. However, before the Fundamental Code, only the parents of the *attending* children had to pay; those who did not send their children to school bore no financial liability. This key difference was the source of much contention. Surprisingly, in the 1876–77 uprisings, resistance did not come only from families that did not want their children to attend school. The leaders of these protests were village elites, most of whom had for decades invested large amounts of money in their children's education, and many of whom had contributed money to establish new schools in the early Meiji period. Furthermore, the villages that supplied the bulk of participants in these uprisings generally had higher levels of school attendance both before and after the Restoration than did surrounding areas that did not participate in the uprisings.[28] Protesters were not opposed, in other words, to the idea of schooling their children outside the home or to the notion of paying the individual who provided that service.

Rather, the 1876–77 uprisings emerged from the contradictions inherent in early Meiji educational policy. The Fundamental Code was based on the concept of centralizing education so that it might serve the interests of the state. At the same time, the Fundamental Code stipulated that most of the costs relating to education would be borne not by the state but by the people (using *minpi*, or popular funds, as opposed to *kanpi*, or government funds). People perceived a contradiction between local funding and central control; the 1876–77 uprisings expressed both recognition and disapproval of this contradiction. The protesters, for example, destroyed only newly constructed school buildings and left intact those new schools that were held in old buildings. Hori Kōtarō notes only one case, in an uprising in Gifu, in which protesters targeted an old school building, and in that instance protesters destroyed only the new school equipment housed inside the building and carefully avoided damaging the building itself.[29] Protesters also expressed resentment over the contradiction of local funding and central control when they chose not to destroy schools taught by teachers from their own villages and instead focused their wrath on schools taught by "outsiders" who had received their teaching certification from prefectural normal schools.[30] Occasionally protesters made this point explicitly, as they did in Mie by burning new schools while chanting "Destroy and burn everything that belongs to the government!"[31]

The protesters were expressing, in other words, their perception that the new schools belonged not to them but to the government (*kan*). Indeed, they were correctly reading the intent of the Ministry of Education, which created the Fundamental Code with the assumption that the local school would serve as an apparatus of the state. This intention was not always at the forefront of government rhetoric on educational reform, particularly in the Preamble of the Fundamental Code, which justified the expense of public schooling in terms of the schools' benefit to the individual instead of to the state. However, government officials assumed that the state would run education for its own benefit. Occasionally, this sentiment found its way into the open; for example, in 1875 a government official named Nakajima Nobuyuki declared bluntly, "Schools do not belong to the people!"[32] This attitude contrasts with that common in the Tokugawa period, when the state exercised no institutional control over commoner education, and tuition-based funding and the absence of any legal compulsion to attend school resulted in local schools that conformed to the demands of the families that supported them. Partly because of the tax-based system of funding and more generally because of the government's clear regulation of the new schools, many people undoubtedly felt that the new schools did not, in fact, belong to them. Indeed, had people felt a sense of ownership or identification with the new schools, they would not have destroyed them. Attacking newly built schools, especially those staffed by teachers from outside the local area, was a strategic and symbolic act: the protesters were destroying an institution they felt should be controlled locally, for their own benefit. In contrast to earlier incidents, the 1876–77 uprisings were not expressing absolute opposition to the new schools. Rather, they represented merely the most visible manifestation of what would be an ongoing struggle between ordinary villagers and local elites, on the one hand, and prefectural and central government officials, on the other, to reshape the local school to further their own expectations.

Resistance in Nagano and Chikuma

Neither Nagano nor Chikuma experienced large-scale, violent opposition to the new school system during the first few years of the Fundamental Code. It is this fact, combined with high enrollment figures and the favorable response of prefectural officials and local activists to central reforms, that led both the Meiji government and postwar Japanese historians to view Nagano and Chikuma as "model" prefectures. From this perspective, we might be inclined to view Nagano and Chikuma, as James Baxter has done with Ishikawa and Neil Waters with Kawasaki, as areas in which (in Waters's words) "nothing happened."[33] Nagano and Chikuma would thus seem inappropriate case studies for examining the role of resistance in the local experience of state formation.

It would a mistake, however, to conclude from the lack of large-scale, violent opposition that the establishment of the Meiji educational system in Nagano and Chikuma was a smooth, consensual process. First, there were many small-scale expressions of opposition to the new educational policies in Nagano and Chikuma. In addition, if the definition of resistance is broadened to include not just open conflict but also low-key, passive techniques of ignoring or deflecting the power of dominant groups, then individuals and communities in Nagano and Chikuma can be seen as resisting the demands of the central and prefectural governments.[34] Finally, local cooperation with central policy does not necessarily imply consensus. Local cooperation in the effort to build the new educational system was based on a variety of goals and motivations, many of which differed considerably from those of the Meiji government. Local initiatives toward integration often involved efforts to contest and influence the terms of that integration, and cooperation was often temporary or conditional, with room for future conflict whenever personal or local interests diverged from those of the state.

One form of resistance to the Fundamental Code involved some of the more than 2,000 teachers left unemployed because of the abolition of pre-existing schools. As noted in the preceding chapter, some of these teachers responded by finding other forms of employment, and others were able to find work at the new elementary schools after obtaining a license from the prefectural normal schools. Still others attempted, often unsuccessfully, to receive permission from the prefectural government to continue to operate their old schools as private schools. A few, however, chose to defy the new regulations by continuing to operate their old schools without permission. These illegal schools usually left no documentary trace, since what made them illegal was the absence of formal, written documentation and approval from the prefectural government.[35] However, evidence of these schools occasionally crops up in the voluminous documents produced by the day-to-day administration of education at the prefectural level. For example, in spring 1879 the Chikuma prefectural office received two "letters of apology" from Kitajō village. Both letters concerned the unlicensed operation of a private school; one was written by the teacher, Ōta Shin'eiji, and another by several other residents of Kitajō. Ōta's letter expressed his contrition:

Even though we received and understood the kind instructions [about the Fundamental Code] from the prefectural office at this time of educational progress, Takeda Tashichi and several other people from the village came to me and entrusted me with their children. I gathered the children together at my home and taught them only reading and writing. Then the prefectural authorities admonished me, saying that without a license, such activities are very inappropriate and are contrary to imperial will. I am very grateful for the admonition, and from now on I will forgo such activities.[36]

The second letter was from the parents who had sent their children to Ōta's school. Their letter explains that they entrusted their children to Ōta out of "nostalgia for the ways of the old-time school-teachers."[37] Both Ōta and the parents promised to "rid ourselves of past tendencies."

Ōta appears to have abandoned his school after a single scolding, but other renegade teachers were less repentant. News of one such teacher in Higano village reached the Nagano prefectural office in 1874, in the form of an attendance investigation report for the recently established Nisshin Elementary School in Higano. The parents of several children in Higano, when asked by the local school administrators why the children were not attending the new school, responded that their children were studying at a school taught by an individual named Kitajima Jun.[38] On receiving the report, the educational official for the district began investigating the matter.

The district official learned that Kitajima had been causing problems for village officials ever since the promulgation of the Fundamental Code. When, in early 1873, officials began collecting funds to build a new elementary school, Kitajima assembled the people of Higano, spread rumors about the new school, and urged them not to contribute. Kitajima apparently voiced a number of complaints about the new educational system, but, according to the report, his opposition stemmed fundamentally from the fear that the new school "would strip him of his livelihood."[39] When officials told him that all pre-existing schools must close, Kitajima falsely claimed to have received permission from the prefectural government to continue to operate his school. Consequently, even though village officials managed to raise enough money to build a new school, many parents continued to send their children to Kitajima. Because of Kitajima's prestige in the community, village officials were afraid to confront him and called in the *torishimari* to reprimand him. Under threat of punishment, Kitajima personally escorted his students to the new elementary school and promised to stop teaching. However, only a few months later, Kitajima had convinced students to leave the new school and study under his tutelage. The *torishimari*, arguing that such behavior "impedes the development of the new school" and "insults the authority of the prefectural office," urged the prefectural authorities to summon Kitajima and punish him.

The prefectural government apparently did not respond decisively in this matter, and soon Kitajima devised a new scheme to continue his former occupation. In 1877, the *torishimari* informed the prefectural office that Kitajima had obtained the school sign and a license of a school that had closed and reopened his old school in his own house, this time with the sign from the other school hanging in his window.[40] Once again, Kitajima began voicing complaints about the new school system to people in Higano and other nearby villages and encouraged parents to send their children to his school. As a result, the district official noted, "criticisms of public education in the village have been unceasing, and the collection of school funds has stagnated." The investigating official expressed the fear that "if this kind of insidious character is allowed to continue unchecked, it will affect not only Nisshin Elementary School but other schools as well, and ultimately bring about the decline of public education." The district investigator's fears were justified. Not only did Kitajima not participate in the new system but he openly criticized it and advocated past educational arrangements as a legitimate alternative. As a man of status within his community, one with a long history of educational leadership, he was in a powerful position to convince local people not to accept the new government's assertion of a monopoly over schooling.

A more pervasive expression of local opposition to the new educational system was the refusal to pay for it. As noted in the preceding chapter, elementary schools were funded mainly through voluntary contributions and mandatory school levies. Since most elementary schools received minimal support from the central government, they were heavily dependent on these funds. In the first few years of the Fundamental Code, officials from hundreds of schools asked the prefectural authorities to take action against villagers who either would not pay the school levies or, in the case of voluntary contributions, refused to honor their pledges. Nearly every school that petitioned the prefectural office listed at least a half-dozen (and sometimes as many as twenty or more) individuals who had repeatedly neglected to pay the school levies or contributions. In most cases, this refusal to pay school fees persisted despite multiple scoldings by village- and district-level authorities; these petitions to the prefectural government were a last resort, in the hopes that the threat of punishment from prefectural authorities might compel local recalcitrants to comply. Those who were delinquent in the payment of voluntary contributions were particularly troubling to local authorities: since such contributions tended to come from among the wealthy residents of a school district, authorities worried that they might set a pattern of noncompliance for the rest of the local population.

In one case, village officials in the Azumi district of Chikuma prefecture complained in 1876 to the prefectural authorities that one of several villagers who had refused to continue his annual contributions was a former district head. According to local officials, the high status of the offender had led a number of other villagers to follow suit.[41] In Shimadachi, a village near the city of Matsumoto, village officials petitioned the prefectural office to take action against a recalcitrant who was "a man of influence" and therefore needed to be reprimanded "in order to prevent his behavior from infecting others in the village."[42] The offender, a man named Asada Yoshi, subsequently explained that he could not afford to pay because he had sent his son to Tokyo to study under a well-known doctor—an apparently persuasive excuse, since the prefectural office waived Asada's financial obligation to the school. In other cases, nonpayers cited a preference for pre-Meiji educational arrangements as grounds for refusing to pay their levies or contributions. For example, in one village in Chikuma district, local officials complained to the prefectural office about two wealthy landowners who had criticized the new educational system and refused to pay their contributions to the new school. Following a scolding from prefectural authorities, the two men promised to resume their payments, but only after the authorities had given them permission to send their own children to what they called a "traditional" school.[43]

By 1876, these various forms of noncompliance with the Fundamental Code—many of them by village elites—had apparently become such a serious concern in Nagano and Chikuma that *torishimari*

and prefectural officials initiated discussions of it at district and prefectural assemblies. In 1876 a *torishimari* in Chikuma prefecture submitted a lengthy document to the prefectural office entitled "A Proposal for the Revision of Educational Affairs."[44] Concerned about the
problem of "shallow knowledge of education and enlightenment"
among the people in his jurisdiction, he suggested a number of measures to demonstrate the importance of public education. Much of his
proposal, however, addressed the problem of individuals who refused to participate in the effort to implement the Fundamental Code.
The author named several different types of offenders: (1) those "who
scorn the Fundamental Code, spread fallacious rumors about it, and
throw regulations into disorder"; (2) those "who criticize new teaching methods, treat teachers with contempt, and obstruct school attendance"; (3) those "who encourage students not to attend [the new
schools] and block the road to and from school"; (4) those "who, by
expressing their own selfish feelings, overshadow the constructive
zeal of others"; (5) those "who do not join in efforts to collect school
funds or to build new schools"; (6) those "who open unlicensed private schools and thereby obstruct the attendance of school-age children [at the new elementary schools]"; and (7) those "who spend
money unnecessarily on Buddhist festivals, theatrical productions,
and so on, which are irrelevant to education." The author's need to
classify the different types of deviant behavior suggests that anti–
Fundamental Code sentiment was broad enough to manifest itself in
several different forms of common subversive activity.

These acts of opposition and recalcitrance constituted the more
overt forms of resistance to the Fundamental Code: the individuals
involved positioned themselves outside the government's project,
openly criticized it, and espoused alternative forms of education.
Other individuals chose to participate in the new system—for example, by contributing to the local school endowment or even by assuming an administrative role in the schools—but challenged specific aspects of the Fundamental Code, usually in an attempt to
persuade the prefectural government to allow their own local
schools to deviate from central government policy. Their opposition
was often based on local exigencies, but their requests often reveal a
concept of "school" that differed from that in the Fundamental Code.
Such individuals seldom challenged the authority of the government

to make educational policy, nor did they reject the goal of a nation-wide, compulsory school system. Rather, they operated from within the new system, encouraging its local implementation while seeking to alter the terms of that implementation.

The most common example of this kind of activity can be found in what I call the "school deconsolidation" movement, which occurred in the first years of the Fundamental Code. This movement stemmed from the tendency of prefectural authorities and *torishimari* in Naga-no and Chikuma to draw elementary school districts that encompassed several pre-Meiji villages. In doing so, they were deviating from the letter of the Fundamental Code, which advocated smaller districts that were intentionally incongruous with pre-existing village boundaries. Their goal, however, was to create a broader financial base for the new, larger, better-equipped elementary schools envisioned in the Ministry of Education's regulations. Establishing and operating such schools involved extensive cooperation among the officials of several different villages as they hashed out such critical issues as the location of the school and the relative financial burden of each village. Such situations were rife with the potential for conflict. In the spirit of possibility and collective ambition that pervaded Nagano and Chikuma in the aftermath of the Restoration and the promulgation of the Fundamental Code, village elites seemed willing to work through such disagreements and forged ahead to establish hundreds of new elementary schools. Soon, however, rifts began to appear, and village leaders petitioned the prefectural government for permission to secede from the local elementary school district and establish a school in their own village.

In some cases, officials petitioned to build a branch school, arguing that the distance from the main school (*honkō*) caused hardships for local children. The Fundamental Code had acknowledged that branch schools (called *bunkō, shikō,* or *hashutsujo*) might be necessary after the school districts had been established, since they would shorten commuting distances and, in the process, remove a potential obstacle to school attendance. At the same time, the official designation of these schools as "branch schools" and their listing in the Fundamental Code under the heading "irregular schools" stigmatized them as temporary, as "not quite a school." This designation also allowed the government to eliminate these schools more easily once the new system was firmly in place. Perhaps in order to emphasize their provisional nature, branch schools were to be supported by funds and taught by the teacher(s) from the main school.

Since the Ministry of Education had set fairly high financial qualifications for villages seeking to establish a main school, most villages could not realistically hope to afford one. However, hundreds of villages throughout Nagano and Chikuma prefectures applied to the prefectural office during the early to mid-1870s requesting permission to open branch schools. Prefectural officials were willing to grant such requests, since branch schools were consistent with the intent of the Fundamental Code. Yet a branch school served the interests of the village as well by shortening the commute of local children and giving the residents of a particular village a sense of control over their own school—even if it was an "irregular" school theoretically under the administrative authority of the main school. And in fact, many villages subtly contested this distinction by specifying in their applications that the new branch school be funded not with money from the main school but with private contributions from within the village.[45] Even if this act did not openly challenge the relegation to branch school status, it secured a greater degree of local control for the village.

Many villages took the next step of contesting the designation of "branch school" in the hopes of upgrading the status of their school. For example, the officials of Ushiroku village in the Saku district of Nagano prefecture petitioned the prefectural office in 1878 requesting that their local school, the Seirin Branch School, be recognized as a main school. The officials explained that at the time a main school had been established in a nearby village in 1873, the people of Ushiroku "had no idea what a school was and lived their lives mired in conservatism," and therefore they had not established their own school.[46] According to the officials, "the people have now come to realize that they should not neglect their education," but the mountains surrounding the village on all sides prevent their children from attending the main school. "Consequently," they reported, "the whole village has chipped in, and as you can see from the appended documents, we have raised the funds to build a new school building and establish it independently as a main school." The officials appended extensive data on the various sources of the school's endowment, as well as detailed population statistics and geographical information on their village. The village was rewarded for its diligence: the prefectural office approved the petition without investigation—despite the fact that the new "Seirin Elementary School" reported an endowment of only ¥300, far below the prefecture's requirement of a minimum endowment of ¥1,000.

Village officials in Inabe village petitioned the Chikuma prefectural office to request a similar change of status for their village school, the Kamimaki Branch School. The officials reported that a prefectural inspector had visited the school and urged that it be consolidated with nearby Inazawa Elementary School. At the time, remarked the officials, they supported this measure.[47] When they discussed the matter with local residents, however, "people expressed a number of objections and spread fallacious rumors; so in the end we were unable to come to a decision." The officials decided to call off the merger and petitioned that their school become a "main school." They also asked permission to withdraw the ¥200 they had contributed toward the establishment of a consolidated school and add it to the endowment of their own school. The prefecture seems to have hesitated in granting the request, for several months later the officials submitted another petition. This time they emphasized the hardship caused by the commute: "We are isolated from neighboring villages, and in winter the snow accumulates on the steep mountain roads, making travel very difficult. We think that this could result in obstructing the progress (*shinpo*) of the students and the school."[48] This time, the prefectural office approved the request, despite the fact that the school's endowment and number of students fell far short of prefectural guidelines.

One complaint, usually left unstated, behind the deconsolidation movement concerned the inclusion of *burakumin* communities in the same school districts as non-*burakumin* communities. As noted above, the liberation of the *burakumin* had been a major factor in the uprisings of 1873. In Nagano and Chikuma, this issue did not lead to open revolt. Instead, village officials sought to manipulate the drawing of school district boundaries to exclude the children of *burakumin*. One of the few examples of this kind of conflict to appear in the documentary record occurred at Nisshō Elementary School in the Minochi district of Nagano prefecture. The dispute first came to the attention of the prefectural government in 1878, when two representatives from a *burakumin* community (referred to in these documents as *shinmin,* or "new people") petitioned the prefectural governor for permission to attend the school:

Since the opening of Nisshō Elementary School in 1873, we have pleaded [with the school authorities] a number of times, but the people are unable to rid themselves of their old customs. Even though the prefectural officials have urged us to begin attending the school . . . the school representatives, Makino Tōbei and Tamura Takezaburō, stirred up resentments and refused [to let us attend]. We have already paid our school contributions, but they still decided to exclude us. . . . Our houses are the only ones raising un-schooled children. And if they do not know about schooling, they will be ignorant and unlawful; they will not understand human morality and will be inferior even to wild beasts.[49]

The petitioners asked the prefectural authorities to summon school officials to the prefectural office and compel them to accept children from the *burakumin* community. These *burakumin* representatives were obviously well versed in the new discourse of enlightenment and education propagated by the Ministry of Education and made use of this rhetoric in their efforts to integrate the school.

The two administrators from the school did not deny the legitimacy of these requests. However, in their response to the petitioners' complaints two months later, they remarked that the choice to exclude the *burakumin* children had not been "an arbitrary decision"; rather, it had been made "from the point of view of the entire population." If the *burakumin* children were allowed to attend the school, "it would lead to other objections, and we fear that it could ultimately result in the failure of the school."[50] Consequently, they requested that the *burakumin* community be instructed to rent a house in their own village and establish a branch school; in return, the main school would send its teacher to the branch school on a regular basis to teach the children there. The prefectural office agreed, remarking that the separation of the schools was "unavoidable" given the "sentiment of the general population."[51] This was, in fact, a decision reached elsewhere in Japan as well and led to the widespread creation of separate "*buraku* school districts" (*buraku gakku*). Administratively these districts were the same as any other district, but they were populated only by *burakumin.*[52] This compromise was apparently acceptable to all three parties: the non-*buraku* communities were able to exclude the *buraku* children (at the expense of having to support the *buraku* school financially); the *buraku* community received its own school, which would have been impossible without the financial resources of the main school (at the expense of perpetuating their own social segregation—although this was not a matter in which they had a choice); and the prefectural government forestalled a possible obstacle to the popular acceptance of the educational reforms (at the expense of compromising the revolutionary intent of Meiji social and educational policies).

These examples from the school deconsolidation movement illustrate how cooperation and resistance functioned as complementary strategies in negotiating the local implementation of educational reform. On the surface, these villages' demands for their own elementary schools appear to provide evidence of grass-roots support for the Meiji government's project in education. Villages were willing to observe proper administrative practices (petitioning, recordkeeping, statistical surveying, and so on) and to adopt officially sanctioned rhetoric ("progress," "curricular regulations," "imperial will") in an effort to obtain their own schools. Since the dissemination of these practices and words was a key strategy in the Meiji government's effort to make its new concept of "school" appear legitimate and commonsensical, it would seem that the Fundamental Code was working according to plan. But the deconsolidation movement also represented a strategic attempt to appropriate the terms of the dominant group in an effort to further local interests. Rather than reject government regulations outright, villages in Nagano and Chikuma manipulated the system from within in order to acquire their own school in their own village, paid for by themselves. As is evident in the case of the Kamimaki Elementary School, villages might petition the government several times, each time adopting a different rhetoric and rationale until they found the one that worked. Predictably, once villages discovered that the issue of avoiding the hardships of commuting constituted an acceptable justification in the eyes of the prefectural government, the form and language of the school deconsolidation petition became conventionalized—even among those villages for whom the commuting issue was irrelevant. Indeed, after being inundated with petitions that cited this excuse, the prefectural office realized that it needed to send *torishimari* to investigate the geography of each school district in order to verify the legitimacy of these claims.[53]

Of course, in order to view the government's decision to accept these petitions as a compromise with local interests, we must keep in mind that the Meiji government's aim was not simply to bring schooling to an unschooled people—even though this is how authorities usually represented it. Had this been the sole intent, the decision of prefectural governments in Nagano and Chikuma to permit a village to establish its own school would not have been much of a compromise, for it would have been consistent with the goal of more schools and greater attendance. The Fundamental Code was not, however, a project intended to introduce the concept of schooling to the Japanese people; rather, it was an attempt to displace pre-existing schooling patterns and transform the assumptions that underlay them. In this light, school deconsolidation was a significant compromise on the government's part, since it allowed villages to establish schools that were smaller, closer, and subject to greater local control—in other words, schools that were more consistent with pre–Fundamental Code schooling experiences.

The Hotaka Elementary School Incident

Among the hundreds of examples of local conflicts over education in Nagano and Chikuma, the case of Hotaka Elementary School was the most prominent and acrimonious. The numerous struggles and debates surrounding the school spanned several years, involved fifteen villages, resulted in a number of arrests, and produced several hundred pages of documentation. This example is particularly noteworthy because the school had been celebrated by the Chikuma prefectural government as a "model school." Indeed, in a petition to prefectural authorities requesting their presence at the opening ceremony of Hotaka Elementary, one of the founders justified the request on the basis of his desire that the school "become a beacon for elementary schools throughout the district."[54]

Although Hotaka Elementary officially opened in 1873, the school had been operating as a *gōkō* for more than a year before the promulgation of the Fundamental Code. This particular *gōkō* had opened in 1871 through the combined efforts of two individuals we have encountered earlier. One was Fujimori Jūbei, a former schoolteacher from a wealthy commoner family who had written the government of Matsumoto domain in 1870 with a proposal to establish a system of primary schools throughout the prefecture; schools were necessary, he argued, to "cleanse ourselves of two hundred years of evil customs" and to counter the moral decline that had weakened "our imperial nation."[55] The other founder was Takahashi Keijūrō, the regionally renowned scholar and former samurai from nearby Takatō domain who wrote a similar petition in late 1871 to the newly established Chikuma prefectural government; in it he argued that schooling was "in conformity with the law of civilization and enlightenment" and constituted a form of "service to the imperial public."[56]

Although the Fundamental Code forced their school to close temporarily, Fujimori and Takahashi were not discouraged. Rather, they used the opportunity to enlarge the scope of their school, enlisting the cooperation of leaders from fifteen different villages in an effort to establish a new elementary school that conformed to the principles and curricular regulations found in the Fundamental Code. With this large financial base, they were able to organize the construction of a new, two-story school building, complete with a globe, a clock, a blackboard, and other equipment recommended by the Ministry of Education; the structure was completed in late 1873, at the cost of over ¥1,000.[57] Takahashi had studied at Tokyo Normal School and was one of the few teachers in Chikuma or Nagano to understand Western textbooks and pedagogical techniques. The names of many future educational leaders of Chikuma and Nagano prefecture appear on the class rosters of Hotaka Elementary as either teachers or students.[58] In spring 1878, an article in the Matsumoto-based *New Day Newspaper* praised the school's accomplishments, noting that only nineteen of the school's 759 students had failed their recent promotion examinations.[59]

Although Hotaka Elementary School was celebrated as an example of progress, an outpost of enlightenment in the middle of the mountains, it soon became apparent that the school was not entirely a welcome presence among the local people. Only four months after the laudatory newspaper article, four representatives from Yabara village (one of the fifteen villages in the Hotaka *kumiai*) submitted a petition to the prefectural government to complain about Hotaka Elementary School and to request permission to establish an independent school in Yabara.[60] The petition began with an expression of support for the new educational system, praising the new government for its policies, which had encouraged the establishment of schools and thus had "opened the path to enlightenment." The petition acknowledged the past accomplishments of Hotaka Elementary School; in the years since it was established, the school "has flourished and been of great benefit" to the area. The petitioners argued, however, that because of "the unfairness of the school's regulations," Hotaka Elementary "has lost its way, and the students have not progressed."

The petitioners leveled several specific complaints against the operation of the school. Like other deconsolidation petitions, this one raised the issue of distance. The petitioners noted that the commute to Hotaka Elementary was causing local children great hardship. The petitioners even suggested that this physical distance might lead to an emotional distance from the new state: "We fear that [the distance] stifles the gratitude in the people's hearts toward the government and could lead them to unwittingly contradict the imperial will." In addition, they expressed disapproval of the cost of the school, arguing that the financial burden was especially heavy for the people of Yabara village and caused great hardship. This burden was especially galling because, according to the petitioners, the funds were wasted on the excessive salaries paid to school administrators and teachers. These salaries, they contended, were extracted from people such as day laborers who lived from day to day without a stable income and from impoverished parents who had to sell themselves or their children into slavery in order to pay the school tax. In general, the petitioners painted a highly unfavorable portrait of Hotaka Elementary and its teachers and *sewayaku*. They noted the "strict" and "imposing" manner in which the school levies were collected. They decried the "harsh" practice of fining the parents of absentee children and making them sweep the school floor. They argued that the people were "afraid of the intimidating rules of the school's teachers and administrators." For all these reasons, the representatives of Yabara village asked "to be allowed to obey the imperial will, to work diligently in their agricultural tasks, and to collect funds to secede [from Hotaka school] and build our own independent school."

The prefectural offices in Nagano and Chikuma had approved hundreds of similar petitions during the preceding five years. Perhaps because of the prominence of this particular school and the individuals involved, however, this particular petition did not go unchallenged. The first disapproving voice came from Nakajima Yūji, the *torishimari* responsible for Hotaka Elementary. After investigating the petition of Yabara village, Nakajima wrote a detailed refutation of the various claims made by Yabara and attached the report to the Yabara petition before passing it on to the prefectural office.[61] In his report, Nakajima questioned the claim that the commute to Hotaka Elementary School was a hardship for the children of Yabara. Nakajima drew a map of the fifteen villages in the Hotaka village group to illustrate his point and noted that Yabara was in fact adjacent to the village in which the school was located and separated from it by flat ground—there was "not the slightest inconvenience to commuting children." He then countered the claim of excessive school levies: the great number of students at the school made it necessary to employ several teachers and to equip it with the latest facilities. Moreover, the school regulations were in conformity with those recommended by Tokyo Normal School. He even supported the practice of requiring the families of absentee children to sweep out the school on the grounds that the measure "was decided by all the *sewayaku* together" and was "a good strategy for encouraging attendance." Finally, he suggested that the complaints were "not entirely about schooling." Without being specific, he said that "a few misguided individuals . . . have incited the people of the entire village" and concluded by expressing the fear that this problem might spread to other villages.

This was precisely what happened. Within a month, five representatives of Kashiwahara village, Yabara's neighbor to the north, submitted a similar petition to the prefectural office. They, too, argued that Hotaka Elementary School was "in an inconvenient location" and requested permission to secede from the school and build a new school more conveniently located in the center of their own village of Kashiwahara. A few weeks later, the *sewayaku* from eleven other villages in the Hotaka village group submitted a joint complaint about Hotaka Elementary School to the prefectural office entitled "Under the Yoke of Hotaka School."[62] In the preface to the document, they claimed that the teachers and administrators "control every little detail" of the school and "shackle and stifle the people." The petitioners were writing the document in order to "summarize the elements of the oppressive system that have fomented dissent among the people." The five articles of the petition dealt mainly with the high salaries and incompetence of each of the different administrators and teachers at the school. The district head, for example, collected a monthly salary of ¥12 but only worked part time. The chief school administrator (*kanji*) also received ¥12 per month but "does not interact whatsoever with the people" and "has no idea what a school is supposed to be." The head teacher, Taka-hashi Keijūrō, received ¥25 per month, but he, too, was distant from the people and was "in collusion with (*nareai*) the district head and chief administrator."[63] These practices, argued the petitioners, had "raised suspicions among the people" and had led each of these eleven villages to demand permission to secede from the main school. Some meetings of representatives of the seceding villages be-came raucous demonstrations and ended with the arrest of a few of the alleged ringleaders. Hotaka Elementary, established as a beacon of enlightenment and a model of local cooperation with central ex-pectations, had become a site of intense, violent controversy.

School administrators and prefectural officials feared that since the Hotaka school had "acquired great fame in the area as a model school," the "spirit of dissent might spread to other schools."[64] Con-sequently, they investigated the sources of the opposition to the school and sought to settle the growing conflict. They concluded that the hostility derived not from the imperiousness of the teachers or the hardships of the commute but from the inflated salaries of the teachers and administrators at the school: "If we revise the salaries of the teachers and administrators, which is the most important ele-ment in the complaints about Hotaka school, then the situation will calm down."[65] They also suggested that the recent absorption of Chi-kuma prefecture into Nagano prefecture and the consequent demo-tion of Matsumoto from a prefectural capital to a district outpost had inaugurated a wave of popular anti-government sentiment that had now spread to Hotaka Elementary.

The district head, a former village league headman (*ōjōya*) named Gō Den—who himself had been instrumental in organizing the school in 1873 and whose inflated salary was being challenged by the other villages—proposed a somewhat different interpretation of the conflict. In a detailed memo to the prefectural office, Gō sug-gested that the protest was indeed about money.[66] He argued, how-ever, that the problem was not that of inflated salaries—an under-standable opinion, considering that his salary was one of those under scrutiny—but the people's unwillingness to contribute village moneys to a multivillage school. Pre–Fundamental Code schools, he pointed out, had been funded solely by the tuition payments of attending children, and collective village funds could be used for "Shinto shrines, festivals, and other social gatherings, as well as pilgrimages and theatrical productions." Since those funds were now invested in Hotaka Elementary, Gō argued, villages could no longer afford such things and were resentful of this fact. Gō's account is significant, for it suggests that local opposition to the new schools was informed by the assumptions that underlay pre-Meiji schooling arrangements—in particular, the notion that attendance should be voluntary, that schools should be supported by tuition, and that schooling should coexist unproblematically with long-standing religious practices and popular entertainments.

Gō's memo also pointed to another layer of motivation behind the deconsolidation movement: local elites' resentment of early Meiji reforms in the structure of local government and changes in personnel. "Among the former village officials," he wrote, "there are some disreputable ones who are always inciting the people to complain about everything and to oppose the will of the government." He suggested, in other words, that these "former officials" were causing trouble precisely because they were "former" officials—village leaders left without a job after the reorganization of village government in 1871–72. Another investigation report, written by four officials of Hotaka village, made this point explicit in addressing the grudges (*shukui*) held by the ringleaders of the secession movement against the district head, Gō Den.[67] Since Gō had been a former village group headman who had stepped into the position of district head after the reforms, many individuals blamed him for blocking their attempt to find a new position. Personal resentment against Gō, however, extended beyond frustrated professional ambition. According to the report, one ringleader held a grudge against Gō because Gō had caught him stealing rice from the village storehouse and scolded him severely in public. Another blamed Gō for a failed business venture. Another was resentful because Gō had upbraided him in public and fired him from his position as village elder for snoring during a village group meeting. Another held Gō responsible for breaking up his son's engagement. The authors of this report claimed that these spiteful rabblerousers had devised a plan to avenge past wrongs by stirring up popular sentiment against one of Gō's pet projects, Hotaka Elementary.

Whatever the motivations behind the dissent, the prefectural government was in a quandary over how to deal with the situation. Takahashi, the head teacher at the school, had entreated the prefectural government not to give in to the demands of the leaders of the deconsolidation effort. He argued that if the original contract holding the fifteen villages together around the school were broken, the people "would come to distrust the government."[68] The prefectural government, however, seemed to fear the backlash that might result if it rejected the petitions. It sought to contain the incident as much as possible and seemed concerned more about alienating the people—particularly those disenfranchised local elites who led the movement—than about preserving the initial spirit of the Fundamental Code. Takahashi himself, concluding that "there does not seem to be a resolution of this conflict," submitted his resignation in what appears to have been a last-ditch effort to defuse the conflict.[69]

In spring 1878, 98 officials and educational administrators from all fifteen villages met and hashed out a new arrangement detailing each village's financial obligations to the main school.[70] The contract granted a few of the villages permission to establish independent elementary schools and ordered the authorities in Hotaka to return those villages' contributions to the Hotaka Elementary School's endowment. A few other villages were allowed to establish branch schools; although they continued to make payments based on their original contributions to Hotaka Elementary, the interest rate was sharply reduced, and the control over the capital contributions reverted to the villages. The prefectural government, eager to find a solution that would curb further disorder, accepted the new contract.[71]

This one-sided compromise must have been disheartening for Fujimori, Takahashi, Gō, and others who had invested so much into Hotaka Elementary School only to see their bastion of enlightenment and modernity torn into pieces by what they perceived to be the narrow-minded, selfish criticisms of a few spiteful individuals. For the leaders of the deconsolidation campaign, the results were favorable: some villages were able to secede fully from Hotaka Elementary and establish their own schools; others received permission to maintain branch schools and reduced their financial obligations to the main school. For the Ministry of Education and its effort to displace preexisting schooling patterns with a singular, hegemonic conception of "school," the results were mixed. The deconsolidation campaign had followed proper administrative procedures and made use of officially sanctioned arguments and rhetoric to bolster its case—both of which should have functioned to entrench the Ministry of Education's conception of the school in local society. In the process, however, this conception expanded to accommodate alternative understandings of the nature and purpose of the local school.

Conclusion

The struggle over the fate of Hotaka Elementary School encapsulates the full range of local responses to the Fundamental Code seen in this and the preceding chapter. The school was a symbol of the active, constructive response to the Fundamental Code in Nagano and Chikuma, a direct product of the vigorous movement to implement central reforms in local society. It had been founded through cooperation between local activists and prefectural officials—a collegial group mobilized for the cause of educational reform even before the promulgation of the Fundamental Code—and was guided by the rhetoric of imperial restoration as well as civilization and enlightenment. For the school's founders, the unprecedented scale of Hotaka Elementary reflected their ambitions to contribute their energies in the service of a newly expanded public.

Their vision, however, was not shared by everyone. Their project encountered intense opposition from other segments of local society. These included not only ordinary villagers who resented having to pay for this new school and to send their children outside their own villages but also village leaders who had been sidelined. Neither group rejected the Meiji government and its educational reforms absolutely, as had participants in the first round of uprisings against the new order in other parts of the country. Instead, their goal was to modify the new regulations to serve the interests of their own villages, and their method was to work within the framework of procedures and rhetoric established by the Fundamental Code. Furthermore, the conflict was not principally between the mutually antagonistic parties of "local society" and "the state"; rather, underlying conflicts *within* local society were compounded and transformed by the expansion of the central government into new areas of local life.

The Hotaka Elementary School incident also reveals the layers of factors that informed local resistance to Meiji educational reform. Scholars who have studied the uprisings against the new order have suggested a number of reasons for the early Meiji resistance—the unfulfilled promise of the Restoration, the hostile and disruptive intent of the Meiji reforms toward premodern village culture, popular resentment against the lack of local control over the momentous and revolutionary changes being instituted by the new government, and the exploitative nature of the Meiji land tax and its destruction of the security offered by the premodern moral economy. Although the Hotaka incident can be seen as manifesting all these elements, other motivations were also at work. Some people opposed the diversion of village funds away from popular entertainments and cultural practices that had previously been central to village life. Many village elites were resentful of losing their jobs and wanted a separate school in their own village in order to create new leadership opportunities for themselves. Still others held personal grudges toward the teachers and administrators of Hotaka Elementary and sought to avenge past wrongs by destroying the school. These motivations were not, of course, mutually exclusive, and occupational or personal concerns frequently informed more abstract, principled statements of opposition. Finally, much of the discontent focused on the school itself. Some people did not want their children to commute outside their villages. Others were intimidated by the harsh regulations of the Hotaka school and the attitudes of its instructors and administrators. Many resented their lack of input into the operation of the school. Many of the objectives of the deconsolidation campaign—shorter commutes, less rigid attendance policies, more village-level control over the school, funding through voluntary contributions rather than mandatory levies—were clearly shaped by pre-existing schooling patterns and assumptions. These assumptions continued to influence both local practice and central policy over the next decade, as the educational system settled fitfully into the form it would hold until the end of the Pacific War.

Negotiating "School"
in Mid-Meiji Japan, 1876–1890

In late August 1876, Aoki Teiichirō, a *torishimari* based in the former castle town of Iida, learned that Chikuma prefecture no longer existed. As part of the Meiji government's decision to reduce the number of prefectures from 72 to 46, Chikuma had been amalgamated into Nagano prefecture, and the prefectural office in Matsumoto relegated to the status of a branch office of the prefectural government in the capital city of Nagano. Aoki's thoughts immediately turned to the educational implications of this development. He and three other *torishimari* in his middle-school district quickly produced a list of queries for the prefectural office in Nagano: Do the old prefectural directives still apply? Is Nagano's stance on school deconsolidation different from that of Chikuma? What will become of our proposals that were being discussed by the prefectural office in Chikuma? Should we change the prefectural name on school signboards from "Chikuma" to "Nagano"? Once again, a decision by the central government sent local authorities scurrying to figure out how to carry out their goals within new legal and geographic parameters. Aoki expressed a bit of exasperation at this latest turn of events. In a letter he and his colleagues addressed to a group of *torishimari* in a neighboring district, he wrote of his feelings of disappointment, if not disillusionment. "Oh, these times of change!" he exclaimed. "All of our toils have, in an instant, been rendered for naught. It is deeply regrettable!"[1] His sentiments appear to have been common: other *torishimari* reported a precipitous rise in "antipathy toward the new schools" after the amalgamation of the two prefectures,[2] and resentment over this development was later cited as a factor in the Hotaka Elementary School incident.

From the perspective of the central government, the reduction in the number of prefectures was merely one of many steps in the ongoing restructuring of local administration. For local officials and activists, however, such decisions had major consequences. As they had the abolition of the *gōkō* four years earlier, many local activists saw the amalgamation of the two prefectures as nullifying their efforts. The decision tested their commitment to the new order. After the closing of the *gōkō*, most activists quickly reconciled themselves to the new policy, since they perceived that their own interests and ambitions were served by the Meiji government's educational goals. And despite opposition from other segments within local society, they worked vigorously to implement the Fundamental Code.

By the late 1870s, however, the context was substantially different. The structure and orientation of local leadership had changed considerably: the boundaries between different leadership functions had become clearer, and local personnel—teachers, in particular—had begun to specialize and develop an identity as professionals. The political environment had also changed: many local elites who had previously been mobilized for the project of state formation were beginning to reorganize in opposition to the Meiji government. The central government, too, was undergoing significant transformations; in the area of education, changes in attitude and personnel within the Ministry of Education would soon have a major impact on local schools. Many ordinary people, meanwhile, remained either skeptical or indifferent toward the new system. Despite the flurry of activity during the preceding years, pre-Meiji patterns of school attendance persisted, for example, and would continue to do so for another decade and a half. This chapter explores these developments and examines the changing responses of local society toward education and its continued influence on central policy during this period of consolidation.

Revising the Fundamental
Code: Compromise in the Late 1870s

The late 1870s witnessed a reconceptualization of the administrative relationship between central and local government. Prompted in large part by the local response to earlier reforms, this process led to major revisions of several key policies inaugurated earlier in the decade. This development was felt first in the area of political administration. Many Meiji leaders who had previously sought to centralize the government and uproot premodern patterns of local autonomy began, in the mid-1870s, to support a limited redistribution of power to local government. After the Restoration, Kido Takayoshi, for example, had emphasized Japan's need for a highly centralized political system. Now he argued that a decentralized form of government, complete with elected assemblies at the prefectural, district, and village levels, was necessary to integrate local society into the modern state.[3] Similarly, Ōkubo Toshimichi concluded that the Meiji government's centralizing policies were a major cause of the widespread agrarian unrest and local opposition to the new government. By the mid-1870s, he had come to believe that local assemblies and a degree of local autonomy in certain administrative matters might curb opposition to the government and help foster a sense of allegiance and identification with the Meiji state.[4] Inoue Kaoru, another architect of early Meiji centralizing policies, echoed this sentiment in a letter to Ōkubo: having completed the "great reforms" of the early 1870s, he argued, "some of the authority of the center can be given to local areas so that a gulf will not emerge between the government and the people."[5] Of course, these leaders were motivated by the desire to consolidate the authority of the central government and to integrate local society more fully into the life of the nation. Nonetheless, their shift in attitude can be seen as a retreat, one informed by local resistance to the Meiji government's centralizing policies.[6]

This Meiji government affirmed this stance by promulgating the "Three New Laws" in July 1878. In addition to providing for prefectural assemblies, the Three New Laws reformed the structure of local administration. Most notably, they abolished the large district/small district system, which tended to ignore customary patterns of local organization. In Ōkubo's opinion, these districts were "not favorable to popular feeling," and their elimination would quell popular dissent.[7] In the place of the district system, the laws established the district (*gun*) as the larger subprefectural administrative unit and restored the village (*mura*) as the smaller administrative unit of local society. In fact, since localities had often ignored the earlier territorial arrangements, these laws in some ways simply recognized existing realities.[8]

A similar shift was under way in the realm of educational policy. Criticism of the Fundamental Code had begun immediately following its promulgation. The first critiques came from Kido Takayoshi and other members of the Iwakura Mission; while in the United States, they grew less convinced that extreme "civilization and enlightenment" policies were appropriate for Japan.[9] Over the next few years, the Ministry of Education was flooded with questions and complaints from local authorities struggling to adapt the Fundamental Code's rigid guidelines to local circumstances. In response, a number of key figures in the Meiji government began to reconsider their earlier stance on centralized schooling. Ōki Takatō, initially one of the most important supporters of the Fundamental Code, remarked in 1873: "There are hundreds of thousands of differences among the Japanese people, yet we are trying to follow fixed rules for primary schools—some of which are excessive, and others insufficient." "I now realize," he stated, "that the Fundamental Code was wrong. Primary schools must follow convenient and appropriate rules."[10] A similar critique was leveled by Nishimura Shigeki, a renowned expert on Western Learning who, by the mid-1870s, had begun to emphasize the importance of Confucian moral training in public schools. Nishimura criticized the inflexibility of the Fundamental Code, arguing that each community should be allowed to adjust the curriculum and schedule of its school to fit local needs. He even cited pre-Meiji commoner schools as a model and questioned the decision to abolish old schooling arrangements.[11]

The head of the Ministry of Education, Tanaka Fujimarō, shared these concerns. His views were influenced, in part, by local opposition to the Fundamental Code. Particularly troubling to him was the fact that, after an initial rise during the first few years after 1872, enrollment rates had begun to level off in many parts of the country; in a few areas—including Nagano and Chikuma—enrollment had actually declined from 1876 to 1878. Upon observing such developments, Tanaka commented: "The organization of local elementary schools in strict conformity to a fixed system . . . has resulted in serious objections to the plan."[12] To soften such opposition, he argued that "the practical operations of education should be conducted in accordance with experience and carefully adjusted to the exigencies of different localities."[13] For example, he praised the adjustments made in the schoolyear in some areas "so as not to interfere with the occupational pursuits of people in rural areas."[14] Tanaka argued that the content of primary education should be allowed to vary, with different schools using different textbooks "according to the conditions of the people."[15] Before embarking on a revision of the Fundamental Code, he dispatched ministry officials throughout the country to investigate local conditions, so that the new educational policies would be based on the actual needs and circumstances of the people.[16]

This educational vision was embodied in the Kyōikurei, or Educational Ordinance, of 1879. Like the Three New Laws, the Educational Ordinance took into consideration many of the complaints raised against the reforms of the early 1870s. For example, among the major objections to the Fundamental Code were that attendance requirements interfered with agrarian labor patterns—specifically, the contribution of children to the household labor force; that the curriculum laid out in the Fundamental Code was overly complex and irrelevant; and that school districts did not correspond to pre-existing patterns of local organization. In response, the Educational Ordinance shortened the period of compulsory attendance from four years to sixteen months, reduced the number of required subjects and allowed localities to adapt subject matter to practical needs, and abandoned the "school district" system and restored the village as the basic unit of local educational life. In contrast to the Fundamental Code's categorical opposition to pre-existing schooling arrangements, the Educational Ordinance implicitly sanctioned them by allowing a community not to establish a new elementary school if it already had a private elementary school. Finally, the Educational Ordinance provided for the creation of locally elected school boards (*gakumu iinkai*), which gave residents more control over their school.

On all these counts, the Educational Ordinance represented a significant concession to local dissent on the part of the central government. As we shall see, some of this opposition arose from the Popular Rights Movement. Among the dissenting voices, however, were village leaders and ordinary people who demanded a school that was more adaptable to local conditions and more consistent with pre-Meiji schooling patterns. Tanaka and his supporters, of course, did not see the Educational Ordinance as a compromise with the demands of unenlightened local people. Just as Kido's conversion to the cause of limited local autonomy was informed partly by his study of developments in the West, so Tanaka and other likeminded educators who advocated a degree of local independence in education often based their views on what they perceived to be the most progressive Western theories. As Michael Lewis points out, what attracted reformers to the concept of "local autonomy" was its newness; it was a "bright and shiny import, forward-looking and modern."[17] Indeed, Tanaka's views were deeply shaped by his observation of the decentralized school system he had discovered in America when he toured the country in 1876. On the other hand, there were many Western models; the fact that the American model made so much sense to Tanaka was due in large part to the unfavorable local response to the radical centralization imposed by the Fundamental Code. In this sense, local opposition contributed significantly to this major shift in central government policy at the end of the 1870s.

According to the prefectural inspectors who investigated local schooling in the aftermath of the Educational Ordinance, a large segment of local society apparently did, in fact, view this policy shift as a surrender by the central government. For those prefectural officials and local activists who had invested so much in the effort to implement the Fundamental Code and rid local society of its backward, narrow-minded schooling practices, this concession to popular opposition was lamentable. In Nagano, for example, prefectural inspectors reported dire results. A report from an inspector in the Chiisagata district is typical. As a result of the Educational Ordinance, he argued, "People now have the misconception that education is something to be left up to each individual's convenience. Consequently, not only do they neglect attendance, but they even complain about the schools. If we do not change the situation, we will not be able to halt this deterioration."[18] An inspector in the Saku district commented on the confusion caused by the ordinance, noting with regret that "each area uses whatever teaching methods it sees fit."[19] An inspector in the Chikuma district remarked that the ordinance had incited "groundless rumors" among the people and that many were using these rumors "as an excuse not to pay the school fees."[20] These rumors may have been similar to those uncovered by an inspector in the Azumi district, who reported that the Educational Ordinance had "led some people to say that we should abolish public schools in order for private schools to flourish."[21] An editorial in a Nagano newspaper described the situation in vivid, tragic terms, using the physical condition of a local school as a metaphor: "The windows and walls [of the schools] are cracked, allowing the wind and rain to leak in. The school flags are torn and no longer flutter in the breeze. Now the children simply babysit and sing noh songs."[22]

Educational Freedom, Local Autonomy, and the Popular Rights Movement

Not everyone concurred with this negative assessment of the impact of the Educational Ordinance upon local schooling, even among this group of inspectors dispatched by the Nagano prefectural government. One inspector in the Chikuma district, for example, commended the ordinance for "taking into consideration local realities" and "ameliorating the inconveniences caused by standardization."[23] In fact, although some viewed destandardization as a step backward, an inspector in Chiisagata interpreted it as a sign of "the progress of local autonomy."[24] Whereas some lamented that the softening of regulations on compulsory schooling had led to a decline in attendance, an inspector from Ina district praised the ordinance for ending the "attendance-in-name-only" phenomenon—that is, children enrolled in the schools who rarely if ever attended.[25] Finally, although most officials felt that the ordinance had resulted in a decline in school endowments and a deterioration in school facilities, the Ina inspector remarked that "expenses have been pared down to what is appropriate," and as a result, "The outside [of the school] is not much to look at, but the heart [of the school] offers hope for the future."[26]

These divergent assessments of the consequences of the Educational Ordinance did not result primarily from actual variations among the districts of Nagano prefecture. Even if localities responded to the Educational Ordinance in different ways, it is unlikely that dramatic differences would have been visible within a few months of the ordinance's promulgation. Rather, the variations in the assessments reflect a rift within the educational leadership of Nagano prefecture. On one side were leaders who continued to hold to the ideal of standardization and believed that this goal could best be achieved through the intervention of enlightened elites into the affairs of each community. These ideals had been embodied in the Fundamental Code and had informed the initial movement to implement it in Nagano and Chikuma. On the other side was a group who argued that each community must be allowed the freedom to discover the value of schooling on its own and to adapt its school to local conditions. As might be expected, prefectural officials tended to favor centralization. And although the community perspective could be found among officials at the district level, it was most common among teachers or local activists and intellectuals who did not hold (or who no longer held) an official position. This was precisely the social milieu that provided the local leadership for the Popular Rights Movement in Nagano prefecture. Furthermore, the concepts of educational freedom and local autonomy were shaped by popular rights ideology—and vice versa.

Educational issues were central to the Popular Rights Movement from its inception. In the mid-1870s, Itagaki Taisuke, Ueki Emori, Nakae Chōmin, and other key figures in the movement explicitly addressed the relationship between education and popular rights. Itagaki emphasized the importance of education in inculcating a spirit of independence within each individual.[27] Ueki and Nakae saw education itself as a natural right and chastised parents who, by keeping their children at home, violated that right.[28] Like Tokugawa-era ideologues and local elites, leaders of the Popular Rights Movement assumed the inseparability of politics and education. But to these advocates of popular rights, education was not simply a tool in the repertoire of governance. It was a matter of political debate, a means of cultivating a new political subject, and an organizing principle for an oppositional political movement. Accordingly, they criticized the Ministry of Education's repeated attempts to separate education and politics—oppositional politics, at least—into two distinct realms of activity.

At the local level, the Popular Rights Movement overlapped with dissenting voices on education, and the two mutually influenced each other. One of the first stages in the development of this relationship can be seen in a shift in attitude among local educational leaders toward both the Fundamental Code and their own role in the new educational system. Early evidence of this change can be seen in two mid-1870s petitions by one of the many educational assemblies that sprang up in Nagano prefecture after the promulgation of the Fundamental Code. In 1874, this group of teachers and educational officials petitioned the prefectural government for permission to form a group to talk about education. Like most early assemblies, this one was intended as a forum for discussing the new educational policies to better equip local educational leaders to implement those policies in a consistent fashion. This petition began: "It goes without saying that the teacher should carry out school rules in conformity with [the Ministry of Education's] educational regulations" and proceeded to justify the assembly in terms of ensuring local conformity to central guidelines.[29] Only one year later, however, the rationale for this particular assembly had changed. The 1875 petition explained, "Our land of Shinshū [Nagano] is nestled among the mountains, and many areas are isolated from important roads. Consequently, areas differ from one another in many respects, from popular sentiments and morals to standards of living to landscape to population density." "Therefore," the report continued, "it is difficult at present to make education uniform."[30] This group of educators and local officials concluded that the purpose of the assembly should not be to standardize local schooling but to examine the conditions in each locality and discuss how to adapt central regulations to fit local needs. Whereas the first petition illustrates the tendency among local educational leaders in Nagano and Chikuma to identify themselves eagerly with the center and to view their role in terms of bringing the center to the locality, the second reveals an inclination to identify with the locality and, from that position, to evaluate central policies critically.

During the second half of the decade, this emphasis on local adaptation of central policies developed into a more pointed critique of the Fundamental Code. Within this critique was the now-familiar call for flexibility in the implementation of central regulations; as one newspaper editorial put it, "What is appropriate for the people of Matsumoto is not necessarily appropriate for the people of Onimusato village [an isolated hamlet in the Chikuma district]."[31] Influenced by the new pedagogical doctrine of "developmentalism" and its emphasis on the individual learning needs of the child, these critics advocated an education oriented toward the actual lives of children.[32] One local commentator mocked the Fundamental Code for "trying to turn all the children of the state into scholars." The school subjects outlined by the Ministry's 1872 plan were "noble-sounding," he argued, but the vast majority of children did not stay in school long enough to learn them. As a result, the practical value of education was completely lost, and many children "end up unable to write their address or even their own name."[33] Because the content was so irrelevant to the daily lives of ordinary people, other commentators argued, children did not attend of their own volition; consequently, the state's only recourse was to encourage attendance through exhortation or intimidation. One editorial pointed out that if a child attends school simply because of the fear of punishment from parents or authorities, then "the child's heart is merely a spectator" in the learning process. Instead of forcing children to go to school and receive a uniform education, the writer argued, parents and teachers "should foster an independent learning spirit" in children, so that they understand the value of learning and attend school willingly.[34]

These criticisms of the Fundamental Code did not, in the late 1870s, imply a radical critique of the central government. Indeed, they were close to the views of Tanaka Fujimarō and other reformist officials within the Ministry of Education. Among regional circles of educators and activists, however, these opinions often carried political overtones. For example, many of the discussions among educators and activists—or, between educators and activists on one hand and prefectural authorities on the other—were framed in terms of a debate between "freedom" (*jiyū*) and "intervention" (*kanshō*). In education, "freedom" was a code word for a laissez-faire approach by the government toward schooling, on the grounds that education could have a transformative effect only if it was undertaken at the initiative of the individual and the community. "Intervention," in contrast, echoed the sentiment behind the early movement to implement the Fundamental Code. Since schooling was essential to the strength and prosperity of the nation, interventionists (*kanshō shugisha*) believed, it was too important to be left up to families and communities; consequently, they argued that the government needed to take an active role in bringing children into the schools and ensuring that all children received a certain level of schooling. The distinction between these two positions was not as clear-cut as it might seem, however. Popular rights advocate Nakae Chōmin, for example, urged the government to intervene in popular schooling—specifically, to use its coercive powers to make schooling compulsory—precisely because he believed that education was a natural right of the individual. On the other hand, he stated, "We should not construe this as meaning that the state has a right or duty to control the rules regulating the organization of educational practices and teaching materials."[35] Local activists in Nagano could be found on either side of this debate.

The language of "freedom" versus "intervention" was, of course, easily transferable to the realm of oppositional political movements. Popular rights advocates employed a similar rhetoric to advocate the political freedom of the individual against the intervention of the state, and activists in Nagano applied it to a different, but related, political cause: local autonomy.[36] Local autonomy, they argued, was a precondition for individual freedom: self-government (*jichi*) at the local level, autonomous from central government intervention, was essential for the cultivation of free, independent, self-reliant individuals. The cause of local autonomy was a natural fit for local educational activists who saw their own role not in terms of implementing policies created by the center but in terms of adjusting those policies to fit local circumstances. These three issues—educational freedom, popular rights, and local autonomy—informed one another in various ways. Educational debates were infused with the language of popular rights; the Popular Rights Movement fed off burgeoning cries for local autonomy; the concept of local autonomy tapped into an earlier movement among teachers that advocated an educational policy adaptable to local needs and conditions. Occasionally, all three issues came together in one voice, as in an essay by an activist in Nagano: "It is our first priority in education . . . to transform the government's 'intervention' into 'delegation,' and its oppression into freedom." This delegation of authority to the locality, the writer argued, "will provide both the foundation and the preparation for the future opening of the national assembly."[37]

Often implicit in the call for freedom from state intervention was a desire among teachers for greater professional autonomy. Such a concept would have been quite foreign only a few years earlier: not only did most late Tokugawa–era teachers not recognize a clear distinction between teaching and other forms of local leadership, but the initial movement to implement the Fundamental Code assumed a collegial interaction among officials, teachers, and educational administrators in pursuit of a common goal. By the late 1870s, however, teachers had begun to distinguish themselves clearly from political officials. As one educator commented in an editorial, "It is wrong to think of the teacher as an official." The teacher is not an employee of the state, he continued; rather, he "establishes a public elementary school in cooperation with the local people" and "conducts education based on a contract with the children in his school."[38] Whereas in the first few years of the Fundamental Code many teachers had requested the presence of district or prefectural authorities at local schools to help enforce the new regulations and to impress on the locals the importance of schooling, by the second half of the 1870s teachers complained that the presence of officials at examinations and other occasions interfered with the normal operation of the school.[39] Reflecting this newfound sense of professional identity, prominent educators in the Matsumoto area created two journals devoted to education; one of these, *Gekkei shinshi*, had a run of over two years (1879–81), and more than a hundred issues appeared.[40]

This shift in the attitudes of teachers was due, in part, to the changing demographic makeup and educational experiences of teachers. In the first two years of the Fundamental Code, roughly half of all elementary school teachers (and nearly two-thirds of those of commoner background) in Nagano prefecture were over 40, and their assumptions about curriculum and pedagogy were deeply rooted in pre-Meiji schooling practices.[41] By 1877, however, 90 percent of all teachers were under 40, and more than half were under 25; furthermore, almost all had graduated from the prefectural normal school.[42] The image of the "teacher" had changed rather dramatically in only a few years. These new teachers had not been part of the *gōkō* experiment or the initial movement to implement the Fundamental Code, both of which had involved close interaction among teachers, local activists, and district and prefectural authorities. And even though these new teachers had received their early education at pre-Meiji schools, they were shaped more deeply by new assumptions about teaching—one of which was that teaching was a specialized endeavor, distinct from other areas of knowledge and other forms of leadership activity. As Mark Lincicome points out, this new sense of professionalism was reinforced by pedagogical theories that stressed not broad erudition but a mastery of specialized techniques—a novel form of expertise that could be possessed only by those who had received proper training.[43]

It is ironic, of course, that these new teachers evoked consternation among the prefectural and central authorities. In the first few years of the Fundamental Code, the new schools were staffed primarily by former teachers and other local literati who did not, for the most part, fully accept the government's educational vision. The Ministry of Education, as well as enlightened officials within the prefectural government, eagerly awaited the day when such scoundrels were replaced by teachers trained in normal schools according to the guidelines of the Fundamental Code and Tokyo Normal School. That day would mark the definitive break from Tokugawa-era schooling practices and alternative educational visions, thus eliminating a potential source of opposition to the new educational system. However, the training of a new cohort of teachers led to a new, perhaps equally troubling, source of opposition. Not only did these new teachers assert their professional autonomy from the state, but they proved a receptive audience for political movements that claimed other forms of autonomy from government intervention, either on the basis of individual liberty or localism.

The sites for the exchange of new ideas about education and politics were the hundreds of associations and study groups that sprang up in Nagano prefecture in the second half of the 1870s. These organizations drew upon patterns commonly found in pre-Meiji educational arrangements: some consisted of a few local elites studying under the tutelage of a regionally prominent intellectual; others were closer to social gatherings of local literati over poetry and sake. Another model for these political associations were the early Meiji educational assemblies, which had been formed by local educators, educational officials, and activists for the purpose of addressing problems encountered in implementing educational reform within their communities. These assemblies created an opportunity for interaction and discussion among local leaders and intellectuals; this, in turn, often led to the formation of new groups devoted to issues other than education, such as local economic development, famine relief, and, increasingly, politics.[44] Educational assemblies also provided a model for structured debate on issues of public concern. Whereas the initial assemblies were rather informal, by 1875 most groups had established detailed procedural rules. There were extensive guidelines, for example, on seating arrangements, the order of the speakers, the time allotted each speaker, procedures for rebuttal, and acceptable methods of argumentation.[45]

Within a few years, these models for structured debate on public issues among local elites were being applied to the realm of politics. Some assemblies, in turn, developed into formal political organizations. Most prominent among these was the Shōkyōsha, or the Society for Encouragement and Rectification. The Shōkyōsha took shape as a "political speech society" (*enzetsukai*) in 1877, attracting a handful of local intellectuals from in and around the city of Matsumoto. It was founded by Matsuzawa Kyūsaku, a young man from a wealthy soy sauce–brewing family in the village of Hotaka (the site of the school secession controversy discussed in the preceding chapter). At the time he founded the Shōkyōsha, he was managing a newspaper in Matsumoto—a job he had inherited from a former Tosa samurai who had been involved with Itagaki Taisuke and his popular rights organization, the Risshisha.[46]

The Shōkyōsha announced its founding in the main Matsumoto newspaper and invited other likeminded individuals to attend: "We hereby announce the opening of our speech assembly, which will be held every Saturday evening on the balcony of the silk-spinning factory at number 13, Minami-Fukashi ward. We will meet for the purpose of learning (*gakumon*) and study (*kenkyū*)."[47] Although this public announcement made no explicit mention of politics, the group's internal manifesto was more specific about its goals: it would "discuss issues over tea," seeking ultimately to "expand popular rights" and to "unite the people of Nagano prefecture in support of a national assembly."[48] In order to attain these goals, many of the Shōkyōsha's founding members traveled around the prefecture, delivering speeches and using local connections to form ad hoc political study groups. Others founded newspapers, many of which were short-lived but helped to publicize the Shōkyōsha's message and to draw other local intellectuals into the movement. Within a few months of the group's founding, its membership had risen from fifteen to over a thousand. The Shōkyōsha's status among other regionally based political societies in Japan had risen considerably, and its leaders had formed close ties with the leaders of other prominent popular rights organizations.[49]

From its inception, teachers formed the core of this popular rights organization. Nine of its fourteen founding members were employed as teachers in and around Matsumoto, most of them connected with Kaichi Elementary School, which also served as a branch of the Nagano Prefectural Normal School. In Matsuzawa's words, the Shō-kyōsha "burst forth from the trees around the normal school."[50] Although the number of teachers relative to the total membership declined as the organization grew, teachers continued to provide the core of the Shōkyōsha: at its height in 1878–79, teachers and educational administrators accounted for 219 of the group's 1,069 members.[51] Furthermore, Shōkyōsha activists often used schools as the sites for both its regular meetings and the ad hoc study sessions and political speeches they organized as they traveled throughout the prefecture. In doing so, they targeted teachers, local intellectuals, and students as potential supporters.[52]

One of the key vehicles through which the Shōkyōsha spread its message was the private school. The most prominent of these was opened by Ina-district native Takei Yōsetsu, a longtime educator in Shinano who had participated in each stage of educational reform over the previous decades. Before the Meiji Restoration, he had operated a nativist-oriented private school and trained many of the nativist ideologues in southern and central Shinano. In the early Meiji, he was hired as the head instructor of a *gōkō* in the Kiso valley. Then, after the promulgation of the Fundamental Code, he was invited by a teacher and future Shōkyōsha member in Toyoshina village (just west of Matsumoto) to teach at a private school there called the Yūkō gijuku, or Academy for Further Prosperity.[53] Under Takei's leadership, the school became a training ground for future Shōkyōsha members. After the establishment of the Shōkyōsha in 1877, members circulated in and out of the Yūkō gijuku as guest teachers, and the school itself was used as a forum for the exchange of ideas among popular rights activists. The school's regular curriculum, however, did not revolve around popular rights ideology. In fact, Takei revised the curriculum in 1878 so that it resembled that of his pre-Meiji private school.[54] Students learned poetry and history from nativist texts and also learned to write in classical Chinese (*kanbun*). His courses on composition and ethics were based on Confucian texts, including the Four Books and the Five Classics. Takei's pedagogy also conformed to an earlier model, employing conventional methods like lectures (*kōgi*) and recitation (*sodoku*)—although his new school now included "speech" (*enzetsu*) and "debate" (*tōron*) among its methods of learning. In embracing a curriculum and pedagogical approach rooted in pre-Meiji schooling practices, the Yūkō gijuku presented a double challenge to the Meiji government: not only did it serve as a vehicle for political activism, but it embodied an oppositional vision of "school."

Another private school closely associated with the Shōkyōsha was an academy that shared its name, the Shōkyōsha gijuku. This school was founded as the government was growing increasingly intolerant of regional popular rights organizations like the Shōkyōsha. Fearing a crackdown on the Shōkyōsha's political activities, members met in April 1880 to discuss alternative strategies to continue pressing for the organization's goals without attracting undue attention from government authorities.[55] They decided to establish the Shōkyōsha gijuku to focus on the educational goals of the movement and leave the political activities to the Shōkyōsha itself. This school was somewhat different from the Yūkō gijuku. Although the school's mission statement included the goal of "expanding popular rights," its political rhetoric was significantly toned down. Furthermore, the school was oriented more toward vocational training than toward the political instruction of elite literati and intellectuals. The schedule, for example, was arranged so as to encourage the attendance of children and young adults whose work prevented them from attending ordinary elementary schools. The curriculum, although it included courses in oration and government, focused more heavily on reading, industrial arts, agricultural studies, morality, law, and other subjects that served the practical needs of the individual in his occupational and social life. Employing the rhetoric of "educational freedom," the founders sought to create a school "in accordance with local conditions and popular feelings and customs," one that would be "appropriate to the occupations of the local people."[56]

The Shōkyōsha gijuku and the Yūkō gijuku were only two of dozens of politically oriented private schools that sprang up throughout the country during the second half of the 1870s.[57] Their emergence owed much to new kinds of political activism among local elites—not all of it on behalf of the Popular Rights Movement. As Motoyama Yukihiko has shown, some private schools, like the Seiseikō

Academy in Kumamoto prefecture, were established in the late 1870s to counter popular rights ideology. The Seiseikō, for example, viewed its purposes as cultivating virtue and preparing students for service to the state; it espoused a kind of statist nationalism that stood in direct contrast to the ideological orientation of private schools associated with the Popular Rights Movement.[58] Regardless of their political orientation, however, all these private schools intentionally positioned themselves outside the public school system and the authority of the Ministry of Education. This was true even of the Seiseikō, whose teachings were consistent with the political and ideological synthesis that eventually took shape in late Meiji Japan. To highlight their position external to the new educational system, the Shōkyōsha gijuku and the Yūkō gijuku intentionally adopted the status of an "irregular school" (*hensoku gakkō*), the title given to all private schools that did not conform to the Ministry of Education's guidelines (and thus could not substitute for public middle schools). Indeed, these schools seemed to celebrate this designation and, in the case of the Yūkō gijuku, made conspicuous efforts to retain it. Beginning in 1872, the Meiji government had attempted to stigmatize irregular schools as part of its effort to espouse a new, abstract conception of school and to marginalize pre-Meiji schooling practices; several years later, schools were now embracing this status in order to make a political statement against the new educational system, based on a variety of political ideologies that ranged from natural rights theory to rightist nationalism.

The critique of the new school system based on an ideology of popular rights and local autonomy shared several strands with earlier forms of popular opposition to the Fundamental Code. Advocates of local autonomy in the late 1870s, for example, had something in common with earlier protesters who had destroyed schools as a statement of opposition to the principle of local funding and centralized control embodied in the Fundamental Code. Parents who sent their children to illegal private schools in the years immediately following their abolition in 1872 might have celebrated those defiant teachers who opened irregular schools in the late 1870s. Families who resented the rigid, imposing, impractical nature of the new schools would likely have welcomed the call for "educational freedom" articulated by the educational wing of the Popular Rights Movement. Based on these similarities, one might conclude, as Irokawa Daikichi and Roger Bowen tend to do, that such various forms of resistance were simply different manifestations of a united voice of popular opposition.[59]

We must keep in mind, however, that the political associations formed in Nagano in the late 1870s were, in terms of their social makeup, elitist; more than half the members were former samurai, and many had held (or continued to hold) some position of local leadership—district chiefs, *torishimari, sewayaku,* teachers, and, after 1878, district or prefectural assemblymen.[60] Most of the rest came from literate, and usually wealthy, families, the kind who would have felt at home discussing Chinese poetry. Even when their rhetoric resonated with issues of popular concern, their understanding of those issues was often quite different from that of most people, for whom "educational freedom" meant that they did not have to attend school if they did not want to. And these elites often found themselves in opposition to ordinary people in conflicts over local schools. A number of the advocates of popular rights and educational freedom had earlier been named as the enemy in school deconsolidation disputes: they were the oppressive officials, pompous inspectors, and outsiders who were resented by local residents for trying to implement the new educational policies. We must not, therefore, assume a united front between—or within—these two segments of local society. There were multiple strains of local opposition to Meiji educational policies, and various local voices contributed to the common, though not unified, effort to negotiate with prefectural and central governments to enact changes in those policies.

The Consolidation of the Educational System in the 1880s

For most historians of modern Japanese education, the 1870s represent a time of possibility. The liberal strains of educational thought imported from Europe and America at this time, as well as the appropriation of those ideas by the educational wing of the Popular Rights Movement, signal to many scholars the potential in early Meiji Japan for the development of a democratic educational system—and ultimately, a democratic society. Most often, however, this era of opportunity is contrasted with the 1880s, when the possibility of a liberal, democratic educational system was supposedly stifled by an increasingly authoritarian central government. In Western-language scholarship, this narrative was first articulated by Herbert Passin, who argued that the "liberal dominance" of the 1870s gave way in the 1880s to a "conservative counterattack" that transformed the educational system along the lines of nationalism, traditional values, and aggressive centralization.[61]

Japan moved from a liberal to a conservative educational system. Morals were made the center of the curriculum, and a particular morality — *sonnō aikoku* (reverence for the Emperor and patriotism) — was established as orthodox. Textbooks were brought under direct government control. Teachers were treated as "officials," servants of the State, and they were forbidden to take part in political activities. Administration was tightly centralized and controlled by the Ministry of Education.[62]

This shift was, according to this narrative, a decisive one, and fixed the key elements of Japan's educational system until the end of the Pacific War, when the U.S. occupation forces transformed Japanese education along democratic lines. In Japanese historiography, the closing of democratic possibilities in education during the 1880s is described in tragic tones, for this closure marked the onset of *tennōsei kyōiku*, or emperor-system education, which led the Japanese people down a destructive path toward ultranationalism, militarism, and war.

A few historians have contested this narrative. By focusing on the debates among elite policymakers during and after the 1880s, Byron Marshall and Motoyama Yukihiko show that the changes in educational policy during this decade did not represent a decisive or unanimous shift within the central government.[63] Mark Lincicome, by tracing the continuing influence of developmentalist pedagogical theory after the Meiji government had supposedly weeded out all heterodoxies from the educational system during the 1880s, demonstrates the limits of government control over educational thought throughout the late Meiji and pre–World War I periods.[64] The remainder of this chapter seeks to evaluate the characterization of the 1880s as a time of inevitable, decisive consolidation in the educational system. I look at three issues that were the focus of much concern and debate in Nagano following the promulgation of the Fundamental Code: school districts, teachers, and school attendance. In each of these areas, the 1880s were certainly a time when the range of possibilities and alternatives began to narrow. As we shall see, however, this process was by no means completed by 1890. Furthermore, the dynamic was not that of an autonomous state acting unilaterally to secure its dominance but an ongoing process of negotiation between the central government and various levels of local leadership.

SCHOOL DISTRICTS AND
LOCAL ADMINISTRATION

In the narrative of "liberal dominance" and "conservative counterattack," a key turning point in the formation of the Meiji educational system was the government's decision to revise the Educational Ordinance in 1880. As noted above, the Educational Ordinance of 1879 had signified something of a retreat by the Ministry of Education from its earlier goals of centralization and standardization. Within a year, however, the influence of the officials responsible for the ordinance had been eclipsed by that of others in the central government who favored a more interventionist role in education for the Ministry of Education. One product of this shift was the Kaisei kyōikurei, or Revised Educational Ordinance.[65] By establishing moral criteria for teachers, lengthening the period of compulsory attendance (from 16 to 24 months), emphasizing the importance of moral education in the elementary school curriculum, and increasing the powers of the prefectural office in local educational administration, the Revised Educational Ordinance signified a shift away from the laissez-faire spirit of the original ordinance.

On the other hand, the revision was not a complete about-face. For instance, the period of compulsory attendance was still considerably shorter than that mandated by the Fundamental Code, and the revised ordinance kept the escape clause in the original ordinance that allowed parents to remove their children from the schools after twelve months if they could offer a valid excuse. In addition, the newly expanded powers of the prefectural government did not lead to drastic changes in local administration. Probably the most visible change at the local level was that school administrators (*gakumu iin*)—who, according to the original ordinance, were to be elected by local residents—were now appointed by the prefectural governor (in practice, elections were still held, but the prefectural office was responsible for choosing two to four administrators from a larger pool of elected candidates).[66] Although this change allowed the prefectural government to exclude well-known popular rights advocates from administrative positions, it was not a major encroachment by the state on local prerogatives in education. Furthermore, it is problematic to lump the prefectural office with the central government as an agent of centralization. Not only did prefectural governments have their own agendas, but the handful of officials in each prefectural office responsible for educational administration were not guided strictly by the goal of consolidating the power of the central government. In Nagano, some of them were normal school graduates and viewed themselves as professional educators; others had a long history of involvement in matters relating to education. This was true at the district level as well, where the recently created position of secretary of educational affairs (*gakumu tantō gun shoki*) was dominated by former *torishimari* and graduates of the prefectural normal school.[67] In other words, those officials often grouped unproblematically within the category of "the state" and viewed as agents of the center were, in fact, influenced by both local interests and professional concerns.

Finally, from the perspective of local educational administration, the Revised Educational Ordinance is significant for what it did *not* change. Namely, it retained the original ordinance's affirmation of the village as the unit of local educational organization.[68] The Educational Ordinance's provision for districts that conformed to pre-Meiji village boundaries was intended to allow communities to return to "natural" patterns of educational organization, but the transition was not always smooth. Like all changes in local administrative structure, this reorganization gave rise to a new round of local controversies, as village leaders in some areas worked to adjust local schooling arrangements to fit new financial and geographic circumstances. In fact, as they had after the promulgation of the Fundamental Code, many local leaders petitioned the prefectural government to permit some flexibility in the application of the central guidelines on school districts. On being flooded with such petitions, the prefectural government in Nagano followed a familiar pattern and wrote to the Ministry of Education to inform central officials of the various problems caused by this new policy.[69] The central government reassured the prefectural office that it was acceptable for a district to have more than one elementary school or for funding arrangements to vary from school to school. Several months later, the Council of State issued a formal directive to this effect, which the prefectural office in Nagano immediately forwarded to district heads.[70] The dynamics of educational policymaking continued to follow the early Meiji pattern: when confronted by a new set of legal parameters, local authorities reported problems in implementation to the central government—which, in turn, usually accommodated such concerns by revising its initial policies.

During the early 1880s, the prefectural and district governments in Nagano continued to urge village authorities to make school districts conform to village boundaries, but with only limited success: in 1884, the prefectural office reported to the Ministry of Education that nearly half the over 800 school districts in Nagano did not conform to village boundaries (many instead were centered on the pre-Meiji village leagues that had often served as the basis for school districts in the Fundamental Code era).[71] More troubling for prefectural officials and prominent educators, however, was the existence of unusually small school districts without the financial base necessary to support a school with up-to-date facilities and curricula. Although prefectural and district officials were able to consolidate a number of schools during these years, many communities responded as they had done in the 1870s—by petitioning to keep the old schools open as branch schools (now referred to as *hashutsujo*), which generally offered a more limited curriculum. The problem of school consolidation was by no means limited to Nagano. An inspector in Ishikawa prefecture reported to the Ministry of Education in 1883 that whenever the prefectural government tried to create larger, consolidated school districts, the boundaries often violated conventional boundaries regulating fishing rights or the use of mountain land, resulting in a great deal of friction both among villages and between villages and the prefectural government.[72] An official in Nagasaki prefecture pointed in 1882 to the sociocultural divisions in local society: "Even if we try to consolidate several towns or villages, customs are different, and thus there are many cases where they just do not get along."[73] This pessimistic outlook was shared by an inspector from Hiroshima prefecture: "People like to do things within their old localities and hate sharing school fees [with other villages]; they also like to fight one another. Consequently, because the popular spirit of cooperation and unification is poor, it is difficult to change [the school districts] suddenly."[74]

The mid-1880s witnessed a renewed emphasis on school consolidation throughout the country. This effort was carried out not in the interests of centralization or administrative rationalization but as a response to the widespread recession that followed the deflationary policies of the Meiji government and its finance minister, Matsukata Masayoshi. In 1884, after three years of recession had severely constrained the ability of local governments to perform their assigned tasks, the Meiji government decided to restructure village-level administration as a means of reducing the cost of local government. Specifically, it required three or four individual village offices to form a Joint Office of Village Chiefs (*rengō kochō yakuba*). Although the law did not cover educational administration, prefectural and district officials in many parts of the country perceived the new policy as an opportunity to reduce educational costs by consolidating school districts as well.

In Nagano, the initiative behind this effort to consolidate school districts came from the district offices rather than the prefectural government. In early 1885, Nagano's sixteen district chiefs met to discuss the redrawing of school districts. Their discussions produced a proposal for uniform funding levels for all elementary schools, with the intent of forcing small schools to consolidate with other schools in order to meet these minimum standards.[75] Not all the district chiefs agreed with this proposal. One opposed the rigidity of the proposal: "Setting a uniform funding level for all schools is impossible. Each school, based on its size, should be able to establish its own method of funding."[76] Another feared the popular reaction to the forced consolidation of school districts: "Weakening the power of previous local groupings is absolutely not desirable. . . . We should leave [the school districts] as they are." "A third major revision [of the boundaries of school districts]," he worried, "will weaken the confidence of the people in the government."[77] The majority of district chiefs, however, agreed with the proposal and expressed the desire that each school district "should collect enough money so that the size of the school should not be an impediment to instruction."[78]

The prefectural government approved the proposal and worked with district offices in 1885–86 to carry out an extensive consolidation of school districts. As a result of these efforts, the number of school districts declined from 836 to only 250, and the size of most districts more than tripled. As a cost-saving measure, the consolidation was a success: total school expenses in Nagano dropped by nearly 40 percent. The prefectural office was quite proud of this accomplishment and reported its efforts in the Ministry of Education's annual report for 1885: "Even though we have faced financial difficulties in recent years, the progress of civilization has demanded greater school-related expenses each year. This pattern was difficult to maintain. Consequently, this year we carried out a major reform [of school districts], making them conform to the consolidated districts for village chiefs."[79]

Some Japanese scholars see this consolidation effort as a decisive moment in the formation of the Meiji educational system. The forced consolidation of pre-existing village communities (*sonraku kyōdōtai*), they argue, contributed to the destruction of those communities, which, in turn, allowed the central authorities to fix Japan's path toward emperor-system education.[80] One assumption behind this argument, of course, is that the preservation of such communities would have served as a bulwark against ultranationalism, an authoritarian government, and militarism. I return to this issue in the Epilogue; at this point suffice it to point out two potential problems with this argument about school district consolidation and emperor-system education. First, the impact of the 1884–86 consolidation effort on local patterns of educational organization was not as great as might be thought. Although the number of elementary school districts declined precipitously, the number of elementary schools did not. As had occurred in previous consolidation efforts, most smaller schools managed to remain open, although they were usually permitted to offer only the first three grades of what was now an eight-grade (3-3-2) elementary-school curriculum. Since schooling was compulsory only for three years, and since the vast majority of children did not proceed beyond this point, the consolidation did not transform the immediate social horizon of most families. Such was also the case with the amalgamation of villages that followed the inauguration of the "local self-government" system in 1888. As Neil Waters points out, this amalgamation often disrupted long-standing patterns of inter-village cooperation and brought dislocation and local conflict.[81] In terms of educational organization, however, the effect was not so dramatic. In fact, the number of elementary-school districts rebounded from 250 to 391 after this round of consolidations. More important, the number of schools continued to remain relatively constant; in fact, many schools that had been demoted in status from "main" to "branch school" during the 1884–86 consolidations regained main school status.[82] This is not to argue that timeless rural communities were able to survive the attacks of a centralizing state but to point out that the consolidation efforts did not immediately and fundamentally change local patterns of educational organization. Like earlier educational reforms, the various policy shifts by the central government in the 1880s did not impose a fixed, completed system on local society; rather, they created new sets of boundaries within which local leaders could maneuver and, in the process, influence subsequent revisions in central policy.

Second, linking school consolidation with the inauguration of emperor-system education tends to obscure the motives of the prefectural and district officials who carried out these consolidations. The consolidation campaigns of the 1880s occurred in the midst of other significant developments in education—for example, greater control by the Ministry of Education over textbook production and selection,[83] tighter regulations for private schools,[84] and an increasing emphasis in the primary-school curriculum on moral education.[85] It would be misleading, however, to link these developments with school consolidation as part of a grand strategy of centralization and indoctrination. The impetus for consolidation came not from the central government but from district and prefectural officials wanting to reduce the burden of educational costs on both local governments and local people. Many of these officials—particularly the professional educators who served as educational administrators in the prefectural and district offices—also pursued consolidation as a way of improving the quality of schooling in the more remote areas of the prefecture. For them, consolidation ensured closer conformity to the enlightened concept of the school manifested in central curricular regulations. Of course, as in the case of the early Meiji *torishimari*, the efforts of these officials undoubtedly served the purposes of centralization and administrative rationalization. Nonetheless, these processes were shaped in dialectical fashion by the active participation of local leaders, who had a wide range of concerns regarding schooling and local society.

TEACHERS, POLITICS,
AND PROFESSIONALIZATION

For those who view educational policy in the 1880s in terms of a fundamental break from earlier trends and an inevitable movement toward consolidation, the Meiji government's effort to regulate the ideas and activities of schoolteachers stands out as a fateful development. Faced with the burgeoning Popular Rights Movement, the Meiji government attempted in the early 1880s to segregate the educational system from oppositional politics. This attempt was, by all accounts, successful. The new constraints on the political activities of teachers did not, however, relegate them to the role, in Passin's words, of "servants of the state."[86] As we shall see, even as teachers in Nagano were increasingly excluded from the realm of oppositional politics, they continued to develop an identity as professional educators. This identity was not fully autonomous from the interests of the state, but neither was it fully encompassed by those interests. With the option of political activism closed off, teachers began to work within the new legal constraints to pursue their goals and to cooperate strategically with the political authorities as a means of influencing educational policy.

The Meiji government adopted two main tactics to curtail the political activities of teachers. The first was to prevent teachers from participating in political gatherings. A series of ordinances, the earliest of which was issued in April 1880, made this illegal; beginning in 1881, the government also forbade the use of school facilities for political meetings.[87] The second approach was to establish moral standards for teachers. This tactic began with the Revised Educational Ordinance of 1880 but became particularly evident with the announcement in 1881 of the "Guidelines for Primary-School Teachers" ("Shōgakkō kyōin kokoroe"). The "Guidelines" stressed the importance of moral character in effective teaching. If teachers do not possess a moral character, the "Guidelines" exclaimed, "How will we rouse a spirit of patriotism and reverence for the emperor? How will we beautify popular morality? How will we enrich the people, thereby increasing the stability and prosperity of the state?"[88]

Such sentiments were not particularly novel. The assumptions that teachers should serve as moral exemplars to their students and that moral inculcation in the school could foster social stability, patriotism, and national strength would have been shared by most educators at that time, either in Japan or in the West. What was significant, however, was that the Meiji government used this emphasis on moral character to purge political activists from the ranks of teachers. Since loyalty to the state was identified as a key virtue in this official definition of morality, oppositional politics could be labeled "immoral" and thus could serve as grounds for dismissal. Prefectural authorities in Nagano applied the new behavioral standards in precisely this manner. In 1883, for example, the prefecture revoked the teaching license of Kiyomizu Ruini, an elementary-school teacher in the Chiisagata district.[89] Kiyomizu, who had presented a poem to the Meiji emperor during an imperial tour of Nagano prefecture in 1878, had opened a private school that often served as a political assembly point for local youth. In the 1879 prefectural educational assembly, in the presence of prefectural officials, Kiyomizu questioned whether the prefectural governor should possess extensive powers over local schooling. The prefectural office did not make public the grounds for its decision to revoke Kiyomizu's license, but by 1883 it would have been clear to teachers in Nagano that open participation in oppositional politics would likely cost them their teaching career.

The crackdown against political activism within the teaching profession, however, came not only from political authorities but also from professional educators. In Nagano, the most significant actor in stemming the tide of political activism was the new head of the prefectural normal school in Matsumoto, Nose Sakae. Nose was decidedly not a heavy-handed bureaucrat dispatched by the government to seize control of the normal school—a breeding ground for political activists during the late 1870s and early 1880s—and make it obedient to the wishes of the state. Having learned English while stationed in Yokohama at the time of the Restoration, Nose traveled to San Francisco in 1870 at the age of nineteen, completed middle school in Oregon, and graduated with a B.S. from Pacific University in 1876.[90] Upon being named principal of the normal school in Matsumoto in 1882, he worked with great determination to disseminate the latest educational methods throughout the prefecture. He frequently brought primary-school teachers from throughout the prefecture to the normal school, gathering them around while he played the violin, conducted calisthenic exercises, and expounded on the developmentalist pedagogical theories of Johann Pestalozzi and James Johonnot.

This earnest, cosmopolitan 31-year-old also worked to curb the spread of political activism among teachers. Contributing to the educational debates played out each week in the pages of local newspapers, Nose lamented in an editorial in the *Shinano Daily News* that many students at the normal school "are learning from fashionable political speakers, fraternizing with members of political parties, and abandoning the work of schooling."[91] Indeed, from 1879 to 1882, 44 percent of all normal-school graduates were members of the Shōkyō-sha, the popular rights organization. Nose's stance against teachers' participation in political movements was based not on opposition to the political vision of the Popular Rights Movement but on his desire to cultivate professionalism among teachers in Nagano prefecture. Professionalism, in his view, required complete autonomy from the realm of politics—both from the influence of oppositional politics and from the intrusion of the government.[92] By the time Nose left Nagano prefecture in 1885 to head the normal school in Fukushima prefecture, he had successfully purged the normal school of oppositional politics—at least in the form of political organizations and popular rights ideology. This "crackdown" was initiated by a reformist educator not to protect the state from political opposition but to shield the noble calling of education from the taint of politics.

Many schoolteachers were quite willing to disavow political activism. Indeed, many teacher assemblies had begun to distance themselves from political affairs even before the prefectural authorities began enforcing this separation in the early 1880s. As early as the mid-1870s, most educational assemblies confined their agendas to education; some even expressly forbade political discussions.[93] By the late 1870s, as some assemblies began to transform themselves into political associations, others limited themselves more explicitly to education. In addition, whereas in the early and mid-1870s most educational assemblies were composed of teachers, *sewayaku*, village officials, and any other local leaders with an interest in educational reform, by the late 1870s some assemblies had confined their membership strictly to teachers. Beginning in 1879, teachers began to expand the scale of their meetings and organize themselves into district-level teacher assemblies (*gun kyōikukai*). In each of these assemblies, organizers divided the district into subsections. Within each subsection, local teachers elected one of their number to participate in a semiannual meeting. Even though the prefectural government in Nagano was still more than a year away from taking steps to forbid teachers from participating in political movements, all these teacher assemblies restricted their discussions to education; most confined themselves even more narrowly to pedagogical issues. The teacher assembly in the Upper Ina district, for example, explicitly cautioned participants: "We will not get into debates about how to change curricular regulations"—debates that, in the late 1870s and early 1880s, almost guaranteed a politically charged discussion of educational freedom and local autonomy.[94] Assemblies strove to represent themselves as professional organizations that gave teachers an opportunity to share ideas about pedagogy and to commiserate with one another about local problems.

Within a year some district-level teacher assemblies grew dissatisfied with this limited role. Instead of joining the ranks of oppositional political groups, however—in 1880 still a feasible alternative for teachers—most of these assemblies chose to involve the political authorities as a means of gaining influence over the formation of policy. The first association to take such a step was the Chiisagata district assembly. The Chiisagata assembly had been founded in 1879 as a forum for discussion of pedagogical matters; in fact, the participants initially called themselves an "instructional assembly" (*jugyō-kai*) to reflect this limited focus. As in most other district-level assemblies, participation was initially confined to local teachers.

By fall 1880, however, local officials—school administrators and village officials—outnumbered teachers three to two in the Chiisagata assembly.[95] Local historians in Nagano see this as signifying the forceful encroachment of politics upon education.[96] Indeed, it was undoubtedly in the interests of the central and prefectural governments to co-opt the activist energies of teachers by channeling them into officially recognized organizations over which the government had some supervisory power. But in this case—as in other district-level teacher assemblies that, beginning in 1880, began to incorporate political officials into their meetings—the political authorities did not initiate the change. Rather, the teachers themselves asked local political officials to participate as a means of expanding the influence of the assembly. As two representatives of the Chiisagata assembly (both teachers) explained, "We decided that by changing our name [from "instructional assembly" to "educational assembly"] and by having school administrators participate, the assembly would be of greater real benefit."[97] A few months later, while discussing the decision to include village officials in their meetings, they argued, "It is appropriate to add village officials to the assembly, isn't it? If we have only [teachers and] school administrators, with no connections to local political officials, we will have problems when it comes to carrying out whatever we decide."[98] Teachers in East Chikuma district referred to this strategic alliance as "the joining of the government and the people" (*kanmin gappei*), a phrasing that differentiated themselves from government officials yet expressed their intent to forge a cooperative, mutually beneficial relationship. The decision to incorporate political authorities into educational assemblies was a pragmatic move by local teachers to gain some amount of systematic influence over the making of educational policy. Gaining access to the policymaking process required them to surrender a certain amount of independence, but many teachers were willing to make such a compromise so that their views as professional educators were reflected in educational policy.

Starting in 1881–82, when the prefectural government in Nagano began to take a decisive stance against the involvement of teachers in the Popular Rights Movement, the advantages of cooperation with local political authorities became even more evident. As the option of exerting influence over educational policy through oppositional politics was closed off, more and more teacher assemblies began to court the favor of political authorities during the early 1880s in the hopes of injecting their voices into the decision-making process. This movement culminated in 1884 with the amalgamation of the various district-level educational assemblies into a prefecture-wide umbrella organization, the Shinano Educational Assembly. According to its charter, the purpose of this organization was to provide advice to prefectural authorities on educational matters so that "civilization might flourish" and the prefectural government "might achieve an intimate understanding of educational conditions in the areas under its jurisdiction."[99] This organization functioned mainly as a consultative body and provided teachers an opportunity to lobby higher-level political authorities on educational policy. At the same time, it served as a professional network among educators, and its quarterly publication, the *Journal of the Shinano Educational Assembly*, provided a forum in which teachers could publish education-related research. It was by no means an independent organization for teachers—the chair of the semiannual meeting was, after all, the prefectural governor. Nonetheless, the teachers used the organization to pursue their professional agendas and to communicate their views on educational policy based on their experience as educators.

Not all teachers were in agreement either with the participation of political authorities in teacher assemblies or with the amalgamation of district-level assemblies into a prefecture-wide organization. In several districts, the decision to involve political authorities led dissenting teachers to form their own private educational assemblies; after the formation of the Shinano Educational Assembly, these private assemblies remained separate, competing with the official, prefecture-wide organization for influence among the teachers of Nagano. One of these private assemblies was started in Chiisagata district in 1884 by the same two teachers who had led the 1880 initiative to include local political officials; four years later, they had apparently decided that their interests were best served by reasserting their assembly's independence from political authorities.[100] Another private assembly was established in Upper Minochi district in 1884 and met on the second day of each month in the city of Nagano. Like other private assemblies, the Upper Minochi assembly confined its membership to teachers only and expanded its purview beyond pedagogy to a broad range of topics relating to educational policy.[101] Following each meeting, a representative would submit petitions to the district chief and prefectural governor so as to communicate the views of the assembly to political authorities. Despite its intent to remain independent, this assembly was by no means hostile to political authorities. An advertisement for the assembly (in the form of an open letter addressed to all teachers in the prefecture) urged "those of common spirit" to join the assembly, so that together they might "work for the spread and improvement of education and promote the well-being of the state."[102] That this explicitly private, independent assembly would explain its purpose in terms of "promoting the well-being of the state" reveals the extent to which the professional goals of teachers in Nagano were congruent with those of political authorities. This correspondence in views tended to diminish the significance of these assemblies' independent status. In recognition of this fact, one private assembly after another voted to relinquish its independence and join forces with the Shinano Educational Assembly. By 1890, all but one had done so; the lone holdout, the association in East Chikuma district—ground zero of the initial movement to implement the Fundamental Code and the hotbed of popular rights activism in the late 1870s and early 1880s—joined in 1898.

This trend toward consolidation and cooperation with political authorities should not, however, be interpreted to mean that teachers in Nagano had abandoned their professional concerns and their critical stance toward educational policy. At the annual meeting of the National Educational Assembly in 1890, 800 delegates (consisting mainly of nominees from each prefectural educational assembly) from throughout the country joined in a discussion of the future of the educational system. The delegates from Ishikawa prefecture raised a question concerning the ideological basis of education: "Should our nation's education be based on statism (*kokkashugi*), or on individualism?" After a number of delegates expressed support for statism, the delegates from Nagano demurred:

We think it is rash to decide such a major issue in only an hour. . . . It is also unwise to draw such a simplistic distinction between the state and the individual. If we are to decide this matter, we should do so only after extensive debate, having been given a clear research agenda and ample time for discussion.[103]

Arai Tsutomu portrays this incident as evidence that Nagano's teachers were resisting the pull of ultranationalism. In fact, Nagano's teachers were, if anything, more consistently vociferous in their support of emperor and nation than teachers in many other parts of the country, stretching back to the bakumatsu period. The point of this anecdote is, rather, that teachers in Nagano maintained a critical professionalism even as they pursued a strategy of cooperation with political authorities.[104] This strategy was not simply the product of the state's coercive encroachment on the realm of education; nor was it based on teachers' abandonment of their professional concerns or on their full agreement with the aims of the central government. Teachers in Nagano sometimes agreed with those aims, and sometimes they did not; in either case, their views continued to be grounded in their professional experience and identity as teachers.

THE REALITIES OF SCHOOL
ATTENDANCE, 1872–90

The 1880s witnessed an ongoing attempt by teachers and village leaders to negotiate the terms of their integration into the new educational system. Ordinary people were involved in a similar enterprise, although their techniques of negotiation were rather different. Unlike teachers and village leaders, most people lacked the opportunity to influence policy directly by lobbying political authorities and striking compromises. Yet because the educational system was created to transform them, they possessed tremendous leverage. If they did not attend the new schools, the educational system would fail to serve its purpose of building a loyal, united, skilled populace, capable of constructive participation in the life of the nation. School attendance, therefore, was of great concern to leaders at all levels of government; yet the goal of universal attendance remained frustratingly elusive. This section traces patterns of school enrollment and attendance in Nagano during the first two decades of the Meiji educational system. These patterns reflect both the degree to which ordinary people were integrated into the new system and the impact of this system on popular conceptions of the school.

The statistics on school enrollment in Meiji Japan can be read in a number of different ways. If we begin in 1873, when less than 30 percent of all children were enrolled in the new schools, and end in the final years of the Meiji period, when enrollment figures topped 95 percent, the situation appears to be one of dramatic growth. It is from this perspective that Meiji Japan is so often read as a success story of rapid, peaceful modernization. If we break this 40-year period into two halves, however, a different picture emerges. To the Meiji government, enrollment statistics in 1890—often cited as the endpoint in the consolidation of emperor-system education—would have appeared quite troubling. Figure 4 traces the changes in enrollment in Nagano prefecture during the first half of the Meiji period.[105] The figure illustrates that, after an initial jump in the first three years of the Fundamental Code, enrollment patterns remained essentially unchanged until 1890 (a trend that continued until around 1893). The national statistics tell a similar story, except that

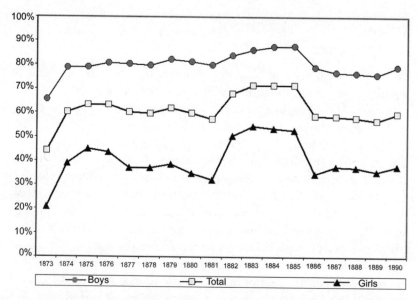

Fig. 4 Enrollment rates in Nagano, 1873–90

the enrollment figures are 10–20 percent lower, and the shape of the curve is smoother.[106] From this perspective, during its first twenty years the Meiji educational system was far from an unqualified success.

In fact, even the initial increase in enrollments from 1873 to 1875 is somewhat illusory, at least in terms of changing pre-existing patterns of school attendance. Particularly in 1873 and 1874, many of the new schools had not yet been established; as a result, the children in those school districts who would eventually enroll in the new schools would not have surfaced in the statistics. Many of them were already attending (or had attended) one of the pre-existing schools in their area that continued to operate in the first two years after the promulgation of the Fundamental Code.[107] As a result, the increase in enrollment during these years was, in part, the result of an effort to establish new schools and enroll children who were participating in older schooling arrangements. The steep incline in Figure 4, in other words, represents not so much an increase in the number of children enrolled in school but the movement of children from old schools to new ones.

The extended period of stagnation continued despite the concerted efforts of authorities in Nagano to enroll children in the schools.

Parents who refused to enroll their children rarely faced serious punishment; *torishimari* suggested that the prefectural government fine
parents who kept their children at home without a valid excuse,[108] but
such measures were never enforced systematically.[109] Nevertheless,
parents would have felt consistent pressure from authorities to send
their children to school. Village-level officials made enrollment charts
each year, and *sewayaku* visited the families of unenrolled children,
both to investigate the reasons for nonattendance and to encourage
them to change their ways. Those who continued to keep their children at home received a visit from the *torishimari* or a letter from the
district chief. Even the prefectural governor himself—or, more often,
one of his deputies at the prefectural office—might visit a district and
both scold and encourage recalcitrant parents.

Among the officially sanctioned excuses for not enrolling one's
children in the new schools were illness, poverty, commuting distance, or household responsibilities.[110] Usually, a number of factors
coincided to make school attendance unfeasible: for example, poverty
and the illness of a parent made it necessary for children to assist in
household chores. For girls, the most common excuse was childcare
responsibilities; often, this took the form of seasonal labor (*hōkō*) in
which a girl was sent to another family to look after the children. In
the words of one family, "We have many children, and if the oldest
doesn't take care of the younger ones, it affects our livelihood."[111] An
additional obstacle to school enrollment in Nagano prefecture was the
spread of the silk industry, in which younger children—especially
girls—could make a substantial contribution to the household economy.[112] The fact that most of the legitimate excuses for keeping children at home were created for girls is telling: not only were families
less willing to lose female children's labor, but the authorities were
more willing to accept female nonattendance as legitimate. Indeed, it
was only in the 1890s that the major gap between male and female attendance rates was widely identified as a problem.[113]

Although officially sanctioned excuses removed the legal obligation of school attendance—an obligation that was, even into the
1890s, neither clearly defined nor consistently applied—most local
authorities in Nagano endeavored to integrate into the public school
system those families who had not previously viewed schooling as
an option. Not only did officials continue their exhortation campaigns, but they also sought to regulate more closely the process by

which families could exempt their children from school enrollment. Indeed, the jump in school enrollment in 1882 was, in large part, the result of such an effort.[114] Furthermore, both the central and the prefectural governments worked to make school more feasible for poorer families. The Ministry of Education, for example, continued to sanction the existence of inadequately equipped branch schools throughout the 1880s and encouraged the establishment of schools that offered classes only in the afternoon or evening. In Nagano prefecture, authorities provided tuition waivers and free textbooks to the children of poorer families.[115] Beginning in the late 1880s, local volunteers even formed "associations for the encouragement of school enrollment" to raise funds to help poorer families pay school fees. Until the 1890s, however, such efforts failed to bring substantial improvements in school enrollment. Compounding the frustration of central and prefectural authorities was the fact that, after a promising increase in enrollment from 1882 to 1885, a second recession sent enrollment rates tumbling to earlier levels, where they would remain for several more years. After nearly twenty years of vigorous effort, authorities were not much closer to the goal of universal enrollment than they had been in the first two years of the Fundamental Code.

Furthermore, when we shift the focus from enrollment to attendance, the results are even less impressive.[116] Prefecture-wide attendance statistics for the first fifteen years or so after the Fundamental Code are either unreliable or nonexistent;[117] however, records for individual schools or districts do allow a glimpse of attendance patterns. For example, records for Shijin Elementary School in the Saku district of Nagano reveal an enrollment of 121 boys and 62 girls. However, over a two-month stretch in late 1874, fewer than half of those children were in school on most days; on some days, the rate was as low as 38 percent.[118] Records kept by one *torishimari* in 1877–78 show the attendance figures for the seventeen school districts under his jurisdiction. On average, there were 176 school-age children in each district, of whom 110 were enrolled in school—an enrollment rate of over 62 percent.[119] Over a three-month stretch in 1877, however, only fourteen of these 110 children attended school at least 60 times (out of a total of 65 school days), and only 39 attended between 20 and 60 times. The remainder of these enrolled children—over 50 percent—were in school fewer than twenty days during this period. In other words, most of the children attended school rarely, if at all. Prefecture-wide records for the late 1880s suggest that these patterns persisted: daily attendance rates (as a percentage of enrolled children) were under 60 percent. If unenrolled children are included, out of a total of over 180,000 school-age children in Nagano prefecture in the late 1880s, only about a third were in school on any given day.[120] Since local officials often excluded from their lists of school-age children those from very poor families for whom school attendance was deemed unfeasible, it is evident that the actual figure was even smaller.[121]

Further obstructing the goals of the new educational system was the tendency of many children to quit school after only one or two years. According to the records of one Suwa district school, around half the 157 boys who entered the school in the first two years after its establishment in 1873 quit school during the first four grades of the eight-grade elementary school curriculum (each grade took six months); only 13 percent of boys finished all eight grades.[122] Predictably, girls were even less likely to stay in school for an extended length of time. None of the 55 girls enrolled in the Suwa district school during this period reached either of the top two grades, and over 60 percent quit school during the first year. Indeed, in the entire prefecture, only nineteen children who had entered the new elementary schools in 1873 and 1874 completed the upper-elementary-school curriculum by finishing all eight grades (four years).[123] By the mid-1880s, the number of children who completed the upper-elementary-school curriculum each year had risen to over 100, but this was only a tiny fraction of the children in Nagano prefecture. As in the late Tokugawa period, there was a gulf between the large numbers of children who attended school for only a year or two and those privileged few who stayed in school for many years and became the literate elite of local society.

Continuities in patterns of school attendance are also reflected in the seasonal fluctuations. For example, records for Tashima Elementary School in the Upper Ina district of Nagano allow us to trace attendance patterns on a month-by-month basis.[124] At the beginning of 1877, there were 278 school-age children in the school district that supported Tashima Elementary; around 180, or some 65 percent, of these children were enrolled in school.[125] From January through March, around a third of all enrolled children attended school on at

Table 1
Enrollment and Attendance in Yoshida Elementary School, 1883

Month	Number of children enrolled	Number of children attending	Average daily attendance
January	100	90	80
February	100	90	50
March	132	120	111
April	119	109	100
May	119	106	93
June	119	80	68
July	119	77	54
August	119	94	75
September	118	89	83
October	118	92	81
November	118	76	66
December	118	87	82

SOURCE: Hayashi, "Gakusei–kyōikurei-ki," p. 15.

least 60 of the 65 school days in this period. Over half of the enrolled children, in contrast, attended fewer than 20 times during this same period; eight of those children did not attend even once. From April through June, the proportion of enrolled children who attended at least 60 times dropped from one-third to one-fifth, a proportion that remained relatively constant during the remaining months of the year. Most parents in this district, it appears, did not feel the need to send their children to school every day, even during those winter months in which the labor of school-age children was less essential. Beginning in the spring, the decreasing commitment of parents to their children's schooling resulted in highly sporadic attendance patterns.

The records of Yoshida Elementary School for 1883 reveal similar trends. The enrollment rate for this school—that is, the percentage of school-age children in the elementary school district enrolled in the school—was 70 percent, which was identical to the prefecture-wide enrollment rate for 1883. Actual attendance rates, however, were significantly lower. Table 1 organizes the school's attendance records into three categories: the number of children enrolled at the school, the number of enrolled children who attended the school at some point during each month, and the average daily attendance for each month. The table shows that the percentage of enrolled children who attended the school at least once during a given month ranged from a high of 91 percent in March to a low of 65 percent in July and November. In July, for example, 42 of the 119 enrolled children did not attend the school even once. The average daily attendance rate (the percentage of enrolled children in school on a given day) varied widely from a high of 85 percent in March to a low of only 44 percent in July. These statistics reveal that, in 1883, attendance still conformed closely to Tokugawa-era patterns: the marked increase in attendance in late winter/early spring, the dramatic drop in late spring through midsummer, the recovery in late summer/early fall, and a second, briefer decrease at harvest time. Despite the concerted efforts of central and local authorities during the first two decades of the Meiji era, the patterns and frequency of school attendance continued to conform to pre-Meiji rhythms.

Conclusion

In the introduction to their edited volume on the Tokugawa-Meiji transition, Marius Jansen and Gilbert Rozman turn their attention to the educational system to illustrate the momentous changes that occurred in Japan during the first two decades of the Meiji period. They describe the educational system, circa 1890, in the following terms: "By middle and late Meiji all children, not just some, trooped off to uniform public schools; there they learned the new national hymn of loyalty, its lyric drawn from a *Kokinshū* poem. . . . They bowed to the imperial picture, and stood to hear their principal read the Imperial Rescript on Education."[126] This picture draws a provocative image of the mid- to late-Meiji educational system and captures what was probably the most significant education-related development of these decades: the nationalization of schooling that resulted in the creation of both a centralized, hierarchical network of schools and administrative structures and a citizenry united in its identification with the Japanese nation.

In two important respects, however, this quote is misleading. First, the notion that "all children, not just some" attended elementary schools is inaccurate: as we have seen, not only were enrollment rates in 1890 still far from universal, but a great number of enrolled children attended only sporadically and usually quit school after a year or two. The system was thus "national" in terms of its structure, but the extent of its reach into the lives of families and communities was still limited. Second, this description of the educational system—children "trooping off" to school, bowing before the imperial picture, listening obediently to an Imperial Rescript concocted by the central government—conveys an image of local schools lying prostrate before the central government, fully obedient to its dictates and wholly defined by its interests. As we have seen, however, the consolidation of the educational system in the 1880s did not signify the subordination of local or professional concerns to the political goals of the state. The suppression of the Popular Rights Movement ensured that educators and local activists could not express these concerns through oppositional politics. Teachers continued their effort to influence educational policy, however, by adopting a technique of strategic cooperation with political officials—while maintaining a strong sense of professional identity. Communities and their leaders continued to maneuver within a constantly changing set of legal and institutional parameters to create schooling arrangements amenable to their local concerns and interests. This negotiation between the central government and various segments of local society continued throughout the 1880s and eventually produced a more enduring legal framework and administrative structure—one that would continue to be shaped, however, by a process of negotiation among competing forces and interests.

The Local in the Nation-State

The year 1890 is widely recognized as a watershed in Japan's modern history, a rough dividing line between the two decades of "structural drama" and a subsequent era in which "stability was wrested from the aftermath of crisis."[1] The promulgation of the Constitution (1889), the opening of the Diet (1890), the Imperial Rescript on Education (1890), and the restructuring of local administration (1888–90) marked a consolidation in the "structures and directions of Japan's modernity."[2] As Carol Gluck and others have pointed out, however, this consolidation signified neither the victory of the Meiji state and its emperor-system ideology over the people nor the cessation of all discussion and debate regarding policy and identity.

Nor did it mean the end of conflict and negotiation over education. The dynamics of negotiation after 1890 followed patterns established during the first two decades of the Meiji era, when the central government and local society engaged in a dialogue about the educational system. Many of the specific points of contention were also familiar and can be traced to the various visions of education and schooling that erupted into the vast, undefined public space created during the last decades of the Tokugawa period and the immediate post-Restoration years. One such point was the issue of school consolidation. The revision of school district boundaries in 1878 and at several points in the 1880s resulted in further controversy and negotiation among local residents, community leaders, educators, prefectural authorities, and the central government. The local government reform of 1888–90 created a new set of legal and institutional parameters within which this dynamic of conflict and negotiation proceeded.

In what was merely one of hundreds of such conflicts in Nagano prefecture in the 1890s and the early twentieth century, the residents of the newly formed Asahi village fought for nearly a decade over the establishment of a new, consolidated elementary school. Five separate villages had been joined in 1890 to form Asahi village after the creation of the new Town and Village System (Chōsonsei). In the two decades preceding this amalgamation, these villages had witnessed numerous changes in the number and type of schools available in the area. Repeated school secessions during the first two decades of the Fundamental Code had resulted in as many as six different schools at one point, and the precise number fluctuated frequently because of changes in local administration and the subsequent redrawing of school districts.[3] In the early 1890s, however, the Asahi village assembly began to feel pressure from district and prefectural authorities to consolidate the schools and build one large elementary school to serve all the children of this new village.

The project faced considerable opposition from the outset. It was not until 1897 that the village leadership seriously considered the matter, and the village assembly immediately splintered once the issue came before it. Assembly members defended their own interests and those of their constituents—which usually meant the people from their own pre-1890 villages. The key points of contention were the issues fundamental to any consolidation: location, control, and money. To some extent, consolidation was objectionable to all residents, since it would result in longer commutes and require families to contribute money to a school that served multiple villages—issues that had long fueled opposition. However, depending on the location of the school, the division of the financial burden among the different communities, and the selection of administrators, virtually any decision would have adversely affected some areas more than others. Consequently, consolidation met with fierce resistance from those assemblymen whose families, friends, and neighbors were unduly burdened by it. Some representatives refused to show up for meetings to prevent a quorum; others withdrew from the assembly in defiance.

In 1899, after discussions had stalled for two years, the village head (*sonchō*) sent a letter of reproof to the village assembly, in which he passionately implored the assemblymen to put aside their parochial interests and press on with plans for school consolidation.[4] "It is an old habit of our nation (*waga kokumin*) to remain in small groups," he wrote. "Those who stick by this principle seek to decrease the scale of education and obstruct its progress." As for the issue of finances: the choices were to allow each pre-1890 village to maintain its own system for funding the school or to institute a standardized levy for the entire administrative area. The second option, he noted, was both cheaper and, in fact, mandated by law. Concerning the construction of a new, consolidated school, he entreated the assembly to think not only of the costs but also of the benefits. "If we consider the future and observe the condition of the state, we have no choice but to adopt the policy of consolidation." The members of the community, however, "view [the situation] of multiple independent schools in the village as being to their benefit, basing [their views] only on the grounds of commuting convenience." The village head concluded that the persistence of this kind of "local isolationism"—which he later contrasted with the positive virtue of "self-governing spirit" (*jichi no seishin*)—"impedes the progress of education . . . and obstructs the realization of village governance."[5]

Over the next two to three years, the village head and his supporters seem to have been successful in winning support for a consolidated school. However, when they tried to designate a site for the new school, opposition arose again. In a report to the prefectural office written in 1902, the village head explained: "Since the incident regarding the consolidation of the three schools, even the ordinary villagers have come to feel the necessity [of the consolidation]." "However," he lamented, "when it comes to the selection of a site for the school building, each district is mired in its own selfish feelings, fighting with the others to have the site close to its own hamlet." Armed with such opinions, the people "have swarmed upon the village office," submitting petitions and expressing their "selfish feelings" to the village officials. The instigators "have incited public sentiment" and "awakened old grudges," thus "destroying harmony within the village," "causing confusion and disarray in village governance," and "interfering with the welfare of the people."[6] Despite the village head's efforts, the resistance to school consolidation persisted, as did the disputatious atmosphere within the village. It was not until 1907 that the village assembly, partly because of pressure from the district and prefectural government, was able to choose a site, set up a budget, and begin construction on a consolidated school—and even then, only after the dissenting parties had bargained for existing schools to remain open as branch schools.

The obvious similarities between the incident in Asahi village at the turn of the century and the consolidation-related conflicts of the mid-1870s might leave the impression that three decades of concerted efforts by the Ministry of Education, prefectural authorities, educators, and local activists had failed to transform popular views toward education and schooling. This impression would certainly be strengthened by the fact that, even after the steady increase in school enrollment rates that began in the mid-1890s, most children attended school irregularly and quit after only a year or two.[7] Because of such evidence, we might be inclined to view the trappings of the Meiji government's hegemonic project in education—all the laws, procedures, rituals, paperwork, textbooks, school buildings, and flagpoles—as nothing more than "a gimcrack facade behind which the common people . . . grumbled and prayed to old gods, untouched by the new legitimation."[8]

In many respects, however, the conflict in Asahi village reveals the extent to which certain elements of the educational system had taken root in local society. For example, all sides in this conflict, in their efforts to argue their case and influence the decision of the prefectural government, followed proper administrative channels and documentary procedures. As in the Meiji- and Taisho-era protests examined by Michael Lewis, the various parties pursued their own interests through the institutional and legal frameworks sanctioned by the central government.[9] In doing so, they participated in what Kären Wigen has characterized as a transformation in the orientation of conflict from vertical to horizontal: rather than opposing the central government itself, localities competed with one another—often with the central government as arbiter rather than enemy.[10] Furthermore, all sides in the Asahi conflict argued their case with concepts and rhetoric fundamental to the Meiji government's vision of education—particularly, its notions of progress and nationalism. One could argue, of course, that local leaders simply manipulated this rhetoric without fully buying into it; indeed, as we have seen, local leaders were quite astute in figuring out the kinds of rhetoric and arguments most likely to be effective in influencing the prefectural or central governments. Local leaders at all levels were, however, quick to embrace many of the basic concepts and goals that underlay this rhetoric. The continuing use of such ideas and rhetoric had, by 1890, contributed to the formation of a common discursive framework for talking and thinking about education. Just as the growth of laws, institutions, and procedures made it more difficult for local leaders to employ irregular or illegal measures to pursue local interests, this discursive framework made it increasingly difficult to imagine and articulate alternatives to the centralized, public school system.

This discursive framework is vividly rendered in an anecdote from a semi-autobiographical novel published in 1901 by Tokutomi Kenjirō. Tokutomi had attended a pre–Fundamental Code commoner school before completing his education during the first decade of the Meiji system. In this novel, he expressed, through the voice of the child-protagonist, his amazement upon seeing a newly constructed elementary school for the first time:

Coming to the new school was like climbing out of the dark depths of a valley to a forest of tall straight trees on a mountainside. . . . The new school wasn't luxurious, but it was new, and built from the start as a school, with a second story and windows all round, which made the rooms almost dazzlingly bright, a playground, imposing black gates with the school's name inscribed on the posts, and a flagpole. It *looked* like a school.[11]

The sort of elementary school described in this passage may have indeed evoked amazement, and perhaps even admiration, among many local residents in the early Meiji period. On the other hand, the passage is of limited value as a window on the experiences of children in this period. No child whose previous schooling had been limited to a commoner school that met in a temple or a neighbor's home would have thought that this new two-story building "looked like a school." Despite this anachronism, however, the passage is illuminating as an expression of the decidedly new assumptions about schooling that Tokutomi had come to internalize during the first three decades of the new educational system. The child-protagonist is articulating a concept of school—not to mention concepts of modernity and progress—that had been fundamental to early Meiji educational policy; by the late Meiji, this concept had become, for Tokutomi, commonsensical.

Perhaps it is not surprising to find such statements in the writings of a cosmopolitan literary figure like Tokutomi, but he was not alone in holding such views. There is evidence that local educators and community leaders in Nagano had come to embrace many of the key assumptions undergirding the public school system. Particularly revealing are the "school histories" (*gakkō enkaku-shi*) that local leaders began to write in the late 1880s. The Ministry of Education initiated this project by calling on local leaders to collect information on pre–Fundamental Code schooling arrangements as part of a nationwide survey—part of a larger venture that ultimately resulted in the compilation of the *Materials on the History of Education in Japan* (*Nihon kyōiku-shi shiryō*). Local leaders in towns and villages throughout Nagano took this responsibility seriously: they conducted extensive surveys of local residents who had taught or attended pre–Fundamental Code commoner schools and submitted the information in narrative form. The format of these narratives would serve as a model for the countless volumes of educational history (*kyōiku-shi*) produced by nearly every prefecture, district, city, village, and school during the past hundred years.

The narratives usually began with a description of the pre-Meiji schools in the area and then chronicled the efforts of local leaders to establish new elementary schools following the promulgation of the Fundamental Code. Often, the account focused on the construction of a new school building, as in this passage from the "History of Naganuma Elementary School":

We were one of the first in the prefecture to attempt this undertaking [the construction of a new school building]. Our building was praised even by the prefectural governor, Narasaki Tomonao. Within a few years, however, neighboring villages began to build huge, tall buildings, and ours came to be viewed as a crude, primitive hut. Truly, the progress of this age does not stop for an instant.[12]

Employing another narrative technique commonly found in these school histories, the writers in Naganuma explained that many people in their community, unable to comprehend the importance of modern education, initially opposed the new schools. Over time, however, the writers noted proudly, the new system "gradually sank into the hearts and minds of parents."[13] Whether ordinary parents and children experienced such a change of heart is debatable; nevertheless, it is significant that the writers, like the Ministry of Education, viewed that change of heart as necessary and inevitable. Echoing these sentiments, as well as those expressed in Tokutomi's novel, in 1911 the authors of "The History of Takai Elementary School" chronicled the challenges faced by community leaders during the early Meiji period.[14] They discussed the local impact of the disruptive changes that followed the Meiji Restoration—including the efforts to establish a *gōkō* in their community, only to have it abolished following the promulgation of the Fundamental Code. As a result of this disruption, "the people's hearts were unsettled," and "we had not yet reached the point where we could build a *real* school (*gakkō rashiki gakkō*)."[15] The authors of this history had come to embrace the conception of school embodied in Meiji educational policy; accordingly, they now viewed pre–Fundamental Code schooling arrangements as unworthy of the title of "school."

It is particularly significant that the writers included the *gōkō* in the category of substandard schools, since local activists had conceived of the *gōkō* as something quite different from pre-existing commoner schools, a product of their own reformist energies in the aftermath of the Restoration. By seeing their *gōkō* as something less than a *"real* school," these men—community leaders who had been a part of the movement to build the *gōkō*—had seemingly come to view their own Restoration-era reformist vision as illegitimate (or at least incomplete). This was, of course, precisely the goal of the project of state formation: to displace and marginalize the ideas and energies released in the late Tokugawa and early Meiji years by creating a singular, authoritative vision of the new political and social order. The formation of a common discursive, as well as institutional and legal, framework in the realm of education and schooling would thus appear to mark the completion of the Meiji government's hegemonic project. As in Nemerov's poem quoted at the beginning of this book, "worlds visible and invisible" had seemingly bowed down before the new image of school embodied in government policy.

Such an impression, however, needs to be qualified. First, the emergence of a common discursive framework in education did not eliminate dissent. Rather, it simply transformed the nature of the resistance and, in some cases, made possible new forms of protest. For example, the internalization of the central assumptions behind the new conception of school allowed nostalgia to emerge as a form of opposition. In the late Meiji period, for example, intellectuals began to reminisce about the merits of the premodern private school—for example, the close, personal link between master and pupil—and they contrasted its virtues with the shortcomings of the modern school system.[16] Also at the end of the Meiji period, some district-level educational associations conducted another round of investigations into pre–Fundamental Code schooling arrangements. This time, however, the investigators represented these premodern schools in a very different light: not as backward customs to be wiped away as local society progressed toward enlightenment, but as objects of ethnographic study that had to be recorded before they, along with other premodern social and cultural practices, became extinct amid the inexorable tide of modernity.[17] The genealogy of late Meiji nostalgia can be traced to early Meiji forms of dissent—for example, the defying of the Fundamental Code by commoner-school teachers who reopened their schools secretly and urged local children to attend, thus expressing implicit support for pre-Meiji schooling arrangements. By the late Meiji, however, the contrast between old and new forms of schooling was explicit. By defining its new, authoritative conception of school in opposition to pre-existing schooling arrangements, the Meiji government made possible the nostalgic representation of those arrangements as an alternative to the modern, public school system.

While recognizing the consolidation of a discursive and institutional framework for education, we must also keep in mind that this framework was itself the product of negotiation, not of autonomous decisions by the central government. Teachers, local officials, and ordinary people participated actively in the formation of the educational system. Through a combination of resistance (usually of a specific, rather than an absolute, nature), strategic cooperation, and local initiative, these various segments of local society were able to exert a considerable amount of influence upon educational policy at several key junctures. The emergence of an institutional and discursive framework in the 1890s did represent the culmination of a process of hegemony—a process through which a new definition of "school" was wrested from the multiple definitions present in the aftermath of the Restoration and, over time, became accepted as common sense. The Meiji government played a central, but not unilateral, role in this process: the hegemony that took shape in the area of education and schooling by late Meiji resembles that described by Florencia Mallon, one achieved only when leaders "effectively garner to themselves ongoing legitimacy and support" by "partially incorporat[ing] the aspirations or discourses of supporters."[18]

If we grant local society some degree of agency in the creation of the Meiji educational system, the question of attributing responsibility for this system becomes more complicated. If the educational system was not unilaterally imposed upon the Japanese people by an absolutist state, we cannot assign to the Meiji government sole responsibility for the negative elements or effects of the system—elitism, excessive centralization, ultranationalism, and militarism being those most frequently mentioned. Of course, assigning responsibility for the Meiji educational system—and, by extension, for Japan's prewar and wartime history—is a highly complicated exercise. On one hand, although teachers, community leaders, and local residents were willing to express opposition to certain aspects of the educational system, they usually did not oppose the spread of quasi-military physical training, moral education, and nationalism in the schools. On the other hand, evidence of popular agreement with militaristic or ultranationalistic education does not necessarily deflect responsibility from the state. Agreement can be interpreted, as it is by many Japanese historians of education, as something akin to a false consciousness resulting from the overwhelming power of the prewar state. In a more novel and persuasive formulation, Michael Lewis argues that local enthusiasm for imperialism and ultranationalism in Toyama was, in part, the consequence of a relationship between state and locality in which local benefits were often secured by expressing support for ideological discourse or political programs emanating from the center.[19]

Lewis's description of the relationship between state and local society in prewar Japan clearly fits the case of Nagano as well. Although this relationship ended up serving the state's needs quite well, the central government cannot claim exclusive credit (or take the exclusive blame) for creating this relationship. In the area of education and schooling, the patterns of interaction between the central government and the various segments of local society were forged through a common experience of crisis during the late Tokugawa era and two decades of vigorous negotiation following the Meiji Restoration. Many local activists, for example, eagerly sought the involvement of prefectural and central authorities in the project of educational reform, based on their shared vision of an educational system coordinated from the center and undergirded by an ethic of service to emperor and nation. Educators increasingly asserted their professional identity but often cooperated with political authorities as a means of influencing policy. Local communities, meanwhile, sometimes clashed with district or prefectural authorities over school fees and commuting distances, but they also fought with one another and appealed to the state to referee their disputes. Localities sometimes reacted to central reforms with dissent, sometimes with eager cooperation. In either case, local people responded actively, negotiating with central and prefectural authorities to shape policy—indeed, to shape the very terms of negotiation. As a result, we must reconsider the assumption that Japan's modern educational system would have been different had local voices not been silenced by the center. Japan's prewar educational system—and Japan's modern history in general—was, to a far greater extent than we usually assume, a product of such voices.

Reference Matter

ॐ

Notes

Abbreviations Used in the Notes

Hattatsu-shi	Kyōikushi hensankai, ed., *Meiji ikō kyōiku seido hattatsu-shi*
NKKS	Nagano-ken kyōikushi hensan iinkai, ed., *Nagano-ken*
NKS	Nagano kenshi hensan iinkai, ed., *Nagano kenshi shiryō-hen*
NKSTH	Nagano kenshi hensan iinkai, ed., *Nagano kenshi tsūshi-hen*

Introduction

EPIGRAPH: Nemerov, *Trying Conclusions*, pp. 49–50.

1. Maynes, *Schooling in Western Europe*, pp. 13–20. These figures are based largely on wedding registration records. As Maynes points out, the aggregate figures are somewhat misleading, since there was wide regional variation in literacy rates in any given country, and the literacy gap between rural and urban areas was considerable.

2. For statistics on literacy in Tokugawa Japan, see Dore, *Education in Tokugawa Japan*, pp. 317–22.

3. The relationship between industrialization and the popular demand for literacy is complex and has been debated at length among historians of education. See, e.g., Anderson and Bowman, "Education and Economic Modernization"; Schofield, "The Dimensions of Illiteracy"; and West, *Education and the Industrial Revolution*. Not only is there some doubt whether industrialization stimulated a demand for literacy, but historians of education are also skeptical that literacy provided real opportunities for economic betterment among working people in industrializing societies; see Graff, *The Literacy Myth*.

4. See Chisick, *The Limits of Reform*; Kaestle, "Between the Scylla"; and Johnson, "Educational Policy."

5. It would be disingenuous to characterize the movement for educational reform in Europe and America solely as a cynical attempt to control the masses. The motivation of many reformers should be characterized as "concern" rather than "fear," and most viewed the school less as a "technique of social control" and more as a "method for solving social problems." A few reformers, like the Swiss Johann Pestalozzi, saw education as a tool for genuine social mobility. On the other hand, it would be unwise to draw a sharp distinction between "fear" and "concern" or between "social control" and "social management." Furthermore, we should separate the *motivations* for school reform from its *effects*. However noble the motives of some reformers, centralized schooling certainly provided a new form of social control.

6. The "political roles" that elites envisioned for the masses in the emerging nation-state were usually quite limited, at least at first, and usually did not entail active participation in political decision making. For many government officials, both in the West and Japan, educational reform was stimulated by the need to prepare the masses for military service, not political participation. Where centralized educational systems did emerge in the context of the rise of a representative political order, schools were intended to function as a mechanism of containment rather than of empowerment or liberation. For example, Bruce Curtis (*Building the Educational State*) shows how educational reform in Canada West coincided with the expansion of representative government and argues that reformers sought to use universal schooling to create responsible, self-regulating citizens whose political participation would not undermine the prerogatives of elites.

7. Some states were much more explicit and aggressive than others in their use of schools as a tool to consolidate political power. In England and the United States, educational reforms were often initiated by private groups outside the government, and although the regulative functions of government expanded during the nineteenth century, the level of centralized control was relatively weak. In revolutionary Mexico, on the other hand, central government officials explicitly conceived of schools as political instruments and teachers as a political vanguard, both of which would be used to carry out land reform, to organize labor unions, to build roads, to promote hygiene, to create a new patriotic culture, and so on; see Vaughan, *Cultural Politics in Revolution*, esp. pp. 25–46.

8. A notable early example of such a recognition can be found in Aizawa Seishisai's *New Theses*, written in 1825. For a translation, see Wakabayashi, *Anti-Foreignism and Western Learning*.

9. For two slightly different summary charts of the types and numbers of schools in Tokugawa Japan, see Passin, *Society and Education in Japan*, p. 14; and Rubinger, *Private Academies*, p. 7.

10. On Confucianism as a source of popular education movements, see Kawamura, *Zaison chishikijin*; on Shingaku, see Sawada, *Confucian Values and*

Popular Zen; on nativism, see Nakano, "Sonraku fukkō." I address these and other educational movements in Chapter 1.

11. Lincicome, *Principle*, p. 9.

12. One book that vividly illustrates this dual nature of modern state formation is Eugen Weber's *Peasants into Frenchmen*.

13. For further discussion of the concept of hegemony within the context of Antonio Gramsci's work, see Femia, *Gramsci's Political Thought*; and Mouffe, "Hegemony and Ideology in Gramsci." For discussion of the application of the concept of hegemony to the study of history, particularly to the issue of state formation, see Corrigan and Sayer, *The Great Arch*; Joseph and Nugent, *Everyday Forms of State Formation*; Lears, "The Concept of Cultural Hegemony"; and Scott, *Weapons of the Weak*.

14. Fujitani, *Splendid Monarchy*.

15. Perhaps the most definitive statement from this perspective is found in Hall, "Changing Conceptions." Sheldon Garon's work has sought to reinsert the issue of agency into our view of modernization, looking at the ways in which people have understood modernization as a concept and applied it in different contexts; see, e.g., "Rethinking Modernization."

16. See, e.g., Haga, *Meiji kokka no keisei*; Kuroda, *Tennōsei kokka keisei*; and Yamamuro, *Hōsei kanryō no jidai*. This perspective can also be found in the works of two influential scholars whose works have appeared in English: see Irokawa, *The Culture of the Meiji Period*, and Ishida, *Japanese Political Culture*. A few Western historians of Japan have also characterized Meiji state formation as a project of domination. The most prominent of these is E. H. Norman, whose *Japan's Emergence as a Modern State* defined the genre. See also Bowen, *Rebellion and Democracy*; and Hane, *Peasants, Rebels, and Outcasts*.

17. Garon, *Molding Japanese Minds*, p. 4.

18. Corrigan and Sayer, *The Great Arch*, p. 195.

19. For a printed copy of this speech, which I discuss again in Chapter 5, see Kamijō, *Mō hitotsu no "yoakemae,"* pp. 79–80.

20. Dower ("E. H. Norman, Japan and the Uses of History") and Harootunian ("America's Japan/Japan's Japan") have explored how this narrative was influenced by the Cold War effort to make Japan into a peaceful and democratic ally in East Asia. They argue that by rewriting Japan's history as peaceful and democratic, scholars could use Japan as a non-communist model of modernization for developing countries—a model that might also function prescriptively to transform and maintain Japan in that image.

21. For an unusually frank analysis of the issue of preconditions as well as of "success stories," modernization, and the Cold War, see Dore's preface to the new edition of his 1965 book, *Education in Tokugawa Japan*, pp. xi–xxi.

22. The term "legacy" is used in the title of the final chapter of Dore's *Education in Tokugawa Japan*, and also in his article, "The Legacy of Tokugawa Education." Passin (*Society and Education in Japan*) uses the term "portents of modernity" to describe the ostensibly modern elements of pre-Meiji education and emphasizes their role in facilitating a smooth transition to the Meiji educational system. Rubinger ("Education") also examines pre-Meiji

education in terms of "modern portents," which are positioned in contrast to "traditional patterns" that were also a part of the Tokugawa schooling experience. Rubinger gives "traditional patterns" and "modern portents" equal treatment and also points out the ways in which the conception of "school" articulated by the Meiji government diverged from pre-Meiji conceptions. On the other hand, his description of Tokugawa education in terms of "modern portents" and "traditional patterns" tends to relegate the latter to a marginal role in the historical narrative—something that will inevitably be overcome during the process of modernization.

23. Passin (*Society and Education in Japan*, pp. 79–80) does point out examples of popular resistance to early Meiji education, but they do not play an important role in his overall narrative of educational modernization.

24. For an extended discussion of this historiography, see Gluck, "The People in History."

25. Ibid.; Waters, *Japan's Local Pragmatists*, pp. 3–30.

26. Gluck, "The People in History," p. 32. Bowen (*Rebellion and Democracy*, pp. 1–7) critiques a different kind of "failure thesis." This "failure thesis" was articulated by early postwar Western scholars who had neglected the study of popular movements because they assumed, given the eventual course of Japan's prewar history, that these movements were not genuinely democratic. Bowen's book attempts to prove that there was, in fact, a genuine democratic spirit in Meiji Japan, one that flowed from the people rather than from the government or the ideologues who supposedly led the democratic movement. In doing so, he argues that these movements were "successful" in the sense that they were genuinely democratic. However, his narrative implies that these popular movements failed to alter the course of prewar history—that the Meiji state had to suppress popular energies in order to build the prewar emperor state. In this sense, Bowen's story closely follows the outlines of the tragic narrative adopted by most Japanese scholars.

27. The majority of books on educational history follow this narrative; this approach comes through particularly clearly in Ishijima and Umemura, *Nihon minshū kyōiku-shi*, since the authors follow the narrative up to the present and explicitly link it with contemporary issues in education. For a similar approach in English, see Horio, *Educational Thought and Ideology*. One Japanese scholar who has not followed this narrative is Motoyama Yukihiko, whose work has been recently translated into English as *Proliferating Talent*.

28. Itō, *Nihon kindai kyōiku-shi*, pp. 2–3.

29. Irokawa, *The Culture of the Meiji Period*, p. 45.

30. Ibid., p. 190.

31. Ibid., p. 272.

32. As James Scott ("Foreword," pp. xi–xii) points out, it is precisely the plurality of "popular" opposition that accounts for its strength.

33. Sayer, "Everyday Forms of State Formation." Timothy Mitchell makes a similar point in "The Limits of the State," in which he calls the state a "discursive effect" and argues that to talk about the state as a historical object (or subject) causes us to see it within its own mystifying discourse.

34. For thorough treatments of some of these conflicts, see Motoyama, *Proliferating Talent*; and Marshall, *Learning to Be Modern*.

35. See, e.g., Tilly, *The Vendée*; and Tilly et al., *The Rebellious Century*. James Scott has also rejected the cooperation/opposition dichotomy, arguing that moments of open resistance are actually the product of a "hidden transcript" of power relations that is always being written and rehearsed by subordinate groups during times of apparent quiescence; see his *Domination and the Arts of Resistance*.

36. Vlastos, "Opposition Movements."

37. Gluck, "The People in History," p. 32.

38. In addition to Lincicome's *Principle* and Motoyama's *Proliferating Talent*, see Lincicome's review of Motoyama's book.

39. Scott, *Weapons of the Weak*, esp. pp. 315–22.

40. Lipsitz, "The Struggle for Hegemony"; Mallon, "Reflections on the Ruins." In *Domination and the Arts of Resistance*, Scott himself speaks in similar terms about a "contract" between elites and subordinate groups, one that makes room for the agency and strategies of subordinate groups, but he seems more reluctant to discuss such an arrangement under the rubric of hegemony.

41. Gluck, *Japan's Modern Myths*, p. 15.

42. Lincicome, "Nationalism, Imperialism, and the International Education Movement"; Motoyama, *Proliferating Talent*, esp. chap. 8; Marshall, *Learning to Be Modern*, esp. pp. 101–6.

43. Williams, "Base and Superstructure," p. 383.

44. Wilson, *Patriots and Redeemers*, p. 10.

45. Harootunian, "Late Tokugawa Culture and Thought," p. 256.

46. Scott, "Foreword," pp. viii–ix.

47. For a more extensive discussion of how Dore and other scholars guided by the concerns of modernization theory framed the Tokugawa legacy in terms of continuity, see Lincicome, *Principle*, pp. 3–9.

48. Walthall, *The Weak Body of a Useless Woman*. Haga Noboru is one Japanese scholar who has also done this, focusing particularly on the social networks of nativism and their extension into the Meiji period; see, e.g., his *Kokugaku no hitobito*.

49. Hall, *Government and Local Power*; Jansen, *Sakamoto Ryōma*.

50. See P. Brown, "Local History's Challenge to National Narratives."

51. For an analysis of this phenomenon as it occurred in Nagano prefecture, see Wigen, "Politics and Piety." For a general analysis of the various factors that have contributed to the local history movement in Japan, see Amino, "Undō to shite no chiiki-shi"; and Kimura Motoi, "Kyōdo-shi, chihō-shi, chiiki-shi." For a discussion of the link between local history and educational history, see Kaminuma, "Chihō-shi to kyōiku-shi."

52. For a review essay of recent scholarship on the relationship between localities and the Meiji state, see Hanes, "Contesting Centralization?"

53. Wigen, "Constructing Shinano."

54. Baxter, *The Meiji Unification*; Waters, *Japan's Local Pragmatists*.

55. Lewis, *Becoming Apart.*
56. Allinson, *Japanese Urbanism.*
57. Wigen, "Politics and Piety," p. 505.

Chapter 1

1. Dore, *Education in Tokugawa Japan*; Passin, *Society and Education in Japan.*

2. See, e.g., John Hall's "Changing Conceptions" (p. 19), the keynote article in Princeton University Press's four-volume series on Japan's modernization. In this article, Hall identifies education and literacy as one of a handful of indices by which we can evaluate the level of modernization in a particular society.

3. On the influence of Dore's and Passin's research on Japanese scholars of Tokugawa education, see Iriye, "Kinsei 1," pp. 83–84.

4. Many historians, instead of using the full term *shizen hassei*, simply use *hassei*, which literally means "growth" or "generation" and is most often used to describe an outbreak of a disease or fire.

5. For discussions in English on the various types of pre-Meiji educational institutions, see Dore, *Education in Tokugawa Japan*; Passin, *Society and Education in Japan*, pp. 13–42; Rubinger, *Private Academies*, pp. 3–14; and Sawada, *Confucian Values and Popular Zen*, pp. 9–27.

6. On the early history of *terakoya*, see Tanaka, "'Terakoya' no kigen"; see also Umihara, *Kinsei no gakkō*, pp. 293–353.

7. Rubinger, *Private Academies.*

8. Monbushō, *Nihon kyōiku-shi shiryō*, vols. 8 and 9.

9. Takamisawa's district-by-district research appeared in a series of articles in the journal *Shinshū daigaku, Kyōiku gakubu kiyō*. In addition, his research on several Shinano districts was never published; I am indebted to his colleague Nagura Eizaburō, who photocopied this unpublished research for me. Some of Takamisawa's aggregate figures can also be found in Nagano-ken kyōiku-shi hensan iinkai, *Nagano-ken kyōiku-shi* (hereafter *NKKS*), 1: 96–97.

The eighteen volumes in *NKKS* consist of six volumes of secondary scholarship (under the rubric of *sōsetsu*, or "general narrative") and twelve volumes of primary sources. When citing from the *sōsetsu* volumes, I follow the standard practice of giving the volume and page numbers. When citing from the primary-source volumes, however, I refer to the volume and document number (rather than page number). The compilers of the primary-source volumes provided titles for each document to give some indication of its content, but many of the documents themselves were not originally titled. In the cases in which an original document was not titled, I include in the footnotes only the volume number and the number of the document; if an original document was titled, I include the title of the document as well.

10. For example, research for *Tochigi-ken kyōiku-shi* has turned up evidence of 449 schools, just over four times the original number of 105 reported in the early Meiji statistics. Similarly, the *Nihon kyōiku-shi shiryō* reports only 239 schools for Kanagawa prefecture (Kaga province), but recent

research by Takada Minoru ("Kanagawa-ken no terakoya") has uncovered 1,231 schools, over five times the original figure. Kaigo Tokiomi (*Japanese Education*, p. 48), a Japanese scholar of educational history, has also suggested that the number of Tokugawa-period village schools may have exceeded 40,000, although much of the local research that supports such a conclusion had not yet been published.

11. Monbushō, *Nihon kyōiku-shi shiryō*, vols. 8 and 9.

12. Ishikawa, *Nihon shomin kyōiku-shi*, pp. 271–73.

13. Ishikawa Ken (ibid., pp. 267–71) presents the *Nihon kyōiku-shi shiryō* statistics in this per annum format in his book.

14. For example, I have found this post-Tempō growth pattern in Gifu prefecture using records of school openings in the *Gifu-ken shi, tsūshi-hen, kinsei 2*, 1078–102. Similar trends can be found in Kanagawa prefecture (see Takada, "Kanagawa-ken no terakoya") and Tochigi prefecture (Iriye, "Kinsei Shimōzuke").

15. *NKKS*, 1: 98.

16. Ibid., p. 95.

17. Takamisawa, whose research forms the basis for these statistics, classifies "farmers" (*nō*) and "merchants" (*shō*) as separate status groups, although by the late Tokugawa period, most farmers—particularly those village elites who were most likely to be teachers—were extensively involved in some sort of commercial or mercantile activity. For a full list of Takamisawa's articles, see the Works Cited.

18. *NKKS*, 1: 98.

19. According to Ministry of Education statistics from the mid-Meiji period, there were nine female teachers in Shinano. Six of these taught alongside a male instructor—in most cases, their husbands. Three female teachers had their own schools, including Tanaka Seki, who taught some 3,000 students over a 50-year period in the castle-town of Matsushiro. See *NKKS*, vol. 8, no. 35.1.

20. District (*gun*) boundaries existed in Shinano before the Tokugawa period but were of no real meaning after the consolidation of the Tokugawa order, because they did not, for the most part, correspond to the boundaries of bakufu and domain lands. I use the geographic unit of "district" here simply because the statistics on commoner schooling are organized by district.

21. Takamisawa, "Shinshū Hanishina-gun," pp. 29–30.

22. Takamisawa, "Fudezuka ni kansuru kenkyū: Nagano-ken Kamitakai-gun no baai," pp. 22–23.

23. Takamisawa, "Fuzezuka o chūshin to shita shomin kyōiku," pp. 4–6.

24. In calculating this figure I have combined the *Nihon kyōiku-shi shiryō* statistics on *terakoya* with those on *shijuku*. Because the percentage of samurai teachers in schools classified as *shijuku* was higher than in schools classified as *terakoya*, the overall percentage of samurai teachers in what I have termed "commoner schools" is slightly higher than that calculated by historians who consider *terakoya* separately. See, e.g., Rubinger, *Private Academies*, p. 11; and Ishikawa, *Nihon shomin kyōiku-shi*, pp. 288–91.

25. Takada, "Kanagawa-ken no terakoya," p. 17.

26. Ishikawa, *Nihon shomin kyōiku-shi*, pp. 290–91.

27. The major exceptions to this two-phase pattern of growth were Edo, Osaka, and Kyoto, where the increase in the number of schools began much earlier and leveled off by the late eighteenth century, and where the status backgrounds of teachers did not change so markedly.

28. Even in the case of Kanagawa, where Buddhist priests far outnumbered commoners among the teaching ranks throughout most of the Edo period, we find a dramatic increase in the percentage of commoner teachers after the Tempō period; see Takada, "Kanagawa-ken no terakoya," pp. 17–20. I have discovered similar late Tokugawa increases in commoner teachers in my research on Gifu, and Iriye has pointed out this trend in Tochigi prefecture, as has Kimura Masanobu ("Bakumatsu-ki Chikugo no nōson") in Shizuoka.

29. Umihara, *Kinsei no gakkō*, pp. 319–20.

30. Tone, *Terakoya to shomin kyōiku*.

31. See, e.g., Komoriya, "Bakumatsu-ki Kitagawauchi nōson"; and Umemura Kayo, *Nihon kinsei minshū*.

32. *NKKS*, vol. 8, no. 40.

33. Population statistics for Matsunojō are found in ibid., 1: 157.

34. This survey is found in ibid., 4: 142–45.

35. Dore, *Education in Tokugawa Japan*, pp. 62–64.

36. See Chihara, *Shinshū no hangaku*.

37. Aoki, "Shinano no rangaku-juku," p. 23.

38. Chihara, *Shinshū no hangaku*, pp. 140–43.

39. Rubinger, *Private Academies*, pp. 41–56.

40. Dore, *Education in Tokugawa Japan*, p. 220.

41. Najita, *Visions of Virtue*, pp. 27–48.

42. For a discussion of the concept of *kyōka* in modern Japan, see Garon, *Molding Japanese Minds*.

43. Dore discusses this incident in *Education in Tokugawa Japan*, p. 232.

44. Chihara, *Shinshū no hangaku*, pp. 17–20.

45. *NKKS*, vol. 8, no. 35.1.

46. Ibid., no. 137.2.

47. Ibid., 1: 118.

48. Ibid., vol. 8, no. 85.2.

49. As Ooms (*Tokugawa Village Practice*, pp. 74–110) points out, the number of such elite families within each village and the nature of their position—both within their communities and vis-à-vis bakufu or domainal authorities—varied in different parts of the country. In particular, he notes the important distinction between "corporate villages" (*sō*) and those villages ruled more autonomously by rural magnates (*dogō*).

50. Takahashi Satoshi, *Minshū to gōnō*, pp. 74–75.

51. On these "characteristic" features of the Tokugawa village, see Smith, *Agrarian Origins*, chaps. 7–9.

52. Ooms, *Tokugawa Village Practice*, pp. 111–21.

53. Watanabe, *Kinsei no gōnō*, pp. 18–20, 120.

54. Ibid., p. 21.

55. Walthall, "Village Networks," pp. 282–90.

56. Several English-language scholars have described the role of commercial activity in linking villages, cities, and regions in Edo-period Japan; see, e.g., Hauser, *Economic Institutional Change*; Wigen, *The Making of a Japanese Periphery*; and Howell, *Capitalism from Within*.

My primary focus here is on proto-industrialization and commercialization as opposed to capitalism. Recently, both William Kelly's *Deference and Defiance* and Howell's *Capitalism from Within* have pointed out the distinction between the two and have emphasized that "it was not the commercialization of exchange, but the capitalist reorganization of production that was the thrust of change in the nineteenth century rural economy" (Kelly, p. 24). However, in my discussion of the transformation of local elites during the eighteenth century and the effect of this transformation on the development of commoner education, it was the formation of elite networks through commercial exchange (and not capitalist production) that was the key process.

57. Here I use the term "region" not in the sense of a formal region such as Kantō, Chūbu, etc., or even a province; rather, I rely here on the notion of a "functional region," described by Wigen as "a contiguous area united by a complementarity of economic and political resources, and integrated through the routine interactions among its constituent parts" (*The Making of a Japanese Periphery*, p. 16).

The obvious exception to this pattern, in which castle-towns served as regional hubs of commercial (and, as we will see later, cultural) activity, is the town of Zenkōji, which was a temple-town rather than a castle-town but whose status as a national pilgrimage site stimulated its development into a major commercial and cultural center for northern Shinano.

58. *Nagano-ken shi tsūshi-hen* (hereafter *NKSTH*), *kinsei* 2, pp. 378–81.

59. Ibid., *kinsei* 3, p. 289.

60. For the case of Iida, see Wigen, *The Making of a Japanese Periphery*, pp. 121–23. For accounts of this trend in other Shinano castle towns, see *NKSTH*, *kinsei* 2, pp. 478–80, and *kinsei* 3, pp. 352–61.

61. Wigen, *The Making of a Japanese Periphery*, p. 71.

62. This practice was known by the term *hōkō*, or domestic service. By the late eighteenth century, the nature of *hōkō* had changed somewhat, as poorer commoners began doing seasonal, manual labor *hōkō* mainly for the purpose of earning cash in the slack agricultural season; see *NKSTH*, *kinsei* 2, pp. 434–45.

63. Kobayashi Keiichirō, "Kinsei kita-Shinano."

64. Nagano-ken shi hensan iinkai, *Nagano-ken shi shiryō hen* (hereafter *NKS*), *kinsei shiryō hen*, vol. 1, no. 289.

65. *NKSTH, kinsei* 2, p. 193.

66. *NKS, kinsei shiryō hen*, vol. 7, no. 716.

67. Ooms, *Tokugawa Village Practice*, p. 184; *NKSTH kinsei* 2, pp. 542–43, *kinsei* 3, pp. 435–36.

68. Bourdieu, *An Outline of a Theory of Practice*, pp. 177–84.

69. Ooms, *Tokugawa Village Practice*, pp. 3–4, 123–24, 126–34, 198–202.

70. Bourdieu, *An Outline of a Theory of Practice*, pp. 177–78.

71. Ironically, later in the period, local poets built numerous memorials to commemorate Bashō's passage through Shinano, and local elites would travel great distances to lay eyes on even a middling poet from Edo or Kyoto; see Kobayashi Keiichirō, "Haikai no ryūsei to shakai," p. 99.

72. *NKSTH, kinsei* 3, pp. 500–501.

73. Kobayashi Keiichirō, "Haikai no ryūsei to shakai," p. 101.

74. This is not to suggest that Edo was the source of all Edo-period culture and that provincial areas like Shinano were simply cultural blank slates, waiting for "Edo culture" to reach the peripheries. Constantine Vaporis ("To Edo and Back") has effectively criticized this notion and argues that "Edo culture" itself was in part the product of the interaction of influences brought from the provinces to Edo.

75. Kobayashi Keiichirō, "Haikai no ryūsei to shakai," pp. 108–9.

76. Ibid., pp. 113–16.

77. For Sōhan's records, see *NKKS*, vol. 8, no. 1.

78. This quote is found in the diary of one of Mutaku's students, a headman and aspiring *haiku* poet in the Northern Ina district of Shinano (ibid., no. 128).

79. Biographical information on Shūsuke and Jiken can be found in ibid., 1: 170–71. As a youth, Shūsuke had studied poetry in Ueda with Kaya Shirao, the *haikai* master mentioned above who achieved fame as an Edo poet while also spending part of each year in Shinano tutoring aspiring local poets.

80. For a discussion of the organization and activities of Shingaku meetinghouses, see Sawada, *Confucian Values and Popular Zen*, pp. 46–48.

81. For Shūsuke's records of his students, see *NKKS*, vol. 7, no. 307.

82. Ibid.

83. Sawada, *Confucian Values and Popular Zen*, pp. 48–50, 91–109.

84. Ibid., pp. 110–40.

85. *NKKS*, vol. 7, no. 328.

86. Aoki, "Shinano no rangaku-juku," p. 25.

87. See, e.g., Stone, "Literacy and Education"; Schofield, "The Dimensions of Illiteracy"; and Laqueur, "Working-Class Demand."

88. *NKSTH, kinsei* 2, pp. 377–406.

89. Ibid., *kinsei* 3, p. 214.

90. Ibid., pp. 214–43.

91. Ibid., pp. 32–36.

92. While Japanese scholars generally agree that school attendance by non-elite villagers began only in the last decades of the Tokugawa period, one can find exceptions to this generalization. For example, Umemura (*Nihon kinsei minshū*) has researched a few late eighteenth- and early nineteenth-century schools in the Kinai region that were attended predominantly by the middle and lower classes within the village; in these cases, the children

acquired the basic knowledge and skills they needed to work as domestic servants in Kyoto and Osaka during their teenage years.

93. Tone, *Terakoya to shomin kyōiku*; Takahashi Satoshi, *Nihon minshū*, esp. pp. 184–92.

94. Smith, *Native Sources*, p. 192.

95. Detailed information on these famines can be found in *NKSTH, kinsei* 3, pp. 102–15.

96. Ibid., p. 114.

97. For example, see Hanley and Yamamura, *Economic and Demographic Change*; Smith, *Nakahara*; and more recently, Saito, "Infanticide, Fertility, and 'Population Stagnation.'"

98. Boli-Bennett and Meyer, "The Ideology of Childhood."

99. For detailed records of tuition fees at specific schools in Shinano, see *NKKS*, vol. 8, nos. 103, 127, and 159.

100. The diary of one teacher includes a kind of "lesson plan" for his students, detailing the characters and texts covered during the first years of a child's schooling. See ibid., no. 216.1.

101. Takahashi, *Nihon minshū*, pp. 220–45.

102. *NKKS*, vol. 8, no. 85.2.

103. Ravina, *Land and Lordship*; Roberts, *Mercantilism in a Japanese Domain*.

104. *NKKS*, 1: 102–5.

105. Ibid., vol. 7, no. 17.1 and no. 369.2.

106. Ibid., no. 373.

107. For documentation on such efforts, see the following sources from *NKKS*, vol. 7: for Iiyama domain, no. 8.1; for Matsushiro domain, no. 26.1; for Ueda domain, no. 36.1; for Komoro domain, no. 43.1.

108. Ibid., no. 129.1.

109. Ibid., 1: 169.

110. Shōzan kept a diary while scouting this area, and his discussion of this particular incident is excerpted in ibid., vol. 8, no. 13.

111. Shōzan mentions this reader in a letter he sent to the teacher, Nakamura Kōeimon. The letter is found in ibid., no. 16, and the reader is found in ibid., no. 184. In the letter, Shōzan urges Nakamura to write another text for the children, one which teaches them common characters in personal names and place-names. Nakamura fulfilled Shōzan's request; the text is found in ibid., no. 185.

112. Quoted in ibid., 1: 168.

113. On the different kinds of reform measures taken by bakufu and domain authorities, see Bolitho, "The Tempō Crisis."

114. Harootunian, "Late Tokugawa Culture and Thought," pp. 182–98.

115. *NKSTH, kinsei* 3, p. 114.

116. Ibid.

117. Ibid., pp. 38–40.

118. Takahashi, *Nihon minshū*, pp. 199–203.

119. Ibid., pp. 140–47.

120. Walthall, *The Weak Body of a Useless Woman*, pp. 104–5.

121. Harootunian, *Things Seen and Unseen*.

122. Harootunian, "Late Tokugawa Culture and Thought," p. 207.

123. Kamijō, "Hirata kokugaku," pp. 9–10.

124. Nakano, "Sonraku fukkō," pp. 109–18.

125. Takahashi, *Nihon minshū*, pp. 203–6.

126. Quoted in Nakano, "Sonraku fukkō," p. 119. For a discussion of Miyaoi in English, see Harootunian, *Things Seen and Unseen*, pp. 296–307.

127. Nakano, "Sonraku fukkō," pp. 121–22.

128. Kawamura, *Zaison chishikijin*, pp. 104–6.

129. Ibid., pp. 140–48.

130. Ibid., p. 105.

131. For the series of documents discussed in this paragraph, see *NKKS*, vol. 8, no. 57.1–6.

132. Ibid., no. 140.

133. Ibid., no. 128.2, no. 85.2.

134. *NKS, kinsei shiryō hen*, vol. 4, no. 1,058.

135. Ibid.

136. Nakano, "Sonraku fukkō," pp. 120–21.

137. Harootunian, *Things Seen and Unseen*, pp. 231–32.

138. Harootunian, "Late Tokugawa Thought and Culture," pp. 204–5.

139. For a recent discussion of this debate, see Umemura, *Nihon kinsei minshū*, chap. 1; or Kawamura, *Zaison chishikijin*, pp. 19–40.

Chapter 2

1. If we are to believe the author, the audience for this family history was his own descendants, rather than his peers or the village at large. At the end of the text, he wrote that his work should be seen "only by our descendants, that they should know about my father's and my grandfather's generation: their circumspection in all matters, their various struggles, their frugality, and their filiality" (Ozawa Watoku, "Tōke shodai kōkodō Shisan ichidaiki" [A chronicle of Shisan, the forbear of this household, and his Love of Antiquity School; hereafter "Tōke"], p. 159). If this sentiment was genuine, the document may have been intended to establish the family's credentials for local leadership in its own members' eyes rather than to make a public claim for specific rights and privileges as village elites. His journals, however, seem to have been written largely for personal recordkeeping purposes (rather than for public consumption). Consequently, I do not believe that we need to suspect self-conscious exaggeration when reading the journals.

2. Patricia Hampl ("Memory and Imagination") argues that it is precisely the subjective nature of individual memory that makes it historically significant. She writes, "But in the act of remembering the personal environment expands, resonates beyond itself, beyond its 'subject' into the endless and tragic recollection that is history" (ibid., p. 201).

3. Ozawa Watoku, "Shoji nisshinroku" (hereafter cited by the title), 1868/7/23.

4. The autographs of Watoku's journals and family history are held by his descendant Ozawa Kazunobu. Photographic copies of the original texts can be found in the Nagano Prefectural History Museum, and portions of the journals and the family history were published in *NKKS*, 8: 492–554. Watoku bound his journal yearly, giving each year's volume a different title. Since the journals are not paginated, I cite entries by the title of that year's journal and date. Watoku's family history, entitled "Tōke shodai kōkodō Shisan ichidaiki," is also unpaginated; in citing it, however, I refer to the pagination I have assigned my copy of this work. For the three successive heads of the Ozawa family, I will use the posthumous names (Shisan, Kameharu, and Watoku) given to them by the local Buddhist temple, presumably in exchange for the family's contributions, rather than the hereditary name of the household head (Danji) with a generation marker (i.e., Danji I, Danji II, etc.). The posthumous names should enable the reader to distinguish the three distinct personalities described in Watoku's family history more easily. They also befit the emphasis of this article on the cultural activities of the three generations, for although Shisan, Kameharu, and Watoku used the name Danji when acting as household head in official matters, they received their posthumous names well before their deaths and used them as pen names when writing poetry.

5. The experience of the Ozawa seems to have been common. According to Takahashi Satoshi (*Gōnō to minshū*, pp. 74–75), many early Tokugawa village elites in Kai and Shinano provinces were former retainers of the Takeda family who settled in rural areas as farmers after their lord's defeat. Ono was a large village and minor post-town along a branch of the Ina Road. The post-town was originally constructed to serve the Nakasendō road but was demoted when in 1615 the Nakasendō was rerouted to pass through Shiojiri (several kilometers north of Ono). Just a few years earlier, Ono had been divided into northern and southern sections; the northern village was incorporated into Suwa domain, and the southern was classified as Tokugawa land (*tenryō*) and administered by the bakufu intendant's office in Iida. On the complex and fragmented political arrangements in and around Ono during the Edo period, see Tatsuno-machi, *Tatsuno-machi shi*, pp. 455–508.

6. Takahashi (*Gōnō to minshū*, p. 74) notes that this was a common strategy for newly rusticated samurai.

7. See, e.g., Mizumoto, *Kinsei no mura*; Watanabe, *Kinsei no gōnō*; and Ooms, *Tokugawa Village Practice*.

8. Kobayashi Keiichirō ("Kinsei kita-Shinano") notes that it was common in Shinano at this time to distribute family wealth fairly evenly among many, if not all, male offspring.

9. Smith, *Agrarian Origins*.

10. In addition to the main heir (Kozaemon), the branch house heir (Shisan), and the two sons sent into adoption, the Ozawas had a fifth son who died unmarried at the age of 25.

11. A generation later, Shisan (the son who had branched off from the main Ozawa family), arranged for the adoption of his son Kameharu into a

samurai family. The adoption was not completed because Kameharu ran away from home to prevent the transaction. His justification was, ironically, filial piety. He is said to have thought to himself, "Because Ryōnosuke [his younger brother who, after the adoption, would have been designated as the main heir] is rude, careless, and spendthrift, it would not be filial for me, the family heir, to go off to this wealthy home and leave my parents in the hands of an unstable person" ("Tōke," pp. 33–38).

12. We can perhaps apply a similar logic to the family's decision to send their only daughter (who, unlike her five male siblings, goes unnamed in Watoku's family history) into a convent at a young age. Considering the family's concern with forging extra-village connections—and considering Walthall's evidence that such connections were commonly established through out-marrying female offspring—it may seem odd that the family did not find her a husband from a wealthy and influential family; see Walthall, "The Family Ideology of Rural Entrepreneurs." Perhaps they tried but did not succeed, for any number of possible reasons: constraints on available dowry funds, unavailability of a suitable mate, or even the girl's physical undesirability due to sickness or disability. Temples and monasteries, however, played an important role in the literary and artistic circles of rural elite society. In the case of the Ozawa family, priests are mentioned repeatedly in Watoku's diary and family history as coparticipants in poetry societies, and local monasteries appear frequently as lenders and borrowers of books. Sending the only daughter into a convent may have served to strengthen the family's ties with these local religious institutions.

13. Akira Hayami ("The Myth of Primogeniture") suggests that primogeniture was in fact not a pervasive pattern in Tokugawa-period rural society. In the case of the Ozawa, the fifth-, sixth-, and seventh-generation family heads were not the oldest son in their respective families; instead, parents either adopted the eldest son out or allowed him to establish a branch house, reserving the household headship for the second or third son.

14. As Ooms (*Tokugawa Village Practice*, pp. 21–22) notes, however, in some areas it was common for ordinary farm families to marry outside their own villages.

15. Toby ("Both a Borrower and a Lender Be") and Walthall ("Village Networks") make similar arguments regarding the importance of regional networks in establishing an elite family's economic and political career.

16. "Tōke," pp. 4–6.

17. For the second son, Gen'iku, who studied medicine in Nagoya and later became a doctor, there seems to have been a more instrumental relationship between education and career. After financing his medical studies, however, his parents sent him into a cotton merchant family as an adopted son, which suggests strongly that they did not intend for him to pursue medicine as a profession. Gen'iku became a doctor only later, after separating from his adoptive family.

18. See Walthall, "The Cult of Sensibility."

19. "Tōke," pp. 4–5.

20. Ibid., pp. 6–7.

21. Ibid., p. 21.

22. Ibid., p. 7.

23. Ibid., pp. 11–12.

24. Ibid., pp. 51–55.

25. Ibid., p. 21. Walthall ("The Family Ideology of Rural Entrepreneurs," p. 467) notes that descriptions of large funerals (and other family ceremonies) were common in village elite diaries, since they provided future generations a concrete measure of a family's wealth and prestige.

26. "Tōke," p. 51.

27. They were short-lived for his troublemaking brother Ryōnosuke as well. After repeated petitions to Edo for reinstatement in his previous job proved unsuccessful, he eventually settled in the Kanda district of Edo and became, of all things, a schoolteacher, instructing the children of both samurai and wealthy commoners.

28. "Tōke," pp. 110–12.

29. Ibid., pp. 139–40.

30. Ibid., p. 141.

31. Ibid.

32. For a chart listing all the teachers in the various villages that now make up the city of Tatsuno, see Tatsuno-machi shi, *Tatsuno-machi shi,* pp. 983–89.

33. For population statistics for Ono, see ibid., p. 677.

34. Ozawa Watoku, "Gakumonjo kyōkun kyosairoku," 1865/1/23. Watoku recorded that beginning students used texts such as *I-ro-ha* (Alphabet book), *Nagashirazukushi* (Book of personal names), *Murazukushi* (Book of village names), and *Kunizukushi* (Book of province names). Students did not use the actual texts. Rather, Watoku owned at least one copy of each of these texts and wrote out excerpts from them to make workbooks (*tehon*) for each student. This task seems to have taken up much of Watoku's time; even on days when no students were in attendance, Watoku almost invariably records that he spent time writing workbooks.

35. For English translations of these texts, see Chamberlain, "Teachings for the Young" and "The Teaching of the Words of Truth."

36. Watoku rarely recorded the exact number of students; usually, he simply wrote, "Tenaraikodomo yohodo mairisōrō" (many students came), replacing *yohodo* with *ōzei, soroi,* and *nokorazu* as increasing gradations of "many."

37. "Shoji nisshinroku," 1868/6/9.

38. Ozawa Watoku, "Nennai shoji nikkicho" (hereafter cited by the title), 1866/3/9.

39. Ozawa Watoku, "Nisshin keikai jichiroku" (hereafter cited by the title), 1863/12/8.

40. Ibid., 1863/12/11.

41. "Tōke," p. 20.

42. Ibid., pp. 157–58.

43. This particular manifestation of student-teacher bonds was also found by the Japanese scholar Takahashi Satoshi in his examination of a village teacher in Gunma prefecture; see his "Mura no tenaraijuku," pp. 22–23.

44. "Tōke," pp. 23–24.

45. "Nisshin keikai jichiroku," 1863/12/11.

46. Rubinger, "Education," p. 210.

47. For this particular incident, see "Tōke," pp. 84–98.

48. Ibid., p. 95.

49. Apparently the authorities were not menacing enough, for one of the perpetrators proceeded to refuse his service the next day. The man, one Jin-gozaemon, instead stayed in Ono, got drunk, and cursed the man Kameharu sent to retrieve him. That night, when summoned again by the authorities (who were still staying at Kameharu's home), Jingozaemon arrived sporting a limp, saying that he was unable to perform his labor obligations because he had fallen out of a tree and hurt himself. The authorities gave another tongue lashing to Kameharu, Jingozaemon, and the latter's two accomplices. The matter was settled only after two more confrontations, with the perpe-trators eventually complying with the officials' orders (though, according to Watoku's account, remaining unrepentant).

50. Ooms, *Tokugawa Village Practice*, p. 241.

51. Sasaki, *Bakumatsu shakairon*, pp. 57–58.

52. Village elites seemed conscious of this fact, as suggested by an entry in Watoku's diary from the fall of 1861 recording a bitter, drawn-out dispute between the headman of Ono and another local notable over who would host a bakufu intendant for tea during his passage through Ono; see Ozawa Watoku, "Shoji kyosai tebikaechō," 1861/10/7.

53. Walthall, "Village Networks," p. 282.

54. "Tōke," pp. 116–40.

55. Ibid., pp. 160–61.

56. Ibid., p. 21.

57. In one such celebration, Watoku, his students, and other villagers in Ono paid homage to the spirit of tenth-century poet and scholar Sugawara no Michizane, deified as Tenjinsama, the god of learning and scholarship. According to Watoku's diary, on this day, children came to Watoku's house early in the morning, and he led them on a pilgrimage to the Tenjinsama shrine—the construction of which he himself had organized. After bringing money and sake to the shrine, Watoku took the children to the Ono River to offer poems and requests to Tenjinsama (poems that Watoku had helped the children write in the days leading up to the celebration). As with other school-centered events, this festival expanded into villagewide feasting, drinking, and socializing.

58. "Nisshin keikai jichiroku," 1863/7–1863/8.

59. Ibid., 1863/10.

60. "Nennai shoji nikkicho," 1867/2–1867/3.

61. "Tōke," pp. 160–61.

62. Ibid., p. 21.

63. Ibid., p. 25.

64. We do not know how Kameharu and Shisan were perceived by the participants of higher status in these social gatherings. Although in Watoku's account they socialized as equals, they may well have been perceived as interlopers. So long as others in Ono heard (and believed) the Ozawa version of the story, the family's prestige would be unaffected, and since subsequent generations of Ozawa would have access only to Watoku's version, the stories would serve to bolster the descendants' self-image.

65. The entire episode was a source of great pride for the Ozawa family, and Watoku recorded it in detail, from Chōgetsu's advice on poetry to his "spotless white silk robe and purple sash." Especially treasured were Chōgetsu's words of praise for Kameharu's poems, which were said "out of genuine admiration, with no trace of insincerity" ("Tōke," p. 46).

66. Miyachi, *Bakumatsu ishinki*, p. 22.

67. On cultural integration, see Berry, "Was Early Modern Japan Culturally Integrated?"; on the reciprocal nature of the cultural exchange between Edo and the provinces, see Vaporis, "To Edo and Back."

68. All the quotations in this paragraph are from "Tōke," pp. 37–38.

69. Kameharu tried several other ventures in his lifetime, including a sake brewery and an inn. The number of different ventures suggests Kameharu's success in raising capital, which was facilitated by his esteemed position within the village as a teacher and his extra-village connections formed through educational and cultural activities.

70. Toby ("Both a Borrower and a Lender Be," p. 507) provides a similar description of a rural banker named Gonbei who had access to capital through such networks of business and culture.

71. Kurushima, "Hyakushō to mura no henshitsu," p. 99; Tsukamoto makes a similar argument in his *Chihō bunjin*.

72. According to Watoku, all of Shisan's and Kameharu's books were lost in the many fires suffered by the family, particularly one in 1834. Watoku writes, "Even though the books no longer exist, I write them down here as a record of what [Shisan and Kameharu] accomplished [in copying the books]" ("Tōke," pp. 159–60).

73. "Shoji nisshinroku," 1868/6–1868/9.

74. For a translation of the Sakura Sōgorō story, see Walthall, *Peasant Uprisings in Japan*, pp. 46–75.

75. "Shoji nisshinroku," 1868/7/14.

76. In fact, Kobayashi Fumio ("Kinsei kōki," p. 29) has specifically emphasized the role of village teachers in this diffusion of the written word into the countryside. On the role of village elites in the formation of what many scholars now refer to as an "information society," see Miyachi, "Bakumatsu seiji katei"; and Takahashi Sadaki, "Bakumatsu-ki nōson."

77. "Tōke," pp. 21–22.

78. Ibid., p. 135.

79. Ozawa Watoku, "Nennai shoji hikae nikki" (hereafter cited by title), 1868/4/22.

80. "Nennai shoji nikkichō," 1866/4/25.

81. "Shoji nisshinroku," 1868/7/25.

82. Ibid., 1868/7/10.

83. "Nennai shoji nikkicho," 1868/5/11.

84. "Nennai shoji hikae nikki," 1868/4/22.

85. Kamijō, "Hirata kokugaku," pp. 9–10.

86. The highest number belongs to Yamabuki-mura, just outside Iida, with 33 disciples; only two other villages had more than 20, and most had only one or two. The castle-town of Iida, the largest town in the area, had 50. See *NKSTH*, 6: 800. Interestingly, Watoku had close connections with both these other centers of nativist thought: he traveled to Iida often on official business, and several times journeyed to Yamabuki to participate in poetry society meetings with friends.

87. Shimazaki, *Before the Dawn*.

88. "Nennai shoji hikae nikki," 1868/3/18.

89. Ibid., 1868/3/20.

90. Ibid., 1868/3/25.

91. While Hanzō eventually grew disillusioned with the long-term re-sults of the Restoration, he initially saw it as "the rising of a sun that would pour the spirit of life back into this ancient and exhausted high-way," comparing it to Jimmu's initial conquest of Japan (Shimazaki, *Before the Dawn*, p. 460).

92. Ibid., pp. 439–42.

93. Watoku also noted that as Iwakura passed through, farmers from Matsushima village wearing raincoats and carrying umbrellas interrupted Iwakura's path and petitioned to change the jurisdiction of the area from bakufu-ruled land to that of Owari domain ("Nennai shoji hikae nikki," 1868/3/1).

94. For the portion of Tōzaemon's diary that deals with the *ofudafuri* and *ee ja nai ka* incidents, see Miwa, "Shinano 'ee ja nai ka.'" For the most exten-sive discussion in English concerning the *ofudafuri* and *ee ja nai ka* move-ments, see Wilson, *Patriots and Redeemers*, pp. 95–121.

95. Miwa, "Shinano 'ee ja nai ka,'" p. 32.

96. "Shoji nisshinroku," 1868/7/25.

97. Ibid., 1868/7/23.

98. Ibid., 1868/8/15.

99. "Nennai shoji hikae nikki," 1868/4/12.

100. Ibid.

101. Ibid.

102. "Shoji nisshinroku," 1868/10/1.

103. Ibid.

104. This comment was made specifically in reference to the former wife of Watoku's uncle Ryōnosuke (the one who had achieved the exalted status of clerk at the bakufu intendant's office, only to lose his job, his sanity, his inheritance, and his wife). After her husband fled to Edo, Watoku's father,

Kameharu, managed to marry her to the master of the *honjin* of a nearby post-town ("Tōke," p. 67).

105. Miyachi, "Bakumatsu seiji katei."

106. Ibid., p. 48.

107. Harootunian, "Late Tokugawa Thought and Culture," pp. 180–81. Miyachi has written at length on this issue, using the concept of the "public sphere" to describe the circulation of political information during the bakumatsu era; see his "Fūsetsu tome."

108. Walthall, *The Weak Body of a Useless Woman*.

Chapter 3

1. Najita, "Introduction," p. 15.

2. This discussion of educational debates within the central government immediately following the Restoration relies on a number of works on early Meiji education. In Japanese, see Kaigo, *Meiji shonen no kyōiku*; Kaneko, *Meiji zenki kyōiku*; and Motoyama, *Meiji kokka no kyōiku shisō*. For an English translation of one of Motoyama's earlier essays on early Meiji education, see Motoyama, *Proliferating Talent*, pp. 83–147. For a succinct synthesis in English of the issues addressed in these works, see Marshall, *Learning to Be Modern*, pp. 27–29; and Rubinger, "Education," pp. 202–4.

3. The early Meiji university in Tokyo consisted of three separate schools: the Main School (Honkō), which sprang from the Tokugawa-period Shōheikō and focused on both Confucian and Shinto scholarship; the South School (Nankō), formerly known as the Kaiseijo, which focused on Western Learning; and the East School (Tōkō), which served as a medical school, inheriting the function of its Tokugawa predecessor, the Igakujo.

4. On the contemporary debates concerning the transfer of the capital to Tokyo, as well as later debates about the respective place of Kyoto and Tokyo in the national imagination, see Fujitani, *Splendid Monarchy*, pp. 34–92.

5. For a full translation of the Charter Oath, see Tsunoda et al., *Sources of Japanese Tradition*, pp. 643–44.

6. Iwakura, "Sakugi," in Iwakura kō kyūseki hozonkai, *Iwakura kō jikki*, 2: 23–31.

7. Iwakura, "Jimu sūken," in ibid, pp. 760–61.

8. Ibid.

9. Here I use Rubinger's translation of Itō's document, found in Motoyama, *Proliferating Talent*, pp. 117–18. For the original document, entitled "Kokuze kōmoku," see Shunpo kō tsuishōkai, *Itō Hirobumi den*, 1: 422–23.

10. Ibid.

11. Kido Takayoshi, "Futsū kyōiku no shinkō o kyūmu to subeki kengensho," in Tsumaki, *Kido Takayoshi monjo*, 8: 78–79.

12. Ibid.

13. *The Diary of Kido Takayoshi*, 2: 118.

14. Kido, "Futsū kyōiku no shinkō," in Tsumaki, *Kido Takayoshi monjo*, 8: 78–79.

15. On the different meanings of "Restoration" in the early Meiji period, see Najita, "Introduction."

16. "The Meiji leaders, aware of the urgent need for a modern unified educational system to catch up with the West, plumped down firmly on the side of Western learning. Even before the Restoration this was becoming clear" (Passin, *Society and Education*, p. 63).

17. Indeed, Kinmoth ("Fukuzawa Reconsidered") has raised questions regarding our application of the label "liberal" to the educational thought of Fukuzawa Yukichi, whose liberal credentials are much stronger than Itō's or Kido's.

18. "Shofuken shisei junjo," in Kyōiku-shi hensankai, *Meiji ikō kyōiku seido hattatsu-shi* (hereafter *Hattatsu-shi*), 1: 228–30.

19. Ibid.

20. On the 1869 directive, entitled "Senkyōshi kokoroesho," see Inoue Hisashi, *Meiji ishin kyōikushi*, pp. 95–97; in English, see Collcutt, "Buddhism," p. 154.

21. For excerpts from the text of the "Senkyōshi kokoroesho," see Inoue Hisashi, *Meiji ishin kyōiku-shi*, p. 95.

22. For Tanaka's statements, see ibid., p. 96.

23. As Helen Hardacre (*Shintō and the State*, p. 46) points out, although the intent of the campaign may have been to make Shinto a state religion, thereby distinguishing it from Buddhism, Buddhist priests and leaders of new religions also served as proselytizers and undoubtedly put their own non-Shinto spin on vague moral precepts issued by the government.

24. Ibid., pp. 44–45.

25. "Daigaku kisoku oyobi chūshōgaku kisoku," in *Hattatsu-shi*, 1: 139–42.

26. Motoyama, *Proliferating Talent*, p. 135.

27. Kaminuma, *Shinshū kyōiku-shi*, p. 176.

28. Bix, *Peasant Protest in Japan*, pp. 194–214; Esenbel, *Even the Gods Rebel*, pp. 139–218.

29. Rubinger, *Private Academies*, p. 5.

30. Chihara, *Shinshū no hangaku*, pp. 7–8.

31. Ibid., pp. 47–50.

32. Ibid., pp. 147–49.

33. *NKKS*, vol. 7, no. 118.

34. Ishijima, "Kōshinchi gōgaku."

35. *NKKS*, vol. 7, no. 67.4.

36. See Roberts, *Mercantilism in a Japanese Domain*, pp. 2–12, for a discussion of the many terms now associated with the nation (including *kokka*) that referred in Tokugawa Japan to the domain and thus manifested the sentiments of domain nationalism.

37. *NKKS*, vol. 7, no. 25.7.

38. Miyachi, *Bakumatsu ishinki*, esp. chap. 1.

39. *NKKS*, vol. 7, no. 126.1 (p. 121).

40. Rubinger, "Education," p. 204. On the Tokugawa antecedents to this kind of educational exchange program, see idem, *Private Academies*, pp. 15–38, 208–23.

41. Kaigo, *Meiji shonen no kyōiku*, p. 99.

42. This quote is from an essay written by Nishi in response to queries from the daimyo of Tsuwano; for excerpts from the essay, see Takahashi Satoshi, *Nihon minshū*, pp. 209–11.

43. Ibid.

44. Rubinger, "Education," pp. 206–7.

45. Kozuka and Terasaki, "Bangumi shōgakkō."

46. Ibid., pp. 142–43.

47. Kurasawa Takashi, *Shōgakkō no rekishi*, 1: 50–51.

48. Rubinger, "Education," p. 207.

49. On the Kitahara family, as well as the relationship between Kitahara Inao and Matsuo Taseko, see Walthall, *The Weak Body of a Useless Woman*, pp. 49–55.

50. Kitahara Inao, "Gakkō hatsujo no chūi," in *NKKS*, vol. 8, no. 120.

51. On the writings of such critics, see Lincicome, *Principle*.

52. Ibid., p. 3.

53. In fact, I would argue that the term *gōkō* (and the similar term *gōgaku*) is used to refer to such a broad array of educational institutions that it is virtually meaningless as a category. Not only were the early Meiji *gōkō* distinct from Tokugawa-era *gōkō*, but even among the Tokugawa-era *gōkō* there are critical differences that render the term of little descriptive value. Ishikawa Ken (*Nihon shomin kyōiku-shi*, chap. 2) divides Tokugawa-era *gōkō* into two major types: those established by domainal authorities as a local outpost of the domain school, with a clientele of samurai; and those established by domainal authorities for the education of commoners. However, these categories do not reveal the variety of schools contained within them: some schools provided basic moral instruction for ordinary commoners; others were intended to provide an advanced education for commoner elites; some were targeted at children, and others at adults; some were established not by the domainal authorities but by the cooperative efforts of commoner elites.

54. Ishijima, "Kōshinchi gōgaku."

55. Kaigo (*Meiji shonen no kyōiku*, p. 114) identifies 428 *gōkō* in Aichi, but Yūki ("Aichi-ken ni okeru gōkō") explains that precise numbers depend on the categorization of the different types of schools in existence at the time.

56. For a discussion of this controversy, see Umemura, *Nihon kinsei minshū*; and Kagotani, "Saikin no 'gōgakkō' no hyōban."

57. *NKKS*, 4: 70.

58. "Kōjō oboe," *NKKS*, vol. 7, no. 172.

59. Ibid.

60. By 1870, the Meiji government had divided Ina prefecture into northern and southern halves and reorganized the northern half into Nakano prefecture. For a fuller treatment of the complex jurisdictional changes in

288 *Notes to Pages 118–26*

modern-day Nagano prefecture during the first few years of the Meiji period, see *NKSTH, kindai 1*, pp. 25–51.

61. *NKKS*, vol. 8, no. 164.1.

62. Ibid., vol. 7, no. 95.1.

63. In November 1870, the domain school decided against establishing new elementary schools and chose instead to focus on recruiting talented students from existing commoner schools. The domain school planned to instruct village officials to identify outstanding students and send their names to the domainal authorities and even designed a standardized form for village officials to use when nominating such students. See ibid., no. 98. For subsequent materials detailing this plan, see ibid., no. 100 and no. 104.

64. Ibid., no. 95.

65. Ibid., no. 185.

66. Ibid., no. 186.

67. "Gakkō sōritsu kokuyusho," ibid., no. 200.

68. "Gakkō nyūhikin sashidashikata torihakarai furui," ibid.

69. "Gakkō-ken besshi no tōri aihakobisōrō aida kokoroesase aimawarisōrō koto," ibid., no. 205.

70. "Gakkō sashikin ninbetsuchō inkō," ibid., no. 202.

71. "Shōgakkō kiritsukin meibo," ibid., no. 224.

72. "Gakkō sekikin jinmeiroku," ibid., no. 203.

73. "Tōke nendaiki," Ibid., no. 210.

74. "Kyōritsu gakkō setsuritsu hōhōsho," ibid., no. 210

75. Nagaoka, "Chikuma-ken no kindai gakkō," p. 28.

76. See, e.g., the response by a committee of *sewayaku* to some of the prefectural office's proposed guidelines concerning the organization and funding of the *gōkō*, in *NKKS*, vol. 7, no. 207.2.

77. "Gakkō sewanin ni mōshitsukesōrō dan mōshikikikomi nado sashidasaresōrō taii," ibid., no. 207.1.

78. Ibid., no. 207.2.

79. For examples of curricular records of *gōkō* in Nagano and Chikuma prefectures, see ibid., nos. 237 and 247.

80. Local organizers may have also selected these sites because they provided more space than did private homes, but most *gōkō* were not, in fact, larger than the average pre-Meiji commoner school.

81. "Mawashijō Chikuma-kenchō," *NKKS*, vol. 7, no. 228.

82. "Fujimori Jūbei to gishite Chikuma kenchō e ageru no sho," *NKKS*, vol. 8, no. 164.2. Since the document refers to the establishment of Chikuma prefecture, it was written after July 1871. The fact that Takahashi neither mentioned the promulgation of the Fundamental Code of Education in August 1872 nor adopted any of the code's rhetoric suggests strongly that it was written before August; as we will see, almost immediately after the promulgation of the code, local educators in Chikuma and Nagano inserted many of its phrases into their own rhetoric of educational reform. The fact that the document is undated and cannot be found among the prefectural

government records suggests that it may not have been sent. One possibility is that Takahashi wrote the petition between July 1871 and January 1872 but decided not to send it after the Chikuma prefectural government issued its directives concerning the establishment of *gōkō* in February 1872 and thereby made some of his own proposals somewhat redundant.

83. Nishihara, "Kyōritsu gakkō setsuritsu kengonsho," *NKKS*, vol. 7, no. 195.

84. Ibid., no. 227.

85. NKKS, 1: 231.

86. Kelly, *Deference and Defiance*, p. 172.

87. Yamamuro, "Meiji kokka no seido," pp. 140–42.

88. One could easily include several other measures in this brief list of crucial reforms during the 1871–73 period: the abolition of the Department of Rites and its incorporation into the new Ministry of Rites and Education (Kyōbushō), the adoption of the Gregorian calendar, the abolition of the Tokugawa-era prohibition on the alienation of land, just to name a few. Most of these reforms were finalized while the key figures in the Meiji government were abroad with the Iwakura mission, even though the caretaker government had pledged to avoid initiating reforms until the mission returned to Japan; see Beasley, *The Meiji Restoration*, p. 371.

89. Curtis, *Building the Educational State*, p. 14.

90. Motoyama, *Meiji kokka no kyōiku shisō*, pp. 54–55.

91. *Hattatsu-shi*, 1: 250–52.

92. Motoyama, *Meiji kokka no kyōiku shisō*, p. 66.

93. Inoue Hisashi, *Gakusei ronkō*, pp. 100–102.

94. Scholars differ on the degree to which the final version of the Fundamental Code corresponded to this original draft. Kurasawa (*Gakusei no kenkyū*, p. 398) emphasizes the differences between the two versions, but Inoue Hisashi (*Gakusei ronkō*, p. 112) stresses the underlying similarity between them. Motoyama (*Meiji kokka no kyōiku shisō*, p. 67) identifies key principles found in both versions but points out that the draft made explicit mention of the value of education for strengthening the state (the final version omitted any such connection) and distinguished between schooling for the wealthy and schooling for the poor (the final version made no distinctions within the general population).

95. The debate within the central government concerning the Fundamental Code played out as a conflict between two consultative bodies within the State Council. The body that supported the Fundamental Code, the Sa'in, was led by Etō Shinpei, who had served as the highest-ranking official within the Ministry of Education at the time of its creation and had played a significant role in formulating its early agenda. The Sei'in, which was a higher-ranking body than the Sa'in, was led by Inoue Kowashi and others who had close ties to the Ministry of Finance and thus were more concerned about the expense of the Fundamental Code plan. This conflict also reflected pre-Meiji domainal ties: the Sa'in was dominated by former retainers of Saga

domain, whereas a clique of samurai from Chōshū and Tosa held sway within the Sei'in. See Moribe, "'Gakusei'-ki no kyōiku hōsei."

96. Quoted in Naka, *Meiji shoki no kyōiku*, pp. 240–41.

97. For the text of the Preamble, entitled "Ōse idasaresho," see *Hattatsu-shi*, 2: 275–77; for an English-language translation, see Passin, *Society and Education*, pp. 209–11.

98. Trans. from Passin, *Society and Education*, pp. 210–11.

99. For similar techniques employed by the British colonial administration in Egypt, see Mitchell, *Colonizing Egypt*, p. 44.

100. See Marshall, *Learning to Be Modern*, p. 33; Passin, *Society and Education*, p. 73; and Rubinger, "Education," p. 208.

101. In most areas, the creation of the *daiku* and *shōku* did not fundamentally alter the administrative patterns of local society. Many long-standing village elites simply assumed new titles while performing essentially similar functions and operating within familiar geographical boundaries and personal networks; see Waters, *Japan's Local Pragmatists*, pp. 58–73.

102. Umegaki, *After the Restoration*, p. 132.

103. Motoyama (*Meiji kokka no kyōiku shisō*, p. 80) argues that the eventual failure of this initial attempt to separate the realms of educational administration and political administration allowed political authorities to interfere unduly in educational matters.

104. Inoue Hisashi, *Gakusei ronkō*, pp. 247–49.

105. Rubinger, "Education," pp. 210–11.

106. On the exclusionary effect inherent in the practice of abstraction, see Sayer, *The Violence of Abstraction*.

107. For a translation of part of this document, see Lincicome, *Principle*, p. 2. For the original text, see *Hattatsu-shi*, 1: 777–79.

108. *Hattatsu-shi*, 2: 23–40. The multiple addressees included in the sample form begin with the university district office (*tokugakukyoku*); in reality, however, the seven university district offices (other than the one in Tokyo) never materialized, and thus the petitions were sent to the educational division (*gakumuka*) of the prefectural government via the district educational administrators (*gakku torishimari*).

109. For the original petitions, see Naka, *Meiji shoki no kyōiku*, pp. 298–303. Naka uses these two petitions to demonstrate the contrast between the "official reality" of the Fundamental Code–period schools and the actual conditions of the schools—which were not, he argues, much different from the schools operating before the promulgation of the Fundamental Code. I agree that these administrative procedures did not immediately transform local practice, but I also argue that they played a key role in the formation of a shared concept of school throughout Japan.

110. Fujitani, *Splendid Monarchy*, esp. pp. 24–28, 121–44, 241–45.

111. Cooper and Stoler, "Tensions of Empire," p. 609; Mitchell, *Colonizing Egypt*; Cohn, *Colonialism*.

Chapter 4

1. Scott, *Domination and the Arts of Resistance*, esp. pp. 70–107.

2. *NKKS*, vol. 9, no. 108.

3. As I discuss in Chapter 6, early Meiji enrollment statistics, especially those from the first few years after the promulgation of the Fundamental Code, are not reliable measures of school attendance. What they do measure, however, is the vigor with which local officials in Chikuma and Nagano approached the task of signing local children up for school—even if those children did not subsequently attend school.

4. "Gakumugakari junkai ni tsuki kokoroesho," *NKKS*, vol. 9, no. 237.

5. Cited in ibid., 4: 141–42.

6. Ibid., vol. 9, no. 237.

7. Naka, *Meiji shoki no kyōiku*, pp. 45–52.

8. *NKKS*, vol. 9, no. 1.

9. "Gakusei ontasshi utsushi," ibid., no. 126.

10. "Gakumon fukyū no mōshisatoshi sho," ibid., no. 127.

11. "Kakku shōgaku kenritsu no gi ni tsuki ōme ukagai," ibid., no. 3.

12. Ibid., no. 124.

13. Such responses were recorded in early Ministry of Education publications, most extensively in the *Monbushō nisshi*.

14. *NKKS*, 1: 491–94.

15. Ibid., vol. 9, no. 8.

16. Ibid., no. 135.

17. Ibid., no. 137.

18. Ibid., no. 192.

19. Naka, *Meiji shoki no kyōiku*, pp. 64–66.

20. The most extensive discussions in English of these registration-district officials are Baxter, *The Meiji Unification*, pp. 100–108; and Waters, *Japan's Local Pragmatists*, pp. 67–68.

21. On the role of village leagues in the establishment of early Meiji schools in Nagano, see Nagura, "Keisei gakkō ki," pt. 1, pp. 14–20. For a general discussion of these village leagues, see Waters, *Japan's Local Pragmatists*, pp. 42–47; and Walthall, "Village Networks," pp. 281–82, 289–93.

22. *NKKS*, 1: 260–68.

23. Chiba Masahiro, *Kindai Nihon chiiki minshū*, pp. 13–16.

24. Waters (*Japan's Local Pragmatists*, pp. 74–75) notes similar adaptations of the Fundamental Code made by local officials in Kawasaki.

25. Kurasawa, *Shōgakkō no rekishi*, 1: 442–3.

26. *NKKS*, vol. 9, no. 37.

27. Ibid., no. 134.

28. A few prefectures, including Ibaraki and Kanagawa, shared Chikuma's interpretation of the Fundamental Code; see Kurasawa, *Shōgakkō no rekishi*, 1: 442–43.

29. Most *gōkō* did, in fact, become elementary schools, but only after they submitted petitions to the prefectural government and received permission to reopen (*NKKS*, vol. 9, no. 148).

30. Whereas Nagano prefecture based its curricular regulations on those used in Tokyo Normal School's laboratory elementary school, Chikuma's were based mainly on the curricular regulations found in the Fundamental Code. On these two sets of regulations, see Lincicome, *Principle*, pp. 28–29.

31. "Shōgaku kagyō ichiran hyō jōshi no gi ni tsuki ukagai," *NKKS*, vol. 9, no. 129.

32. Nagano made two requests to publish new texts locally: see "Shōgaku kyōkasho hankoku no gi ukagai," ibid., no. 27; and "Hankokusho busū zōka no gi ukagai," ibid., no. 53. For Chikuma's request, dated November 1873, see ibid., no. 155.

33. Ibid., no. 155.

34. "Shōgakkō kyōshi no gi ni tsuki ukagai," ibid., no. 735.

35. "Shihan gakkō e seito sashidashi no gi mōshiage," ibid., no. 751.

36. For Nagano's request, see "Sotsugyō seito hashutsu onegai," ibid., no. 753; for Chikuma's, ibid., no. 832. The Tokyo Normal School teacher sent to Chikuma was Kaneko Naomasa, one of the early proponents of the "developmentalist" educational approach and the translator of N. A. Calkins's *Manual of Primary School Instruction* (1875). On Kaneko and Calkins, see Lincicome, *Principle*, pp. 49–54. A close collaborator on this translation was Takahashi Keijūrō, the former *gōkō* teacher from Chikuma who had been sent by prefectural authorities in 1873 to study at Tokyo Normal School.

37. By this time, the Ministry of Education had expressed its intent to establish a normal school in each of the eight university districts but had not issued any formal instructions for prefectural governments concerning normal schools (Moribe, "'Gakusei'-ki no kyōiku hōsei," pp. 133–34). On the early teacher-training initiatives in other prefectures, see Hashimoto, "Meiji shoki no fuken."

38. "Gakkō kenritsu no gi ukagai," *NKKS*, vol. 9, no. 7.

39. Ibid., no. 820.

40. For the figures in Nagano, see ibid., no. 770; for Chikuma, see ibid., no. 832.

41. Ibid., no. 151.

42. Ibid., no. 144.

43. Ibid., no. 151.

44. Ibid.

45. Nagao, "Setsuyu yōryaku," ibid., no. 178.

46. Ibid.

47. Ibid.

48. *Monbushō zasshi*, no. 14 (1874/8/4).

49. "Setsuyu yōryaku," *NKKS*, vol. 9, no. 178.

50. Ibid.

51. Ibid., no. 478.

52. "Kaichi gakkō shinchiku kaienshiki narabi ni iwaikotoba," ibid., no. 547. The Kaichi school cost over ¥11,000 to construct; the bulk of the funds came from the voluntary contributions of local benefactors; see "Kaichi gakkō shinchiku hiyō sōgakuchō," ibid., no. 548.

53. School openings in Nagano prefecture were covered by *Nagano Daily News* (*Nagano mainichi shinbun*), which was similar in ideological orientation to Matsumoto's *New Day Newspaper*.

54. Naka, *Meiji shoki no kyōiku*, pp. 332–35.

55. The Fundamental Code divided the elementary-school course into eight grades (four in lower elementary school, and four in upper elementary school), each of which could be completed in six months. The grades were counted in reverse order, with eighth grade as the lowest, seventh as next lowest, and so on; first grade was the final grade of this eight-grade system. However, I have rendered these grades in ascending order, as is now the pattern in Japanese schools.

56. See, e.g., "Shikenhō," *NKKS*, vol. 9, no. 109.1.

57. *Shinpi shinbun*, 1875/9/8.

58. See Fujitani, *Splendid Monarchy*, esp. pp. 24–28, 42–55, 121–45, 241–45.

59. Other names for this position in different parts of the country include *gakkō shukan, kanji, gakkō gakari,* and *kanji shuho,* all of which carried roughly the same meaning; see Naka, *Meiji shoki no kyōiku*, pp. 29–30.

60. "Kakku shōgaku kenritsu no gi ni tsuki ōmoku ukagai," in *NKKS*, vol. 9, no. 3. A year later, in May 1874, the prefectural government changed its mind, deciding that there should be only one full-time *sewayaku* per school; see ibid., no. 59.

61. *NKKS*, 1: 300.

62. *NKKS*, vol. 9, nos. 133, 171.

63. "Kyōiku jimukai seigian," ibid., no. 344.5.

64. For the diary kept by the *sewayaku* at Isetsu, see ibid., no. 564; for the diary of the *sewayaku* at Sōtatsu, see "Gakkō setsuritsu nisshi," ibid., no. 478.

65. Ibid., no. 478.

66. Ibid., no. 564.

67. In particular, they asked the prefectural office about the collection of school levies. The diary does not discuss the prefectural officials' responses, but it does note that the prefectural office gave them a sample form for recording endowment contributions. Ibid., no. 564.

68. Naka, *Meiji shoki no kyōiku*, pp. 72–74.

69. "Zenkan gakkō torishirabe hyō," ibid., no. 192.

70. Information on the background of *torishimari* is from *NKKS*, 1: 274–94.

71. Ibid., vol. 9, no. 28.

72. For this diary, kept by Nakahara Tomitarō, see ibid., nos. 362 and 363. For a chart that tracks his movements, see ibid., 1: 336.

73. Waters, *Japan's Local Pragmatists*, esp. pp. 73–76.

74. *NKKS.*, vol. 9, no. 136.

75. Ibid., no. 342.3.

76. Ibid., no. 343.2.

77. Ibid., no. 344.

78. Ibid., no. 343.2.

79. Ibid., no. 344.5.

80. Ibid., nos. 350, 344.5, 347.

81. Ibid., no. 344.5.

82. For example, after repeated calls from *torishimari* to make more frequent tours, the prefectural government responded, "We understand your request that we visit each school, but it would be difficult to do so several times; we will conduct such visits only as often as we are able" (ibid., no. 347.1).

83. Ibid., nos. 86, 196, 347.2.

84. Ibid., no. 204.

85. In the conference report of one such assembly, the participants—many of whom were *torishimari*—distanced themselves from their official positions and declared that their participation in the assembly was as *meibō aru mono* ("Chikuma-ken kamon kaigi nisshi," in ibid, no. 348.2).

86. Ibid., no. 341.2.

87. Ibid., no. 133.

88. Ibid., no. 347.1.

89. Ibid., no. 344.3.

90. Ibid., no. 349.

91. Curtis, *True Government by Choice Men?*, p. 188.

92. "Kengon," *NKKS*, vol. 9, no. 343.2.

93. Ibid., no. 136.

94. "Kengon," ibid., no. 343.2.

95. This incident is recorded in ibid., 1: 447.

96. "Osorenagara o motte kakitsuke negaiagetatematsurisōrō," ibid., vol. 8, no. 241.

97. "Otazune ni tsuki rireki kisoku mōshiagetatematsurisōrō," ibid., no. 242.

98. The prefecture's reasoning in rejecting these petitions was as follows: schools like these whose purpose was merely to teach basic reading and writing fell into the category of *kajuku* rather than *shijuku*; consequently, the regulation that allowed teachers to reopen their schools as *shijuku* did not apply in these cases (ibid., no. 241).

99. Ibid., vol. 9, no. 818.

100. Ibid., no. 829.2.

101. Ibid., no. 829.3.

102. For the original text of Chimura's speech, see Kamijō, *Mō hitotsu no "yoakemae,"* pp. 79–80.

103. Ibid., p. 80.

104. In comparison, by 1875 in *Before the Dawn*, Shimazaki Tōson could portray his character Hanzō, also a Hirata disciple and village notable from the Kiso valley, as having long since lost faith in the Meiji government because of what he perceived as a betrayal of the nativist principles of the Restoration.

105. *NKKS*, 1: 839–40.

106. Twenty-nine of the 33 people in the first cohort of students at the Chikuma normal school were samurai; in Nagano, at least 80 of the 103 students who enrolled at the normal school in its first two months were samurai (ibid., pp. 823, 829–30).

107. These and other statistics in this paragraph on the backgrounds of early Meiji schoolteachers can be found in ibid., pp. 829–30.

108. "Kyōka nisshi," *NKKS.*, vol. 9, no. 829.

109. Article 27 of the Fundamental Code listed fourteen different subjects in the lower-elementary-school curriculum; the "Elementary School Curricular Regulations," produced by Tokyo Normal School under the leadership of Marion Scott, simplified the curriculum by dividing it into only eight subjects; see Lincicome, *Principle*, pp. 28–29.

110. For Nagano, see *NKKS*, vol. 9, no. 94; for Chikuma, see ibid., no. 138.2.

111. "Kyōshi seito toriatsukaikata oku kishūkō," ibid., no. 746.

112. Ibid.

113. Ibid., no. 119.

114. See, e.g., ibid., nos. 175, 201.

115. Ibid., no. 746.

116. Ibid., no. 39.

117. For the curricular records of Nakahara Elementary School, see ibid., no. 605.

118. Ibid., no. 633.

119. *NKKS bekkan*, 1: 104–12, 140–53.

120. This was particularly a problem in Chikuma, where 80 percent of the more than 500 schools had only one teacher (*NKKS*, 1: 831).

121. *NKSTH*, vol. 7, p. 114.

122. See Allinson, *Japanese Urbanism*; Baxter, *The Meiji Unification*; Waters, *Japan's Local Pragmatists*; Lewis, *Becoming Apart*; McClain, "Local Elites and the Meiji Transition"; Steele, "Political Localism in Meiji Japan."

123. Waters, *Japan's Local Pragmatists*.

124. Lewis, *Becoming Apart*; Allinson, *Japanese Urbanism*.

Chapter 5

1. This rumor was cited specifically by participants in a riot in Okayama in June 1873 (Tsuchiya and Ono, *Meiji shonen nōmin sōjōroku*, p. 339).

2. Tsurumaki, "Minshū undō," p. 233.

3. Ibid., p. 232.

4. Morikawa, "Gakusei no minshūteki juyō to kyohi," pp. 322–23.

5. Kurasawa, *Shōgakkō no rekishi*, 1: 1004–7.

6. Ibid., p. 1013.

7. Mogi ("Shinsei hantai ikki") argues that, in contrast to the 1873 uprisings, protesters in 1876 were interested in destroying not so much the buildings themselves as the documents (mainly tax documents) stored in them.

8. Ibid., p. 301.

9. Tsuchiya and Ono, *Meiji shonen nōmin sōjōroku*, p. 344.

10. This account of the Tottori uprising was recorded in ibid., p. 467.

11. Both Esenbel (*Even the Gods Rebel*, pp. 219–52) and White (*Ikki*, pp. 193–99) emphasize that, in comparison to Tokugawa-era political authorities, the Meiji state took a more rigid stance toward popular resistance, conceding little to the demands of organized protest.

12. Stephen Vlastos ("Opposition Movements," p. 371) uses this term with hesitation, but Hirota Masaki ("Keimō shisō to bunmei kaika," pp. 351–54) explicitly makes the argument that the *shinsei hantai sōjō* are essentially similar to other antimodernist, anticapitalist rebellions such as the Luddite movement in Britain and the Taiping rebellion in China.

13. Hirota, "Keimō shisō to bunmei kaika," p. 353.

14. Kären Wigen (*The Making of a Japanese Periphery*, pp. 181–82) makes a similar point regarding the local experience of national economic planning.

15. Tsurumaki, "Minshū undō," p. 206; Esenbel, *Even the Gods Rebel*; McClain, "Local Elites and the Meiji Transition," pp. 118–19.

16. See, e.g., Herman Ooms's (*Tokugawa Village Practice*, p. 276) recounting of how samurai excrement fetched a higher price on the fertilizer market than did that of ordinary commoners.

17. Tsurumaki, "Minshū undō," pp. 238–39.

18. Ibid., p. 237.

19. See Toby, "The 'Indianness' of Iberia."

20. Vlastos, "Opposition Movements," p. 372.

21. Makihara, "Bunmei kaikaron," pp. 268–69.

22. Hirota, "Keimō shisō to bunmei kaika," pp. 350–52.

23. Tsuchiya and Ono, *Meiji shonen nōmin sōjōroku*, p. 344.

24. Herbert Passin (*Society and Education*, pp. 79–80) mentions these uprisings briefly; Nagai Michio provides a slightly fuller commentary in "Westernization and Japanization," pp. 54–55.

25. Inoue Masashi, "Meiji zenki nōminsō," pp. 106–8.

26. Morikawa, " Gakusei no minshūteki juyō to kyohi," p. 324.

27. Ibid., p. 325.

28. Hori ("Gifu-ken ni okeru shōgakkō") and Morikawa ("Meiji 9-nen Shinpeki-machi sōdō") have made this observation in reference to uprisings in Gifu and Ibaraki, respectively.

29. Hori, "Gifu-ken ni okeru shōgakkō," p. 24.

30. Ibid.

31. Tsuchiya and Ono, *Meiji shonen nōmin sōjōroku*, p. 305.

32. Quoted in Chiba Masashi, *Gakku seido no kenkyū*, p. 38.

33. Baxter, *The Meiji Unification*; Waters, *Japan's Local Pragmatists*, p. 3.

34. For a fuller discussion of such techniques of passive, low-key resistance, see Scott, *Weapons of the Weak*, esp. pp. 289–301.

35. Hayashi, "Gakusei no happu," p. 37.

36. "Wabishō sho," *NKKS*, vol. 9, no. 598.

37. "Wabishō sho," ibid., no. 599.

38. "Gakkō jin'in torishirabe-hyō," *Gakumu zakken 2, Meiji 9-nen* (1876). All the sources in this chapter entitled *zakken* or *shogan ukagai todoki* are bound volumes of documents (investigation reports, petitions, correspondence with school officials, and so on) that were compiled annually by the Nagano prefectural office during the Meiji period. These volumes are now held at the Nagano Prefectural History Museum (Nagano kenritsu rekishikan), in the town of Kōshoku, Nagano prefecture. Many of the documents in these volumes are untitled; in such cases, I simply cite the volume title.

39. This report is located in *Shogan ukagai todoki 1, gakumu, Meiji 7-nen* (1874).

40. See *Zakken 2, gakumu, Meiji 9-nen* (1876).

41. See *Gakumu zakken 4, Meiji 10-nen* (1877).

42. Ibid.

43. See *Gakumu zakken 3, Meiji 10-nen* (1877).

44. See *Gakumu zakken 2, Meiji 9-nen* (1876).

45. See, e.g., the petitions of Kōmio village in Saku district (in *Shogan ukagai todoki 2, Meiji 6-nen*) and of three neighboring villages in the Hanishina district (in *Shogan ukagai todoki 1, Meiji 7-nen*).

46. "Gakkō bunri ukagai," *Shogan ukagai todoki 2, gakumu, Meiji 12-nen.*

47. The series of documents related to Kamimaki Elementary School can be found in *Shogan ukagai todoki 1, gakumu, Meiji 12-nen.*

48. Ibid.

49. "Onegai," *NKKS*, vol. 9, no. 429.

50. "Rei," ibid., no. 430.

51. "Rei," ibid., no. 431.

52. Yasukawa, "Mikaihō buraku," p. 20.

53. *NKKS*, vol. 9, no. 344.5.

54. Ibid., no. 571.

55. Ibid., vol. 8, no. 164.1.

56. Ibid., no. 164.2.

57. Nagura, "Keisei gakkō ki," pt. 1, p. 29.

58. One reason for this is that the Hotaka school (which was called Keisei school during its early years) also served as a teacher-training institute before the prefecture established its own normal school (ibid., pp. 45–48).

59. *Shinpi shinbun*, no. 142, 1878/5/15.

60. *Gakumu zakken 6, gakumu, Meiji 10-nen*. Also in *NKKS*, vol. 9, no. 574.

61. *Gakumu zakken 6, gakumu, Meiji 10-nen.*

62. *NKKS*, vol. 9, no. 577.

63. These charges of financial impropriety by the Hotaka school administrators and teachers appear to have been valid. As anti-school sentiment rose to a dangerous level in early 1877, the prefectural office decided to open a formal police investigation of the situation. In the police report, the investigator suggested that Takahashi (the head teacher) and Gō (the district head) had misappropriated ¥200 from the school endowment; see *Gakumu zakken 3, gakumu, Meiji 10-nen*; also in *NKKS*, vol. 9, no. 584.

64. *Gakumu zakken 6, gakumu, Meiji 10-nen*; also in *NKKS*, vol. 9, no. 578.

65. *Gakumu zakken 6, gakumu, Meiji 10-nen.*

66. Ibid.; also in *NKKS,* vol. 9, no. 580.

67. "Tansakusho," in *Gakumu zakken 3, gakumu, Meiji 10-nen.*

68. *Gakumu zakken 6, gakumu, Meiji 10-nen;* also in *NKKS,* vol. 9, no. 579.

69. *Gakumu zakken 5, gakumu, Meiji 10-nen;* also in *NKKS,* vol. 9, no. 585. After leaving the Hotaka school, Takahashi was invited by the former governor of Chikuma prefecture, Nagayama Moriteru (now governor of Niigata prefecture) to bring his passion for educational matters to Niigata and help the cause of teacher training and primary education in a less developed area (less developed by educational standards). He later returned to Nagano prefecture as a school principal in the Ina district and then opened up a Chinese Studies *juku;* see Nagura, "Keisei gakkō ki," pt. 3, pp. 31–40.

70. *NKKS,* vol. 9, no. 587.

71. Residual animosities and conflicts were not extinguished completely with the signing of this contract. Four months later, five of the villages had not paid their allotted interest payments to the Hotaka school; according to the administrators of the school, it was "on the verge of financial collapse" (*Gakumu zakken 4, gakumu, Meiji 10-nen;* also in *NKKS,* vol. 9, no. 589). Two years later, a newspaper reported that financial controversies continued to swirl around the school, and as a result, the funds were still insufficient (*Gekkei shinshi,* no. 103, 1880/11/16).

Chapter 6

1. *NKKS,* vol. 9, no. 350.

2. "Kakkō gojunshi o kou jōgen," ibid., no. 246.

3. McClain, "Local Politics and National Integration," pp. 54–55. As McClain points out, Kido's change of heart was not due exclusively to popular opposition; it owed much to his observation of Western political systems in Europe in the early 1870s.

4. Ibid., p. 55.

5. Quoted in Craig, "The Central Government," p. 62.

6. Because Baxter (*The Meiji Unification,* esp. pp. 161–200) emphasizes the logical, progressive nature of this policy shift in terms of the long-term goal of administrative integration, he would likely disagree with this characterization of the Three New Laws as a "retreat."

7. Steiner, *Local Government in Japan,* p. 30.

8. For more information about the Three New Laws, see Baxter, *The Meiji Unification,* pp. 161–200; McClain, "Local Politics and National Integration," pp. 55–56; Waters, *Japan's Local Pragmatists,* pp. 85–91; Steiner, *Local Government in Japan,* pp. 29–31; and Steele, "Political Localism in Meiji Japan," p. 139.

9. Motoyama, *Meiji kokka no kyōiku shisō,* pp. 81–85.

10. Quoted in Kurasawa, *Gakusei no kenkyū,* p. 737.

11. Kyōikushi hensankai, *Meiji ikō kyōiku seido hattatsu-shi,* 1: 462–64.

12. Monbushō, *Monbushō nenpō,* vol. 5, p. 33.

13. Ibid., p. 2.
14. Ibid.
15. Ibid., p. 34.
16. For a discussion of the critique of the Fundamental Code by officials within the Ministry of Education, see Lincicome, *Principle*, p. 57.
17. Lewis, "The Meandering Meaning of Local Autonomy," p. 450.
18. "Gunji gaikyō: Chiisagata-gun," in *Shōmuka, Meiji 13.*
19. "Gunji gaikyō: Kitasaku-gun," in ibid.
20. "Gunji gaikyō: Higashichikuma-gun," in ibid.
21. "Gunji gaikyō: Minamiazumi-gun," in ibid.
22. *Gekkei shinshi*, 1881/6/11.
23. "Gunji gaikyō: Nishichikuma-gun," in *Shōmuka, Meiji 13.*
24. "Gunji gaikyō: Chiisagata-gun," in ibid.
25. "Gunji gaikyō: Shimoina-gun," in ibid.
26. Ibid.
27. Katagiri, "Jiyū minken undō," pp. 362–63.
28. Horio, *Educational Thought and Ideology*, pp. 34–37.
29. "Ukaigaisho," *Shogan ukagai todoki 1, Meiji 7-nen.*
30. "Kengon," *Zakken kon, Meiji 8-nen.*
31. *Matsumoto shinbun*, 1879/12/4.
32. On this doctrine of "developmentalism," see Lincicome, *Principle*.
33. *Gekkei shinshi*, 1879/1/27.
34. *Matsumoto shinbun*, 1879/12/10.
35. Horio, *Educational Thought and Ideology*, pp. 37–38.
36. For a similar relationship between Popular Rights and localism in Kanagawa prefecture, see Steele, "Political Localism in Japan," esp. pp. 141–45.
37. *Matsumoto shinbun*, 1879/12/10.
38. Ibid.
39. See *NKKS*, vol. 9, nos. 563 and 604.
40. *NKKS*, 1: 895–900.
41. Ibid., p. 834.
42. Ibid., p. 841.
43. Lincicome, *Principle*, esp. pp. 68–69.
44. For an example of an assembly whose scope included both education and other matters of public concern, see "Kukai yōryō," *NKKS*, vol. 9, no. 352. On the politicization of these assemblies in Nagano prefecture, see Kaminuma, *Shinshū kyōikushi*, pp. 547–51.
45. See, e.g., "Dai-roku daigakku Nagano-ken kyōiku kaigi shōtei," *NKKS*, vol. 9, no. 344.4.
46. Kaminuma, *Shinshū kyōikushi*, p. 610.
47. *Matsumoto shinbun*, 1877/9/23.
48. Cited in Kaminuma, *Shinshū kyōikushi*, pp. 610–11.
49. Ibid., pp. 612–14.

50. Ibid., p. 619. For a discussion in English of the role of normal schools in the transmission of Popular Rights discourse, see Lincicome, *Principle*, p. 255*n*13.

51. For a list of educators in the Shōkyōsha, see *NKKS*, 1: 885–88. The rest of the members came largely from a stratum of local officials, lawyers, newspaper writers, and other highly educated professionals or local notables.

52. Kaminuma, *Shinshū kyōikushi*, p. 619.

53. Takei was mentioned in Chapter 4 as the associate to whom Chimura Kyokai sent a rough draft of the speech he would later deliver at the opening of Narakawa Elementary School. Because so many Shōkyōsha members had studied under Takei's tutelage, they gave him the honor of naming the organization (ibid., p. 611).

54. The Yūkō gijuku's curriculum was originally published in *Matsumoto shinbun*, 1878/11/20. It can also be found in *NKKS*, 1: 891–92.

55. Kaminuma, *Shinshū kyōikushi*, pp. 619–27.

56. "Shōkyōsha gijuku kisoku," *Gekkei shinshi*, 1880/5/6.

57. On these kinds of politically oriented private schools, see Irokawa, *The Culture of the Meiji Period*, pp. 92–102; Motoyama, *Proliferating Talent*, pp. 148–94; and Rubinger, "Education," p. 221.

58. Motoyama, *Proliferating Talent*, pp. 274–316.

59. Irokawa, *The Culture of the Meiji Period*; Bowen, *Rebellion and Democracy*.

60. On the social and occupational backgrounds of political activists in Nagano prefecture, see Kaminuma, *Shinshū kyōikushi*, p. 613; and *NKKS*, 1: 884–88.

61. Passin, *Society and Education*, pp. 81–86.

62. Ibid., p. 149. On the influence of this narrative among more recent scholars of Japanese education, see Lincicome, "Local Citizens or Loyal Subjects?"

63. Marshall, *Learning to Be Modern*, pp. 52–62; Motoyama, *Proliferating Talent*, pp. 199–237, 354–97.

64. Lincicome, *Principle*, pp. 230–46.

65. For the text of the Revised Educational Ordinance, see Kyōikushi hensankai, *Hattatsu-shi*, 2: 201–6.

66. "Gakumu iin senkyo kisoku," *NKKS*, vol. 10, no. 127.

67. *NKKS*, 2: 376–77.

68. Hijikata makes this point in her *Kindai Nihon no gakkō*, p. 31.

69. "Gakku torisadamekata no gi ni tsuki un'un ukagai," *NKKS*, vol. 10, no. 102.

70. *NKKS*, vol. 10, no. 115.

71. Monbushō, *Monbushō nenpō*, vol. 12.2: 204.

72. Ibid., pp. 504–5.

73. Ibid., *furoku* (1882), p. 192.

74. Ibid., vol. 11, *furoku* (1883), p. 594.

75. "Gakushi teido gaku sekisan hyōjun," *NKKS*, vol. 10, no. 253.2.

76. "Meiji jūhachi-nen jūni-nichi honken shūkai," ibid., no. 253.3.

77. Ibid.

78. "Gakushi teido gaku sekisan hyōjun," *NKKS*, vol. 10, no. 253.2.

79. *Monbushō nenpō*, vol. 13.2: 223.

80. Hijikata, *Kindai Nihon no gakkō*, pp. 54–56; Chiba, *Gakku seido no kenkyū*.

81. Waters, "The Village Consolidation of 1889," pp. 180–84.

82. *NKKS*, 2: 165.

83. Kajiyama, "Kyōkasho kentei seido," esp. pp. 75–82.

84. Rubinger, "Education," pp. 226–27.

85. Patricia Tsurumi ("Meiji Primary School," pp. 247–61) argues that this shift in emphasis from Western utilitarianism to traditional morality is overstated and points out that the content of instruction in morality during the first two decades remained relatively constant.

86. Passin, *Society and Education*, p. 149.

87. For a discussion of these ordinances, see Lincicome, *Principle*, p. 76.

88. Kyōikushi hensankai, *Hattatsu-shi*, 2: 260–61.

89. The following information on Kiyomizu Ruini is taken from *NKKS*, 1: 905–6.

90. Arai, *Shinshū no kyōiku*, pp. 66–69.

91. *Shinano mainichi shinbun*, 1872/11/25; reprinted in *NKKS*, vol. 10, no. 518.

92. On this antibureaucratic strain of developmentalism, see Lincicome, *Principle*, pp. 233–39.

93. *NKKS*, vol. 9, no. 344.3.

94. Ibid., vol. 10, no. 585. Educational assemblies in Eastern Chikuma district and Lower Ina district made similar statements limiting their purview to pedagogical issues. See *Gekkei shinshi*, 1879/7/14; and *NKKS*, vol. 10, no. 594.

95. *NKKS*, vol. 10, nos. 579, 580.

96. See, e.g., Ikeda Jun'ichi's account in ibid., 2: 912–17; and Arai, *Shinshū no kyōiku*, pp. 74–77.

97. *NKKS*, vol. 10, no. 577.

98. Ibid., no. 579.

99. Ibid., no. 177.

100. "Nagano-ken Chiisagata-gun shiritsu kyōikukai kakisoku," ibid., no. 584.

101. "Nagano kyōikukai kisoku," ibid., no. 567.

102. Ibid., no. 568.

103. This incident is recorded in Arai, *Shinshū no kyōiku*, pp. 83–85.

104. For similar observations about elite educators in Tokyo, see Lincicome, *Principle*, pp. 233–47; and Motoyama, *Proliferating Talent*, pp. 317–53.

105. In this figure, I have averaged the statistics of Nagano and Chikuma prefectures for 1873 and 1875 (the two prefectures joined in 1875); in Fig. 2, the figures were kept separate.

106. Rubinger ("Education," pp. 213–14) points out an important regional variation concealed by the national statistics: prefectures with comparatively low enrollment rates in the immediate post–Fundamental Code years experienced more consistent increases in school enrollments during the first

two Meiji decades than those prefectures (like Nagano) that started with higher enrollments.

107. Koganezawa, "Meiji shoki no kyōin," pt. II, p. 41. As I noted in Chapter 4, many old schools continued to exist after these early years, but such schools were not included in official statistics because their existence depended on their not being reported to government officials.

108. *NKKS*, vol. 9, no. 344.

109. Ibid., vol. 10, no. 130.

110. For examples of the excuses used by rural families, see ibid., vol. 9, no. 660, and vol. 10, no. 307.

111. Ibid., vol. 9, no. 421.

112. A journalist in Nagano called attention to this phenomenon in 1891; see ibid., vol. 11, no. 363.

113. Ibid., 2: 324–26.

114. The prefectural government's new policy toward unenrolled children can be seen in ibid., vol. 10, no. 133.

115. Ibid., 2: 322–24.

116. A few English-language scholars have noted this distinction between enrollment and attendance. Rubinger ("Education," pp. 211–14) and Marshall (*Learning to be Modern*, pp. 47–49, 72–73), for example, have corrected a common mistake by translating the Japanese term *shūgaku* as "enrollment" (rather than "attendance"). Because nationwide statistics on attendance are somewhat speculative, however, these scholars trace long-term changes in Meiji education by creating charts for enrollment statistics, and I have done the same in this chapter. Enrollment figures are indeed valuable: not only do they provide some basis for comparison among prefectures, but they also indicate the vigor with which local authorities worked to enroll children in the new schools. They should not, however, be interpreted as accurate indicators of school attendance.

117. *NKKS, bekkan*, vol. 1, table no. 70, provides daily attendance figures for many of the years between 1873 and 1912, but the precipitous drop in daily attendance rates between 1873 and 1885 suggests that the official statistics are inaccurate, at least until the mid-1880s.

118. *NKKS*, 1: 612.

119. Ibid., pp. 612–13.

120. Ibid., *bekkan*, vol. 1, tables no. 64, 70.

121. Hijikata (*Kindai Nihon no gakkō*, p. 52) has found in a study of one Nagano village in 1891 that only 91 percent of boys and 75 percent of girls were included by local officials on their list of "school-age children."

122. *NKKS*, 1: 626.

123. Ibid., p. 627.

124. For these records, see *NKKS*, 1: 614.

125. Because an unknown number of those enrolled in the school were not within the "school-age" parameters, we do not know the exact percentage of school-age children enrolled. However, because the number of enrolled children who fell outside the "school-age" boundaries (ages seven

through thirteen) was usually quite small—prefecture-wide, they constituted only 0.05 percent of all enrolled children in 1878—the enrollment rate
cited above is most likely accurate. For the numbers of non-school-age students in Nagano's elementary schools, see *NKKS*, 1: 602.

126. Jansen and Rozman, "Overview," p. 25.

Epilogue

1. Gluck, *Japan's Modern Myths*, p. 20.

2. Ibid., p. 18.

3. For details about these school openings and separations and closings,
see Asahi-mura kyōiku enkaku-shi kankōkai, *Asahi-mura kyōiku enkaku-shi*,
pp. 69–199.

4. The document is reprinted in ibid., pp. 202–3.

5. Ibid. Here "village governance" refers to the post-1890, amalgamated
village units (*son*), rather than the smaller villages (*mura*) that were generally
consistent with the boundaries of pre-Meiji villages.

6. The document is reprinted in ibid., pp. 205–6.

7. Hijikata, *Kindai Nihon no gakkō*, p. 19.

8. Knight, "Weapons and Arches," p. 59.

9. Michael Lewis (*Becoming Apart*, esp. pp. 118–87) observes a similar pattern in Meiji- and Taisho-era conflicts in Toyama prefecture.

10. Wigen, *The Making of a Japanese Periphery*, p. 216.

11. Tokutomi, *Footprints in the Snow*, p. 59.

12. Portions of this document are reprinted in *NKKS*, 4: 142.

13. Ibid.

14. *NKKS*, vol. 7, no. 199.

15. Ibid.

16. See, e.g., Tayama Katai's novel *Country Teacher*.

17. For a representative example of this kind of ethnographic investigation of premodern schooling practices, conducted by the Lower Ina District
Educational Assembly in the early 1930s, see *NKKS*, vol. 8, no. 137.

18. Mallon, *Peasant and Nation*, p. 7.

19. Lewis, *Becoming Apart*.

Works Cited

Local Histories and Published Document Collections

Asahi-mura kyōiku enkaku-shi kankōkai, ed. *Asahi-mura kyōiku enkaku-shi.* Nagano: Asahi-mura kyōiku enkaku-shi kankōkai, 1971.

Gifu-ken shi hensan iinkai. *Gifu-ken shi, tsūshi-hen, kinsei 2.* Gifu: Gifu-ken, 1969.

Iwakura kō kyūseki hozonkai. *Iwakura kō jikki.* Tokyo: Iwakura kō kyūseki hozonkai, 1903.

Kido Takayoshi. *The Diary of Kido Takayoshi.* Trans. Sidney Devere Brown and Akiko Hirota. Tokyo: University of Tokyo Press, 1986.

Kyōiku-shi hensankai, ed. *Meiji ikō kyōiku-seido hattatsu-shi,* vols. 1–4 (Tokyo: Ryūginsha, 1939).

Monbushō, ed. *Monbushō nenpō.* Tokyo: Monbushō, annual publication.

———. *Monbushō nisshi.* Tokyo: Monbushō, annual publication.

———. *Monbushō zasshi.* Tokyo: Monbushō, periodical.

———. *Nihon kyōiku-shi shiryō.* 9 vols. Tokyo: Monbushō, 1892.

Nagano-ken kyōiku-shi hensan iinkai, ed. *Nagano-ken kyōiku-shi shiryō,* vols. 1–9. Nagano: Nagano-ken kyōiku-shi hensan iinkai, 1978.

Nagano-ken shi hensan iinkai, ed. *Nagano-ken shi shiryō-hen.* Nagano: Nagano-ken shi hensan iinkai, 1982.

———. *Nagano-ken shi tsūshi-hen.* Nagano: Nagano-ken shi hensan iinkai, 1987.

Shunpo kō tsuishōkai, ed. *Itō Hirobumi den,* vol. 1. Tokyo: Hara shobō, 1970.

Tatsuno-machi shi hensan iinkai, ed., *Tatsuno-machi shi.* Tatsuno: Tatsuno-machi shi hankō iinkai, 1990.

Tsuchiya Takao and Ono Michio, eds. *Meiji shonen nōmin sōjōroku.* Tokyo: Nanboku shoin, 1931.

Tsumaki Chūta, ed. *Kido Takayoshi monjo,* vol. 8. Tokyo: Nihon shiseki kyōkai, 1932.

Archival Materials

Nagano Prefectural Government Documents. Nagano. Nagano Prefectural History Museum. (The following sources are bound volumes of documents compiled by the Nagano and Chikuma prefectural governments during the Meiji period.)

Gakumu zakken 2, Meiji 9-nen (1876).
Gakumu zakken 3, gakumu, Meiji 10-nen (1877).
Gakumu zakken 4, gakumu, Meiji 10-nen (1877).
Gakumu zakken 5, gakumu, Meiji 10-nen (1877).
Gakumu zakken 6, gakumu, Meiji 10-nen (1877).
Gakumu zakken 14, Meiji 10-nen (1877).
Shogan ukagai todoki 1, Meiji 6-nen (1873).
Shogan ukagai todoki 2, Meiji 6-nen (1873).
Shogan ukagai todoki 1, gakumu, Meiji 7-nen (1874).
Shogan ukagai todoki 1, gakumu, Meiji 12-nen (1879).
Shogan ukagai todoki 2, gakumu, Meiji 12-nen (1879).
Shōmuka, Meiji 13-nen (1880).
Zakken-kon, Meiji 8-nen (1875).

Ozawa Watoku. Ozawa Family Documents. Nagano. Nagano Prefectural History Museum.

———. "Gakumonjo Kyōkun kyosairoku." 1865/1/1–1865/5/9.
———. "Nennai shoji hikae nikki." 1868/1/1–1868/5/18.
———. "Nennai shoji nikkicho." 1866/1/1–1866/5/11.
———. "Nisshin keikai jichiroku." 1864/7/17–1864/12/20.
———. "Shoji kyosai tebikaechō." 1861/9/29–1862/3/28.
———. "Shoji nisshinroku." 1868/6/2–1868/12/29.
———. "Tōke shodai Kōkodō Shisan ichidaiki." 1867/8/12.

Secondary Materials

Aichi daigaku. Kyōdo Kenkyūjo, ed. *Kinsei no chihō bunka*. Tokyo: Meicho shuppan, 1991.

Allinson, Gary. *Japanese Urbanism: Industry and Politics in Kariya, 1872–1972* (Berkeley: University of California Press, 1975).

Amino Yoshihiko. "'Undō to shite no chiiki-shi kenkyū' o megutte." In Asao Naohiro et al., eds., *Iwanami kōza Nihon tsūshi, bekkan 2: Chiiki-shi kenkyū no genjō to kadai*. Tokyo: Iwanami shoten, 1994, pp. 105–13.

Anderson, C. Arnold, and Mary Jean Bowman. "Education and Economic Modernization in Historical Perspective." In Lawrence Stone, ed., *Schooling and Society*. Baltimore: Johns Hopkins University Press, 1976, pp. 3–19.

Aoki Toshiyuki. "Shinano no Rangaku-juku nyūmonsha ni tsuite." In Aichi daigaku sōgō kyōdo kenkyūjo, ed., *Kinsei no chihō bunka*. Tokyo: Meicho shuppan, 1991, pp. 23–55.

————."Sōmō no rangaku." In Takeuchi Makoto, ed., *Nihon no kinsei*, vol. 14, *Bunka no taishūka*. Tokyo: Chūō kōronsha, 1993, pp. 219–68.

Arai Tsutomu. *Shinshū no kyōiku*. Tokyo: Gōdō shuppan, 1972.

Baxter, James. *The Meiji Unification Through the Lens of Ishikawa Prefecture.* Cambridge, Mass.: Harvard University, Council on East Asian Studies, 1994.

Beasley, W. G. *The Meiji Restoration*. Stanford: Stanford University Press, 1971.

Befu, Harumi. "Village Autonomy and Articulation Within the State." In John W. Hall and Marius Jansen, eds., *Studies in the Institutional History of Early Modern Japan*. Princeton: Princeton University Press, 1968, pp. 301–14.

Bellah, Robert. *Tokugawa Religion: The Values of Pre-Industrial Japan.* Glencoe, Ill.: Free Press, 1957.

Berry, Mary Elizabeth. "Was Early Modern Japan Culturally Integrated?" *Modern Asian Studies* 31, no. 3 (1997): 547–81.

Bix, Herbert. *Peasant Protest in Japan*. New Haven: Yale University Press, 1986.

Boli-Bennet, John, and John Meyer. "The Ideology of Childhood and the State." *American Sociological Review* 43 (1978): 797–812.

Bolitho, Harold. "The Tempō Crisis." In Marius Jansen, ed., *The Cambridge History of Japan*, vol. 5, *The Nineteenth Century*. Cambridge, Eng.: Cambridge University Press, 1989, pp. 116–67.

Bourdieu, Pierre. *An Outline of a Theory of Practice*. Trans. Richard Nice. Cambridge, Eng.: Cambridge University Press, 1977.

Bowen, Roger. *Rebellion and Democracy in Meiji Japan*. Berkeley: University of California Press, 1980.

Brown, Phil. "Local History's Challenge to National Narratives." *Early Modern Japan: An Interdisciplinary Journal* 8, no. 2 (Nov. 2000): 38–48.

Brown, Sidney Devere, and Hirota Akiko, trans. *The Diary of Kido Takayoshi.* 3 vols. Tokyo: University of Tokyo Press, 1985.

Chamberlain, Basil Hall, trans. "The Teaching of the Words of Truth." *Cornhill Magazine*, Aug. 15, 1876, pp. 176–80.

————. "Teachings for the Young." *Transactions of the Asiatic Society of Japan* 9, no. 3 (1881): 223–48.

Chiba Masahiro. "Gakusei gakkō sōsetsu jijō to funjō." *Kōchi daigaku, Kyōiku gakubu kenkyū hōkoku* 42 (1990): 113–20.

————. *Kindai Nihon chiiki minshū kyōiku seiritsu katei no kenkyū*. Tokyo: Azusa shuppanbu, 1996.

Chiba Masashi. *Gakku seido no kenkyū*. Tokyo: Keisō shoten, 1962.

Chihara Masayoshi. *Shinshū no hangaku*. Matsumoto: Kyōdo shuppansha, 1986.

Chisick, Harvey. *The Limits of Reform in the Enlightenment: Attitudes Towards the Education of the Lower Classes in 18th-Century France*. Princeton: Princeton University Press, 1981.

Cohn, Bernard. *Colonialism and Its Forms of Knowledge: The British in India.* Princeton: Princeton University Press, 1996.

Collcutt, Martin. "Buddhism: The Threat of Eradication." In Marius Jansen and Gilbert Rozman, eds., *Japan in Transition: From Tokugawa to Meiji*. Princeton: Princeton University Press, 1986, pp. 143–67.

Cooper, Fredrick, and Ann Stoler. "Tensions of Empire: Colonial Control and Visions of Rule." *American Ethnologist* 16, no. 4 (1989): 609–21.

Corrigan, Philip, and Derek Sayer. *The Great Arch: English State Formation as Cultural Revolution*. Oxford: Basil Blackwell, 1985.

Craig, Albert. "The Central Government." In Marius Jansen and Gilbert Rozman, eds., *Japan in Transition: From Tokugawa to Meiji*. Princeton: Princeton University Press, 1986, pp. 36–67.

———. *Chōshū in the Meiji Restoration*. Cambridge, Mass.: Harvard University Press, 1961.

Curtis, Bruce. *Building the Educational State: Canada West, 1836–71*. Sussex: Falmer Press; London: Althouse Press, 1988.

———. *True Government by Choice Men?* Toronto: University of Toronto Press, 1992.

Dore, Ronald. *Education in Tokugawa Japan*. Berkeley: University of California Press, 1965. Reprinted—Ann Arbor, Mich.: Center for Japanese Studies, University of Michigan, 1992.

———. "The Legacy of Tokugawa Education." In Marius Jansen, ed., *Changing Japanese Attitudes Towards Modernization*. Princeton: Princeton University Press, 1965, pp. 91–131.

Dower, John. "E. H. Norman, Japan and the Uses of History." In idem, ed., *Origins of the Modern Japanese State: Selected Writings of E. H. Norman*. New York: Pantheon Books, 1975, pp. 3–101.

Eklof, Ben. "Peasant Sloth Reconsidered: Strategies of Education and Learning in Rural Russia Before the Revolution." *Journal of Social History* 14, no. 3 (Spring 1981): 355–85.

Esenbel, Selçuk. *Even the Gods Rebel: The Peasants of Takaino and the 1871 Nakano Uprising in Japan*. Ann Arbor, Mich.: Association for Asian Studies, 1998.

Esherick, Joseph, and Mary Rankin, eds. *Local Elites and Patterns of Dominance*. Berkeley: University of California Press, 1990.

Femia, Joseph V. *Gramsci's Political Thought*. Oxford: Clarendon Press, 1981.

Fujitani, Takashi. *Splendid Monarchy: Power and Pageantry in Modern Japan*. Berkeley: University of California Press, 1996.

Garon, Sheldon. *Molding Japanese Minds: The State in Everyday Life*. Princeton: Princeton University Press, 1997.

———. "Rethinking Modernization and Modernity in Japanese History: A Focus on State-Society Relations." *Journal of Asian Studies* 53, no. 2 (May 1994): 346–66.

Gluck, Carol. *Japan's Modern Myths: Ideology in the Late Meiji Period*. Princeton: Princeton University Press, 1985.

———. "The People in History: Recent Trends in Japanese Historiography." *Journal of Asian Studies* 38, no. 1 (Nov. 1978): 25–49.

Graff, Harvey. *The Literacy Myth: Social Structure in the Nineteenth Century City*. New York: Academic Press, 1979.

Gramsci, Antonio. *Selections from the Prison Notebooks*. Ed. Quentin Hoare and G. Nowell Smith. London: Lawrence and Wishart, 1971.

Haga Noboru. *Kokugaku no hitobito: sono kōdō to shisō*. Tokyo: Hyōronsha, 1975.

———. *Meiji kokka no keisei*. Tokyo: Yūsankaku shuppan, 1987.

Hall, John W. "Changing Conceptions of the Modernization of Japan." In Marius Jansen, ed., *Changing Japanese Attitudes Toward Modernization*. Princeton: Princeton University Press, 1965, pp. 7–41.

———. *Government and Local Power in Japan, 500–1700*. Chicago: University of Chicago Press, 1966.

Hampl, Patricia. "Memory and Imagination." In James McConkley, ed., *The Anatomy of Memory: An Anthology*. Oxford: Oxford University Press, 1996, pp. 201–11.

Hane, Mikiso. *Peasants, Rebels, and Outcastes: The Underside of Modern Japan*. New York: Pantheon, 1982.

Hanes, Jeffrey. "Contesting Centralization? Space, Time, and Hegemony in Meiji Japan." In Helen Hardacre and Adam Kern, eds., *New Directions in the Study of Meiji Japan*. Leiden: Brill, 1997, pp. 485–95.

Hanley, Susan B., and Kozo Yamamura. *Economic and Demographic Change in Preindustrial Japan, 1600–1868*. Princeton: Princeton University Press, 1977.

Hardacre, Helen. *Shintō and the State*. Princeton: Princeton University Press, 1989.

Harootunian, Harry. "America's Japan / Japan's Japan." In idem and Masao Miyoshi, eds., *Japan in the World*. Chicago: University of Chicago Press, 1993, pp. 198–221.

———. "Late Tokugawa Culture and Thought." In Marius Jansen, ed., *The Cambridge History of Japan*, vol. 5. Cambridge, Eng.: Cambridge University Press, 1989, pp. 168–258.

———. *Things Seen and Unseen: Discourse and Ideology in Tokugawa Nativism*. Chicago: University of Chicago Press, 1988.

Hasegawa Tsuneo. "Meiji shoki 'gakusei' shita ni okeru gakuhi chōtatsu no ichi keitai." *Shigaku* 43, no. 1–2 (1970): 371–89.

Hashimoto Tarō. "Meiji shoki no fuken ni okeru kyōin yōsei." *Kyōiku kenkyū* 24, no. 3 (1980): 27–48.

Hauser, William. *Economic Institutional Change in Tokugawa Japan: Osaka and the Kinai Cotton Trade*. Cambridge, Eng.: Cambridge University Press, 1995.

Hayami, Akira. "The Myth of Primogeniture and Impartible Inheritance in Tokugawa Japan." *Journal of Family History* 8, no. 1 (1983): 3–29.

Hayashi Tobito. "Gakusei–kyōikurei-ki ni okeru shūgaku jōkyō." *Ina*, no. 727 (Dec. 1988): 9–16.

———. "Gakusei no happu to terakoya no tōsa." *Ina*, no. 778 (Mar. 1993): 22–40.

Hijikata Sonoko. *Kindai Nihon no gakkō to chiiki shakai*. Tokyo: Tokyo daigaku shuppanbu, 1994.

———. "Meiji zenki chōson to shōgakkō no kankei no rekishi." *Higashi Matsuyama-shi hensan chōsa hōkoku* 20 (1979): 1–64.

Hirota Masaki. *Bunmei kaika to minshū ishiki.* Tokyo: Aoki shoten, 1980.

———. "Keimō shisō to bunmei kaika." *Iwanami kōza Nihon rekishi,* vol. 14, *Kindai 1.* Tokyo: Iwanami shoten, 1975, pp. 312–64.

Hori Kōtarō. "Gifu-ken ni okeru shōgakkō setsuritsu katei to Ise bōdō." *Nihon no kyōiku-shigaku* 23 (1980): 12–31.

Horio Teruhisa. *Educational Thought and Ideology in Modern Japan.* Ed. and trans. Steven Platzer. Tokyo: University of Tokyo Press, 1988.

Hoston, Germain. *Marxism and the Crisis of Development in Prewar Japan.* Princeton: Princeton University Press, 1986.

Howell, David. *Capitalism from Within: Economy, Society, and the State in a Japanese Fishery.* Berkeley: University of California Press, 1995.

Ikegami, Eiko. "Citizenship and National Identity in Early Meiji Japan, 1868–1889: A Comparative Assessment." *International Review of Social History,* no. 4, supplement 3 (1995): 185–221.

Inoue Hisashi. *Gakusei ronkō.* Tokyo: Kazama shobō, 1963.

———. *Meiji ishin kyōiku-shi.* Tokyo: Yoshikawa kōbunkan, 1984.

Inoue Masashi. "Meiji zenki nōminsō no bunkai to gakusei shokaikaku no igi." *Kyōtō daigaku, Kyōiku gakubu kiyō* 74, no. 3 (Mar. 1974): 104–21.

Iriye Hiroshi. "Kinsei 1." In *Kōza Nihon kyōiku-shi,* vol. 5. Tokyo: Iwanami shoten, 1982, pp. 82–108.

———. "Kinsei Shimōzuke nōson ni okeru tenaraijuku no seiritsu to tenkai." *Tochigi-ken shi kenkyū* 13, no. 3 (Mar. 1977): 21–46.

Irokawa Daikichi. *The Culture of the Meiji Period.* Translation ed. Marius Jansen. Princeton: Princeton University Press, 1985.

Ishida Takeshi. *Japanese Political Culture.* New Brunswick, N.J.: Transaction Books, 1983.

Ishijima Tsuneo. "Kōshinichi gōgaku no ni-taiyō: Ishin-ki no Yonezawa-han no jirei." *Nihon no kyōikushigaku* 30 (1987): 42–60.

———. "Kyōto-fu bangumi shōgakkō no gōgakuteki ishiki." In *Koza Nihon kyōiku-shi,* vol. 2. Tokyo: Iwanami shoten, 1982, pp. 250–276.

Ishijima Tsuneo and Umemura Kayo, eds. *Nihon minshū kyōiku-shi kenkyū.* Tokyo: Azusa shuppanbu, 1986.

Ishikawa Ken. *Nihon shomin kyōiku-shi.* Tokyo: Tamagawa daigaku shuppanbu, 1972.

Itō Yahiko, ed. *Nihon kindai kyōiku-shi saikō.* Kyoto: Shōwadō, 1994.

Jansen, Marius, ed. *The Emergence of Meiji Japan.* Cambridge, Eng.: Cambridge University Press, 1995.

———. *Sakamoto Ryōma and the Meiji Restoration.* Princeton: Princeton University Press, 1961.

Jansen, Marius, and Gilbert Rozman. "Overview." In Marius Jansen and Gilbert Rozman, eds., *Japan in Transition: From Tokugawa to Meiji.* Princeton: Princeton University Press, 1986, pp. 3–26.

Johnson, R. "Educational Policy and Social Control in Early Victorian England." *Past and Present,* no. 49 (1970): 96–119.

Joseph, Gilbert, and Daniel Nugent, eds. *Everyday Forms of State Formation.* Durham: Duke University Press, 1994.

Kaestle, Carl. "Between the Scylla of Brutal Ignorance and the Charybdis of a Literary Education: Elite Attitudes Toward Mass Schooling in Early Industrial England and America." In Lawrence Stone, ed., *Schooling and Society.* Baltimore: Johns Hopkins University Press, 1976, pp. 177–91.

Kagotani Jirō. "Saikin no 'gōgakkō' no hyōban ni tsuite." *Nihon-shi kenkyū* 215, no. 7 (July 1980): 57–76.

Kaigo Tokiomi. *Japanese Education: Its Past and Present.* Tokyo: Kokusai bunka shinkōkai, 1965.

———. *Meiji shonen no kyōiku: sono seido to jittai.* Tokyo: Hyōronsha, 1973.

Kajiyama Masachika. "Kyōkasho kentei seido no seiritsu to hōkai." In *Kōza Nihon kyōiku-shi,* vol. 3. Tokyo: Iwanami shoten, 1982, pp. 71–100.

Kamijō Hirono. "Hirata kokugaku no hattatsu to Ina-dani no bakumatsu." *Ina,* no. 804 (May 1995): 4–13.

———. *Mō hitotsu no "yoakemae": kindaika to Narakawa no kokugakushatachi.* Tokyo: Kanegawa shobō, 1991.

Kaminuma Hachirō. "Chihō-shi to kyōiku-shi." *Chihō-shi kenkyū* 29, no. 3 (1979): 49–55.

———. *Shinshū kyōiku-shi no kenkyū.* Nagano: Shinano kyōikukai shuppanbu, 1964.

Kaneko Terumoto. *Meiji zenki kyōiku gyōsei-shi kenkyū.* Tokyo: Kazama shobō, 1967.

Katagiri Yoshio. *Jiyū minken-ki kyōiku-shi kenkyū.* Tokyo: Tōkyō daigaku shuppankai, 1990.

———. "Jiyū minken undō no kyōiku shisō." In *Koza Nihon kyōiku-shi,* vol. 2. Tokyo: Iwanami shoten, 1982, pp. 359–81.

Kawamura Hajime. *Zaison chishikijin no jugaku.* Tokyo: Shibunkaku shuppan, 1996.

Kazukiyo Shiga. "Meiji ishin-go no kyōikukan ni tsuite." *Yokohama kokuritsu daigaku jinbun kiyō* 37, no. 10 (Oct. 1990): 1–24.

Kelly, William. *Deference and Defiance in Nineteenth-Century Japan.* Princeton: Princeton University Press, 1985.

Ketelaar, James. *Of Heretics and Martyrs.* Princeton: Princeton University Press, 1990.

Kimura Masanobu. "Bakumatsu-ki Chikugo no nōson ni okeru terakoya no kyūzō to murayakuninsō." *Kyūshū daigaku kyōiku gakubu kiyō* 34 (1988): 45–59.

Kimura Motoi. "Kyōdō-shi, chihō-shi, chiiki-shi kenkyū no rekishi to kadai." In Asao Naohiro et al., eds., *Iwanami kōza Nihon tsūshi, bekkan 2: Chiiki-shi kenkyū no genjō to kadai.* Tokyo: Iwanami shoten, 1994, pp. 3–30.

Kinmoth, Earl H. "Fukuzawa Reconsidered: 'Gakumon no susume' and Its Audience." *Journal of Asian Studies* 37, no. 4 (Aug. 1978): 677–96.

Knight, Alan. "Weapons and Arches in the Mexican Revolutionary Landscape." In Gilbert Joseph and Daniel Nugent, eds., *Everyday Forms of State Formation.* Durham: Duke University Press, 1994, pp. 24–68.

Kobayashi Fumio. "Kinsei kōki ni okeru 'zōsho no ie' no shakaiteki kinō ni tsuite." *Rekishi* 76 (1991): 25–43.

Kobayashi Keiichirō. "Haikai no ryūsei to shakai—Kobayashi Issa o chūshin ni." In Takeuchi Makoto, ed., *Nihon no kinsei*, vol. 14, *Bunka no taishūka*. Tokyo: Chūō kōronsha, 1993, pp. 95–130.

———. "Kinsei kita-Shinano ni okeru kinbun sōzoku ni tusite." *Nihon rekishi*, no. 280 (Sept. 1971): 45–47.

Koganezawa Toshio. "Meiji shoki no kyōin no ninyō o megutte," pt. 2. *Shinano* 23, no. 10 (Oct. 1971): 431–42.

Komoriya Jirō. "Bakumatsu-ki Kitagawauchi nōson ni okeru terakoya no shūgaku ni tsuite." *Chihō-shi kenkyū* 23, no. 2 (Apr. 1973): 31–46.

Komoriya Jirō and Umemura Kayo. *Nihon kinsei minshū kyōiku-shi kenkyū.* Tokyo: Azusa shuppanbu, 1991.

Kozuka Tetsuyo and Terasaki Masao. "Bangumi shōgakkō." In Ishikawa Matsutarō, ed., *Kindai Nihon kyōiku no kiroku*, vol. 1. Tokyo: Nihon hōsō shuppankai, 1978, pp. 141–52.

Kuhn, Philip. *Rebellion and Its Enemies in Late Imperial China.* Cambridge, Mass.: Harvard University Press, 1970.

Kurasawa Takashi, *Gakusei no kenkyū.* Tokyo: Kōdansha, 1973.

———. *Shōgakkō no rekishi*, vol. 1. Tokyo: Japan Library Bureau, 1971.

Kuroda Nobuyuki. *Tennōsei kokka keisei no shiteki kōzō.* Kyoto: Hōritsu bunka-sha, 1993.

Kurushima Hiroshi. "Hyakushō to mura no henshitsu." In Asao Naohiro et al., eds., *Iwanami kōza Nihon tsūshi*, vol. 15. Tokyo: Iwanami shoten, 1995, pp. 69–110.

Laqueur, Thomas W. "Working-Class Demand and the Growth of English Elementary Education, 1750–1850." In Lawrence Stone, ed., *Schooling and Society.* Baltimore: Johns Hopkins University Press, 1976, pp. 193–203.

Lears, T. Jackson. "The Concept of Cultural Hegemony: Problems and Possibilities." *American Historical Review* 90 (June 1985): 567–93.

Lewis, Michael. *Becoming Apart: National Power and Local Politics in Toyama, 1868–1945.* Cambridge, Mass.: Harvard University Asia Center, 2000.

———. "The Meandering Meaning of Local Autonomy: Bosses, Bureaucrats, and Toyama's Rivers." In Helen Hardacre and Alan K. Kern, eds., *New Directions in the Study of Meiji Japan.* New York: Brill, 1997, pp. 440–50.

Lincicome, Mark. "Local Citizens or Loyal Subjects? Enlightenment Discourse and Educational Reform." In Helen Hardacre and Alan Kern, eds., *New Directions in the Study of Meiji Japan.* New York: Brill, 1997, pp. 451–65.

———. "Nationalism, Imperialism, and the International Education Movement in Early Twentieth Century Japan." *Journal of Asian Studies* 58, no. 2 (May 1999): 338–60.

———. *Principle, Praxis, and the Politics of Educational Reform in Meiji Japan.* Honolulu: University of Hawaii Press, 1995.

———. Review of Motoyama Yukihiko's *Proliferating Talent. Journal of Japanese Studies* 25, no. 1 (Winter 1999): 121–29.

Lipsitz, George. "The Struggle for Hegemony." *American Historical Review* 75, no. 1 (June 1988): 146–50.

Makihara Norio. "Bunmei kaikaron." In Asao Naohiro et al., eds., *Iwanami kōza Nihon tsūshi*, vol. 16. Tokyo: Iwanami shoten, 1994, pp. 249–90.

Mallon, Florencia. *Peasant and Nation: The Making of Postcolonial Mexico and Peru*. Berkeley: University of California Press, 1995.

———. "Reflections on the Ruins." In Gilbert Joseph and Daniel Nugent, eds., *Everyday Forms of State Formation*. Durham: Duke University Press, 1994, pp. 69–106.

Marshall, Byron K. *Learning to Be Modern*. Boulder, Colo.: Westview Press, 1994.

Maruyama Yasunari, ed., *Nihon no kinsei*, vol. 6, *Jōhō to kōtsū*. Tokyo: Chūō kōronsha, 1992.

Maynes, Mary Jo. *Schooling in Western Europe: A Social History*. Albany: State University of New York Press, 1985.

McClain, James. "Local Elites and the Meiji Transition in Kanazawa." *Asian Cultural Studies* 20 (1992): 107–35.

———. "Local Politics and National Integration: The Fukui Prefectural Assembly in the 1880s." *Monumenta Nipponica* 30, no. 1 (Spring 1976): 51–75.

Mitchell, Timothy. *Colonizing Egypt*. New York: New York University Press, 1989.

———. "The Limits of the State: Beyond Statist Approaches and Their Critics." *American Political Science Review* 85 (Mar. 1991): 77–96.

Miwa Noriaki. "Shinano 'ee ja nai ka' no ichi yōsō." *Inaji* 37, no. 4 (Apr. 1993): 27–38.

Miyachi Masato. *Bakumatsu ishinki no bunka to jōhō*. Tokyo: Meicho kankōkai, 1994.

———. "Bakumatsu seiji katei ni okeru gōnōshō to zaison chishikijin." In idem et al., eds., *Nihon kin-gendai shi*, vol. 1, *Ishin henkaku to kindai Nihon*. Tokyo: Iwanami shoten, 1993, pp. 29–76.

———. "Fūsetsu tome kara mita bakumatsu shakai no tokushitsu: kōron sekai no tanshoteki seiritsu." *Shisō*, no. 831 (Sept. 1993): 4–26.

Mizubayashi Takeshi. *Hōkensei no saihen to Nihonteki shakai no kakuritsu*. Tokyo: Yamakawa shuppansha, 1987.

Mizumoto Kunihiko. *Kinsei no mura shakai to kokka*. Tokyo: Tōkyō daigaku shuppankai, 1987.

Mogi Yōichi. "Shinsei hantai ikki to chiso kaisei hantai ikki: Ise bōdō o rei ni." In Sakano Junji et al., eds., *Nihon kin-gendai shi*, vol. 1, *Ishin henkaku to kindai Nihon*. Tokyo: Iwanami shoten, 1993, pp. 279–321.

Moribe Hideo, "'Gakusei'-ki no kyōiku hōsei." *Gumma daigaku, Kyōiku gakubu kiyō, jimbun shakaigaku-hen* 42 (1993): 124–26.

Morikawa Teruki. "Gakusei no minshūteki juyō to kyohi." In Kōza Nihon kyōiku-shi iinkai, ed., *Kōza Nihon kyōiku-shi*, vol. 2. Tokyo: Iwanami shoten, 1982, pp. 306–33.

———. "Meiji 9-nen Shinpeki-machi sōdō no kyōiku-shiteki kentō." *Kyōiku undō-shi kenkyū* 15 (1973): 19–29.

Moriya Katsuhisa. "Urban Networks and Information Networks." Trans. Ronald P. Toby. In Chie Nakane and Shinzaburo Ōishi, eds., *Tokugawa Japan*. Tokyo: University of Tokyo Press, 1990, pp. 97–123.

Motoyama Yukihiko. *Meiji kokka no kyōiku shisō*. Tokyo: Shibunkaku shuppan, 1998.

————. *Proliferating Talent: Essays on Politics, Thought, and Education in the Meiji Era*. Translation ed. J. S. A. Elisonias and Richard Rubinger. Honolulu: University of Hawaii Press, 1997.

Mouffe, Chantal. "Hegemony and Ideology in Gramsci." In idem, ed., *Gramsci and Marxist Theory*. London: Routledge and Kegan Paul, 1979, pp. 168–204.

Nagai Hideo. "Tōitsu kokka no seiritsu." In *Iwanami kōza Nihon rekishi*, vol. 14, *Kindai 1*. Tokyo: Iwanami shoten, 1975, pp. 121–66.

Nagai Michio. "Westernization and Japanization: The Early Meiji Transformation of Education." In Donald Shively, ed. *Tradition and Modernization in Japanese Culture*. Princeton: Princeton University Press, 1973, pp. 35–76.

Nagao Muboku. *Setsuyu Yōryaku*. Nagano: Shinano kyōikukai shuppanbu, 1970.

Nagaoka Takeo. "Chikuma-ken no kindai gakkō to gakkō sewayaku." *Shinano* 30, no. 7 (July 1978): 560–75.

Nagura Eizaburo. "Keisei gakkō ki." 3 pts. *Hikaku bunka* 10–12 (1965–67).

Nagura Eizaburo, ed. *Nihon kyōiku-shi*. Tokyo: Hassendai shuppansha, 1984.

Najita, Tetsuo. "Introduction." In idem and Victor Koschmann, eds., *Conflict in Modern Japanese History*. Princeton: Princeton University Press, 1982, pp. 3–21.

————. *Visions of Virtue: The Kaitokudō Merchant Academy of Osaka*. Chicago: University of Chicago Press, 1987.

Naka Arata. *Meiji shoki no kyōiku seisaku to chihō e no teichaku*. Tokyo: Kōdansha, 1962.

Nakano Shinnoyū. "Sonraku fukkō o mezasu kyōiku shisō to sono kōzō." *Kōza Nihon kyōiku-shi*, vol. 2. Tokyo: Iwanami shoten, 1982, pp. 104–26.

Nemerov, Howard. *Trying Conclusions: New and Selected Poems, 1961–1991*. Chicago: University of Chicago Press, 1991.

Nishiyama Matsunosuke. *Edo Culture*. Trans. and ed. Gerald Groemer. Honolulu: University of Hawaii Press, 1997.

Norman, E. H. *Japan's Emergence as a Modern State*. New York: Institute of Pacific Relations, 1940.

Ooms, Herman. *Tokugawa Village Practice*. Berkeley: University of California Press, 1996.

Passin, Herbert. *Society and Education in Japan*. New York: Teachers College Press, Columbia University, 1965.

Pratt, Edward. *Japan's Proto-Industrial Elite: The Economic Foundations of the Gōnō*. Cambridge, Mass.: Harvard University Asia Center, 1999.

Rankin, Mary. *Elite Activism and Political Transformation in China*. Stanford: Stanford University Press, 1986.

Ravina, Mark. *Land and Lordship in Early Modern Japan.* Stanford: Stanford University Press, 1998.

Roberts, Luke. *Mercantilism in a Japanese Domain: The Merchant Origins of Economic Nationalism in 18th-Century Tosa.* Cambridge, Eng.: Cambridge University Press, 1998.

Roseberry, William. "Hegemony and the Language of Contention." In Gilbert Joseph and Daniel Nugent, eds. *Everyday Forms of State Formation.* Durham: Duke University Press, 1994, pp. 355–66.

Rubinger, Richard. "Education: From One Room to One System." In Marius Jansen and Gilbert Rozman, eds., *Japan in Transition: From Tokugawa to Meiji.* Princeton: Princeton University Press, 1986, pp. 195–230.

———. *Private Academies in Tokugawa Japan.* Princeton: Princeton University Press, 1982.

Saito Osamu. "Infanticide, Fertility, and 'Population Stagnation': The State of Tokugawa Historical Demography." *Japan Forum* 4, no. 2 (1992): 369–82.

Sasaki Junnosuke. *Bakumatsu shakairon.* Tokyo: Hanawa shobō, 1969.

Sasamori Ken. *Meiji zenki chihō kyōiku gyōsei ni kansuru kenkyū.* Tokyo: Kōdansha, 1978.

Sato Hideo, ed. *Nihon kindai kyōiku hyaku-nen shi.* 3 vols. Tokyo: Kokuritsu kyōiku kenkyūjo, 1974.

Sawada, Janine. *Confucian Values and Popular Zen: Sekimon Shingaku in Eighteenth-Century Japan.* Honolulu: University of Hawaii Press, 1993.

Sayer, Derek. "Everyday Forms of State Formation: Some Dissident Remarks on Hegemony." In Gilbert Joseph and Daniel Nugent, eds., *Everyday Forms of State Formation.* Durham: Duke University Press, 1994), pp. 367–77.

———. *The Violence of Abstraction.* Oxford: Basil Blackwell, 1987.

Schofield, R. S. "The Dimensions of Illiteracy, 1750–1850." *Explorations in Economic History* 10 (1973): 473–54.

Schweber, Abigail. "Imposing Education: The Establishment of Japan's First National Education System, 1872–1879." Ph.D. diss., Harvard University, forthcoming.

Scott, James. *Domination and the Arts of Resistance.* New Haven: Yale University Press, 1992.

———. "Foreword." In Gilbert Joseph and Daniel Nugent, eds., *Everyday Forms of State Formation.* Durham: Duke University Press, 1994, pp. vii–xii.

———. *The Moral Economy of the Peasant.* New Haven: Yale University Press, 1976.

———. *Weapons of the Weak.* New Haven: Yale University Press, 1985.

Shimazaki Tōson. *Before the Dawn.* Trans. William Naff. Honolulu: University of Hawaii Press, 1987.

Smith, Thomas C. *The Agrarian Origins of Modern Japan.* Stanford: Stanford University Press, 1959.

———. *Nakahara: Family Farming and Population in a Japanese Village, 1717–1830.* Stanford: Stanford University Press, 1977.

———. *Native Sources of Japanese Industrialization, 1756–1920.* Berkeley: University of California Press, 1988.

Staubitz, Richard. "The Establishment of the System of Local Self-Government (1888–1890) in Japan." Ph.D. diss., Yale University, 1973.

Steele, William. "Goemon's New World View: Popular Representation of the Opening of Japan." *Asian Cultural Studies* 17 (1989): 69–83.

———. "Political Localism in Meiji Japan: The Case of Yoshino Taizō." *Asian Cultural Studies* 20 (1992): 137–55.

Steiner, Kurt. *Local Government in Japan.* Stanford: Stanford University Press, 1965.

Stone, Lawrence. "Literacy and Education in England, 1640–1900." *Past and Present,* no. 42 (Feb. 1969): 66–139.

Strumingher, Laura. "Square Pegs Into Round Holes: Rural Parents, Children and Primary Schools: France, 1830–1880." In Marc Bertrand, ed., *Popular Traditions and Learned Culture in France.* San Francisco: Anma Libri, 1985, pp. 133–47.

Sugano Noriko. "Terakoya to Joshishō." *Hitotsubashi ronsō* 111, no. 2 (Feb. 1994): 240–56.

Sumiya Takeo. "Tempō-ki no nōka no ichinen: Miyata-mura no aru nōka no ichirei." *Inaji* 27, no. 5 (May 1983): 31–37.

Taira, Koji. "Education and Literacy in Meiji Japan: An Interpretation." *Explorations in Economic History* 8 (1974): 371–94.

Takada Minoru. "Kanagawa-ken no terakoya: Fudezuka chōsa o chūshin ni shite." *Kyōdo Kanagawa* 27 (June 1990): 17–20.

Takahashi Sadaki. "Bakumatsu-ki nōson ni okeru jōhō shūshū katsudō to sono shakaiteki haikei." *Chihō-shi kenkyo* 46, no. 4 (Aug. 1996): 65–89.

Takahashi Satoshi. *Minshū to gōnō.* Tokyo: Misosha, 1985.

———. "Mura no tenaraijuku." In *Asahi hyakka Nihon no rekishi bessatsu: rekishi o yominaosu.* Tokyo: Asahi shinbun, 1995.

———. *Nihon minshū kyoiku-shi kenkyu.* Tokyo: Miso shakan, 1978.

Takamisawa Ryōichirō. "Fudezuka ni kansuru kenkyū: Kamiminochi-gun no baai, dai 1–bu." *Shinshū daigaku, Kyōiku gakubu kiyō* 20 (Oct. 1968): 19–45.

———. "Fudezuka ni kansuru kenkyū: Kamiminochi-gun no baai, dai 2–bu." *Shinshū daigaku, Kyōiku gakubu kiyō* 21 (June 1969), pp. 25–54.

———. "Fudezuka ni kansuru kenkyū: Nagano-ken Hanishina-gun Shimo-Matsushiro chiku." *Shinshū daigaku, Kyōiku gakubu kiyō* 29 (June 1973): 1–22.

———. "Fudezuka ni kansuru kenkyū: Nagano-ken Kamitakai-gun no baai." *Shinshū daigaku, Kyōiku gakubu kiyō* 23 (June 1970): 19–43.

———. "Fudezuka ni kansuru kenkyū: Nagano-ken Sarashina-gun no baai." *Shinshū daigaku, Kyōiku gakubu kiyō* 26 (Oct. 1971): 7–44.

———. "Fudezuka o chūshin to shita shomin kyōiku no jōtai: Saku-gun no baai." *Shinshu daigaku, Kyōiku gakubu kiyō* 18 (Oct. 1967): 1–16.

———. "Shinshū Hanishina-gun Matsushiro-chiku no terakoya shishō to fudezuka." *Shinano* 25, no. 10 (Oct. 1973): 25–41.

Takeuchi Makoto, ed. *Nihon no kinsei,* vol. 14, *Bunka no taishūka.* Tokyo: Chūō kōronsha, 1993.

Tanaka Katsuyoshi. "'Terakoya' no kigen to gogen o megutte." *Tetsugaku* 91 (Dec. 1990): 527–46.

Tayama Katai. *Country Teacher*. Trans. Kenneth Henshall. Honolulu: University of Hawaii Press, 1984.

Tilly, Charles. *The Vendée*. Cambridge, Mass.: Harvard University Press, 1975.

Tilly, Charles; Louise Tilly; and Richard Tilly. *The Rebellious Century*. Cambridge, Mass.: Harvard University Press, 1975.

Toby, Ronald P. "Both a Borrower and a Lender Be: From Village Money-lender to Rural Banker in the Tenpō Era." *Monumenta Nipponica* 46, no. 4 (Winter 1991): 483–511.

———. "The 'Indianness' of Iberia and Changing Japanese Iconographies of Other." In Stuart Schwartz, ed., *Implicit Understandings*. Cambridge, Eng.: Cambridge University Press, 1994, pp. 323–51.

Tokutomi Kenjirō. *Footprints in the Snow*. Trans. Kenneth Strong. New York: Pegasus, 1970.

Tone Keizaburō. *Terakoya to shomin kyōiku no jisshōteki kenkyū*. Tokyo: Takeyama kyaku shuppan, 1980.

Tsuda Hideo. *Kinsei minshū kyōiku undō no tenkai*. Tokyo: Ochanomizu shobō, 1978.

Tsukamoto Manabu. *Chihō no bunjin*. Tokyo: Kyōikusha, 1977.

Tsunoda, Ryusaku; Wm. Theodore de Bary; and Donald Keene, comps. *Sources of Japanese Tradition*. New York: Columbia University Press, 1958.

Tsurumaki Yoshio. *Kindaika to dentōteki minshū sekai*. Tokyo: Tōkyō daigaku shuppanbu, 1992.

———. "Minshū undō to shakai ishiki." In Asao Naohiro et al., eds. *Iwanami kōza Nihon tsūshi*, vol. 16, *Kindai 1*. Tokyo: Iwanami shoten, 1994, pp. 215–47.

Tsurumi, E. Patricia. "Meiji Primary School Language and Ethics Textbooks: Old Values for a New Society?" *Modern Asian Studies* 8, no. 2 (1974): 247–61.

Umegaki, Michio. *After the Restoration*. New York: New York University Press, 1988.

Umemura Kayo. *Nihon kinsei minshū kyōiku-shi kenkyū*. Tokyo: Azusa shuppanbu, 1991.

Umihara Tōru. *Kinsei no gakkō*. Tokyo: Shibunkaku, 1988.

Vaporis, Constantine. "To Edo and Back: Alternate Attendance and Japanese Culture in the Early Modern Period." *Journal of Japanese Studies* 23, no. 1 (Spring 1997): 25–67.

Vaughan, Mary Kay. *Cultural Politics in Revolution*. Tuscon: University of Arizona Press, 1997.

Vlastos, Stephen. "Opposition Movements in Early Meiji, 1868–1885," In Marius Jansen, ed., *The Cambridge History of Japan*, vol. 5. Cambridge, Eng.: Cambridge University Press, 1989, pp. 367–431.

———. *Peasant Protests and Uprisings in Tokugawa Japan*. Berkeley: University of California Press, 1986.

Wakabayashi, Bob Tadashi. *Anti-Foreignism and Western Learning in Modern Japan*. Cambridge, Mass.: Harvard University, Council on East Asian Studies, 1986.

Walthall, Anne. "The Cult of Sensibility in Rural Japan: Love Poetry by Matsuo Taseko." *Journal of the American Oriental Society* 117, no. 1 (1997): 70–86.

———. "The Family Ideology of Rural Entrepreneurs in Nineteenth-Century Japan." *Journal of Social History* 23, no. 3 (Spring 1990): 463–83.

———. "Village Networks: Sōdai and the Sale of Edo Nightsoil." *Monumenta Nipponica* 43, no. 3 (Fall 1988): 279–303.

———. *The Weak Body of a Useless Woman: Matsuo Taseko and the Meiji Restoration.* Chicago: University of Chicago Press, 1998.

Walthall, Anne, ed. and trans. *Peasant Uprisings in Japan: A Critical Anthology of Peasant Histories.* Chicago: University of Chicago Press, 1991.

Watanabe Takashi. *Kinsei no gōnō to sonraku kyōdōtai.* Tokyo: Tōkyō daigaku shuppankai, 1984.

Waters, Neil. *Japan's Local Pragmatists: The Transition from Bakumatsu to Meiji in the Kawasaki Region.* Cambridge, Mass.: Harvard University Press, 1983.

———. "The Village Consolidation of 1889: The Institutionalization of Contradiction in Local Administration." *Asian Cultural Studies* 20 (1992): 177–88.

Weber, Eugen. *Peasants into Frenchmen.* Berkeley: University of California Press, 1976.

West, E. G. *Education and the Industrial Revolution.* London: Batsford, 1975.

Wigen, Kären. "Constructing Shinano: The Invention of a Neo-Traditional Region." In Stephen Vlastos, ed., *Mirror of Modernity.* Berkeley: University of California Press, 1998, pp. 229–42.

———. *The Making of a Japanese Periphery.* Berkeley: University of California Press, 1995.

———. "Politics and Piety in Japanese Native-Place Studies: The Rhetoric of Solidarity in Shinano." *Positions* 4, no. 3 (Winter 1996): 491–517.

White, James. *Ikki: Social Conflict and Political Protests in Early Modern Japan.* Ithaca, N.Y.: Cornell University Press, 1995.

Williams, Raymond. "Base and Superstructure in Marxist Cultural Theory." In Robert Con Davis and Ronald Schleifer, eds., *Contemporary Literary Criticism.* New York: Longman, 1989, pp. 378–90.

Wilson, George. *Patriots and Redeemers in Japan.* Chicago: University of Chicago Press, 1992.

Yamamuro Shin'ichi. *Hōsei kanryō no jidai: kokka sekkei to chi no rekitei.* Tokyo: Bokutakusha, 1984.

———. "Meiji kokka no seido to rinen." In *Iwanami Kōza Nihon tsūshi,* vol. 17. Tokyo: Iwanami shoten, 1994, pp. 113–48.

Yasukawa Jūnosuke. "Gakkō kyōiku to fukoku kyōhei." In *Iwanami kōza Nihon rekishi,* vol. 15: *Kindai 1.* Tokyo: Iwanami shoten, 1976, pp. 213–58.

———. "Mikaihō buraku no kyōiku-shiteki kenkyū." In Buraku mondai kenkyūjo, ed., *Buraku mondai no kyōiku-shiteki kenkyū.* Tokyo: Buraku mondai kenkyūjo shuppanbu, 1978, pp. 12–66.

Yasumaru Yoshio. *Nihon no kindaika to minshū shisō.* Tokyo: Aoki shoten, 1974.

Yūki Rikurō. "Aichi-ken ni okeru gōkō no hattatsu to sono igi." *Nagoya daigaku, Kyōiku gakubu kiyō* 18, no. 3 (March 1972): 187–98.

Index

Aizawa Seishisai, 268*n*8
Allison, Gary, 20, 183
Attendance, school: at Tokugawa-
  era schools, 31–34, 49–53, 77–79,
  276*n*92; patterns for girls, 32,
  248–51 *passim*; attempts to encourage, 156, 162, 224, 249–50; at
  Meiji-era schools, 169, 182, 247–
  53, 258, 291*n*3, 302*n*116. *See also*
  Enrollment
Azumi district, 30, 33, 221

Bakufu, 56, 83, 94, 96; encourage-
  ment of schooling, 23, 36, 55, 56
Bakufu intendants, 54–56, 74
Bakumatsu period, 17, 93, 96
Baxter, James, 20, 195
Bix, Herbert, 109
Book lending, 88–89
Bowen, Roger, 270*n*26
Bourdieu, Pierre, 42
Branch schools, 201–3, 236, 239, 250,
  258
Buddhism, 4, 58, 78, 107; priests, 24,
  28, 30; anti-Buddhist sentiments,
  93, 119, 126, 151
Burakumin, 186–93 *passim*; 203–5
Bureaucratization, 161, 169–72

Castle-towns, 68–69; and early
  growth of schooling, 26, 30, 33,

35–38, 64, 66, 72, 76; and regional
  culture, 39–46 *passim*
Centralization, 4–5, 135, 140, 145,
  151, 172, 184, 220, 222, 233–39
  passim, 263
Charter Oath, 103
Chiisagata district, 29, 220, 221, 243,
  245
Chikuma district, 29, 30
Chikuma prefecture: establishment
  of, 120; amalgamation into
  Nagano prefecture, 145, 210,
  215–16
Chimura Kyokai, 175–76, 300*n*53
Chinese Learning, 103–4, 113–14,
  177–78
Chinese Studies Institute (Kangakusho), 103
Christianity, 187–88
"Civilization and Enlightenment"
  (*bunmei kaika*), 105, 119, 127, 157–
  58, 168, 172, 189–90, 207, 213
Commercialization, 24, 39–41, 48–51
  passim, 64
Commoner schools (Tokugawa era):
  growth in numbers of, 23–28, 30,
  34, 47–48; Japanese terms for,
  24–25, 82, 136–37; definition of,
  24, 82; official encouragement of,
  36–38, 53–56; and economic
  development, 39–40, 48–53; and

Harvard East Asian Monographs
(* out-of-print)

Harvard East Asian Monographs

Harvard East Asian Monographs

Harvard East Asian Monographs

Harvard East Asian Monographs

181. Soon-Won Park, *Colonial Industrialization and Labor in Korea: The Onoda Cement Factory*

182. JaHyun Kim Haboush and Martina Deuchler, *Culture and the State in Late Chosŏn Korea*

183. John W. Chaffee, *Branches of Heaven: A History of the Imperial Clan of Sung China*

184. Gi-Wook Shin and Michael Robinson, eds., *Colonial Modernity in Korea*

185. Nam-lin Hur, *Prayer and Play in Late Tokugawa Japan: Asakusa Sensōji and Edo Society*

186. Kristin Stapleton, *Civilizing Chengdu: Chinese Urban Reform, 1895–1937*

187. Hyung Il Pai, *Constructing "Korean" Origins: A Critical Review of Archaeology, Historiography, and Racial Myth in Korean State-Formation Theories*

188. Brian D. Ruppert, *Jewel in the Ashes: Buddha Relics and Power in Early Medieval Japan*

189. Susan Daruvala, *Zhou Zuoren and an Alternative Chinese Response to Modernity*

190. James Z. Lee, *The Political Economy of a Frontier: Southwest China, 1250–1850*

191. Kerry Smith, *A Time of Crisis: Japan, the Great Depression, and Rural Revitalization*

192. Michael Lewis, *Becoming Apart: National Power and Local Politics in Toyama, 1868–1945*

193. William C. Kirby, Man-houng Lin, James Chin Shih, and David A. Pietz, eds., *State and Economy in Republican China: A Handbook for Scholars*

194. Timothy S. George, *Minamata: Pollution and the Struggle for Democracy in Postwar Japan*

195. Billy K. L. So, *Prosperity, Region, and Institutions in Maritime China: The South Fukien Pattern, 946–1368*

196. Yoshihisa Tak Matsusaka, *The Making of Japanese Manchuria, 1904–1932*

197. Maram Epstein, *Competing Discourses: Orthodoxy, Authenticity, and Engendered Meanings in Late Imperial Chinese Fiction*

198. Curtis J. Milhaupt, J. Mark Ramseyer, and Michael K. Young, eds. and comps., *Japanese Law in Context: Readings in Society, the Economy, and Politics*

199. Haruo Iguchi, *Unfinished Business: Ayukawa Yoshisuke and U.S.-Japan Relations, 1937–1952*

200. Scott Pearce, Audrey Spiro, and Patricia Ebrey, *Culture and Power in the Reconstitution of the Chinese Realm, 200–600*

201. Terry Kawashima, *Writing Margins: The Textual Construction of Gender in Heian and Kamakura Japan*

202. Martin W. Huang, *Desire and Fictional Narrative in Late Imperial China*

Harvard East Asian Monographs

203. Robert S. Ross and Jiang Changbin, eds., *Re-examining the Cold War: U.S.-China Diplomacy, 1954–1973*

204. Guanhua Wang, *In Search of Justice: The 1905–1906 Chinese Anti-American Boycott*

205. David Schaberg, *A Patterned Past: Form and Thought in Early Chinese Historiography*

206. Christine Yano, *Tears of Longing: Nostalgia and the Nation in Japanese Popular Song*

207. Milena Doleželová-Velingerová and Oldřich Král, with Graham Sanders, eds., *The Appropriation of Cultural Capital: China's May Fourth Project*

208. Robert N. Huey, *The Making of 'Shinkokinshū'*

209. Lee Butler, *Emperor and Aristocracy in Japan, 1467–1680: Resilience and Renewal*

210. Suzanne Ogden, *Inklings of Democracy in China*

211. Kenneth J. Ruoff, *The People's Emperor: Democracy and the Japanese Monarchy, 1945–1995*

212. Haun Saussy, *Great Walls of Discourse and Other Adventures in Cultural China*

213. Aviad E. Raz, *Emotions at Work: Normative Control, Organizations, and Culture in Japan and America*

214. Rebecca E. Karl and Peter Zarrow, eds., *Rethinking the 1898 Reform Period: Political and Cultural Change in Late Qing China*

215. Kevin O'Rourke, *The Book of Korean Shijo*

216. Ezra F. Vogel, ed., *The Golden Age of the U.S.-China-Japan Triangle, 1972–1989*

217. Thomas A Wilson, ed., *On Sacred Grounds: Culture, Society, Politics, and the Formation of the Cult of Confucius*

218. Donald S. Sutton, *Steps of Perfection: Exorcistic Performers and Chinese Religion in Twentieth-Century Taiwan*

219. Daqing Yang, *Technology of Empire: Telecommunications and Japanese Imperialism, 1930–1945*

220. Qianshen Bai, *Fu Shan's World: The Transformation of Chinese Calligraphy in the Seventeenth Century*

221. Paul Jakov Smith and Richard von Glahn, eds., *The Song-Yuan-Ming Transition in Chinese History*

222. Rania Huntington, *Alien Kind: Foxes and Late Imperial Chinese Narrative*

223. Jordan Sand, *House and Home in Modern Japan: Architecture, Domestic Space, and Bourgeois Culture, 1880–1930*

224. Karl Gerth, *China Made: Consumer Culture and the Creation of the Nation*

225. Xiaoshan Yang, *Metamorphosis of the Private Sphere: Gardens and Objects in Tang-Song Poetry*

Harvard East Asian Monographs